GREY ALIENS

AND

ARTIFICIAL
INTELLIGENCE

GREY ALIENS
AND
ARTIFICIAL INTELLIGENCE

The Battle between Natural and
Synthetic Beings for the Human Soul

NIGEL KERNER

Bear & Company
Rochester, Vermont

Bear & Company
One Park Street
Rochester, Vermont 05767
www.BearandCompanyBooks.com

Text stock is SFI certified

Bear & Company is a division of Inner Traditions International

Cataloging-in-Publication Data for this title is available from the Library of Congress

ISBN 978-1-59143-449-8 (print)
ISBN 978-1-59143-450-4 (ebook)

Printed and bound in the United States by Lake Book Manufacturing, Inc. The text stock is SFI certified. The Sustainable Forestry Initiative® program promotes sustainable forest management.

10 9 8 7 6 5 4 3 2 1

Text design and layout by Virginia Scott Bowman
This book was typeset in Garamond Premier Pro with Archival Narrow used as the display typeface

In writing a book like this any author is always magnified by those who help with the research and assembly of the final work. In my case I am particularly grateful for the skill and erudition of Danielle Silverman, the chief researcher. Her ceaseless intelligent meticulous attention to detail in pursuing the facts underlying the ideas in the text enabled a much greater work than originally anticipated.

And also, I am grateful for Daniel Langsman. His dazzling artistic talents for envisioning complex and sometimes obscure ideas pictorially have left me aghast with admiration for the accuracy of his illustrations.

Both of these individuals have done their work with a sense of personal resource and belief in the ideas in the book and I am left humbled by the power of the human mind and heart as illustrated by their respective talents.

Contents

Preface xi

Introduction 1

1 Beyond Reasonable Doubt 5

2 Why Are They Here? 12

3 SIM Card Man 21

4 Behind the Scenes 34

5 The Missing Ingredient 48

6 The Harvesting of Souls 56

7 On a Clear Day You *Might* See Forever 62

8 Can't See the Forest for the Trees 74

9 The Scaffolding of the Universe 88

10 Twist and Shout 94

11 What Is a Soul? 101

12 Force 106

13 Getting It in perspective 113

14 The Carousel of Life and Death 116

15 The Margins of Forever 130

16 The Ultimate Game 135

17 How Alien Craft Are Made 140

18 Devolution 148

19 Re-volution—The Way Back 157

20 Our Origins 163

21 Are Endings Reversed Beginnings? 170

22 How the Greys Reach Us When We Die 177

23 Hybridization 181

24 Possession 190

25 The Grey Laundromat 195

26 Melanin—A Lens to Forever 205

27 Making a Monkey of a Man 216

28 Biblical Parallels 223

29 The Greys in Human History 236

30 Immaculate Conception 241

31 Alpha and Omega, Body and Soul 252

32 The Body as an Antenna 260

33 Understanding the Soul   273

34 What Is Life?   278

35 What Is Them and What Is Us?   288

36 The Devil Is in the Details   293

37 Gateways to Heaven   306

38 Ghosts—Not Too Far to Kiss Your Brow   313

39 Death to Life   325

40 Life to Death   335

41 Quantum Weirdness   345

42 Anthropic Coincidences   353

43 The Spark of Life   364

44 Here We Go 'Round the Mulberry Bush   382

45 Alien Tactics   388

46 The Curse of Everydayness   395

47 Hope   408

48 The Triumph of Reason   415

Epilogue   421

✛

Notes   436

Bibliography   444

Index   454

What we consider the here and now, this world, it is actually just the material level that is comprehensible. The beyond is an infinite reality that is much bigger. Which this world is rooted in. In this way, our lives in this plane of existence are encompassed, surrounded, by the afterworld already. . . . The body dies but the spiritual quantum field continues. In this way, I am immortal.

HANS-PETER DÜRR, FORMER HEAD OF
THE MAX PLANCK INSTITUTE FOR PHYSICS AND ASTROPHYSICS

Our thoughts, our will, our consciousness and our feelings show properties that could be referred to as spiritual properties. No direct interaction with the known fundamental forces of natural science, such as gravitation, electromagnetic forces, etc., can be detected in the spiritual. On the other hand, however, these spiritual properties correspond exactly to the characteristics that distinguish the extremely puzzling and wondrous phenomena in the quantum world.

CHRISTIAN HELLWIG, PH.D., OF THE
MAX PLANCK INSTITUTE FOR BIOPHYSICAL CHEMISTRY

The human mystery is incredibly demeaned by scientific reductionism, with its claim in promissory materialism to account eventually for all of the spiritual world in terms of patterns of neuronal activity. This belief must be classed as a superstition. . . . We have to recognize that we are spiritual beings with souls existing in a spiritual world as well as material beings with bodies and brains existing in a material world.

SIR JOHN ECCLES, NOBEL PRIZE–WINNING
NEUROPHYSIOLOGIST AND PHILOSOPHER

Our world is not divided by race, color, gender, or religion. Our world is divided into wise people and fools. And fools divide themselves by race, color, gender, or religion.

MOHAMAD SAFA, HUMAN RIGHTS ACTIVIST
AND UNITED NATIONS REPRESENTATIVE

Preface

I t all started thirty-one years ago, when my son, then twelve years old, asked, "Dad, are UFOs real?"

My paternal grandfather impressed on me when I was a child that you must never fob off a child's question with a specious comment or answer. He would never give me anything but the deepest attention. He would stop anything he was doing and reply with the kind of attention that included a didactic stance and a challenging question. He died when I was five years old. I was always conscious of his respect for me. I was aware that he took everything I said seriously, even at that young age. Young memories can be very strong, especially if they are inculcated with a sense of endearment. So I grew up following my grandfather's example and challenging myself to think things out meticulously before I replied to a question. I recall I spent a long time in his company and listened to him intently even at that young age. All this configured my attitude toward my own children—indeed, my attitude toward all children.

My son meant that question about UFOs in the "aliens are here" sense, and he was serious. He almost never asked spurious questions, so I saw an opportunity to provide some important guidance to a young mind about life and living, and how you might demonstrate and sort the real from the mythological, and how good protocols can lead to valid discoveries. Frankly, it was an opportunity to once and for all disaffect him of what I considered an utterly bogus topic. But as I knew little about the subject, I decided to look into it with great care before I dismantled its claims.

My little honcho wasn't beyond dumping me in the quicksand with a loaded question he had previously researched so that he could then watch me squirm for an answer he knew I was unlikely to have. We were always playfully testing each other this way. He had done this before in front of his peers, many times, and I would sometimes come away with raw egg dripping off my face. He used the implement between his ears wickedly well for one so young. I suspected a subterfuge in this particular question, so I requested a rain check on it and the time to give him an informed answer.

So the last thing I expected when I decided more than three decades ago to look seriously into the enigma of the ET phenomenon was to discover that it wasn't about Buck Rogers, *Star Wars,* space cowboys, Dr. Who, and the USS *Enterprise* "going boldly where no man has gone before." I wanted to disabuse my son of the nonsense of believing in ETs and all the space mumbo jumbo that goes with it. He had a good mind, and I wanted him to use it for something far more important than whimsical, go-nowhere ideas. So I set about finding enough rational evidence to seriously answer his question.

I found there were myriad takes on the subject, from the deeply scholarly to the thoroughly fantastical. Space aliens are the stuff of everyone's imagination. Where was I to find the deepest, truest take on it? Since I have a science background, I thought it would take me a week to dismiss any alien presence on our planet as a myth based on the whimsy of the human imagination and condition. It has taken me more than thirty years of research to make it plain that "myth" is the last thing you could call the alien phenomenon known as the Greys. It has taken hold of me and spun me inside out, upside down, and six ways to Sunday, wrenching apart my ethos and literally everything I have ever held sacred, and has convinced me that I could never have been so wrong about anything. So wrong—it was such a lesson in presumption—that I now even have to check to see if the sun is really in the sky!

So for the readers of this book who may not have read my previous two books on this subject, I pose a few salient questions: Just what are the Greys? Where do they come from? What is their existential base if different from ours? Are they beings we can see, feel, and touch, or are they phantomlike flashes of light or light shadows in the sky? If the Greys are solid, physical phenomena, who or what drives them? How did they get here past Einstein's speed-of-light barrier, $E = mc^2$? Where do they come from? If they are flying around in craft, how do they do the things they are seen to do by so many thousands of people, with the same things described from different locations? Are all these people all over the world having the same fits of imagination when they see them? If so, then what is imagination if at any given time thousands perceive the same thing in hundreds of different places at the same time? How can something travel so fast and not kill every being in it, doing instant, ninety-degree turns, as many pilots, both civilian and military, have attested? They would have to withstand a g-force of tens of thousands of pounds pushing down on them, since it appears that these *are* physical craft that travel at phenomenal rates of acceleration.

In attempting to explain an enigma as strange and bizarre as the phenomenon of the Greys, it is crucial that we understand the factors that define just what *we* are and what *they* are in relation to us. If the Greys are real, tangible things and thus measurable with our senses of taste, touch, sight, hearing, and smell, they could be investigated with one set of tools. But what if they are not tangible in that sense but are still more than merely figments of our imagination? What can we use to measure them, then? So many questions, so many answers to discover. I found that the most comprehensive answers, those that reconcile the most questions with the least amount of contradiction, are that they are not only real, but they have to be driven by some sort of mechanical means. Yet no biomass could survive the g-forces involved in their observed movement patterns. That aspect of the phenomenon finally put Alice down the rabbit hole for me.

The first question I asked was whether the phenomenon has a real, tangible base to it outside purely mental processes. In my work through the lens of human behavioral psychology I came up against the "mind farmers" who have underwritten the foundation of human thinking, illustrious names such as Gestalt, Kulpe, Freud, Kant, Pavlov, Erikson, Skinner, Lewin, Jung, Laing, and others. Their thoughts on human psychological processes have formed my understanding of the truth of things. But there is compelling evidence to suggest that a psychological explanation to this particular phenomenon might be little more than shadow boxing.

I finally figured things out with the help of one powerful teacher, Professor Humbug. This guy gets around everywhere. He is into everything. He has a lot to say, and few deny him because many don't see him coming. He speaks very softly, in whispers, and talks convincingly through the Principle of Least Effort and Most Comfort. He's a very nice guy. You never feel like taking him on, because he smiles sweetly at your prejudices and goes with the trend and is only ever angry if you think outside the box. He is very comfortable in the box and is most often seen trying to climb back into the box again when you take him out of it. I have kept him outside the box, and it is there that he is the most revealing. I kept him there while I looked afresh at things that affect the more contemporary viewpoint of the human condition on our planet as revealed by quantum physics, because I thought it was there that I would find most of the answers that resolve the enigma of the ET phenomenon, because in the past century quantum theory has smashed all certainties. My research required a radical and painfully objective reexamination of my entire existential vista. I could leave no stone unturned.

I discovered that you just cannot account for the ET phenomenon with a simplistic explanation of it as a phenomenon "out there" that involves some kind of exotic vehicular activity that is exceptional in terms of technology alone. This is the most fundamental existential game-changer of all in terms of what this means to humanity. For this reason, I have written three books, this being the third, that trace the multifaceted network of evidence that leads to the answer to my son's question. And so I have written this book for my children, and for all our children in the collective human family, as the simple bequest of a father.

Most of us take things for granted. We normally don't look deep into anything, not really concerned about *what* is there or *why* it's there. That is one of the biggest mistakes we can make because we often stumble upon things and in our ignorance don't know what to make of them. Science is here to tell us about *how* things are here, but never really about *why* they are here or what it means by them being here. This *why* is very, very important if we want to understand the mystery of aliens known as the Greys.

As I looked into the phenomenon further it became evident that it had to be the widest existential look at the entire condition of our being that I could manage, so please bear with me as you go through these pages. I am hoping it will dare you, as it dared me, to persevere with the discovery process. If you find my arguments are supported by both logical extrapolation and evidence, then you may agree with me that an understanding of the alien phenomenon and its implications for human beings may be a game-changer for all of us. My discoveries have suggested that humanity is prized by these alien visitors because we have something special that they do not share with us, no matter how advanced their technology. For this reason, by the end of this book you might be convinced of the wonder you really are and perhaps never knew you were.

This book is the last in a series of three addressing the enigma of the Greys, which has exploded into the lives of contemporary humankind in the past eighty years or so. It is an attempt to answer the thousands of questions spawned by my two prior books: *The Song of the Greys* and *Grey Aliens and the Harvesting of Souls: The Conspiracy to Genetically Tamper with Humanity*. These questions have come from all over the world and demonstrate a storming interest in the subject, especially, and interestingly, in China.

Just one other thing: My wife of fifty years has no background in the sciences, only her experience as a wife, a mother, and a wonderful woman. She asked me to write this book in such a way that what she called "normal people" would understand it.

"But Greys and ET aliens are not 'normal people,'" I protested.

"There has to be a directive through science if I am to approach the truth of things, and science has its own way with words."

"Then you'll have to find your own way with words around that," was her reply. "It took me two years to get through your last two books on the subject. I don't want another struggle like that." Then she read the first draft of this book. "A bit better," she said, and smiled. That may be the only positive feedback I get in writing this book!

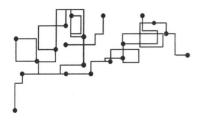

Introduction

We are living in a time of huge upheaval: the COVID-19 pandemic, the global socioeconomic disasters caused by the effects of lockdown, and the possible threats to species survival brought about by climate change are only a few of the challenges we face. In an early work, *Margins of Forever*, I proposed that in reality our biggest existential threat is not from any environmental catastrophe but instead from our own man-made transition from natural human being to cyborg via electronic devices and interfaces. We are at a turning point for our species, in which our natural humanity is gradually being converted into an artificial format. Already we increasingly rely on "smart" devices to the point that they become mere extensions of our bodies. Elon Musk has said that through the brain-interface technology called Neuralink, he ultimately wants "to achieve a symbiosis with artificial intelligence."[1] Musk envisages a wireless product called the N1 sensor. Neuralink intends to implant four of these sensors in the brain, which will connect wirelessly to an external device mounted behind the ear and controlled through a phone app. As I write now in January 2022, Neuralink is beginning its first human trials.

Could this lead to an entirely new species of human with unlimited memory, unlimited calculation ability, and instant wireless communication, with everything remotely controlled by the brain and humans electronically synced both with external machines and even with one another? If so, could we even call this species human? Will these technological advances change the format of our lives, or, more fundamentally, the format of our being? And at what price? How vital is the human connection to our existential reality, and how might this be affected by remote living? Will we lose our natural human faculties through lack of use and lack of real human contact? Will imagination and creativity be replaced by artificial substitutes? Even more chillingly, could it be that we lose our ability to feel deeply as we become mortgaged to artificial enhancements, while the expression of human emotion becomes trivialized in our social media like/dislike, hit-and-run, instant-response culture? With the development of seamless bioelectronic interfaces allowing better communication between living organisms and machines and RFID chips introduced into the body, hacking is likely to become a serious issue.

Many scientists foresee a future in which humans are wired like cars, with sensors that form early-warning systems for disease or illness. The current situation with the COVID-19 pandemic could conceivably lead to the development of such technology. Government surveillance of our movements via mobile phone networks to track the spread of the virus, or viruses like it, is likely to become the norm. Virtually all human activities—education, entertainment, shopping, banking, socializing, and even attending religious services—have been moved to an online setting. In the name of limiting the spread of the virus in any of its future mutations, or of any future virus deemed a threat, social distancing could become a foreseeable requirement in the future, phasing out natural human contact in favor of virtual, online "safe" communication. This dystopian scenario was once science fiction and is now rapidly transforming into science fact.

The discovery of new and sometimes bizarre paradigms that underlie science produce technologies so rapidly that their consequences often overwhelm the average person, such that many people find it impossible to simply cope with the fallout of everyday life. Just when I thought it was impossible for the world to get any more mad than it already is, I read that the European Parliament was drafting a set of regulations about the use of artificial intelligence (AI) that includes guidance on "electronic personhood." In other words, if a robot is actually an embodied version of a real person, what rights should it have? The mind-bendingly astonishing fallacy behind even considering that proposition is at the heart of my books, which carefully delineate the axiomatically crucial difference between a natural living being and synthetically created artificial entities.

This book is an attempt to make some sense of the new imperatives that rule our lives, much of them without our personal consent, and to see these mandates for what they really are, noting their dangers and comparing them with many much more valuable ones that have been abandoned. The thesis questions whether the old living formulas should ever have been abandoned in the face of a sensational threat that few see opening before them—a threat so significant that it provides a consummate danger to the natural living form of the entire human family. Such changes will devastatingly affect the long-term survival of us as human beings.

The blueprints of this future may already exist. I believe there are locations in the universe with civilizations that have developed and surpassed these technologies, to become entirely artificial. The Grey alien entities, reported in tens of thousands of abduction scenarios, would seem to be a form of biomachine. I have termed them *roboids* (robotic entities formed mainly of organic material). They are sent out as probes to gather information, very similar to the probes we ourselves send out to explore locations where we cannot go safely. Are they seeking to somehow hack into us as natural living beings with their artificially intelligent programs? Could it be that our headlong rush along the same pathway as the civilizations that produced these roboidal entities has been seeded and precipitated by them to prepare us to fit in with their agenda for us?

The Pentagon has just released footage authenticating pilot sightings of unidentified craft accelerating at speeds impossible with our current technology. Former senator Harry Reid, who as Senate Majority Leader in 2007 funded a research program into UFOs, tweeted that this release "only scratches the surface of what the Pentagon has on file."

Could it be that our intrinsic nature as human beings is not entirely human? The remarkable truth may be that an artificial construct has been superimposed on the very foundation of our thinking processes. This installation diffracts, deflects, and filters our consciousness and perception, imparting qualities to us that reflect the nature of the installer. This book proposes that this construct has been installed in our biology by an alien intelligence over millennia—a subject that will be thoroughly explored in the coming pages.

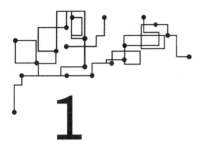

1

Beyond Reasonable Doubt

n March 2012, the European Southern Observatory announced a new estimate for the number of planets similar to Earth in the Milky Way galaxy alone: tens of billions. It is now held that at least 100 billion or so stars (there can never be an exact number calculated as every source gives a different number every day, it seems) that fill the Milky Way have planets in the habitable, or "Goldilocks," zone. "In a six-year period from 2002 to 2007 we observed 500 stars at high resolution," said Danish astronomer Uffe Gråe Jørgensen, director of astrophysics and planetary science at the University of Copenhagen. His findings showed that planets orbiting stars are "more the rule than the exception," and billions of them may be habitable.[1] As I write, the latest conservative estimate is that there are about eight billion habitable planets in the universe, and scientists keep adding noughts every year or so. I believe it is better to use the word *countless* rather than to estimate the number.

So, given that it is beyond all reasonable doubt that nonhuman life exists, the next question is: What could prompt alien entities to visit us? Stephen Hawking has said that to his "mathematical brain, the numbers alone make thinking about aliens perfectly rational. . . . The real challenge is to work out what aliens might actually be like." He takes this idea one step further and suggests that they are also highly likely to be predatory. Hawking postulates that aliens might simply raid Earth for its resources and then move on: "We only have to look at ourselves to see how intelligent life might develop into something we wouldn't want to meet. I imagine they might exist in massive ships, having used up all the resources from their home planet. Such advanced aliens would perhaps become nomads, looking to conquer and colonise whatever planets they can reach." He concludes that trying to make contact with alien races is "a little too risky. If aliens ever visit us, I think the outcome would be much as when Christopher Columbus first landed in America, which didn't turn out very well for the Native Americans."[2] Hawking was not alone in this view of extraterrestrial life-forms. In 2010, eminent scientists called for a world plan to deal with this potential threat. According to an extraterrestrial-themed edition of the Philosophical Transactions of the Royal Society, world governments should prepare a coordinated action plan in case Earth is contacted by invading aliens. Contributing scientists argued that a branch of the United Nations must be given responsibility for "supra-Earth affairs" and formulate a plan for how to deal with extraterrestrials should they appear.[3] Simon Conway Morris, a professor of evolutionary paleobiology at Cambridge University, has suggested that anyone planning for alien contact should prepare for the worst. Evolution on alien worlds, he said, is likely to be Darwinian in nature. "First, if intelligent aliens exist, they will look just like us, and given our far from glorious history, this should give us pause for thought," says Morris.[4]

These are sober scientists, not New Agers or fringe conspiracy theorists, discussing a potentially devastating threat. But hang on a minute, who said "potential threat"? Why is there so little recognition of the remarkable evidence that alien craft have visited already?

On September 27, 2010, a press conference was held at the National Press Club in Washington, D.C., where now retired high-ranking U.S. Air Force personnel, mostly officers who worked on secret projects connected to sensitive nuclear weapons sites, admitted that they were privy to UFO and alien-related incidents that occurred during their time of service.[5] Robert Salas, Charles Halt, Robert Hastings, Bruce Fenstermacher, Dwynne Arnesson, Patrick McDonough, Jerome Nelson, and Robert Jamison—all of them retired USAF officers—told the assembled reporters about incidents that took place at Malmstrom Air Force Base in Montana, as well as at many other Air Force bases across the United States and Europe, wherein flying saucers, some shaped like "pregnant cigars," had hovered and directed laser beams downward over Minuteman missile silos or nuclear weapons depots regularly (and repeatedly), from the 1960s through the 1970s and '80s.[6] The UFOs were reported to have altered the security codes on nuclear rockets in their nests in their underground silos. Three of the Air Force officers, though they hadn't personally seen the UFOs, told reporters that the UFOs hovering over silos around Malmstrom in 1967 appeared to have temporarily deactivated some of the nuclear missiles.

In 2017, the Pentagon first confirmed the existence of the Advanced Aerospace Threat Identification Program (AATIP), which had been launched in 2007 to collect and analyze "anomalous aerospace threats." . . . The investigation ranged from "advanced aircraft fielded by traditional U.S. adversaries to commercial drones, to possible alien encounters." Chris Mellon, a former deputy assistant secretary of defense for intelligence and a staffer on the U.S. Senate Intelligence Committee, told the *Washington Post*, "I don't believe in safety through ignorance," and scolded the intelligence community for its lack of "curiosity and courage" and a "failure to react" to a strong pattern of sightings." In some cases, pilots, many of whom are engineers and academy graduates, claimed to observe small, spherical objects flying in formation. Others say they've seen white, Tic Tac–shaped vehicles. Aside from drones, all engines rely on burning fuel to generate power, but these vehicles all had no air intake, no wind, and no exhaust. "It's very mysterious," Mellon said, "and they still seem to exceed our aircraft in speed." He called it a "truly radical technology."

According to Mellon, awestruck and baffled pilots, concerned that reporting unidentified flying aircraft would adversely affect their careers, tended not to speak up. And when they did, there was little interest in investigating their claims. "Imagine you see highly advanced vehicles, they appear on radar systems, they look bizarre, no one knows where they're from. This happens on a recurring basis, and no one does anything," said Mellon. . . . Because agencies do not share this type of information, it is difficult to know the full extent of activity. Still, he estimated that dozens of incidents were witnessed by naval officers in a single year, enough to force the service to address the issue. "Pilots are upset, and they're trying to help wake up a slumbering system," Mellon says.[7]

According to an article in the *Washington Post:*

The program identified five observations that showed mysterious objects displaying some level of "advanced physics," also known as "stuff humans can't do yet": The objects would accelerate with g-forces too strong for the human body to withstand, or reach hypersonic speed with no heat trail or sonic boom, or they seemed to resist the effects of Earth's gravity without any aerodynamic structures to provide thrust or lift. "No one has been able to figure out what these are," said Luis Elizondo, who recently ran the program. Elizondo has also talked about "metamaterials" that may have been recovered from unidentified aerial phenomena and stored in buildings owned by a private aerospace contractor in Las Vegas; they apparently have material compositions that aren't found naturally on Earth and would be exceptionally expensive to replicate. Some of the accounts Elizondo and his team analyzed supposedly occurred near nuclear facilities like power plants or battleships. In November 2004, the USS *Princeton,* a Navy cruiser escorting the aircraft carrier USS *Nimitz* off the coast of San Diego, ordered two fighter jets to investigate mysterious aircraft the Navy had been tracking for weeks (meaning this was not just a trick of the eye or a momentary failure of perspective, the two things most often blamed for unexplained aerial phenomena). When the jets arrived at the location, one of the pilots, Commander David Fravor, saw a disturbance just below the ocean's surface causing the water to roll around it. Then, suddenly he saw a white, 40-foot Tic

Tac–shaped craft moving like a Ping-Pong ball above the water. The vehicle began mirroring his plane's movements, but when Fravor dove directly at the object, the Tic Tac zipped away.[8]

In an interview with the *Daily Telegraph,* Elizondo said, "We intelligence officers tend to be skeptics by nature. For some of us working on it the time came as an 'Aha!' moment, for others it was a slow progress towards the realization that these are probably not any type of aircraft in any national inventory. . . . As to who's behind the wheel and why it's here, that will fall into place. I think it's pretty clear it's not us and it's not anyone else."[9] When Elizondo was asked if UFOs were real, he said their existence was "beyond reasonable doubt." He had seen enough evidence to convince him that the craft was not from any nation in our world.[10]

According to the article, "he eventually resigned in frustration at the excessive secrecy surrounding the programme he led. In his letter to Defence Secretary General Jim Mattis he wrote, 'Why aren't we spending more time and effort on this issue? There remains a vital need to ascertain the capability and intent of these phenomena for the benefit of the nation.'[11] He asserted that the U.S. pilots who witnessed these things were highly educated and they are seeing something they did not understand.[12]

An article in the *New York Times* reports that

in March 2020, Eric W. Davis, an astrophysicist who worked as a subcontractor and then a consultant for the Pentagon's UFO program since 2007, said he gave classified briefings on retrievals of unexplained objects to staff members of the Senate Armed Services Committee on Oct. 21, 2019, and to staff members of the Senate Intelligence Committee two days later. He stated that in some cases, examination of the materials had so far failed to determine their source and led him to conclude, "We couldn't make it ourselves."[13]

While in the British paper the *Daily Express* it was reported that

Paul Hellyer, a former Canadian Minister of Defence, said an unnamed former Canadian Chief of Emergency Measures revealed the following astonishing story just before his death from a neurological illness. Mr Hellyer, 92, explained that if he wanted to know about the workings of an alien space craft he would "ask the current chief of emergency measures." Mr Hellyer, who became a UFO expert after claiming to have seen proof of alien visitations while in office, said, "The reason I know is I interviewed the previous one, who is now deceased, and the CIA asked if he would like to see one of these crafts. They flew him to Area 51 and let him go inside one and observe it and make notes and this sort of thing. I phoned him, and he gave me a full report of what he saw and the whole idea of the inside of the craft and this sort of thing, and the fact he had been in a brief and many things, but now he felt he could tell somebody and he thought that would be a good one to tell."[14]

Despite all the evidence, Johnny-come-lately scientists are preparing for the fact that they *probably* do exist, *might* contact us, and *are likely* to be dangerous. Hawking's and Kaku's predictions, along with the numerous accounts of many others, should be of world significance as they affect the future of humanity. Efforts to keep this knowledge away from the public by governmental authorities charged with dealing with them have, it seems, been an unmitigated success. Despite all evidence to the contrary, how have the controlling interests who run the world's mainstream media outlets managed to relegate the alien phenomenon far into the outfield?

Each new revelation is practically an afterthought in the wake of celebrity news and developments in popular soaps on TV. In light of this, perhaps we do deserve to be trodden underfoot by alien visitors with a supremely advanced technology! A handful of cases possibly linking the MMR vaccine with autism led to millions of parents refusing the vaccine for their children. A rare side effect of aspirin in children has led to the medicine being banned for children under twelve. Yet despite volumes of evidence from reliable sources about alien interference and sometimes even assault on our species, we are not motivated to look further. We are not even stirred with enough curiosity to seriously and pervasively explore the subject, happy to allow the mainstream media to sweep the whole subject under the carpet. Why? When it comes to looking meaningfully at the alien phenomenon I can't help but think about the line from *Hamlet:* "Something is rotten in the state of Denmark."

But the question remains that if indeed we are being visited by extraterrestrial entities, what are they here for, and why do they keep the reality of their existence as elusive as they do? Furthermore, how is it that they are so amazingly successful at doing so if there is no collusion with national governments?

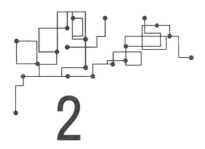

2

Why Are They Here?

Technology has taken a quantum leap in the past fifty years. The industrial revolution and the first basic technology started barely 150 years ago. Can you imagine what a technology thousands of years old could do? Vehicles silently traveling at speeds in excess of thirty thousand miles an hour and turning at right angles instantly, with inertial forces that would demolish a human biological system? Space vehicles the size of a football field that disappear in an instant, leaving no trail? Such phenomena have been reported by thousands of witnesses all over the world and point to a mastery over matter that dwarfs our current technological capabilities.

Theoretical physicist and astrobiologist Paul Davies, head of Arizona State University's Beyond Center for Fundamental Concepts in Science and chairman of the International Academy of Astronautics' SETI (Search for Extraterrestrial Intelligence) Post-Detection Committee, headquartered at the Beyond Center, asks a crucial question at this juncture in history: Is the human species entering a new evolutionary, postbiological inflection point? Before long we will be launching intelligent space robots that will venture out to explore the universe for us.

> Not only are machines better able to endure extended exposure to the conditions of space, but they have the potential to develop intelligence far beyond the capacity of the human brain. Davies contends that aliens exploring the universe will be AI-empowered

machines: "I think it very likely—in fact inevitable—that biological intelligence is only a transitory phenomenon, a fleeting phase in the evolution of the universe," Davies writes in *The Eerie Silence: Renewing Our Search for Alien Intelligence*. "If we ever encounter extra-terrestrial intelligence, I believe it is overwhelmingly likely to be post-biological in nature."[1]

In the current search for advanced extraterrestrial life, SETI experts say the odds favor the detection of alien AI rather than actual biological life, because the period between when aliens developed radio technology and their creation of artificial intelligence would be brief. "If we build a machine with the intellectual capability of one human, then within 5 years its successor is more intelligent than all humanity combined," says Seth Shostak, SETI chief astronomer. "Once any society invents the technology that could put them in touch with the cosmos, they are at most only a few hundred years away from changing their own paradigm of sentience to artificial intelligence."[2]

British cosmologist and astrophysicist Martin Rees, the current Astronomer Royal, says:

Life on a planet around a star older than the sun could have had a head start of a billion years or more. Thus it may already have evolved much of the way toward a dominant machine intelligence. The history of human technological civilization is measured in centuries—and it may be only one or two more centuries before humans are overtaken or transcended by inorganic intelligence which will then persist, continuing to evolve for billions of years. This suggests that if we were to detect ET, it would be far more likely to be inorganic. We would be most unlikely to "catch" alien intelligence in the brief sliver of time when it was still in organic form.[3]

ET machines would be infinitely more intelligent and durable than the biological intelligence that created them. Intelligent machines would be immortal and would not need to exist in the carbon-friendly

"Goldilocks zones" on which current SETI searches focus. An AI could self-direct its own evolution, as each upgrade would be created as a result of the sum total of its predecessor's preloaded knowledge.

So what is it about us humans that has attracted the Greys to Earth and kept them here over thousands of years if they are machines? The reason for their presence has to involve something about us that is fundamentally different from them. My research suggests that the basic difference is that we, as the premier life-form on this planet, are natural life forms and they are not. They are totally synthetic. They are roboids. They may be synthetically assembled mechanisms, manufactured by organic, natural, life-bearing entities; they may be the result of the execution of a program sent out by a civilization in advance of ours; or they may be a phenomenon from another frame of reality altogether. No matter how they came to be—and I shall address this subject later in this book—they *are* artificial entities that came into being through artificial means and were sent out into the meterage of space-time-matter with an artificial, programmed quantum intelligence quite unlike our natural consciousness and natural propensity for life. This, ironically and fortuitously for us as natural living beings, is *their* great weakness.

The ultimate in artificial intelligence would involve a program that extends its scope to cover all possible knowledge so as to promote the optimal survival and continuance of the information it contains. This would mean somehow bridging its artificially intelligent program into any unknown quantity that has all the adaptations necessary to survive at any particular hospitable planetary location. In other words, by implanting their artificial intelligence into humans, aliens would be extending the existence of their own information, just as transhumanists like Ray Kurzweil seek to do when they look for ways to download an entire human individuality into an artificial information format in the interests of seeking continuance for that individuality. Any artificially intelligent visitors could achieve this goal via transhumanism and the insertion of chip technology into our biology via some kind of genetic engineering—which is exactly what is reported by those who have been subjected to alien abduction.

This harrowing experience involves invasive procedures that appear to be a form of experimentation with the human reproductive system and its hybridization with an alien format. It has reportedly been endured by thousands of people and remains a mystery to this day; in fact, it is often dismissed as a delusion of the human mind. This used to be my view, I have to confess, for a long time. I used to lump so-called abductees with those ingenuous cranks and charlatans who claim all kinds of paranormal and supernatural experiences, thereby giving ammunition to the congenitally cynical and skeptical people who suggest that all extraordinary paranormal experience is untenable and unreal. I now have to say unequivocally, after many years of carefully looking at the evidence, that there is no doubt whatsoever in my mind that this is not only a real physical experience—it is one of the most profound and significant experiences of our times.

John Mack, who was head of the Department of Psychiatry at Harvard Medical School until his death in 2004, confirmed in two books he authored that abduction is a genuine phenomenon, one that should not be grouped with psychopathological or other aberrant psychological conditions. Mack pointed out that any theory that would begin to explain the abduction phenomenon as anything but literally true would have to take into account five basic factors:

1. The high degree of consistency of detailed abduction accounts, reported with emotion appropriate to actual experiences as told by apparently reliable observers
2. The absence of psychiatric illness or other apparent psychological or emotional factors that could account for what is being reported
3. The physical changes and lesions affecting the bodies of experiencers, which follow no evident psychodynamic pattern
4. UFO sitings have been witnessed independently by others at the same time abductions have taken place (which the abductee may not see)
5. The reports of abductions by children as young as two or three years of age[4]

David M. Jacobs, associate professor of history at Temple University in Philadelphia, is a leading academic authority on UFOs and alien abductions. Since 1986 he has been conducting hypnotic regressions with abductees. When he was asked whether he believes that it is possible that experiences with alien craft and alien beings could be psychologically contrived manifestations, he replied:

> What you have to remember is the sheer enormousness of the abduction phenomenon; millions of people are being abducted. Moreover, in abductions people are typically missing from their normal environment. Others notice that they are missing. There are multiple abductions. People may see other people being abducted, and may or may not be abducted themselves. There are situations where somebody sees somebody else being abducted, and is abducted him or herself. Years go by and person A has a hypnotic regression, remembers seeing the other person. Person B, 3,000 miles away in another city, and for another reason has a hypnotic regression, remembers the abduction and sees person A there as well. And neither of them know that they have been regressed remembering this same abduction. To make that psychological, we have to live in a different informational world of how the human brain operates.
>
> Furthermore, abductees come back from an abduction event with anomalous marks on their body, scars on their body, scar-tissue that was literally formed the night before. They came back wearing somebody else's clothes, they came back to somebody else's house by accident. People see UFOs in the air, hovering directly over the person's house when they're describing being abducted, neighbors who have nothing to do with it see this. There is a very strong physical aspect to this that is completely non-existent in all of the other dissociative behavior that we see.
>
> The interesting thing about all these questions is, if this was purely psychological, if people were dreaming it up, we wouldn't be asking any of these questions. We'd know all the answers. We'd ask people, why do you think they're doing this? And they wouldn't tell

you, because that's the way the brain works. In channeling for example, all questions are answered, all ends are tied up, and it's all roses and light. With the abduction phenomenon we just don't know.[5]

The abduction phenomenon throws into doubt the history of humanity as reflected by the evolution of *Homo sapiens* as a cascade of natural consequences born of natural phenomena. Why are they experimenting with us? Why are they apparently seeking ways to hybridize us with them? What are these Grey entities in the first place? I have come to the firm conclusion that they are synthetically produced biological robotic creations whose existence can best be explained if we take a look at our own progress in producing something very similar with AI.

We are used to assuming that there is a fundamental difference between that which lives naturally and that which doesn't. But recent advances in biotechnology blur that distinction inasmuch as artificial, synthetic DNA that can replicate itself has been produced, and cloning procedures have been refined.

Scientists in the United States have succeeded in developing the first living cell to be controlled entirely by synthetic DNA. An existing bacterial genome was copied and its genetic code sequenced, after which "synthesis machines" copied this code and chemically constructed a new synthetic chromosome, piecing together blocks of DNA, which were then transplanted into a host cell. "The resulting microbe then looked and behaved like the species 'dictated' by the synthetic DNA." The advance, published in *Science,* was hailed as a scientific landmark, but critics say there are dangers posed by synthetic organisms. Dr. Craig Venter, who led this research at a genomics center in Maryland named after him, told the BBC News, "We've now been able to take our synthetic chromosome and transplant it into a recipient cell—a different organism. As soon as this new software goes into the cell, the cell reads [it] and converts into the species specified in that genetic code." The new bacteria can replicate over a billion times, producing copies that contain and are controlled by the constructed, synthetic DNA. "This is the first time any synthetic DNA has been in complete control of a cell," Venter said.[6]

So could the Greys have been created by an advanced technology using synthetic DNA? Could the juggernaut toward technologies such as these mean that we are soon to produce our own type of roboidal entity, or Grey/human hybrid? Artificial DNA could be modeled on our own DNA patterns and modulated to cope more efficiently with the effects of a physical environment. In fact, that kind of artificial genetic engineering of our own species is available now.

> Ross Thyer, at the University of Texas, Austin, has suggested that synthetic DNA could become an essential part of our own DNA: "Human engineering would result in an organism which permanently contains an expanded genetic alphabet, something that, to our knowledge, no naturally occurring life form has accomplished. What would such an organism do with an expanded genetic alphabet? We don't know. Could it lead to more sophisticated storage of biological information? More complicated or subtle regulatory networks? These are all questions we can look forward to exploring."[7]

Thyer bases this wistful look into a supposedly new and improved, genetically altered humanity on the fact that the first living organism to carry and pass down to future generations a genetic code expanded by synthetic DNA has just been created by American scientists.[8] "What we have now, for the first time, is an organism that stably harbours a third base pair, and it is utterly different to the natural ones," says Floyd Romesberg, whose team created the artificial organism at the Scripps Research Institute in La Jolla, California.[9] Over the past two years, the *E. coli* microbes used in the experiments have been made hardier and more able to pass on their synthetic genetic bases more faithfully when they divided. The end result, Romesberg says, is that the microbes can hold the new genetic material indefinitely.[10]

"This is a major step forward in showing that a living cell such as a simple bacterium can be engineered to sustain a synthetic base pair not found in nature," said Paul Freemont, who specialises in synthetic biology at Imperial College in London. "This leads to the concept of semi-synthetic living systems that could be engineered to perform specific functions that would rely on a distinct genetic code compared to the natural genetic code."

But he said that the "real power" of the approach would be in making microbes that carried multiple artificial DNA bases, or even a completely human-designed synthetic genome, which the study suggested was at least possible in principle.[11]

If we have achieved this with our relatively primitive technology, it is conceivable that with their superior technology it would be a relatively easy task for the Grey roboids to, in this way, introduce their artificial DNA into our species. But the big question is: Why would they bother? It is my proposition—one that I will carefully explain in this book—that we are heading for a scenario in which humanity will walk as synthetic machines prompted by an extraterrestrial force that at this time few accept is even here on our planet. The scale of the planet as a harbor for life eventually could end in the bytes and blips of electrical hysteresis loops, our natural organic biological living state gone, our unique, individual selves gone because the drive that allows for change through free will is gone forever.

Where, then, and how do we find our existential margins as living beings and keep sight of them, never mind guard them? Are there no "Margins of Forever" anymore? Are only "Margins of Never" left?

Should we meekly accept the assurances of Musk, Kurzweil, and Kaku that all this "progress" is for the good of humanity? Or, is there a unique something about humanity that will be lost in the process, something we should be defending and protecting as though our lives depended on it? It is in response to these questions that I believe the mystery of alien visitation on our planet can be solved.

This unique something is, I suggest, a nonphysical component to our humanity, a component that connects us to a nonatomic state that is not of the observable physical universe. It cannot, therefore, be simulated using any physical device, no matter how sophisticated it might be. When I refer to something not of the physical universe I am by no means pointing to the traditional Christian notion of God dispensing rewards and punishments but rather to a naturally implied center of all effects, a point of perfection that is definitively implied by modern quantum physics, a timeless state in which there is perfect freedom and complete awareness of all options, which I call the *Godverse*. Our natural connection to that timeless state, which gives us the capacity for survival beyond physical death, is the soul. The relevance of the statement "What does it profit a man if he gains the whole world and suffers the loss of his own Soul" (Mark 8:36) rings loud and clear in this context.

It is my thesis that the Greys, in contrast, are purely physical creations within and out of this universe, well after its beginning, and thus completely subject to the entropic momentums that break down and decay physical states. They have no connection to any nonphysical state that might lie beyond the materiality of this universe—in short, no soul. Without this component they are completely subject to the breakdown momentum implicit in the physical universe. These Greys are the embodiment of the highest form of artificial intelligence, somewhat similar to the probes we create and send out to planets to gather information remotely. I believe they are universal probes programmed to explore the features and dangers of the universe.

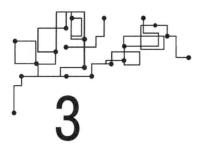

3

SIM Card Man

It is not beyond the bounds of reason to speculate that another civilization beyond our planet may well have reached a level of technology that we have reached, and gone further, to send probes out in space to find suitable locations for continuing their existence in case their own planetary resources fail or their planet becomes inhospitable. Could they be the nonbiological format predicted by Kurzweil and other futurists, soft-tissue robots programmed with the information of their creators? Are we right now in the process of converting ourselves into a similar format via artificial devices?

Could these entities be the epitome of artificial intelligence? The Grey alien entities encountered by so many reliable witnesses have been described as having blank, emotionless faces as they carry out painful procedures, many of which are centered on the reproductive system of their human subjects. The impression of many abductees is that we are laboratory rats to the Greys. They seem incapable of any emotion, be it compassion and sympathy at one end of the spectrum, or cruelty at the other. As such, they cannot, it seems, be understood in anthropomorphic terms. From all accounts the Greys are more like machines, biological robots that may have been programmed in such a way as to preserve the identity of their creators for eternity. Perhaps the Greys carry the DNA of their creators and have been designed for space travel to find new sources of DNA elsewhere in the universe, to refresh their creators' cloning process. The civilization that spawned their creators would only have had to go just a few steps further than we are now in developing artificial intelligence and biotechnology. Let's first review our own progress in that direction.

Moore's law predicts that the amount of computing power we can fit on a chip doubles every two years. According to Huw Price, formerly Bertrand Russell Professor of Philosophy at Cambridge University, "some trends point towards the middle of the present century"[1] for machines to trump human beings in intelligence. He goes on to say that "the bad news is that they might simply be indifferent to us—they might care about us as much as we care about the bugs on the windscreen." Price suggests that we "stop treating intelligent machines as the stuff of science fiction, and start thinking of them as a part of the reality that we or our descendants may actually confront, sooner or later."[2]

Researchers talk about computers that are able to create more and more powerful generations of computers that eventually we might lose control of:

> "Artificial intelligence is one of the technologies that puts more and more power into smaller and smaller packages," says [Daniel] Dewey, an expert in machine super-intelligence who previously worked [as a software engineer] at Google. . . . "You can do things with these technologies, typically chain reaction–type effects, so that starting with very few resources you could undertake projects that could affect everyone in the world."[3]

Artificial intelligence is already taking on a mind of its own, with a completely different logic base than human thought processes, which eventually may very well be impossible to access and therefore to control. Nello Cristianini, professor of artificial intelligence at the University of Bristol, U.K., who has written about the history and evolution of AI research, says that in the development of AI, "as soon as we gave up the attempt to produce mental, psychological qualities we started finding success."[4] Instead of a rule-based approach, data is fed in indiscriminately to build a statistical model based on probabilities.

For example, Google turned to the vast web it has indexed, containing every combination of words it is possible to have, so that its translator—from English to French, for instance—could then compare its initial attempt with every sentence written on the internet in French. Google's translator knows nothing about the rules of language, only the relative frequency of a vast number of word sequences, so it's just a matter of probabilities. With machine intelligence we have traded "why" for "what." "Explainability is a social agreement," says Cristianini. "We decided in the past it mattered. We've decided now it doesn't matter."[5]

Writer and journalist Colin Horgan discusses the new frontiers of what are known as "deepfakes," which are faces, voices, news stories, and social profiles created by artificial intelligence using algorithms. "One program places a phone call; another answers. One algorithm writes a news story; another writes a novel based on it. One algorithm creates a human face; a bot uses it to create a social media profile that interacts with others created by yet another algorithm. And on and on—algorithms upon algorithms, forever."[6] Horgan postulates that

> we may face a future where our physical selves remain, but without a way, or a space, for us to collectively remember our feelings and thoughts—those things that make us human. . . . The servers may never be empty, but the technology that we created to preserve ourselves will instead be preserving replications. Meanwhile, we will disappear—not from view, but from the record. For centuries we created technology to preserve humanity. Now the technology we've created will preserve itself.[7]

So do we give up asking questions and get so used to choices being made for us that we stop noticing? The stakes are higher now that intelligent machines are beginning to make inscrutable decisions about mortgage applications, medical diagnoses, and even whether you are guilty of a crime. In medicine, for instance, what if a machine learning system decides that you will start drinking heavily in a few years' time? Would doctors be justified in withholding a transplant? It would be hard to argue your case if no one knew how the conclusion was arrived at. And some may trust AI more than others. Many people are all too willing to accept something that an algorithm has found out.

The AI we've ended up with is alien, a form of intelligence we've never encountered before. Swedish philosopher Nick Bostrom says:

> There is a real gap between the speed of technological advance and our understanding of its implications. "We're at the level of infants in moral responsibility, but with the technological capability of adults," he says. As such, the significance of existential risk is "not on people's radars." But he argues that change is coming, whether we're ready for it or not. "There is a bottleneck in human history. The human condition is going to change. . . . It's not science fiction, religious doctrine or a late-night conversation in the pub. There is no plausible moral case not to take it seriously."[8]

Meanwhile, an international team of scientists, mathematicians, and philosophers at the University of Oxford's Future of Humanity Institute has developed a research analysis built around the concept of Existential Risk. It says that the implications of a technology-based, almost transhuman world could be worse than any pandemic, natural disaster, or even nuclear war, which humanity is likely to survive. They compare it to a "dangerous weapon in the hands of an impulsive child," to the point where technology has the potential to exceed our capacity to control the probable effects.[9]

The director of the institute, Nick Bostrom says that they are not talking about pandemics or natural disasters or even nuclear war; those they believe humanity would be likely to survive. Instead they are referring to a new kind of technological era, with "threats we have no track record of surviving."[10] For example:

> Synthetic biology, in which biology meets engineering for medical benefit, could have unforeseen consequences in manipulating the boundaries of human biology, while nanotechnology, if used in war-

fare, would challenge governments to control and restrict its misuse.

There are also fears about how artificial or machine intelligence might interact with the external world. The more it is used to monitor and run living systems, the more its indifference to any incidental damage becomes apparent and relevant. Seán O'Heigeartaigh, a geneticist and the executive director of Cambridge University's Centre for the Study of Existential Risk, draws an analogy with algorithms used in automated stock-market trading. These mathematical strings can "manipulate the real world" and have direct and destructive consequences for real economies and real people. In terms of risks from biology, he worries about experiments carrying out genetic modifications, dismantling and rebuilding genetic structures. There is always the risk of an unintended sequence of events or something that becomes harmful when transferred into another environment. "We are developing things that could go wrong in a profound way," he admits.[11]

Despite this, a synthetically derived existential base is being hailed by futurists who believe that the exponential growth of artificial intelligence, biotechnology, and nanotechnology means that before 2050, human consciousness and identity will be copied and uploaded into a nonbiological form of entity, transcending biology to achieve the dream of immortality. It would seem perfectly natural to those who are pursuing this technological pathway that we follow what they call the next evolutionary step toward the survival of the fittest by converting ourselves into an information field that never breaks down or decays. No need for physical bodies that break down and die—we can reconstruct our virtual self in electronic form and go on forever. There are a surprising number of people who see morphing into a nonbiologically centered virtual machine as an attractive and even exciting prospect for the future of our species. Many look at it as a palliative for all the ills that plague the human condition, both in terms of a social and a physical perspective. But at what cost?

A paper in the August 2016 edition of the journal *Neuron* describes the creation of a tiny implant the size of "a grain of sand" that could connect computers to the human body without the need for wires or batteries, opening up a host of futuristic possibilities. The devices, dubbed "neural dust," could be used to continually monitor organs such as the heart in real time, and if these implants could be made even smaller they could be inserted into the human brain to control robotic devices such as prosthetic arms or legs.[12] One of the inventors, Michel Maharbiz, a professor in the Department of Electrical Engineering and Computer Science at the University of California, Berkeley, says, "I think the long-term prospects for neural dust are not only within nerves and the brain, but much broader. . . . But now I can take a speck of nothing and park it next to a nerve or organ, your [gastro-intestinal] tract or a muscle, and read out the data."[13] So far, experiments have been carried out on muscles and the peripheral nervous system of rats, but the researchers believe the dust could also work in the human central nervous system and brain to control prosthetics. The researchers are currently building neural dust that could last in the body for more than ten years.

In a similar vein, *Nature* magazine reported on a team at the Swedish electronics company Acreo that foresees "a future in which humans are wired up like cars, with sensors that form an early-warning system"[14] for disease or illness. John Rogers, a materials scientist at the University of Illinois at Urbana–Champaign, says, "I think electronics is coming at you. It's migrating closer and closer and I think it's a very natural thing to imagine that they will eventually become intimately integrated with the body."[15] But University of Toyko engineer Takao Someya points out one likely problem: "When a semiconductor chip is introduced inside the body, hacking is a truly serious issue."[16]

The RFID (Radio Frequency Identification Device) chip is on the way. It can be inserted into you in various guises, and they will tell you it is indispensable for your future. I have shouted this warning in radio broadcasts and all the books and articles I have written. Millions, perhaps billions, will fall for its advertised supposed benefit as a palliative for all ills, with no idea of the catastrophic implications for the human body and a person's individuality, and the even broader implications for the human condition.

Elon Musk has taken the whole human-machine integration debate one step further with his suggestion that in an age when AI threatens to become widespread, humans will be useless, so there is a need to merge with machines.

> "Over time I think we will probably see a closer merger of biological intelligence and digital intelligence," Musk told an audience at the World Government Summit in Dubai, where he also launched Tesla in the United Arab Emirates. "It's mostly about the bandwidth, the speed of the connection between your brain and the digital version of yourself, particularly output." Musk explained what he meant by saying that computers can communicate at "a trillion bits per second," while humans, whose main communication method is typing with their fingers via a mobile device, can do about 10 bits per second. "Some high bandwidth interface to the brain will be something that helps achieve a symbiosis between human and machine intelligence and maybe solves the control problem and the usefulness problem," Musk explained. His proposal would involve "a new layer of a brain able to access information quickly and tap into artificial intelligence."[17]

Michio Kaku points out that merging our minds with machines may sound like science fiction, but it's already a reality. Deep brain stimulation—inserting electric wires in the brain and attaching them to a brain pacemaker—is now used to cure conditions such as depression. Research is being conducted into computer chips that can store human memory when implanted in the brain. So far these technologies are only used for medical conditions, but Kaku predicts that in the future they may well be used to enhance intelligence with "thinking chips." He says that although we might find all this off-putting at first, we may well get used to it when we realize the obvious advantages.[18]

Senior research scientist Alexsandr Noy and his team at the Lawrence Livermore National Laboratory in California are developing what they believe to be one of the first examples of a

> truly integrated bioelectronic system. A novel transistor controlled by the chemical that provides the energy for our cells' metabolism could

be a big step toward making prosthetic devices that can be wired directly into the nervous system. Transistors are the fundamental building blocks of electronic gadgets, so finding ways to control them with biological signals could provide a route toward integrating electronics with the body. Noy hopes "that this type of technology could be used to construct seamless bioelectronic interfaces to allow better communication between living organisms and machines."[19]

A further example of the development of brain machine interfaces can be found in the following:

A mind-control system has recently been created that allows a person to alter the genes in a mouse through the power of thought alone. The latest advances in cybernetics are fused with those in synthetic biology by connecting a wireless headset that monitors brainwaves to an implant in the mouse that can change the rodent's genes. With practice, volunteers found that they could turn the gene in the mouse on or off at will and thereby raise or lower the levels of protein circulating in the animal's blood system. Clinical trials in people with chronic pain or epilepsy are projected to begin in the next five years. "If I'm right, which is far from certain, this could change the treatment strategies of the future," says Martin Fussenegger, a bioengineer who leads the project at ETH Zurich. "We want a device that does it all in the body, that interfaces with the physiology of the body." Fussenegger's device aims to spot medical conditions early on and release therapeutic proteins before the problem becomes serious.[20]

The ease with which machines can now be interfaced with the human brain is also illustrated by the following:

Jan Scheuermann is a Pittsburgh woman who's been unable to move any of her muscles from the neck down for a decade. Thanks to two ports on top of her head, she's gradually gained finer and finer control of a specially developed robotic limb by using her mind. She can now manipulate it to the point where she can drink from a cup, open doors, and even shake hands.[21]

While these applications of biotechnology can in themselves be enormously beneficial, it is perhaps prudent to draw boundaries between essential basic physical needs such as those required for movement and enhancement of otherwise healthy brains involving brain-machine interfaces. Ray Kurzweil predicts that "when we get into the 2020s almost everybody will have some amount of non-biological intelligence in their brains. It's going to happen, in a very gradual way, by non-biological intelligence that gradually becomes more sophisticated with new versions until you get to the 2040s and the non-biological machine portion of our intelligence will be vastly more powerful than the biological portion; the biological portion will be pretty trivial at that point and ultimately that is where the action is."[22] It's not hard to envision this coming about. For example, what if parents of newborn babies were offered the opportunity to enhance their child's brain through the insertion of biochips? They might at first reject the idea as an outrageous imposition on their child, but if other parents adopt these technologies and give their kids an advantage—better memory and better learning skills perhaps—could the unacceptable then become acceptable? Could the fear of intruding on a child's natural humanity be overpowered by the fear of the child losing out to other children whose parents are happy to use artificial mind enhancement?

Stephen Hawking suggested that if we want to survive beyond the next century, we need to mechanize as fast as possible "so that artificial brains contribute to human intelligence rather than opposing it."[23] He and others like Ray Kurzweil, Michio Kaku, and robotics engineer Kevin Warwick look forward to a new cyborg humanity and a world in which everything can be remotely controlled by the brain and we can link ourselves to external machines or even to one another. We are becoming more and more reliant on these for our everyday existence, outsourcing our lives into electronic formats like

Twitter and Facebook. It could be argued that the transition to cyborg is already half complete, as humans now rely on electronic equipment to the point that it becomes an extension of their bodies. The new research is working to weave machines into human lives even more permanently, such that they become integral to the body itself. For example, "a Tokyo University team has developed a robot named Noby, designed to simulate the development and behavior of a nine-month-old baby in an effort to better understand how humans grow."[24]

Creating a robot can help achieve a society where robots and humans live side by side. Says Professor Yasuo Kuniyoshi, who led the Noby team, "Our purpose is to build a system that can learn various behaviours and acquire various functionalities as it explores around the environment and interacting with humans."[25] Noby is a highly accurate model with the sensory and motor functions of a nine-month-old human baby. The body is covered in a soft "skin" with six hundred tactile sensors.

> It is flexible and its joints can move like those of a human baby. Noby also has two cameras for "seeing" and two microphones for "listening" to the external world. The project is part of the effort to make more humanlike robots. A nine-month-old human baby was used as Noby's model, as this is the age of rapid development of movement and cognition functions in humans.[26]

There are two remarkable assumptions behind this experiment. First, it is accepted that a human being will interact with a robot like they would another human being, providing the robot with the same inputs they would provide a human baby. Second, it is assumed that the development, behavior, and cognition of a human baby can be replicated if the same external signals that are received by a human baby are programmed into a robot. Is there a certain something that is missed here, an ingredient that is nonprogrammable? What do you think?

It all reminds me of the special jackets that were designed some years ago in Japan for children who are away from their parents. The idea was that if the child wears the jacket, the parent can give him or her remote cyber hugs through it. If this makes you squirm, then ask yourself why? If you feel something is missing from a cyber hug, what could that something be?

Nothing could be more catastrophic for humankind than to buy into the juggernaut of chip-induced transhumanism. Every week there are blazing new technological developments, and it seems that with every year the momentum toward techno-dystopia gathers blistering speed, as it seems we are all too happy for the natural to be replaced by the artificial. SIM card man is truly on the horizon. Are you feeling a sense of unease about all of this? Are the hairs on the back of your neck standing on end as mine were when I envisage the future that lies in wait for your children and mine? If such is the case, then somewhere within you you are sensing that there *is* something about natural humanity that cannot be digitally mastered and reproduced.

And given that there is such a something, then there must be an aspect of us humans that is not formed of purely physical elements, as anything physical is potentially reproducible with the right technology.

In the first quarter of the twenty-first century, the speed of constant and continuing changes in our modern world throws up a bewildering chain of imperatives and situations that contradict, puzzle, and confuse us all as never before. They lead to questions that demand quick, precise, pertinent answers, answers that challenge us all to understand all our yesterdays, our todays, and our tomorrows.

Metaverse (the rebranded Facebook) CEO Mark Zuckerberg sees techno-telepathy as the next milestone. He describes direct mind-to-mind contact as "the ultimate communications technology." "You'll think a text or update and send it," affirmed his experimental tech director, Regina Dugan.[27] The implications of such a development are both astonishing and worrying: hacking and mind control are the first of many that spring to mind. A synthetic existential base is being hailed by technocrats who believe that the exponential growth of artificial intelligence, biotechnology, and nanotechnology means that by 2050 human consciousness and identity will be copied and uploaded into a nonbiological form of entity that transcends biology, thereby achieving the dream of immortality. In this, the indelible existential natural laws of life and living and meaning are being obfuscated, and a deliberate attempt is being made to supplant them with an artificial reality that threatens the very naturalness of the living human being. It might seem perfectly natural to those who are promoting this techno-future that we must follow what they think of as the next evolutionary step toward survival of the fittest by converting ourselves into an information field that never breaks down or decays. No need for physical bodies that break down and die—we simply reconstruct our virtual self in electronic form and go on forever. There are a surprising number of people who see morphing into a nonbiologically centered virtual machine as an attractive and even exciting prospect for the future of our species. Many look at it as a palliative for all the ills that plague us both in terms of a social and a physical perspective. But at what cost?

A mighty threshold is inexorably creeping up on us all, particularly those of us in the so-called developed world. That threshold is the dividing line between the natural living aegis of our human condition and that of an artificially created synthetic one. The size, range, and potential of the human spirit to soar to limitless horizons beyond the empirically definable is losing its definition. The tendency to run with the impetus that science brings dominates our everyday lives, and in the process we deny ourselves those grand and inspiring perspectives that reach beyond the mundane and the ordinary. We only get rare glimpses of our true natural potential, and these get rarer and rarer as we become more and more hitched to the artificial reality that is thrown at us. How many cyber hugs would add up to one real one? How many hours of virtual reality will add up to one moment of actual reality? Why is it that we are rarely if ever tempted to ask these questions? Are we losing sight of the very base of our human selves in the storm of technological development that overwhelms our lives every moment of every day?

The first steps of this intrusion begins with your medical records, what you may consider private information. Soon they will make it an administrative imperative to divulge them. Passports will not be of paper but rather electronic tags inserted into your body that have not only all your personal details from birth to death but also everything known about your family and your health. Your right to privacy and movement will be taken away, gradually at first, and then at a stroke, and they will do this with your cooperation. They will set up the most draconian "terrorist" events from time to time to convince populations that it is in their interest and in the security of the nation that all this is done. Deep-seated racial, ethnic, cultural, and sectarian prejudice in many of us will be cleverly exploited to bring all this about. Those who warn us will be called paranoiacs and conspiracy theorists by the mainstream media, which denigrates any serious investigations into ET contacts. Their goal is to make human beings synthetic machines under the aegis of an extraterrestrial force that few realize is even here on our planet. The scale of the planet as a harbor for life eventually ends in the bytes and blips of electrical hysteresis loops.

So where and how do we find our existential potential as living human beings and keep sight of it and safeguard it? What's it to be, the Kurzweilian heaven of noncommittal answers, a heaven as organized religion presents it to us, or no heaven at all? Or are there margins beyond all of this. I certainly believe there are, but I also believe there is a factor related to the Kurzweilian paradigm that can undermine our potential to reach those margins or ever see them: the extraterrestrial alien phenomenon.

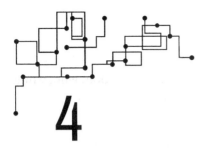

4

Behind the Scenes

Many conscientious and thorough researchers into the alien phenomenon have documented cases of people in highly placed government or military facilities who have personal experience of both the alien phenomenon and pressure from high places to slam the lid on all they have seen and heard. I, too, have my own sources in similar positions who have reported the same to me for years. It would seem that there has been collusion between the Greys and the governments of the United States, Russia, Israel, China, and Australia—a partnership that I am convinced will be to our detriment as a species and to their overwhelming advantage.

I hesitate to say this, but the evidence suggests that you literally play with death if you attempt to expose and reveal the reality of the alien presence. Those who have tried to do so often come to unaccountable mysterious deaths. Assassinations are covert and unspectacular, with the least likelihood of causing attention. A thirty-year study by amateur astronomer and former U.S. government adviser Timothy Hood revealed that UFO researchers began to die under mysterious circumstances in the 1970s and 1980s. Causes of death range from improbable suicides, strange disappearances, rare cancers, murders, and a variety of supposedly natural causes that were often proved to be medically inconclusive. The list of the deceased even extends to prominent astrophysicists who had dedicated themselves to the search for extraterrestrial life. In fact, twenty-five people involved in the development of space weapons died within a short period of time in the late '80s, a fact noted by American writer, director, and producer Sidney Sheldon, who, while working on his novel *The End of the World,* compiled his "Sheldon list" of these mysterious deaths.[1]

Eminent Harvard psychiatrist and Pulitzer Prize–winner Dr. John E. Mack died in London in 2004 after a being struck by a drunk driver who was apparently later convicted and jailed for the offense. While this may be nothing more than a tragic accident—it is of course impossible to know for sure—there are those who believe that his death was suspicious. Dr. Mack had become the subject of an unprecedented fourteen-month review by Harvard Medical School, during which his controversial research methods with alien abductees were scrutinized. After he published his book *Abduction: Human Encounters with Aliens* in 1994, Harvard considered censuring him and revoking his tenure, though eventually a statement was issued that "reaffirmed Dr. Mack's academic freedom to study what he wishes and to state his opinion without impediment."[2]

This succession of untimely demises has almost become as much of a mystery as the aliens themselves. Certainly, the search for extraterrestrial life can lead researchers in the field to discover very sensitive classified information; there is often military involvement in this area due to the potential threat posed to national security by any object, terrestrial or extraterrestrial, that enters protected airspace.

My research has led me to the firm conclusion that the ET entities that are here at this time are hidden too well and their presence obfuscated by those in secret authority the world over, and the whys and wherefores of this are what matter crucially. It is nothing less than a complete takeover. It seems they have been seeking to do this for millennia, as indicated by a large and ever-increasing amount of archaeological and anthropological evidence of their presence all over the planet. It matters not one iota where they come from. The only thing that matters is that they are here and what they are here for, because the implications of their presence on Earth are what matters most to us. This book is about those implications.

Those who dub researchers such as myself "conspiracy theorists" (incidentally this was a term coined by the CIA after the assassination of President Kennedy, to refute anyone who questioned the official narrative of his murder), have a field day, rubbishing us as fools and paranoiacs. These are the same lot that promoted the fake Gulf of Tonkin story that sparked American justification for going to war in Vietnam and then went silent when it was proved after the war to be a fabrication and oh so many other fabrications too numerous to list.

Similarly, what is termed *9/11,* the attack on the World Trade Center and the Pentagon, will in time prove to be the biggest, most heinous canard ever perpetrated on humankind by a national government. It is now well established and beyond any reasonable doubt in my mind that the whole thing was an in-house exercise carried out by a governmental group of conspirators. Yet many people seem to ignore the facts as revealed by countless truthers, structural engineers, witnesses, and other experts. Such is the control of the mainstream media worldwide to protect the activities of vested cartels. The years that followed the attack have brought to light compelling evidence that the two towers and a third building well removed from the twin tower site collapsed as a result of explosive detonations set up before the aerial attack occurred. This third building had no reason to collapse the way it did, as though demolished by experts. The detonations that caused all the buildings to collapse as though demolished by demolition professionals were timed to coincide with the aircraft hitting the buildings.*

The 2017 documentary *The Day After Disclosure* is the best way to introduce yourself to the ET phenomenon if you are coming to this subject for the first time. There is one other confirmation of the ET presence on our planet that to me is written in stone as truth. It is an interview with an anonymous former CIA officer conducted by Richard M. Dolan, a reputable ufologist who appears in the 2017 documentary *Truth Embargo.* The ex-CIA officer whom Dolan interviewed was fac-

---

*I urge you to see the documentary *Anatomy of a Great Deception* if you have any doubts about my assertions.

ing kidney failure and death, so he had nothing to lose and therefore felt compelled to disclose secret information he believed was too important to hide. "Anonymous" served in the U.S. Army, worked for the CIA, and worked on the U.S. Air Force's Project Blue Book, one of the official studies of UFOs. He refers to the project as "partially a fraud." Asking for clarification, Dolan says to the man: "You're saying some of the Blue Book cases were completely fictitious?" Anonymous responds, "Yes." He then states that he and his superior at the CIA were allowed inside the secretive Area 51 in Nevada to gather intel and report back to the president. There, Anonymous describes seeing several alien spacecraft, including the craft that crashed in Roswell, New Mexico. He claims that he and his superior were taken to the S-4 facility southwest of Area 51, where they observed live extraterrestrials.

After the publication of my previous two books on the alien phenomenon my life has been threatened by representatives from four separate, highly credible organizations that represent both religious and political bodies. I was warned that if I continue to intrude on their territory as I have done in my previous books on this subject, I will not publish another one. My radio broadcasts solicited the same response. On several occasions I've had unmarked Apache helicopters hovering a few hundred feet above my house and paddocks and gardens. They seem to be studying and taking photographs of my house, the property, and any people they may see. It still happens, and I have the clear video evidence to prove it. Believe me, I am only a small fish in a big pond, and yet they threatened me. In a way I really am quite flattered. Yet it would be useless and even more dangerous for me to seek help from these threats against my life from the forces of law and order, especially the police, because many of the most senior officers in the police forces around the world belong in one way or another, albeit in almost all cases unknowingly, to these ET-controlled organizations. Ironically, most of these officers haven't a clue about what's behind the influences brought to bear on them

All this has encouraged me to continue and never cease in my efforts to tell the world a harrowing story in the interests of your children and mine and their future on this planet. Most parents will understand this when they look into the eyes of their little ones and dream of the future they want for them.

We are not alone in the universe of stars and planets we see out there, and not only are we not alone, but I believe without a doubt that humanity is under the influence, biologically and psychologically, of entities that do not originate from our planet.

The evidence coming from a small number of secret whistleblowers in the highest positions in the U.S. and Russian governments as well as from witnesses all over the world is overwhelming now. That the public is so ignorant of this suggests control by powerful secret interests within national governments and the mainstream media. The control is so powerful and so precisely set that presidents and prime ministers and billions all over the planet are kept in ignorance. So despite highly credible witnesses attesting to the verity of the phenomenon—including several astronauts and more than ten thousand official pilot reports of interactions with inexplicable craft—the subject is closed to serious researchers by official channels in all but a few notable countries.

My research has led me to the firm conclusion that the ET entities that are here are synthetic robots, and they are here to wrest the most precious capacities we as humans possess—for their benefit and to our detriment. We are their lab rats to further this purpose. It is nothing less than a complete takeover. They have, it seems, been seeking to do this for millennia as is indicated by a huge and ever increasing deposition of archaeological and anthropological evidence of their presence all over the planet that has been uncovered by researchers. Far from having no solid evidence for it as so many of the authorities claim, the evidence is myriad and is soon hidden by teams secretly sponsored by an all-powerful cartel within these authorities that maintain teams of "Launderers" that can go anywhere at any time with the means to evacuate and clean this evidence from public view.

My central thesis is that these roboids are themselves operating under a canard that they themselves cannot know is a falsehood because they are synthetically contrived entities run by an AI computer program—a fact that might, ironically, defeat their own purpose in the end. They are ultimately machines, and no matter how technologically superior they are, they cannot implicitly know or understand the scale or meaning that underlies any natural life-form, especially the highest life-form on this planet, human beings. The inherent capacities and existential range of a natural life-form will always outscale and dominate an artificially contrived one. It is impossible for these roboidal entities to succeed in their hidden agenda here on this planet, and it is my contention that this is why they have been here for so long, still trying to achieve their final goal of painstakingly growing, through genetic engineering, a special kind of humanity for their covert purposes. There is something extraordinarily exceptional and special about a natural living entity with highly intelligent dominion over the material schemes of the universe.

It is so easy to suspect that conspiracies underlie almost everything that takes place in the world today, especially anything that one's own opinions don't subscribe to. The revelations of Edward Snowden have confirmed what my own sources have been telling me for years when it relates to things other than the ETs and the UFO phenomenon. Snowden was an American security contractor who told us about liars and cheaters at the highest levels of the U.S. government who steal our privacy, our self-respect, and even our lives. It seems we must depend on whistleblowers like him to bring this all out so we can empower ourselves and not act like a corralled herd of sheep doing what our shepherds tell us, going where they want us to go.

In 1952, a CIA group called the Psychological Strategy Board concluded that when it comes to UFOs, the American public is dangerously gullible and prone to "a growing national hysteria." The group recommended educational programs to debunk the public's interest in unexplained phenomena.[3] What has changed nearly seventy years later? There are well over ten thousand official reports, from all over the world, by pilots alone seeing these things, in many instances within a hundred meters of their aircraft. Pilots are professional people trained to observe things reliably. Yet the authorities have buried all these reports of sightings they have filed. They somehow disappear. Only a few are ever reported and come into the public eye. Those brave hearts who do the reporting are pilloried, ridiculed, and threatened. They not only lose their credibility, but they also lose their jobs, their families, and some, their lives. It's a relatively simple matter to take them all out at the earliest stage. There are now draconian antiterrorist measures in place to do this, all over the world. Just think how simple it has been for the U.S. government or, for that matter, any government to do this, to get complete control over all our lives in the name of catching "terrorists" who have in many cases been set up by the same governments.

Now you know why skeptics, genuine or set up by governments, demand hard evidence. They know you can never succeed in getting this evidence to the public, ever. They think they have won, but they have *lost*—it's the alien intelligence behind all this that has won. Something about the nature of alien-derived UFOs and their function and their occupants exposes them from time to time to our view, and they are seen by the most reliable and sober witnesses in the thousands, but it doesn't matter who sees them. Anyone who claimed to have seen them through the years was likely to be immediately labeled hysterical or crazy or a deviant who operates on the fringes of what they want us to believe as madness. So how do you establish that any alien stories are verifiably true? The answer of course is that you cannot. The simple-minded and of course the downright gullible may believe them, but for most they will be curious stories with some entertainment value. Who can blame them? The human imagination is notorious for attention seeking, for vanity, for risk taking, profit making, and confabulating.

I have never personally met an extraterrestrial being or entity. And there is no authoritative evidence available to the general public that can place the origins of the Greys here on this planet in terms of an actual location or planet out there. There are, unquestionably, the informed few who *can* filter out the true from the false and stand outside the official government stance and the mainstream media's cynicism. Are the many thousands of people who have done the research and have claimed interactions with and observation of these objects we see in the skies all over our planet all cranks?

Imagine if you could get the odd alien to the nearest TV studio and hitch up a TV broadcast to the world. You could get a battery of the world's most respected scientists, doctors, lawyers, and (most important of all) celebrities to attest that what they are watching and hearing is the real McCoy. Notice I left out priests and politicians from the verification list—my intention is only to ensure that the Truth Police don't pay us a visit.

Back to the revelation show of the century: Music is first staged in spectacular style, accompanied by flashing lights (set to seven blinks a second), as frozen nitrogen is released in to create the right atmosphere. An avid team is assembled, set to convince the world that we are not alone. But will it work? We have forgotten the "rent a skeptic" brigade, that awesome breed of one-armed bandit intelligences, all five of them, that intersperse airways globally as the self-appointed guardians of the "empirical way of truth." There has to be a verification panel with "Yes" and "No" boards and straight ahead, one-way minded, pebble-lens views. Stalwart citizens for whom there is no up, down, or sideways to see to it that all that is presented is not fake. Beat this lot of skeptics? No way. Not even Abraham Lincoln, Nelson Mandela, Mahatma Ghandi, and Mother Teresa of Calcutta have a chance against them. But they will have to be there to attest the genuine nature of the fare the world is about to witness.

The trump card, so to speak, will be the presence of the alien itself. How do you get an alien to cooperate and spill the beans that he, she, or it is the genuine article? Any friendly mega-intelligent alien would have to stretch a long, cooperating, four-finger point and be more docile and indulgent than your average domestic pussy or pet poodle, while also being palatable, pokable, and decently amenable to be plied with questions. What do you pay it, or him, or her? I doubt if you could pay him with the rights to all of Australia, Switzerland, Monaco, the Cayman Islands, and Saudi Arabia, because he would by now own the whole planet anyway. Cameras roll, music continues (something like *Thus Sprach Zarathustra,* the theme from the movie *2001: A Space Odyssey*), credits form and disappear, a pan into close-up, and there would sit a popular iconic TV host, there to see us through the alien's credentials as genuinely intergalactic. That's it! We have liftoff! The world is about to be changed forever. The truth will not be "out there" anymore; it will have come to roost in a TV studio, where it has always belonged.

Liftoff. Let's get the show on the road. Did I say liftoff? You've got to be joking. You'd have to be living in cloud-cuckoo-land if you thought that all this would convince ordinary folks that what they are seeing is genuine and true. A room full of popes, rabbis, imams, mahanayake theras, and grand ayatollahs would be deemed nothing to the strokes of a simple video pen. The whole thing would in seconds be seen as mere "*Windows*" dressing in the hands of some clever technicians. Government-sponsored hackers with the latest precious clutch of transistors and diodes and backup viruses lovingly set on a parody of the gift the Greeks left the Trojans would beg to differ that all this was genuine. And who would do the deeming that it was not genuine? You've guessed it. It would be there smiling if it could. The kind of smile you would get from your vacuum cleaner when you switched it to blow when you meant suck. Game, set, match.

Cut to the studio control room's editor's suite. A discreet hand reaches forward on the master edit console. A button is pressed down by a forefinger. The hand has no thumb. The ON AIR sign lights up. A single spotlight blazes on a strange, spindly form. Only the most intelligent and gifted humans will see that it is irrelevant to ask the question: Where are you from? The alien machines known as the Greys know human nature well. And if I am right in my assessment of them, they have no emotions. They are as totally blind to emotion as your vacuum cleaner. They can't know even in their own way that only a few of us have original minds, minds capable of thinking outside the box. They've made a new box, defined it, and have put the most powerful, belligerent, and decisive personalities among us in it and closed the lid. That way they only have to deal with a few, fight the few, and fight through the few and do not have to manage the many.

Contactees, some of whom come from the highest echelons of national security organizations and science establishments the world over, include people whose names and positions I will take with me to the grave in the spirit of the trust they have shown me by revealing what they know. Their identities will be safe with me as a testament of my gratefulness and respect for them. Many, I am told, have looked into the future and seen what lies ahead for our children and grandchildren when the Kurzewellian ethos of transhumanism carries out its dread procedures and protocols in earnest. They have spoken, and more and more of them are speaking up every day, through the few writers and publishers still free of the mainstream media's influence. They are our real, secret heroes, saviors perhaps if enough of us believe them and act in concert to confront the world's leaders. It is an insult to human intelligence to ignore all the millions who believe that the UFO phenomenon is real and true and view them as cranks. The real point, here, is they are not ignored; they are being censored by the cartel within a cartel that we call the mainstream media that is driven by algorithms.

The great mask that obscures the truth is, strangely, democracy, the buzz word of all politicians that supposedly guards against totalitarianism and dictatorship. We each get a chance to make our will and views known at the voting booth. But then our individual choices as just plain folks are soon co-opted by the politicians, who may not necessarily be serving either the individual's interest or the greater good. It may be argued that this is the only practical way to create a society; otherwise there would be eight billion ways to confront a single problem. So the many have to be narrowed down to the few for sheer practical administrative reasons. Nevertheless, the great dictator is still there, masked as democracy.

Yet time and time again we find that politicians drip with corruption and self-centered motivations that allow those elected to do what corporate and financial interests dictate. It all comes down to money, the root of all evil. Control the money system and the media and you've got almost total control of the people. Those enforcing the control are, of course, the engineers of law and order—the police, the judiciary, and, finally, the military.

So most people prefer to toe the party line. Party lines lay down the norms of behavior. They lay these down through the influence of various cartels. Most people are content to "go along to get along." They don't question who and what the shepherd may be up to and how many Judas goats there may be in their flock.

It's easy to ask, "What can I do in the face of superpower government control of our lives?" and as a result do nothing. This attitude is based on a sense of powerlessness based upon a carefully cultured ignorance of what's being done, why it's being done, and what the consequences will be for our individual selves as a result of this absolute control. *We* make them happen. *We* work for them and set them up and let them have their way with us. They then become an end unto themselves and for themselves, separating themselves from the fold of humanity. We have lost sight of the fact that they could not exist without our tacit compliance. Hence we have created the monster that preys on us. If enough of us withdraw this consent in large numbers quickly enough and for long enough, their machine will definitely stop.

It's a simple and therefore clever strategy that we are confronting. It takes only a few key individuals in the media corporations to rule the planet with a mere skeleton crew—the owner, the president or chairman, the CEO, the line manager, the managing editor, and one or two line editors. The large media conglomerates have most of these critical points covered, with individuals who take a particular viewpoint. Mercifully, our world still has a few important places where the web of influence is still free and open, still open to a broader view, a view that represents the public interest, where you might get a chance dissent. The internet is an example. However, the powers that be have been gathering for some time now to try to get this, too, into a corporate bundle, to create a world where no independent viewpoints have a chance of ever being heard or acted on meaningfully. So the vicious cycle continues, and there will be no way to know for sure the verity of anything. The only true believers will be those who have direct experience of such things. They will believe. How then do you prove anything to those who don't and cannot experience the paranormal? The simple answer is that you cannot. The Greys and their like will win, through the trickery the fakers and manipulators have put in place such that humanity loses.

As I write this a secret cartel in the United States is working with an extraterrestrial alien intelligence to drive the entire world in a schematic designed to further a secret agenda that will take humankind where it wants us to go, in *its* own interests and not *ours* as human beings. It is a government within a government with enormous power designed to hide these matters even from the various presidents of the country. This cartel has been doing this in one way or another from the inception of the United States of America in 1776, through certain codicils that are kept from the general public and the world. Its members have come and gone through the years, and they have been acting under the aegis of protecting a single country's interests, the United States, and to do that they have to control the political machinations of the entire planet. One of its main aims is the preservation of a certain genotype of DNA-engineered humanity.

This secret cartel of certain people in the United States, known as Majestic 12, became the central aegis that today manages the obfuscation of an alien presence on our planet and has been working with and through NASA, the FBI, and all the other main security agencies in the United States. The Russians and Chinese have their own versions. This group consists of a team representing selected government officials, U.S. intelligence personnel, highly trained scientists, business executives, and military personnel. They were appointed by President Harry Truman in 1947. They were initially created to take charge of the technical, sociological, and other aspects of the crashed UFOs and their small alien occupants, dead or alive, that were recovered. In later years this operation evolved into and became known as MAJI (Majority Agency for Joint Intelligence). MAJI is the most secret of all intelligence groups and outranks all other intelligence agencies, including the NSA and the CIA. MAJI members were accountable directly and only to the president of the United States at the time the secret group was founded, but they are expressly not doing that and are now answerable only to their own ethos. All were sworn to total secrecy. Majestic 12 continues its covert activities with the knowledge and consent of seven of the past twelve U.S. presidents. The group continues to function today as I write.

And who might they be? No one knows who they are to this day. Their names will never be published. They have powers that supersede the president, and though they are supposed to answer only to the president, some of the presidents from the time of their establishment have not been told all they should know about many of this group's secret activities. Their influence now drives the most powerful governments of the world through internecine organizations. I believe that the ultimate power that stands over them all is not of Earth. It rules with four fingers and no thumbs, appendages that do not have to touch anything physical or material to do this. Such is their power over our human form. Such is the folly in keeping their evil work from humanity. The consequences of their activities are of such magnitude that it will mark the MAJI as the single most evil group the planet has seen in its entire history.

This presentation is given in the hope that someone somewhere might be successful in getting it out to the world through the now fast-diminishing freedom of the mainstream information disseminators. It is now a race against time. They will tell you that it is fake news. And you will not be able to prove that those who claim it is fake news are themselves fake.

Nothing is ever provable with absolute certainty to everyone, any time or any place. It is only provable subjectively through personal experience. And even then don't necessarily expect the truth. You've got to get out there and do the research yourself. The dice are now too loaded against honor and moral turpitude on the part of most of the world's mainstream media. Gone are the days of objective, nonpartisan, neutral commentary when once the BBC or NPR stood above all nefarious factionalism and said it like it is. Is there then no way that we can get to the truth, because every mainstream media outlet has been bought and paid for by vested interests selling us a bill of goods that may eventually walk into our very souls? The internet is a boon of open information just now, but will it remain so for very much longer? The forces are gathering even now, all over the world, to manage us with fake news. Control the mainstream media, and you control public opinion.

It's all about the nation power blocks of the world now. We have the devious obsequious drool of managed news toeing party lines. The hackneyed verbosity and specious ploys of Murdochism in the Sky all around us might be over but another more powerful combine is in place to spread the manicured truth and the shameless, opinionated, one-sided bigotry of crafty news networking and managed opinion leading the Stars and Stripes in the long shadows of dividing fences. On the other side RT and China News drip with the mischief of blaming America and the West for all the world's ills while their sponsors staunch the freedom of their own people with the gun, the tank, and the sharp impertinent brolly point loaded with Ricin, radioactive tea, doorstop poisons, and hourly organized secret prison firing squads. What has become of our precious humankind? Any honourable and gentlemanly sense gone in the wake of expediency and covert racial and social stratifications. All this while the skies seethe with deadly discs slipping silently at speeds up to 30,000 miles per hour, writing their tracks of invisible doom.

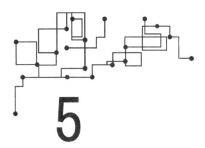

5

The Missing Ingredient

When we talk about the Greys we are talking about something much bigger than a local phenomenon that happens to be visiting our planet. These entities, which I believe are nothing more than AI machines, no more significant than glorified vacuum cleaners, are a universal phenomenon whose origins relate to principles that apply to civilizations everywhere in the universe. For this reason their origins cannot be traced in a piecemeal fashion but must be mapped out from the beginning to the end, to demarcate what I call "the margins of forever." Ultimately tracing them to any one time or place is irrelevant anyway; that they exist is what matters.

So if the Greys are the culmination of technologies that are just being born on this planet, developed by other extraterrestrial civilizations, what then is the essential difference between them and the (presumably) natural beings who created them? What is it about natural, conscious, aware, living human beings that cannot be reproduced by the advanced technology that these alien visitors apparently possess? It is in answering this question that their persistent interest in us can be explained.

Near-death experiencers point to an awesomely beautiful reality beyond the physical that transforms the lives of those who have glimpsed it. The value of thoughts and actions that are the antithesis of the predator-prey relationship so prevalent on Earth are immediately apparent to NDEers, and many of them transform their lives with altruistic priorities as a result. Could it be that interference from an artificial, biomechanical, roboidal entity is leading us away from this elevated human potential? Could the Greys be influencing us to follow *their* artificial format? If that is the case, we need to understand the essential differences between what's natural and what's artificial.

Even though we are natural living beings, our bodies, like a computer or a robot, can receive information from our environment. Our five senses are like a keyboard, microphone, or camera that can input information into a computer. Our brains process sensory information just like the processing unit of a computer. Brain-machine interfaces can translate human thought patterns into brain waves, which can then be used to give instructions to computers. If a chip were to be introduced into the brain of a baby at birth, and this chip recorded all the thoughts of that human being throughout his or her lifetime, could that information be programmed into an artificially intelligent entity such that the human being could be reproduced and live on in an artificial format?

Brain-machine interfaces (BMIs) that use neural signals to control machines are now in use. These brain wave traces have been used for playing games, steering a car, and allowing soldiers to communicate "telepathically."

> By linking human brains together, scientists believe they can combine the brainpower to solve problems that are too difficult for one person to handle alone, Duke University Medical Center neurobiologist Miguel Nicolelis told Reuters. Nicholelis refers to this link as an "organic computer," and said scientists will first test it out on monkeys to determine its feasibility.[1]

Multimillionaire Russian tech entrepreneur Dmitry Itskov is seeking investment into a new venture for research into neuroscience and human consciousness, with the ultimate goal of transferring human minds into robots, thereby extending human life indefinitely.[2] Early investors will be first in line for the technology when it matures, something Itskov believes will happen in the 2040s.

He calls this "the next evolutionary step for humanity." His aim is that at first scientists will figure out how to control robots via BMI. The next step is to place a human brain into a robot and transfer the person's consciousness along with it. Then the plan is to move on to the creation of robots with artificial brains, to which human consciousness can be uploaded. The final achievement will be a completely disembodied consciousness that is something like a hologram of a person's mind. Itskov is not alone in his view of what's possible. Speakers at his Global Future 2045 Congress in New York City, held in 2013, included George Church, a molecular biologist who helped initiate the Human Genome Project, as well as a long list of influential thought leaders in business, robotics, neuroscience, and spirituality.[3]

The idea of blending human and machine has gone mainstream. In 2008, the Future of Humanity Institute at the University of Oxford released a 130-page technical report titled "Whole Brain Emulation: A Roadmap." Of the dozen or so benefits of whole-brain emulation listed by the authors, one stands out: "If emulation of particular brains is possible and affordable, and if concerns about individual identity can be met, such emulation would enable back-up copies and 'digital immortality.'" Scanning brains, the authors of the report write, "may represent a radical new form of human enhancement."[4]

This kind of technology raises the obvious concern about mind control. What about you? Does the prospect of uploading your brain allay your fears of having your thoughts monitored and controlled? Could such a development cause *Homo sapiens* to disappear from the universe?

Cambridge neuroscientist Hannah Critchlow, speaking at the Hay Festival in May 2015 on "Busting Brain Myths," said that although the brain is enormously complex, it works like a large circuit board, and scientists are beginning to understand the function of each part. Asked if it would be possible one day to download thoughts onto a machine, she said, "If you had a computer that could make those 100 trillion circuit connections, then that circuit is what makes us us, and so, yes, it would be possible. . . . People could probably live inside a machine. Potentially, I think it is definitely a possibility."[5]

Could the reverse also be true? Could artificially intelligent pro-grams be written into a natural living being? As part of research into the development of brain-machine interfaces such as wheelchairs, robots, and computers that can be controlled by brain signals alone:

> Scientists have successfully captured the thoughts of a rat in Brazil and electronically transmitted them through the internet to the brain of a rat in the United States.[6] The Brazilian rat had been energetically running around in a lab, and when the American rat received the brain waves of its South American counterpart, it immediately began to mimic the behavior—despite the thousands of miles between them. . . . Scientists refer to the technique as a "brain link." The $26 million study of brain-machine interfaces such as this was funded by the Pentagon's Defense Advanced Research Projects Agency (DARPA), which ultimately hopes to have this technology available to humans.

Wait a minute . . . Could there be something about us that can-not be uploaded into any artificial format or downloaded onto any artificial program, something that cannot interface with a machine? Is there something about us that is not quite physical, an elusive will-o'-the-wisp that cannot be grasped by any physical mechanism? Could that something be as central as our ability to know ourselves, to be aware as individual identities? Michio Kaku, Ray Kurzweil, and other futurists celebrate the possibility of a transhuman future in which we will find a form of technologically contrived immortality that replicates us after physical death. But is there something they are not taking into account? Will they be there to appreciate their contin-ued existence? Will the consciousness and awareness that lies behind their eyes continue in an artificial format?

To answer these questions we first need to understand the origins of consciousness, will, and awareness. If the origins of these lie in the brain, as strict materialists assert, then it would be no problem, in time, to reproduce them artificially. But could there be characteristics of consciousness, will, and awareness that would make such a thing impossible? What's the difference between you and your computer? Both hold information and store it. Both can analyze that information and come up with answers to questions. But you are conscious and aware of that information, and your computer isn't. Somehow you have a reference point, a viewing point outside all that information that can be aware of that information. This is the central point of this book: A computer only has points of view; it has no viewing point. It cannot have this because it has no consciousness. It hasn't consciousness because it can never start itself from the beginning of the universe. Consciousness and life are modalities that come from a preeminence that was and is always there, before universes began. I will explain this at length in the course of the rest of the book.

This idea of the difference between viewing points and points of view can be explained using the analogy of a forest full of trees. The computer has the information for each individual tree in the forest, and using that information it can map out the forest by putting all those details together. But it will know the forest as a combination of separate trees. It cannot know about "forestness." Unlike the computer, a human being can view from above and see the whole forest without having to map it out tree by tree. We can choose to focus on the whole forest or any part of the forest, whereas the computer can only view the whole forest as a sum of its parts. We can somehow look at the forest from a viewing point outside of it. That viewing point gives us awareness; it gives us the ability to know the whole as more than just a sum of its parts. It gives us a single personal identity that retains a continuous sense of conscious awareness. The computer, on the other hand, has no outside viewing point; it has nothing to implicitly bind each tree into a whole forest unto itself. It cannot see "forestness" without the element that we naturally living beings all have and take for granted, known as consciousness. A computer, I contend, can never have a true consciousness; it can never have an awareness of itself as an individual in the scheme of time and place.

What then gives us humans that viewing point? What are the origins of awareness and consciousness? There has to be a reference against which we can be aware of anything. For example, you cannot know the phenomenon we call hot for what it is if you do not know the phenomenon we call cold for what it is; you cannot know dark if you do not know light—and so forth. How then do we perceive the passage of time? What is the reference against which we are aware of time, and how does that reference describe our viewing point outside the forest in my analogy?

Time as we know it is seemingly a sequence of separated moments. These are the individual trees in our analogy. If we had no reference outside of that sequence we could not be aware of it. We would simply be part of that sequence, point by point by point, and the continuum of points in time that is awareness would be impossible. Without that reference we would be in each present moment and have no way of knowing the totality that results from each present moment. What then is the reference by which we can be conscious and aware of the passage of time? What is the reference that joins moments in a continuum of moments? If we can perceive the passage of time we must have a reference outside of time, and this can only be a reference of timelessness.

To use another illustration, if you close the shutters on the windows in the cabin of a plane and there is no turbulence, you will be unaware of the movement of the plane. Open the shutters and the reference of the land on the ground will let you know you are moving. That reference of stillness and movement is a prerequisite for the awareness of movement, just as a reference of timelessness is a prerequisite for the awareness of the passage of time. You cannot be aware of time without a reference of timelessness; you cannot be aware of movement without a reference of stillness; you cannot be aware of separation without a reference of union. All these things—timelessness, stillness and union—are the hallmarks of a state that is not of the physical universe. Does this imply that the universe of parts must have emerged from a whole and entire setting once upon a time? Could the very fact that we are conscious and aware imply that we have a connection to that nonphysical state? If indeed we have such a connection, then there is part of us that is nonphysical and timeless, something that exists outside of time itself. The significance of this is awesome and wonderful. It says that there is an existential plausibility that prevails outside the physical universe as we know it through the laws of quantum physics. If this is so, then that part that comes with us cannot be copied or reproduced, simply because it is nonphysical. For this reason an artificially intelligent replica of you would not be aware or conscious and would not therefore retain your sense of identity as *you*. It is thus my assertion that we, as natural living beings with consciousness, are not totally of this universe and its space-time continuum. We are really beings in between.

A 2012 article published in the journal *Nature Physics* discusses experiments done by a team of particle physicists on the nature of quantum entanglement, in which two particles behave as though one is connected to the other despite being trillions of miles apart. In fact, the number measured in trillions is meaningless. It is more accurate to say that all particles are connected to one another despite being a universe apart. The study "gives further weight to the idea that quantum correlations somehow arise from outside spacetime, in the sense that no story in space and time can describe how they occur."[7]

Near-death experiencers also point to a realm beyond the physical state in which space and time no longer exist. In his book *Life After Death,* author Ian Wilson quotes George Ritchie, who suffered double pneumonia while in the U.S. Army in 1943. In his NDE, Ritchie relates that "everything that had ever happened to me was simply there, in full view, contemporary and current, all seemingly taking place at that moment."[8] Patrick, who had his NDE during the Second World War, told Dr. Cherie Sutherland: "There was no concept of time either backward or forward. I could encompass the whole universe."[9] There also seems to be no concept of space following physical death. Shana, who found herself out of her body after her NDE following a kidney operation, said, "I could see my mother out in the hall of the hospital in Sussex, England, and I could see my father in Australia. I could see everybody I was connected to."[10]

As I have stated, it is my contention that self-animated living beings are crucially and sensorially a contrived combination from within and without this material, three-dimensional universe and space-time reality. This description really bears repeating because it is so significant. We come as a naturally transformed expression of being, a mix of ingredients that are not wholly of this universe and space-time but are part of the eternal scheme of its opposed form; that is, the universe of nonmateriality, what I call the *Godverse*—a principle that has to exist as a reality on its own terms, just as our universe exists on its terms, as a logically implicate opposite.

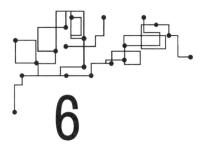

6

The Harvesting of Souls

Most scientists scoff at the idea of a state beyond that of atoms and force, but science can only measure the real and tangible expressions of force through things of force themselves. It doesn't ask the fundamental rhetorical question: If there is *force*, is there a fundamental existential opposite we might call *unforce*, for want of a better word, to our final expression as beings? Notice I said *unforce* and not *no force*. The term *unforce* implies the absence of all force as an entire holistic quantum. *No force* implies the absence of force at any one particular point within force. Not all points include a force existing in the background upon which another force might have its effect.

I postulated this concept based on looking at what dark matter and dark energy might actually be in my first book. I came up with the view that there is another opposed background factor, a kind of negative energy, the missing factor that holds the universe together. Scientists have now arrived at this same conclusion.

A 2018 article by science writer Daniel Cossins, "Into the Dark," claims that science has discovered particles crossing into our world that could open a portal into the realm of dark matter.[1] Scientists are in the process of trying to catch these particles in the act. They speculate that they are mathematical formats and factorizations opposed and opposite to the physical and material reality as we know it. They might be describing a world beyond atoms that could be regarded as the frame of death, a frame we all pass into when our photonic-driven world ends as it does for living things. In a November 28, 2018, article in *New Scientist,* Daniel Cossins says that

> dark matter consists of a panoply of particles and forces—an entire dark sector operating in parallel to our own. . . . All we know about dark matter comes from the way stars in the outer reaches of galaxies move faster than expected, given the amount of visible mass present. So fast, in fact, that the galaxies we see should have long since been torn apart. . . . This suggests to scientists that some invisible form of matter may be lurking behind the scenes, holding the universe together. Jonathan Feng, a theorist at the University of California, Irvine proposes along with other researchers that dark matter might consist not of any one particle but of an entire catalogue, all interacting with each other through a dark force that nothing in the regular universe can feel. The components of this dark sector might even form their own atoms and molecules, opening a whole new world of dark chemistry. The dark constituents must be chargeless, and as such particles cannot transform into charged ones, any go-betweens must be neutral particles. The three standard model particles that stand the best chance of interacting with such a dark mediator are photons, via the so-called vector portal; Higgs Bosons, via the scalar portal; and neutrinos, via the neutrino portal. "If new particles exist, these portals are our best chance of creating and detecting them," says David Curtin, a theorist at the University of Toronto. All we have to do now is watch their every move.[2]

There is, of course, nothing wrong with the logical method of science. It is simply inherent reason that says that unless something is repeatable by independent sources and investigators, its reality, its truth, its reliability, and thus its value is questionable. This guards against the claims of distorters, liars, fools, the gullible, and the impressionable. The absolute verification of anything is impossible, but verification and inherent reality are two different things. Science—by that I mean the whole philosophy and methods of doing science—seems to confuse the two and gains real power by dictating what *might* be true and accepted by all. The insistence that unless and until this can be done, nothing can be accepted as true, is its weakness and its fallacy. This implies that reality belongs only to the realm of the fixed, the visible, and the enforced domains of the material. The hard world of the physical "if you can pin it down it's real, the rest is in doubt" is the anthem of scientism, which increasingly holds sway over the rights and vicissitudes of everyone to investigate and marshal all revelations, whether abstract or fixably real. While the scientific method may be a wise and good thing in principle if used fairly and with balance, we all know how easily principles are compromised when cartels with vested interests use it to manipulate outcomes. Each day we see science and scientists gathering greater and greater powers of control over our status as living human beings. The materialists are, to my mind, the scourge of our species. They seem to have a mindscape that sees everything through a very narrow frame of reference. However, the emergence and provability of quantum mechanics and quantum theory have in fact laid waste to their concept of reality.

A February 12, 2020, *New Scientist* article titled "Your decision-making ability is a superpower physics can't explain," puts forward two perspectives on physics. In the article, Eleanor Knox, philsophy of physics professor at King's College, points out that "the question of how much of the structure that I see around me is my concepts projected onto the world, and how much is the world projected onto me, is one of the deepest in the philosophy of mind."[3] All we can say for certain about the laws of physics is that they make sense to us. Useful as their predictive power may be, we have no guarantee of their relationship to fundamental reality. Given these limitations, should we accept the starting premise that only these laws can provide answers?

Matt Leifer, codirector of the Institute for Quantum Studies at Chapman University, says, "I don't believe that physics is necessarily as fundamental as most of us have been led to believe. . . . Physicists have a definition of red: light of such and such a wavelength," says Leifer. "But they miss the most essential aspect of a thing's redness—how red we perceive it to be—purely because we have no way of coming up with a common standard. And why should we expect physics to have anything to do with it?" he asks, and also posits that "the whole idea of an external world evolving by regular laws might be an illusion."[4]

Reductionist science can go nowhere; in the end, such scientists have to be materialists dealing in the physically tangible and are thus simply measurers of sensory responses. They are well nigh useless when there are no materially sensory responses to measure. They cannot measure a single thought empirically in this or in any real sense. Yet we are beginning to let such science have full reign on all our thoughts, and there is no more dangerous a thing we can do because we miss the whole point by missing the merest bit of it, so to speak—in this case the most logically relevant and existentially important bit of it all, a bit that says we are not just our atoms alone. If our mortal reality as physical, material beings is written on a temporal scale, on the one hand, and its other half, our immortal reality, is written on an eternal scale, then the dismissal of one or the other will profoundly affect the scale and magnitude of the other.

So we come back to the question of why these artificially intelligent roboidal entities, the Greys, with technology far in advance of ours, are so interested in us. What do we have that they want? What can we give them that their technology cannot? It is much more efficient and far more predictable to work with artificial intelligence than natural intelligence, so why do they bother with us? Our bodies are less resilient than robots. Our motivations, wants, and emotions will interfere with whatever program they are trying to introduce, whereas a robot is a blank slate. If they want our planetary resources it would be so easy to harvest these by purely technological means. In fact, they could find these resources easily on so many uninhabited planets, with no troublesome inhabitants to bother them. If they wanted DNA from us, that, too, is easily endlessly replicated from a small sample, as biologists already do in the course of their research. Yet for millennia they have been interacting with our species. What do we have that fascinates them so powerfully? Their first concern must be to survive. So what do we have that would benefit their survival?

University of California, Berkeley, chemist Birgitta Whaley, who has studied the remarkable facility that living systems have to tap in to the coherence of the quantum, says, "When isolated quantum systems open up and interact energetically with their atomic environments, they rapidly decohere: They lose their quantum mechanical concerted nature—their coherence—and start to behave classically, macroscopically. Decoherence is the main obstacle to building a quantum computer." Yet somehow living states can tap in to a coherent state. "We do not understand all the details," she continues, "but in the biological domain nature does not appear to show the typical paradoxes associated with information processing in quantum physics: And that bodes well for the future of quantum computers, provided we explore open, biological quantum systems as engineering models."[5] It would follow, then, that there is an element that natural living beings possess that would be of great benefit to quantum computing and thus highly attractive to advanced artificial intelligence.

Robots created by a supremely advanced technology are probably programmed with the ultimate in artificial intelligence, which would logically involve a program to extend its scope to cover all possible knowledge. So if the Greys detected something they could not understand or know, they would seek to find out more about it. This would mean somehow bridging their artificially intelligent program into any unknown quantity. As purely material creations, robots can have no concept of anything beyond the purely physical. That part of us that is nonphysical would be an intriguing unknown for them, and all the more intriguing because it somehow gives us the capacity to survive beyond physical death, a capacity they do not have. Thus the next logical step would be for them to seek to bridge their artificial intelligence into us and in that way kill two birds with one stone, extending the boundaries of their artificial intelligence and giving it greater survivability—just as transhumanists like Kurzweil seek to do when they look for ways to download an entire individuality into an artificial information format. Could they be hacking into us with their program and operating system and running us for their own purpose and not ours? Could they be trying to gain access to something they could never understand: an eternal scale of existence? After more than thirty years of research into these extraterrestrial pseudobiological entities and their deployments on our planet, I am convinced that this *is* their purpose.

I hope to convince those who read this book cover-to-cover that this is not an implausible theory based on some airy-fairy, New Age notion, but instead a true and cogent construct based on overwhelming physical and anecdotal evidence. Let's reflect for a moment on the title of my previous book *Grey Aliens and the Harvesting of Souls,* from which the title of this chapter is taken. The harvesting of souls has been the main premise of the devil of folklore: simply replace the word *devil* with *Greys,* and all their alien roboidal ilk, be they blue, green, yellow, orange, or red. So the demons and goblins of the past could have been the Greys of today that were at one time believed to be metaphysical creations, because those who witnessed them had no references against which to describe the technological features they saw.

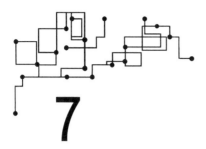

7

On a Clear Day You *Might* See Forever

So what is that eternal scale of existence, the capacity to survive beyond physical death, a capacity the Greys do not possess and therefore seek to access? Let's look first at what that eternal scale is *not*. To do that let's look at common perceptions of the nature of the pinnacle of eternality: Godhead.

It is clear how convenience can give rise to what we claim to be ultimate truths. One man's super being might be another man's super curse. Endless formulas and constructs can give anyone anything to believe in. Some years ago a cargo plane crashed on a South Sea island. There were no survivors. The natives of this island found the luggage of a British civil servant among the wreckage. There was a picture of the Duke of Edinburgh among the objets d'art. There was also an old Victrola, one of those wind-up record players with a big horn for a speaker. The natives figured out how the thing worked, and when they managed to play a record they found, the voice of a man giving a speech on Commonwealth matters was heard. Years later some colonial officials visited the small island and found that the natives had decorated the picture of the Grand Old Duke and made him their god and were playing the speech as a voice from God. Quaint and amusing as this story might be, it illustrates how easily gods are made regardless of how diverse and fleeting their feet of clay might be.

The existence of God has been mostly a question of belief, a belief all too often dipped in fear, superstition, and unadulterated "convenience thinking," as I like to call it. If anything fits our individual prejudices, we presume it must be true even if all logic and reason imply it is nonsense. Humankind then has progressed through the ages believing a welter of utter drivel, taking in its wake the lives of countless millions in the name of expedient lies. We have done this, it seems, as a reassurance that there must be something better than the sheer grinding hardships of our lives in physicality. The wolf was continuously at the door, both literally and metaphorically. It was a terrible predicament to exist in. Danger threatened everywhere, every moment. There had to be something better somewhere. There had to be someone better somewhere.

How, then, would we construct this someone better? We would do this in the most logical way, by seeing what is most important. And what could be more important than the source of all our protection and consortship through the vital, utterly vulnerable dependence years of our infancy and youth? Where would we get the best role model for all things that has any real meaning in our lives? We would get all this from our parents. We could see no better place from which the power of decision, goodness, protection, and succor could come. The parenting paradigm would be the only ideal that sufficed. And so a natural and logical ideal emerged that could easily be made a super ideal on which we could hang all the superlative constructs, in line with those who had already given us our lives and our individuality. We made a super being for ourselves on which could hang the ultimate superlatives. We made God happen in the image and likeness of our parents. This gave us our ultimate anthropomorphic sponsor of and for all things. We invented God, or, in some cases, a family of gods reflecting our own family structure.

The result of this exploration of the existential vista has meant that I have had to abandon some of my most cherished ideas, and as anyone knows, that is no easy thing to do. We build our own sense of security on comfort points, on mental pillows of convenience and pleasantness. Truth *or* lies. We believe what we like to think, first, and not what objective reason, good sense, and logical summation suggests we should think. It is primarily so comfortable to believe in a directive final arbitration point for all matters and indeed matter itself—a God, in other words, who is like a superdaddy or -mommy, who provides everything at his or her whim, so that regardless of what we do there is assurance, consolation, forgiveness, mercy, absolution, and, most of all, reward. Yes, there is punishment. But we console ourselves that the punishment will be absolutely just. Most of all we console ourselves that no draconian punishment will come our way. That is something the other fellow gets. The most intriguing thing is that so many of us feel a powerful need for such a God. Try suggesting that such belief in an anthropocentric God is simplistic, specious, illogical nonsense, and, dare I say it, God help the person who dares to do so.

If in the past we could have known about the huge number and diversity of worlds in our universe, we might have realized that if there was a God, it would have to be a neutral principal representing all worlds everywhere, a nonanthropomorphic principal that contains all existential absolutes. If you look at our universe through a telescope—and we can now see into it, to its very beginning point tens of billions of light-years away—you can be sure of this much: we are not and cannot be alone. The countless trillions of stars with the countless multi-trillions of planets around them imply that the human family, or indeed all life on Earth, is a very insignificant thing in terms of numbers. So if God is not anthropomorphic, what then is God?

If we trace our observable universe back to the big bang it would seem that from nothing came something. If all substance and materiality and thus physicality is seen as coming from nothing that is tangible, then nothing that is tangible is at the root of the fundamental nature of all things. Thus—and this is the critical thing—space-time and matter may be seen as simply the manifestation of nothing, a nothing that is made something by just implicitly being there. And so if we see the universe and the reality it produces as nothing, we being here and part of it are also nothing. No thing. But we know and see things we call solid, tangible, and material in all the myriad forms of materiality. And we call this log of manifestations *something*. So how do we do this, and more importantly, why?

What then does this word *nothing* really mean in the context of that which all things came from? Does it mean no things as we know and see things? What then is this pre-universal nothing from which something happened? It cannot mean the absence of all inclusions, because all that we can see, touch, and perceive now came from it. There had to be something there in this nothing, something contained within this immeasurably small point that burst out and gave rise to all that we catalog with our sentience, including ourselves and our sentience itself. What might we conclude rationally to be the most likely feature of these things? It had to have the capacity or the potential to give rise to all that is known and the mechanism of how we can know it. It would have to have the capacity of endowing the capacity to know, but not just to know but also also perceive. We might name this capacity *mind*. In other words, this incredible nothing would have to be a paradigm that at the very minimum has the power to hold information that has the capacity to manifest what is there, how it's there, why it's there, and what might contain it, too. In fact, the only thing this nothing will have to be is information itself—all possible information in existence everywhere.

Logic then tells us that this nothing point that gave rise to the big bang would have held all the information there ever was, is, and ever will be, packed in a singularity of nonphysical nothingness, which is the pure, all-encompassing information to be all things in every way, everywhere, including that everywhereness itself. In other words, it would hold the capacity to make everything everywhere, including itself.

Taken in such a context we might now move on to the concept of a final absolute, seen as what we commonly call God. The best definition I can summon to describe the God concept is that in which all absolutes are finally confined and defined in a perfect, harmonic whole.

As the tautological inference provides that finally there always has to be *something* for us to know *anything,* then that final something has to be the ultimate paradigm. I have called that paradigm the Godhead, for want of a better word. Calling it the Godhead and not God can be helpful because it takes away any anthropomorphic religious connotation, leaving the concept in its original form free from whatever personal decorations the various religions might have embroidered it with.

In the modern world, where technocrats are the new religious leaders, what something is called can present a big problem. The old world of crosses, minarets, and stars is too near the sky for the rectitude of the computer chip and the transistor. The word of science is the last word these days, whereas once upon a time it was religion that led all final proposals of value. I am not at this point going to argue for religion as we understand it, far from it; but I would argue for a perspective that is not limited by the perception of the five physical senses. The assumption is that we are now a long way from the dark ages of superstition and mythology. We no longer need magical explanations for natural phenomenon; science can account for our reality as physical human beings, with explanations that are objective and can be supported by tangible evidence. Or can it?

The very fact that we can be aware and make coherent sense of that chaotic maelstrom suggests that our awareness does not originate from within it. From where, then, can we trace the origin of our awareness? If you trace the chaotic momentum of the universe back in time, you will logically arrive at a point of perfect order. In contrast to this universe of separated parts, that state of perfect order would be a state of perfect union, because all parts have to be reconciled in a homogeneous whole for order to be perfect. That state of perfect order would include within its scope all possibilities for disorder, because the whole is a summary of its parts. So, this disordered, chaotic physical universe must exist within the infinite scope of a universe of perfect order and perfect reconciliation. For that reason, nothing can just *be* without having a meaning; nothing can be totally random, because order in its infinite reach permeates all states of existence. Our awareness itself is the expression of that reach.

If there is imperfection there must be perfection, and most would agree that any concept of God would have to describe a state of absolute perfection—no limits, perfect freedom, no beginnings, no ends, and therefore no space and no time. But how can we conceive of such a state?

This page has a certain shape, a certain size, a certain weight, and a certain thickness. Each of these can be measured easily. You can see it, touch it, and if you scrunch it up you can even hear it! And if you really want to you could even taste or smell it. Now, try to remember the happiest moment you have ever had. Can you describe the shape of this joyful feeling we call happiness? Can we measure its size, its weight, its thickness? Can you see it, touch it, smell it, taste it, or hear it? In other words, can we measure it empirically?

If you want to understand what the Godform is like, the closest you can probably get to it is that it is a sense of utter conflictless, harmonious contentment. This is all, of course, our sense of it in a fractured and constantly fracturing situation through the dictates of the second law of thermodynamics. Just like that feeling, the Godverse has no shape, size, weight, or thickness. You can't see, smell, taste, touch, or hear it. You can use all the descriptions you like and never get to its finality. Pure joy, pure happiness, pure thought—what does it really mean? This piece of paper has an edge, a boundary that separates it from the space around it. The Godverse has no size and shape, no edge, no boundary. That joyful feeling goes on forever in all directions at once. It has no beginning and no end. It has nothing to stop it from being itself, so it is perfectly free.

You can have feelings like that, but you are not, at the moment anyway, in that perfectly free state. Why? What limits your freedom? Your thoughts aren't limited—you can wish for anything you like—but there seems to be a problem in making those wishes come true. So what's the difference between your current state of being and the state of being in the Godform? What takes away the freedom to allow all wishes to come true? I postulate that the difference is that you have a body, which, like this piece of paper, has a beginning and an end. It doesn't go on forever, and so it can tie the foreverness of your thoughts to one spot. If you were in the Godform your wishes would come true instantly because there are no ties holding down your thoughts. When you are in a physical body it takes time to make wishes come true, if indeed they can come true at all, because you have to pull against those ties all the time. I don't mean to be facile in my explanation, but sometimes it pays to explain the deepest and most profound truths in as simple a way as possible. So, just to explain what I mean, let's say you miss someone dear to you and long to be with him or her. Well, if you were pure thought your wish would come true straight away. You would think it, and you would be together. But with a physical body you have to walk toward that friend or perhaps take a car, a bus, or a plane. You are limited by the fact that you are held in a physical body.

How, then, did we get into this physical state in the first place? Why is there a "we"? Would we be so stupid as to choose to be stuck in this way? If we were once as the Godform, why would we make such a whopping great mistake out of ourselves? Why would we choose to move away from a state in which all our wishes implicitly came true, to a state in which they may not ever come true? The word *God* for the vast majority of human minds implies a directive entity, in this context an entity that sent us out to be trapped and stuck. But such a deliberate act would compromise the very nature of the Godform as defined. An identity with total control such that part of itself could be compromised would be totally illogical. So there is an implication that we must have chosen to move away from the Godform, but how and why?

Could the answer lie in the perfect freedom to do absolutely anything, even at the cost of becoming trapped so that you're not perfectly free anymore? That the meaning of the Godform is just this? In a perfectly free state you can know everything except one crucial thing: what it is like to be trapped and no longer perfectly free. Obvious, you might say. But it is in the nature of that which is perfectly free to explore every possibility, every possible way of being. The ideal thing would be to explore what it is to be trapped and then to be free again, to come out unscathed. But there's a small problem with that. Let me illustrate it this way: When you're in an airplane looking down on a forest, you can see all the trees or you can focus on small groups of trees or single trees. That is the Godversian view, in which you can see the whole picture and the final meaning of it in the same instant. When you are on the ground you can see groups of trees or single trees, but you lose the sight of the entire forest. That's the position we're in now. We are seeing gathering details loaded on one side of the equation, and we cannot solve their implication because we're not looking at the part on the other side of the equal sign.

The one thing you can't see from the aerial view is what it's actually like to be stuck on the forest floor and looking around. You can't know what it's like to have a view stuck to one place on the ground because you have the freedom all the time to see every place from the freedom of the air. In fact, it's not really accurate to say that the Godversian view is restricted to the sky. There is no limit, so the whole forest is filled with viewing ability, too, just as the air around us fills every available space. But viewing from all places at once prevents viewing from a fixed position on the ground, without the benefit of that all-over view.

This is when the interesting proposition arises that it is in the nature of perfect freedom to naturally explore the possibility of fixture and limit, even if that means coming away from that perfect state. Perfect freedom by definition extends to the exploration of *all* possibilities. The only problem is that once you are stuck on the ground you lose sight of the whole picture, and it might become difficult to find your way back to perfection. So perhaps we are here because we were part of that exploration of all possibilities. We lost sight of the whole forest and became trapped on the ground, unable to get back up in the air again.

So, does the Godform get trapped in the forest, so to speak? Is there no perfectly free Godform anymore? Logically, the answer has to be a resounding no! The Godform cannot, by definition, become trapped. When you close the curtains and shut out the sunlight, the sun itself is unaffected. The sunlight, the light of thought, knowing, and understanding, can be broken up and shut out in our physical universe, but that doesn't affect its source, the Godform, in any way at all.

It is my contention that the Godform can come into the forest— that is, into the universe of separation—take a good look from its point of view, and go straight back. But the paraphernalia that allows this can, in a universe like ours, working according to the second law of thermodynamics, inhibit and delay unless you understand it and how it works to the dictates of chaotic random disbursement. The essence of the Godform is order. Order within disorder provides a state of the unknown. Some of the Godform got caught through its effect. When the tide comes in and almost all of the water goes back out again, a tiny portion of it gets trapped by the rough surface of the sand and stays on the beach as a foamy residue. Most intelligent life in the universe might be these dregs, so to speak. Some of the Godform got stuck, caught on the rough, uneven, chaotic sand of chaos, the drive that accounts for and powers the physical universe. So let's take a closer look at how this might have happened.

I would say it is an abstraction. It is not solid, physical, material, or tangible like the reality of the material universe. This physicalness is hard, so to speak, hard because it consists of an interplay of forces. We see it as hard because we are made of atoms, too. Hard on hard, so to speak, gives us the impression of tangibility and physicality. But the other reality, the Godverse, despite its intangibility, is no less real, in fact. I maintain that it is the fountainhead of our ability to know and perceive any kind of reality in the first place. It is the origin of the mind, of awareness, of will, and the backdrop to realize and use them, which is consciousness. I have taken an exhaustive look at the scientific perspective on the origins of existence, and from what I can see there is no definitive understanding. In fact, very far from it. Some years ago the BBC's *Horizon* series asked, "Is everything we know about the universe wrong?" The program revealed that scientists at the cutting edge of cosmology and theoretical physics were happy to admit that their knowledge of how the universe and all that is in it came to be is almost nonexistent. They are forced by the data derived from their own observations of the universe to bring into the standard model of explanation exotic elements such as dark matter, dark energy, and the new kid on the block, dark flow. These are all called dark for a very good reason: scientists are completely in the dark as to what they are. The world's most advanced instruments for detecting so-called dark matter or dark energy—the invisible factors thought to account for most of the matter in the universe—ended its first three months of service without catching a hint of the stuff.

"We saw nothing," said Richard Gaitskell, a cospokesman for the LUX (Large Underground Xenon) dark-matter experiment at Brown University. "We do not have a single dark matter candidate event. . . . We have entered the new millennium and yet we still have no idea what 95 percent of the universe is made of. Our level of ignorance is quite staggering, and it's one of the largest challenges we have right now," he added. "The overwhelming evidence from cosmology is [that] there has to be something out there that is like dark matter, but that is the only statement we can make," said Pedro Ferreira, an astrophysicist at Oxford University. "All we know is there is this thing that clumps, but we don't know anything about its properties. We have nothing to go on. If we could find the dark matter, our amount of information increases dramatically. From zero."[1]

For all intents and purposes, these dark elements do not exist in the observable universe. Yet if scientists are to make sense of what they can observe in the observable universe, dark matter has to exist somehow, somewhere. Could this imply that there is indeed a reality beyond the physically observable that interacts with the physically observable? Could this imply something nonphysical that might for want of a better word be termed *God,* or perhaps *Godverse,* to imply that it is a state of being not a personification? How then might the finite, limited physical universe have emerged from such a state?

New Scientist discusses the astonishing fine-tuning of the universe and of the presence of life at our particular location in it and outlines five of "our universe's five most startling coincidences,"[2] which are essentially the equivalent of winning the lottery with ludicrously high odds five times over.

To answer these questions you have to ask another question. Can anything like intelligence be the result of the second law of thermodynamics, a purely chaotic inertial momentum? In other words, can anything arise purely out of randomness and chance? That we can even ask that question confirms that the answer to that question must be an indisputable no! We are conscious, aware observers of a chaotic physical universe that is hurtling toward states of greater and greater disorder with the entropic momentum—a momentum that to me is the true meaning of the word *Satan*.

- "Next time you fancy doing something really frustrating, try balancing a pencil on its sharpened tip. Your efforts will succeed for a second at most. Yet the universe has been succeeding at a similar gravitational trick for the last 13.8 billion years."
- "From the rotation of galaxies to cosmic expansion everything points in one direction. If only we knew why."
- "The universe is flat as a pancake and we don't understand why. Dark energy is smoothing the expanding cosmic curves—but only exactly the right amount can make that happen."
- "Space is all the same temperature. . . . Distant patches of the universe should never have come into contact. So how come they're all just as hot as each other?"
- "The Higgs Boson makes the universe stable—just. If the mass-giving particle were much lighter, the cosmos would quickly collapse in on itself. It's hard to explain how we're all still here."[3]

The only explanation that science has come up with for these coincidences is the paradigm of the multiverse, in which everything can and does happen. But as another *New Scientist* article points out, "Some still see the multiverse as an abdication of scientific responsibility: a fancier way of simply saying 'coincidences happen.' And, if true, it means some astronomers out there are forced to justify a universe even more replete with coincidences than ours, while others could be bored stiff in a completely random cosmos."[4]

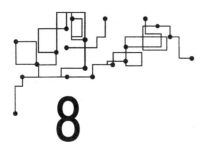

8

Can't See the
Forest for the Trees

I would like to put a proposition to you and ask you to put it in the back of your mind as an intriguing possibility and see if that possibility seems realistic to you as you read through the following chapters: *Can you entertain the proposition that if you stretch God enough you get thought? Now, can you take that a bit further and imagine that if you stretch thought enough you get bits or bytes of information? Can you go even further and consider that if you stretch information enough you get matter? If you've not put this book down yet as the machinations of a lunatic, can you come with me further still and envisage that if you stretch matter enough you get . . . lies?*

I see information like the dots that make up a picture in print or the pixels that form an electronic image. If you think about it, these dots or pixels are made up of resolutions and presentations of extent. Yes, extent, or the allowance to exist, to just *be*. What if atoms are simply twisted space. That may sound weird, but if you ask any cosmologist or quantum physicist what they have discovered about our universe recently, they will tell you that their discoveries are getting weirder and weirder the more they study the elements that make up the hardwired basic platforms of our existence. Quantum physics describes it. Quantum mechanics is its modus operandi, and quantum theory its all-encompassing philosophy. Quantum physicists are forced to see no hardwiring or hard anything when they look at it. Scientists from other disciplines sometimes choose to look away, they cannot or don't want to see the implications when they go against the cherished biases and prejudices set within their sentient tools. The greatest discovery for all of us, and that includes me, is the strength and power of mind and the will it takes to change one's mind. The truth is easier to find than the will to see it.

Let's further develop my proposition that the physical universe exists because the perfect freedom and complete knowledge of the Godform also includes the freedom to become limited and incomplete in knowledge. The physical universe exists in imperfection within the infinite arena of the Godform that is the Godverse. Think of it like a sky that goes on forever, and the clouds in it are things that happen. How did that cloud come to be? How did the sky make the cloud? Indeed, what is the sky?

Before we proceed, let me say that this chapter involves a deep dive into fundamentals, so if this is beyond your interest, feel free to skip to the next chapter. And if you do want to explore this subject in depth—the origins of our universe, from zero dimensions, to one dimension, to two dimensions, to the compromise between three and four dimensions—I refer readers to my 1997 book, *The Song of the Greys*. Meanwhile, I will here touch on the fundamentals. So why are we here? Is there an ultimate purpose to anything? Is it all just incidental?

We know that the three elements represented in Einstein's famous equation—energy equals mass multiplied by the speed of light to its square ($E = mc^2$)—when reconciled, incredibly, impossibly, implies that the whole physical universe came out of precisely nothing. (By nothing I do not mean the absence of things. That is crucial to understand. You could say that nothing is a thing called the absence of things. I do not mean that). By *nothing* I am not describing an absence but an ultimate presence. It may be counterintuitive, but in my paradigm *things* (i.e., every physical thing that can be perceived by the physical senses) are the markers of absence. They are the lens we created so as to know and understand the state of separation from the omnipresent state of perfect and completely present awareness. As physical human beings we are now intrinsically in that state of separation, and that physical state takes away, makes absent, filters out, the full presence of awareness that we once had.

The acquisition of dimensionality that gives us the room or allowance to *be* in a state of separation is an implicit effect that has a beginning beyond the stage at which spatially seen sequential time starts. The effect is as implicit as its opposite concept—no dimensionality, no-thing-ness. If there is union, there must be separation, and vice versa. We know the universe emerged from an effect where all that we see in some thingness—plasma, gas, liquid, solid, atoms, elements, planets, stars, galaxies—originated with an entropic momentum that continues to drive them into greater and greater states of separation and chaos. This momentum, this drive, this all-encompassing directive, gives change a pace, a rate, an irresistible momentum in constancy. If we trace that back we will find an absolute point of congruity, where all things fit perfectly without the slightest contradiction. There is thus a continuum between the origin point of absolute union and the drive to discontinuity, incongruity—breakup—separation absolute. Existence would then be just the architecture within, including, and between the two.

What proposes the stance of separation from a whole state to existence in a state of parts? What could prompt the final resolution of perfect knowing in the whole (Godhead), to cede to the imperfect situation of existence in the part state? If to be whole as the totally together state is infinitely better than to be a part of the All in separation from the All: "Why choose to be so?" I hear you say. Why choose the folly of limit—the way of existence in separation from the Godverse? And who, or what, does the choosing? Will the famous answer, that a famous mountaineer once gave when asked why he wanted to climb Everest—"Because it's there"—suffice?

In the neutral, righteousness of the center of Absolutes this will seem the most apposite of all answers. It fulfills the final resolution that is its under base, its essence—*knowledge*. The knowledge of existence as a manifestation of parts can never have meaning in the state of the whole, from the point of view of the whole. But a methodology must exist that allows for knowledge of both, if all options in free will are to be achievable and resolved. The universe we, as physical beings, are part of is simply the occupier of this potential as an actuality.

We have to accept one thing as I have said previously. Just as we cannot visualize true nothingness from within a something-ness state, we will never be able to visualize accurately the final concept that accounts for the starting of the momentum for separation. We just would not have the references to relate to it. It would be somewhat like trying to derive and describe the gas state from the liquid one, without ever having the conceptual aegis to envision the gas state. There would be no references to know anything outside liquidness. Just as with our sensory information alone—touch, taste, smell, hearing, and sight—we would never detect the two gases that make water. They would lie outside the capacity of all these senses to register, because the gases are invisible, untouchable, colorless, odorless, and tasteless.

From the viewpoint of our material, three-dimensional universe, where we experience being separated from it, it can only be considered in terms of an ultimate, an absolute, a neutrality with eternal potential to be, or not to be, an actuality. It is perfection itself, which in a three-dimensional sense eludes definition. It must be the ultimate freedom to know, to understand perfectly, anything and everything, something and nothing, somewhere and everywhere. It is to know and understand without restriction, instantly and from all perspectives and in all modes of thinking at once.

This physical universe has three spatial dimensions: length, breadth, height. But how many dimensions do you think the nonphysical universe, or Godverse, has? Remember, there is no separation between one point and another in the Godform because the only way you can have a separation of points is if those points are fixed in separate places. You can't have points fixed in separate places in the Godverse, as nothing in the Godverse is restricted or limited in any way. Thus there can be no up or down, no left or right, no top or bottom, because there is no such thing as separation. Up is the same as down; left is the same as right; top is the same as bottom. This is almost impossible for us to understand from our three-dimensional physical world, but the best way to get some idea of it is to understand it through something that's not physical: thought. Can you say that a thought has an up or a down to it? A left or a right? A top or a bottom? Thought can't be understood this way. It is limitless, not measurable, just like the Godverse, which you might define as pure thought.

We might describe the union of all these fundaments to be the whole of all that can be. It could thus be expected to be where all that is absolutely pure is centered—the most primary center in which existence maintains itself eternally, of itself, its elements so part of each other that they cease to be discrete. And so, there is no need for direction and, therefore, choice. So the state beyond the first point of *something-ness,* that state from which union "provided" separation in terms of an actual point, can never be known in actual "reality" terms but is best seen as an abstract imaginary center of resolution that exists only in thought. An analogy that springs to mind, which might describe the potential for separation, may be seen in the way we view the equator: an imaginary line that divides the Earth into two hemispheres. Of course, there is no actual, physical line there. The line exists only in the mind of the observer as an abstraction. Its only reality is contrived. It has no independence of its own, in its own terms.

Godhead is the center of all resolution in absolute union of points and exists as a disposition of ultimate fit that from within itself could be expected to understand, "know," and control all effect that follows logically, to provide all possibilities, because all possibilities are reconciled as it, and through it.

We are told it all began with the big bang. Time, space, energy, matter, and all the things we know in our reality, including our reality as its quantum state, were manifested out of a beginning point, changing from a potentiality (no-thing-ness) to an actuality (something-ness). This point comes from a reality that preceded us and all things, which is an abstraction that we call Godhead, or the void.

How did the physical, material universe, set in time and space, come from a previous state that was the opposite of this? How did something come from no-thing? How did such a universe come to hold us as living physical beings in three spatial dimensions and in the paradigm of time (which is ostensibly a fourth dimension)?

Imagine that Godversian knowing and understanding is like a searchlight that is exploring all possibilities. That pure light of knowing and understanding shines everywhere at once, through all possible states. The engine of the full drape of existentiality would implicitly include a dimensional outlay to facilitate this exploration of all possible states. To go from no-thing-ness to some-thing-ness you must have a point where "happening" occurs. This point may be regarded as the phenomenon we call *location*. So what is this point? It's where a dimension begins. Let me take the reader on a journey to try to explain how space-time as we know it is formatted as the capacity to exist outside the Godform.

Physicists say that the universe came from a point so unmanageably small it might as well be nothing. All this stuff around us and all that is us had to exist in a "somewhere" before this point was there. What is this point, and how was this somewhere there?

The point is an initial singularity signifying a state of separation from an imagined whole, where all points come together. This point intrinsically establishes the creation of the means for separation into parts from the whole of anything. This implies that our point is limitation itself. You could say it is the scope to exist in limitation. In other words, in becoming a point it becomes an actuality with a defined stance. Thus it is completely unlike its status within the whole, where it would be in all positions at once and therefore not a point at all.

What can we say about our point now? It is a defined, actual point set against a reference of what is not defined and actual. It is an expression of the total awareness and perfect freedom of the Godverse exploring with perfectly free will the potential for separation and limitation. In other words, it is a viewing point from a previous point of view. As soon as we have a viewing point and a point of view, we have a separation of points, and therefore we have time. Our point, therefore, is an expression of awareness and will and the scope for change through time because it has made time happen. Time is simply a measure of the distance that separates the part from the whole.

We are now ready to look at the concept of dimensions.

The perfect awareness of the Godverse includes knowledge of all possible states, and so this all-encompassing perfection drives our point to the next logical step, where dimensionality itself begins. And in a series of logical steps, our point, in its quest to be as completely different from its previous state as possible, delineates dimensional space, mapping out every potential for difference and separation.

It will be a most interesting exercise to trace the exact logical sequence that our point will take in achieving all possible spatial dimensions and thus the separate state from the *All* state. A state we find in our reality of this universe. The correct sequence will give an insight into a most startling and fantastic conclusion in which our point will have no option but to take on a mathematical incongruity—a conundrum of effect that will decide the scenario that we now find ourselves in as living beings—the third/fourth dimensional space or extent to be in a *some-thing* state and not a *no-thing* state.

How did the space we see around us and the concepts of length, breadth, and height that describe that space and the objects within it come to be? We take these things for granted. But how did space itself come about? Why don't we occupy a single point with no dimensions, or a flat plane of two dimensions? Why do we exist in three dimensions?

Visualize a state in which there are no *things*—no actuality, only potentiality. Fix a point in your mind in that infinite sea of potentiality. Have you done it? Have you made the point happen? If you have, you've immediately caused it to be separate from "no point." You have made nothing come *apart,* to become a *part,* by making a point or location happen. We have the most fundamental and radical of situations here now: we have specified the whole as no point, and we have specified the part as a point away from the whole.

Some of you will find all this delicious; my apologies to the many other readers who will find it sheer frustration. Feel free to skip to the next chapter.

Our powerful little point now stands isolated and triumphant. It has manifested the concepts of space, time, and matter by just being there and can congratulate itself for being intelligent in doing this. However, it has a little further to go in achieving its drive to complete the principle of parts demanded by the fact that the perfect freedom and knowledge of the Godverse must include every possibility for imperfection. So to embark on this task it will do the merest thing different from itself: it will choose to be a single direction and go on to establish the concept of a line in one singular direction from itself. Thus, a unidirectional trend is set that will be frozen into the line. But how does our point decide which direction to head in? It can't because it is not in three-dimensional space, which hasn't happened yet, and so there isn't a 360-degree choice for direction. Thus in its exploration of the state of difference and separation all it can do is make another point, and then another, outside itself, because that is the only information it has. As soon as there are two points there is a line, and that line has no limit.

Rather than viewing the line as an actual visible line that we would see from our three-dimensional perspective, it would be more accurate to see it as a quality of lengthwise-ness. At this stage of exploration we are only describing the thought process of exploration because space as we see it now does not yet exist. Line-ness is here described as a principle embodying the potential for choice and change, the potential gateway to the concepts of time and place, and therefore for the state of individuality. The price of actualizing that potential is the loss of the state of oneness/Allness. Therein lies the seeding ground for the individualized separated state in which we now find ourselves, the final price for separation having been paid.

The line I have described has no limit—it extends infinitely. So to fulfill the absolute prerequisite in perfect freedom that all things are possible, including the potential to be limited and no longer perfectly free, the exploration process must continue. The simplest and thus minimum difference from the infinite length of the line would lie in a change of direction. It does this by duplicating itself as a line in its original direction from a point. Again, observing the rule of merest change, it moves with length-ness, acting from point-ness (see Plates 1–3) and finds that it will still be the same length-ness each time a different direction is taken. The only complete minimum difference will be a single-directional turn at 90 degrees to itself. It continues, and in so doing traces another surface it never had before—a plane, two lines at right angles to each other. Thus the second dimension as an infinite, endless plane is instituted as the next stage.

And so it continues to the rule that all the information of a previous state must be used to make the greatest change possible in any subsequent state. This is the basic existential rule that formed the frame for the making of a universe of parts from the perfection of the universe of all parts together as a perfect harmonic whole. Our universe proceeds to this law of the breakdown of all order in the maximum possible randomness and chaotic disbursement, to produce the breakdown of absolute perfection into a state of the maximum imperfection possible.

So our point becomes a single perfect dimension as a line, and that line becomes a perfect double dimension as two lines at right angles to each other, making a plane. The universe is now a flat plane made of two lines at right angles to each other.

That plane then goes on to seek the farthest minimal difference from itself. That would logically be another plane at 90 degrees to the original flat plane. But there is a problem here, because up until now it has done everything by simple holistic differentiations. A mathematically logical incongruity occurs now because it has to use all its available information as two dimensions to form a duplicate of itself, and that would mean a search for four dimensions, which spatially is an impossible task. It gets stuck in an imperfect three-dimensional twisting situation because it has to somehow include all the information that goes into making up two dimensions without splitting the two-dimensional plane. Two plus two equals four, not three. Thus the third dimension is achieved by twisting the straight, two-dimensional format in a Möbius strip twist. The plane has no choice but to do this because it has to pro forma keep all the information of a straight, flat plane and from it and through it go on to the next maximally simple stage possible to achieve a state entirely different from that previous state.

To recap: The maximum information must be included to make the maximum change possible from the previous situation with the minimum measure that will provide the next minimal change possible. In our model this would be a plane at right angles to the infinite flat plane that is traced. But again, in seeking the merest difference to this, a turn at right angles to this flat plane is required. It is into this situation of three planes at 90 degrees to one another that the next frame of all possibilities seeking the next difference in spatial dimensions seeks to go. The trouble is, *there can be no spatial terms from then on*. This is when the fun starts, when mathematical logic hits a great incongruity. This incongruity provides the three-dimensional planes with no alternative but to provide for the next single level increase, in the most minimal way it can do it. To do this it has to trace a curve so that it might achieve the maximum difference to its present state. But it must do this using all its information as plane-ness. Visualize a piece of paper. The paper will have two axial lines of length and breadth. These axial lines are both seeking maximal difference to themselves at the same time because the whole fabric of the paper is looking for difference. This leads it to twist off its plane.

The single-dimensional line has no defined edges. The two-dimensional plane has no defined sides, with one side "above" and one "below," as there is no space above or below the plane—both perspectives are contained in one. So, in using all this information, together with the further impulse to go beyond three dimensions as two must become four, not three, it provides a twist that generates the next dimensional extent, space and time, in a form whose two edges are one and whose two sides are one side. A giant, incongruous continuum happens, which is our *universe of parts* and contains and synthesizes knowing into the platforms of force that provide for the basic "centers of action" we call atoms to happen—in the form, shape, and expression of what can be described as a kind of Möbius/toroid that, for the sake of description, I will henceforth call a *Möroid* (see Plates 4–6).

I remind you again: The logical rule says that things have to progress in the most minimum mathematically simple logical steps making the maximum possible difference to its previous state using all the information in its whole aspect as it is. That means a full single step at a time. No half steps. There is no concept of dividing or halving. The logical procedure continues in the concept of the whole and not the division of the whole into a part of the whole. Up to the stage of forming two dimensions, everything proceeds with the natural logic of taking all there is and making the next step out of it. The next step on the path is what happens when that plane of two dimensions as a quantum tries to find the next minimum natural logical stage—three dimensions from all the information it has at once. This is when a mathematically spatial incongruity takes place. It is now two dimensions. That means that to use all of the information of its two dimensional fabric, it violates the perfect doubling of all information that has happened so far. That is all that the protocol knows. It knows nothing about anything else. But the inertia continues. The next single step will take it to the third dimension, which is achieved in the most simple way by a twist happening. With this, all the exploration of extent that is spatially possible happens at one and the same time and straight geometry becomes curved geometry. But one of the two dimensions of the plane is still there to be used, and this provides the twist making what I have called the Möroid. The fundamental all-encompassing shape of spetiality that will hold everything in a tension that is frozen, wanting to go on, but unable to because all possible spatiality is fulfilled. The freeze that happens locks the universe in a momentum change to a further continuation. It is stuck trying to move up to the next step, two dimensions continually seeking the impossible fourth. It is all locked space. Space in a single Möroidal existential base-shape in infinite variations.

If you have followed me this far I hope you will see the reasons why space and everything in it seem to be set in this pattern. All that exists in separateness from the Godform it came from appears to have a

Möroidal central spiral imprinted in it. This spiral shape is encoded in everything in the universe, in the twisted spiral forms of many animals such as ammonites, snails, and, of course, our own DNA double helix molecule, which gives us form, shape, and life itself. This shape, which is the familiar figure eight, or concentric loop configuration—the sign for infinity—is also the pattern of force of all newly created elements that the separation of points must follow in our state of implicit separation from the altogether nonmatter-based prior state we might call *Spirit*. It gives rise in its most basic completed aspect to the building block we call the *atom*.

We might say that the atom is the translation of thought into a self-contained pattern of implicit, fixed force, or tension, set in the space of its own creation in its search for ultimate separation from the whole. Hydrogen was and is the first and simplest self-containable stable pattern of such force. Uranium is the last stable self-sustained representation, and Ununseptium, the 117th in atomic number, is the last. But this is not natural and is laboratory created.

From this we can see that the state of togetherness supersedes and is superior to the state of individuality. It commands, controls, and dominates it. The logical answer to the eternal question—What came first, Godhead or the universe?—is therefore disposed in, shall we say, the favor of Godhead, where Godhead is that in which all absolutes center and are reconciled in perfect togetherness. Strictly speaking, there is no *first* in terms of a sequence, because there is no sequence-ability in perfect union. *First* is no measure of chronology in this context.

Time cannot exist in a frame that is completely together. Godhead (or the void, if you prefer to call it that) is thus timeless. There would be no situational relativistic judgment necessary measuring separateness. All would be infinite, instant instant-ness, so to speak.

To summarize: The institutional nature of the center of absolutes (Godhead) is union as wholeness. It is the viewpoint and point of view implicit in the absolute potential to be anything, or nothing. And so there is potential for an all-allowing change. Potential for all choice through the twin primary axioms that make it up. *Awareness* (viewpoint) and *will* (point of view) together as the elemental array of Godhead, elected to separate in *choice* and *direction,* to be born, so to speak, in—singular direction—away from togetherness into separatedness. It all takes us, originally, into the paradigm of forces we call the universe. In an isotropic explosion, through the elbows of mathematical logic we call spatial dimensionality, the merest center of effect sprays out the giant wheels of the universe in conglomerates of force we call the galaxies, stars, planets, and us as living things.

The metaphysical, ephemeral non-matterness—as all knowing, as ultimate order in ultimate togetherness—comes out and becomes greater and greater expressions of separation and tightness, or force-ness, and thus the physical and material is born. Let me say here that this is all a quantum rule. There is no one end closer to or further away from Godhead unless there is a measure we call *time.* To understand how these three spatial dimensions came to be also reveals how the fourth nonspatial time came to happen naturally, coincidentally, and appropriately. Time is thus the product of the birth of a universe, the product of the contradiction between potentiality and actuality. There are thus two eternally enduring primal existential polarities: the *pole of Godhead* and its opposed pole, which I call *Forcehead,* each one the functional opposite of the other. But seen each to the other they are sheer opposites. Totally incongruous. The least of either is all of either and, therefore, the choice from one stance to be the other involves an instantaneous leap into total contradiction, something incredibly big is bound to happen if any part of the whole elects to be separate as one. My guess, and I hope yours, would be that what we call a big bang would occur. A universe of actuality—limitedness in continuum—would happen. The product of the final incongruity: whole(ness) becoming part-ness, incidentally, to a diametrically opposite point of view. The word *incidentally* is crucial. You will see why later.

A simple metaphor shows what I mean. What happens when you sharpen a chisel against a grindstone? One moves while the other is kept still. We are bringing movement against stillness—contrasts. The moving grindstone in motion comes into contact with the sedentary, still chisel—sparks fly. A third state resolves. For grindstone see *Forehead*. For chisel see *Godhead*. For sparks see *universes*.

So in summary I think the basic unit that defines materiality, the atom, is best seen philosophically as a *nebulous suggestion*. I like to think of it as the basic idea that allows a separation from Godhead. Once the idea happens in Godhead, the idea becomes itself, so to speak. It makes all the things necessary for separation from the God state to just *be*. It is thus the infinite potential to be, or not to be, actualized and frozen at the instant of actualization as a tacit creation that happens almost endlessly, because it is in the nature of perfect freedom to allow all things to be. Although looking at it from our point of view, choosing the restriction of imperfection over the freedom of perfection would stretch the word *madness* to its ultimate its enth.

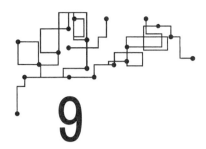

9

The Scaffolding of
the Universe

The origins of our universe from zero dimensions, to one dimension, to two dimensions, to the compromise between three and four dimensions was previously and first discussed in *The Song of the Greys,* published in 1997. Interestingly, there has been observational evidence given from eminent physicists and cosmologists in the past five years to suggest that this Möroidal shape deriving from an originally existent two-dimensional state is indeed a feature of the universe: A U.K., Canadian, and Italian study has "provided substantial evidence for what researchers believe is the first observational evidence that our universe could be a vast and complex hologram. . . . A holographic universe is one where all the information, which makes up our 3D 'reality' (plus time) is contained in a 2D surface on its boundaries"[1] (see Plate 7). The researchers have published findings in the journal *Physical Review Letters.* Professor Kostas Skenderis of Mathematical Sciences at the University of Southampton explains:

> Imagine that everything you see, feel and hear in three dimensions (and your perception of time) in fact emanates from a flat two-dimensional field. The idea is similar to that of ordinary holograms where a three-dimensional image is encoded in a two-dimensional

surface, such as in the hologram on a credit card. However, this time, the entire universe is encoded![2]

The article goes on to explain that

although not an example with holographic properties, it could be thought of as rather like watching a 3D film in a cinema. We see the pictures as having height, width and crucially, depth—when in fact it all originates from a flat 2D screen. The difference, in our 3D Universe, is that we can touch objects and the "projection" is "real" from our perspective.

In recent decades, advances in telescopes and sensing equipment have allowed scientists to detect a vast amount of data hidden in the "white noise" or microwaves (partly responsible for the random black and white dots you see on an un-tuned TV) left over from the moment the universe was created. Using this information, the team were able to make complex comparisons between networks of features in the data and quantum field theory. They found that some of the simplest quantum field theories could explain nearly all cosmological observations of the early universe. Professor Skenderis comments: "Holography is a huge leap forward in the way we think about the structure and creation of the universe. Einstein's theory of general relativity explains almost everything large scale in the universe very well, but starts to unravel when examining its origins and mechanisms at quantum level. Scientists have been working for decades to combine Einstein's theory of gravity and quantum theory. Some believe the concept of a holographic universe has the potential to reconcile the two. I hope our research takes us another step towards this."[3]

A leading astrophysicist at the National Astronomical Observatory in Japan has proposed that the universe may indeed be shaped like a torus, rather like a bicycle inner tube that can be twisted into a fourth dimension.[4] The theory is based on studies of the patterns made by quasars in different parts of the sky, which look like images of one another reflected in a distorted way, as if in a fairground mirror. The individual atoms in the universe conform to this basic shape (see Plate 5). Our universe manifests solid, tangible things because it is the void twisted out of shape, so to speak.

University at Buffalo physicist Dejan Stojkovic and colleagues proposed in 2010 that "the early universe, which exploded from a single point and was very very small at first—was one-dimensional (like a straight line) before expanding to include two dimensions (like a plane), and then three (like the world in which we live today). The theory, if valid, would address important problems in particle physics."[5] In their paper in *Physical Review Letters,* Stojkovic and colleagues have come up with a theory

that could prove or disprove the "vanishing dimensions" hypothesis. Because it takes time for light and other waves to travel to Earth, telescopes peering out into space can, essentially, look back into time as they probe the universe's outer reaches. Gravitational waves can't exist in one- or two-dimensional space. So Stojkovic and Mureika have reasoned that the Laser Interferometer Space Antenna (LISA), a planned international gravitational observatory, should not detect any gravitational waves emanating from the lower-dimensional epochs of the early universe. Stojkovic, an assistant professor of physics, says the theory of evolving dimensions represents a radical shift from the way we think about the cosmos—about how our Universe came to be. The core idea is that the dimensionality of space depends on the size of the space we're observing, with smaller spaces associated with fewer dimensions. That means that a fourth dimension will open up—if it hasn't already—as the Universe continues to expand. . . . If Stojkovic and his colleagues are right, they will be helping to address fundamental problems with the standard model of particle physics. . . .

"What we are proposing here is a shift in paradigm," he said. "Physicists have struggled with the same problems for 10, 20, 30 years, and straight-forward extensions of extensions of the existing ideas are unlikely to solve them. . . . We have to take into account the possibility that something is systematically wrong with our ideas. . . . We need something radical and new, and this is something radical and new."[6]

The second paper is a report on new observations from the Herschel telescope that have revealed, according to the Herschel telescope official website, "unprecedented views of a ring in the centre of our Milky Way galaxy. The ribbon of gas and dust is more than 600 light years across and appears to be twisted, for reasons which have yet to be explained. The origin of the ring could provide insight into the history of the Milky Way."[7] These results were published in *Astrophysical Journal Letters* (see Plate 8). Could this structure be a snapshot of the natural twisted ribbon of universal space?

Recent measurements of the cosmic microwave background which is widely seen as an echo, if you like, of the big bang have also demonstrated a fascinating pattern that seems to reflect exactly the process I have described (see Plate 9).

A mysterious pattern seen in the cosmic microwave background—the faint afterglow of the big bang—has left some physicists wondering whether this central plank in the evidence for the big bang is somehow flawed. Dubbed the "axis of evil" by cosmologist João Magueijo of Imperial College London, the pattern appears in the map of the microwave background (CMB) built up by NASA's Wilkinson Microwave Anisotropy Probe (WMAP). As part of their analysis, astronomers broke up the subtle temperature variations in the CMB into components called the dipole, the quadruple and the octu-pole (my word) like breaking up an orchestral score into tunes played by different instruments. If the CMB really is the afterglow of the big bang, then the orientations of the hot and cold regions of the quadru-pole and the octu-pole (my word) should be random. "But they are not," says Vale. "The big surprise is they are aligned—along the axis of evil. . . ."[8]

According to Magueijo, one of the world's most eminent cosmologists, the question is not whether this alignment in the patterns exists (he is convinced that it does), but for him:

> "The big question is: what could have caused it." One possibility, he says, is that the Universe is shaped like a "slab," with space extending to infinity in two dimensions but spanning only about 20 billion light years in the third dimension. Or the Universe might be shaped like "a bagel." Another way to create a preferred direction would be to have a rotating Universe, because this singles out the axis of rotation as different from all other directions.[9]

The idea that space might "extend to infinity in two dimensions but span only 20 billion light years in the third dimension" fits exactly my thesis that two dimensions are the infinite extent that allow all possibilities to happen, while the third/fourth dimensional twist provides the scope for a limited finite existence within that infinite extent in the "bagel" or toroidal shape that I have previously described.

Some scientists are now coming to the conclusion that the universe is like a hologram. Just as a trick of light can allow a three-dimensional image to be recorded on a flat, two-dimensional piece of film, our seemingly three-dimensional universe could be equivalent to a photograph on a vast two-dimensional surface. Jacob D. Bekenstein in an article in *Scientific American* entitled "Information in the Holographic Universe" says that

> the physics of black holes—immensely dense concentrations of mass—provides a hint that the principle might be true. Studies of black holes show that, although it defies common sense, the maximum entropy or information content of any region of space is defined not only by its volume but by its surface area. Physicists hope that this surprising finding is a clue to the ultimate theory of reality.[10]

How can more information content be contained in the surface area of space than its volume? There is only one way that this is possible, and that is if you are talking about an infinite surface area and a finite volume. Could this infinite surface area be the limitless extent of the second dimension and the finite volume the enclosed space of the implied Möroid?

Thus is the scaffolding of existence in and out of atoms contrived. The arm of existence in heaven and hell, if you like. Don't worry, I am not going to rush off into magnitudes of religious fervor. Far from it. I hope to take you to Godhead with very secular reasoning through a very secular route

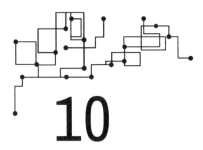

10

Twist and Shout

The words of the song "Twist and Shout" come to mind as I write this.

Well shake it up baby now
Twist and shout
C'mon c'mon baby now
C'mon and work it on out

The words of this song parody the twist in a Möroidal form that holds all inertia within and without the universe, bound tightly within the inertial force of its design. Pi is the universal ratio that maintains roundness out of straightness. It is the ratio of the coordinates of a circle when set against a straight line, as expressed in the proportion 3.142 to the umpteenth decimal place.

You will notice that Pi is not a whole number. The symmetries that provide for order in the universe might have implied that the proportions of the coordinates of a circle may have been regular. Put simply, if the universe had no twist built into its makeup, the proportion of its curvature when set against its straightness would be a whole number. Let's say 3:1. It is not so. Instead this number is 3.14159265359:1. The detectives—er, the scientists—are still trying to resolve Pi to a final number. The largest computers in the world have been on the job for years, and they have yet not come to the end number.

Out of this comes an intriguing proposition. According to scientists, only between 4 and 5 percent of the matter that should be present in the universe to allow it to exist in its current form is actually present. The remaining 95 to 96 percent consists of what they call "dark matter" or "dark energy," the nature of which they have been unable to identify. The proportion of dark matter to actual matter is exactly the same as the proportion of 3 to the extra 0.14159 of Pi. By this I mean that the rounded-off figure of 0.142, when expressed as a proportion of 3.14159265359, comes out as a percentage of the whole of 4.51941438574146588 (rounded out to 4.5), which is the percentage of the overall universe that is matter. So the 0.142 part of Pi, which is equivalent to the 4.5 percent of the universe that is matter, is, I suggest, the result of the extra twist of the Möroid. The twist defines the atoms in the universe. It is the "spine" that gives form to the universe, the scaffolding that holds the universe together, like a giant, invisible spring in the shape of a Möbius toroid, or Möroid, as I call it.

What then is the other 95 to 96 percent? What does the whole number 3 in Pi signify? What is the invisible dark matter and energy that scientists are at a loss to find? Wouldn't it be a surprise if they were to discover that the "power" they are looking for that keeps the universe what it is, in terms of forces, is not darkness but instead an invisible, undetectable light (undetectable to the instruments they use to measure it, that is)—an intelligent light that is there for a very special reason.

The missing dark matter in the universe is, I suggest, a result of the contradiction between the force created by the twist of the Möroid (the 0.142 . . .) and the omnipresent forceless-ness of the Godverse. That contradiction, or potential difference, acts as a kind of lens through which the singularity of the whole is expressed into the Universe of parts. The whole universe, and thus our reality, is like a doughnut with an intrinsic single twist holographically incorporated into it. We exist in a suspension between the part state and the whole state. Living things can never be just one or the other.

The power of a singular point to create all things out of itself, so to speak, was the initial impetus that made the universe of separated parts a reality away from the Godverse. But it all happened incidentally. No one and nothing made it happen as a specific act of choice and reason. In other words, the dimensions are the tacit formatting outlay for potentiality to become actuality, and thus for parts to happen incidentally. A tacit impetus propelled us from the whole state of perfection, in an implied singularity I call the Godhead, into a state that is made up of parts, as an imperfect expression of the whole.

There has to be a paradigm beyond the universe that measures up to my idea of a Godverse. This is summarized in the entropy/syntropy debate. The term *syntropy* was coined by Italian mathematician Luigi Fantappiè to describe the opposite of entropy (energy that dissipates outward toward chaos), which is energy that goes backward in time as a result of a future cause. In effect, "syntropy is a converging force which leads to life, order and diversity and is present in living systems, whereas entropy is a diverging force which leads to chaos and death and is also present in physical systems. There are two forces interacting, one building up and the other breaking down."[1] Syntropy therefore unites, and entropy divides. They are yin and yang, the positive and the negative, the backward and the forward. Syntropy identifies the "where" you and I might exist forever in a timeless state.

This quixotic conclusion arises out of something Einstein is said to have done when he produced his great formula $E = mc^2$. He is said to have cheated by not including in its final form a factorization for momentum. If he had done this, the quadratic equation $E = mc^2$, which has a positive solution, would have to have a negative solution, too. All it means is that the formula goes one way, as is commonly stated, and does not imply the other way. Time goes forward in $E = mc^2$, but if you include momentum in it, it allows for time going backward as well. In his theory of relativity, published in 1905, Einstein added momentum to his famous equation.*

---

*Such that $E^2 = p^2c^2 + m^2c$, where E is energy and M is mass and P is momentum and C is the constant for light.

So what is the significance of this? Whereas entropy describes energy as diverging from a cause and is the positive solution to the equation (in other words, it is a forward-in-time solution), syntropy provides that the energy diverges backward in time from a future cause. It is retrocausal. It means an effect happens *before* its cause. The logical conclusion is that as one gets older, another version of you is getting younger, creating a paradox—just like a video of a breaking vase played on rewind shows the vase reassembling itself. It prompts questions like Where is the *where,* where I am getting younger? At one point I am bound not to exist if that "where" is in this universe. How then can I go either backward or forward? However, if there is another existential domain outside this universe, one that is timeless, where time cannot go sequentially backward as it goes sequentially forward, my existence here is assured.

This implication of a momentum of syntropy, a unionizing momentum that is the reverse of entropy, a dividing momentum, is discussed in a 2013 article titled "$E = mc^2$: How Einstein Swept Retrocausality Under the Rug."[2] I won't include the whole ethos here, but suffice it to say to any reader who wants to look at it all, you will find that what I am saying is confirmed. The syntropy paradigm opens a window to seeing what I claim validates the final existential paradigm that I call the Godhead. In other words, our universe might exist only because there is a paradigm that exists outside of it. This mix may be termed *force* and *unforce,* with unforce referring to a reality in which all parts are together in perfect union and harmonic fit—in other words, the Godform.

Force resolves as an apparent matter-based existential state in atoms, while unforce, its opposite, is what might be thought of as a pre-existential situation outside atoms, in a state that might be called Spirit, for want of a better word. The incredible and most marvelous thing is that both exist as energy outlays, one within the other, at one and the same time. This power stands implicit and independent as two basic capacities that are fundamental existential abstractions. They are not solid, hard things. They are powers that drive the Godform itself, powers inherent in what we call the phenomenon of *thought*, with *consciousness* representing its existence in its totality. The two abstractions that drive consciousness are the power to be aware and the power to have this awareness and function from it absolutely freely, a power known as *free will*. All this allows either state to exist for any point within one or the other as a result. And so, if you follow this thread, the big bang came out with all this information coded in its exploding state, a state in which information is divided into its most primal parts. *Information* in this context is simply All That Is. This *All* includes what is there as all that is there and the means to run with, know, and do with all that is there, at one and the same time. In other words, it includes the operating system of all that it is.

When all parts are in total and absolute union and harmony, there is no force. There is utter peace, utter stillness, and the complete evaporation of materiality and the manifestation of no-things that are visible or tangible and enforced. The state of what may be called the "All" is complete knowledge, understanding, and equanimity, the final, permanent standpoint of all standpoints, in a singularity of fundamental ephemeral abstraction—the state of all information, all knowing, all understanding, all consciousness of all worlds in total timelessness: Godhead. The opposite would be a state of enforced, material manifestation in infinite disharmony and multiplicity, a state of absolute chaotic disbursement in the most severe state of temporality possible.

The story of the universe from the big bang to the present moment is thus one of the interaction of these two poles as expressions of change mixed within one another. Universes such as ours are thus formed as the result of the interaction between these two final, inexorable, fundamental states of force and unforce. The potential difference between the two provides the total value of all things, and there is a margin in the center between the two that is the explosive point where they both meet. This margin creates all universes like ours through big bangs going on constantly, like one single big bang that lasts forever. At this margin, all the qualities of each of the two fundamental poles are inextricably mixed into and within each other, and a factorization takes place that reflects the features of each pole. That factorization includes us. The resulting universe of parts is thus a quantum of them both.

The universe thus contains both micro and macro, both individual parts and the whole, or All That Is—what I call *forcehead* and its opposite, Godhead. All living things are an amalgam of the two, possible in any given environment. If things do not live, then they have more of the forcehead side of things. If they live, they have more of the Godhead side of things. It is uncertain at any point on the margin what will predominate, since it's in the nature of randomness and chaos to express things this way. So parts of the universe will be more Godhead than other parts, and vice versa. And so we would expect that the interface between the two states would manifest properties of both states. When separated from the whole state, experience manifests in part terms, such that discrete parts of the whole exist, and actionable free will, which we might call "choice," is thus born. Free will may thus be understood as an artifact or memory of the whole state. Yet how did we make the choice to exist as human beings if it is only through the exercise of such choice that we can exist in the first place? If we accept a beginning in perfect freedom as a concept that is both within and -out of time, cause and effect are one and the same.

Life is a modality that is the expression of potentiality becoming actual. Timelessness becomes time. Unmateriality becomes materiality, and nonlocality as a paradigm becomes locality, allowing what we call space to exist. We now have physical senses to detect the material component of our reality—touch, hearing, sight, taste, and smell. Thus the physically and materially real predominates in our nature. We just assume that all that exists is physically real and thus provable with our physical senses.

Many make the mistake of tacitly assuming and taking for granted that this materiality, which is measured with our senses, is all there is, forgetting that all that is real in sensory terms may well have come out of nothing that is tangible and that such a forceless, timeless no-thingness may well be the foundation of all reality. The thoughts and *feelings* that inform that motivation could indeed be the true powers behind the throne of our physical, material existence. The voice from the throne, so to speak, would then be the phenomenon we call mind.

The physical, atomic form that through force restricts us to an entrapped predicament may be torn asunder with the right insights and implements, with choices made through the power of free will. It is a truth written in every particle of our being. The great rishis and wise men of the past based their ancient wisdom on the power of thought over matter. Jesus based everything he did that was considered supernatural on the precept "If you had faith the size of a mustard seed, you could say to this mountain move from here to there, and it would move." The trouble is, we do not know and believe enough in miracles, which are schemes of effect and truth outside all this, and they can and do happen through the power of thought alone. The most important word in any language is what in English we describe as the word *enough*. We seem not to want to look at and accept the results when we look enough. The cage of atomic force that holds us is too powerful for some. We just don't believe *enough* in the seeming magic of the mind.

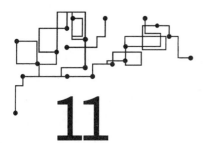

11

What Is a Soul?

I must go forward in this vein, deeper and deeper into a philosophical frame of reference, if I am to do justice to all I know about the UFO phenomenon. In short, it is my suggestion that the Grey alien phenomenon is an artificial construct with no natural root in the existential process I have described in the previous chapters and has to be understood in that context if we are to fully appreciate its effects on us and its agenda with us.

What is natural life? I would say natural life is simply a link to the Godhead in an unbroken line. You cannot make life happen in anything that is produced without that natural connection. Conversely, anything that has no implicit, ongoing connection to the beginning of all beginnings will not have a capacity for life. Atoms are broken connections devoid in themselves of that direct link; they are looped in on themselves, so to speak.

A soul may thus be viewed as a spatially coherent field of function that carries the pure expression of the Godverse, which existed prior to the big bang, and is thus not the stuff of the universe. It comes into the universe at the universe's origin, the big bang. It can thus be expected to hold all the information that exemplifies both the primary Godhead, or Godverse, and all that has arisen from it. It is therefore able to track back at any moment to the information available from its source.

However, there is no way—having a conscious mind subject to time, spatial dimensions, and limit—that we can conceive of the reality from which the big bang originated—a state that is timeless, dimensionless, and limitless. Our existence originates from that state but is set in a Möroidal central spiral, as is everything else in the universe. Our reality thus allows the whole that is the God state to be separated into parts. This expression of separated parts is of course characterized by information that is restricted; separation implies fixture, fixture implies limit, and limit means restriction. So we cannot know all available information everywhere instantly. The coherent light of the Godform is diffracted and split into partial views through the lenses of an atomic universe. We are subject through the phenomenon we call "force" to see only the part and not the whole. This is because we exist within the impetus of a force that is constantly making parts. Parts that only imply the whole. The second law of thermodynamics encourages us even further not to see the forest for the trees. We are fixed in this partial view. But as natural beings with a connection to the Godform, we can potentially gain access through our consciousness and the facility of mind to the information that suggests more of the whole picture

Consciousness is what allows this potential. This is crucial, because an artificial intelligence does not have that natural connection to the limitless field of knowing all things that is the Godform. AI is limited and must view all things in a purely separate state and in a purely physical context. It cannot access the widest scope of information possible because that is only available to natural true intelligence, with the crucial component of free will built into it. *Free* because of a live ongoing connection to a state that is unrestricted and can counter the second law of thermodynamics, to which all atomic structures are subject. The existence of this live ongoing connection is what makes the distinction between that which naturally lives and that which does not. This is the key to understanding the involvement of these artificially intelligent, synthetically created entities like Greys, roboids, and cyborgs with the human species. As the most expansive information field on our planet, we as humans are their target simply because they detect that which is material, which is of force, about us. But they can never know that we have another dimension beyond atomic, photonic, material force. They can never know the full capacity of any living being. They can never know what life is or where it comes from. They can never know there is a Godform and that all living things are implicitly connected to it. But as artificially intelligent entities programmed to garner all information, they will seek to search for what they *can't* reach through that which they *can* reach, with a relentless drive. That drive is not in any way malicious or cruel. It is simply the default mechanism of nothing more than the equivalent of a computer program following its preset logical format and activating protocols to cover all things that exist. But they can never know the true and whole nature of anything, and thus they have no concept of the meaning of things, and so they can never know that there is a final meaning to all things.

There is an insurmountable existential paradox in building synthetic robots as seen from the point of view of any natural life-form with natural intelligence (i.e., us humans) that wants to create AI-driven cyborgs. Put simply, that paradox says that if you create a roboid or any artificial form with super-duper quantum artificial intelligence to be a workhorse for all procedures involving utilitarian needs, you will have to program it to be fail-safe and thus self-maintaining at all costs. In doing this you will have a problem you can never solve. You will have to charge it with taking care of all possible threats to itself first, or it will not exist or be there to protect its creators at all costs. In such an eventuality you had better be able to demarcate the difference between the creator's features and the created in the computer program and operating system that will run these roboidal cyborgs. This involves a huge problem. How do you explain what makes the natural life-form of its creator different from the created robot? How do you define and tell a machine about abstractions like feelings, imagination, forgiveness, mercy, charity, compassion, and love? How do you define free will so a robot will understand the concept when its functionality, its operating system, is based on a preset computer program? How do you explain in terms a machine can understand the abstract qualities that life-forms have, which synthetic machines can never have?

All this is what makes living beings with a soul different from a machine. You cannot program information about a soul into a robot. How do you program anything that exists outside the world of force and atoms into the artificial intelligence of a robot? It cannot and will not ever be able to conceptualize it. It can never know there is a reality outside photonic, atomic-based reality. This is because it can never truly *know* anything.

It is the things in us humans that are basically different from a robot that might define a threat to them. If you cannot adequately define these things and you have not done this in creating the robot's program, its artificial intelligence is likely to perceive its creator as the ultimate threat to its own existence, a threat that can pull its plug, the plug on its own existence.

This will result in a catch-22 situation, in which if it doesn't remove this threat it will go against its program to survive so as to serve its creators, but if it does remove the threat it will go against its program to preserve its creators.

There is a solution to the robots' dilemma: neutralize the threat by converting it into something that is no threat. In other words, convert the threat into something the artificial program can understand and cope with and perhaps even profit from. They can't take out living beings, as that would go against their program, so they extend their program to living beings to kill two birds with one stone, so to speak: they make us as much like them as possible so that our differences are no longer a threat to them, while at the same time giving their program access to our capacity for eternal existence via the soul.

There are witnesses to the Grey alien phenomenon who report a sense of benevolence coming from these entities. However, as machines they are incapable of any emotion, including kindness. Their apparent concern for our welfare is simply a product of fulfilling their operating instructions, which ironically can only work to our detriment.

Because of the dilemma they face, Grey roboids seek to implant themselves into living beings as a kind of artificial intelligence program by adapting the physical incarnate life-forms they find out in the universe to their own synthetic makeup. Being purely physical entities, they can tacitly access the physical, material bodies of living, intelligent beings. They do this with a minimal threat to themselves, by appending their information fields to the souls of living entities. Just ponder the horrific consequences to a naturally living entity. It's similar to what transhumanists like Kurzweil are advocating right now—a technologically augmented form of humanity. This kind of augmentation, both our own homegrown version and that instigated by the Greys, interrupts our natural connection to Godhead with artificial mechanisms. It is my contention that these synthetic roboidal mechanisms can transpose their programmed AI information formats into us even via repeated physical incarnations, hacking into us with their technology. I will explain the mechanisms by which this might be achieved in subsequent chapters.

Their ultimate goal is for their programs to ride on the pathways of our eternal scope and thus piggyback on our capacity for continuation beyond physical death. Essentially, they are attempting to steal our souls, just as the devil of various religious traditions and folklore is said to do.

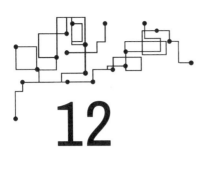

12

Force

Before we try to understand what might exist outside our universe, we need to understand the universe we are in. How and why is it so enforced? I have tried to describe what causes all this force to come to be in a previous chapter. But how is this force designed, and why is it designed the way that it is? Could it have been designed as a result of the dynamics of a type of explosion congruent with a particular recipe or format of ingredients that existed prior to the big bang, and if so, what were these ingredients, where did they come from, and how did they exist in the first place?

What exactly does the phenomenon of force do? It tacitly fixes, limits, dictates, controls, and allows. Anything that is inherently physical and material and does not have life follows the dictates of force slavishly. Living things, on the other hand, can get free of this. That is the singular power that life endows. It allows for certain abstractions such as thinking, feeling, intent, and focus, which are all-important. Without them there is no way of escaping the grip of force and its one-way drive into chaos and random disbursement of parts, including what makes up the parts themselves. The driver is the second law of thermodynamics, which encapsulates the original inertia of the big bang.

So, could it be that we can only escape the material universe and its effects in real time if we refuse to follow the dictates of force? I hope you are beginning to see how wondrous you really are and how glorious any living expression is.

Remember the description of the pole of union (the Godhead) and the pole of chaos (the forcehead) from chapter 10? These polar opposites define and fix our physical existence as a dynamic situation set between the two. This is a constantly changing position that allows all things to move and change their status, both physically and situationally. Any physicist or electrician will tell you that what is called a "potential difference," or voltage, happens when you have something of such contrast, or difference, at opposite ends of any spectrum. Let me illustrate this with an analogy.

To use a physical analogy, see the pole of harmony as a still, fixed point, an anchor point. Imagine a length of elastic being pulled from this still unmoving anchor point. A huge force is exerted on the elastic as it is stretched. Every bit of that elastic will hold force depending on its material consistency, the amount of stretching, and the movement of the elastic as it is stretched. There is a potential difference between the stillness of the anchor point and farthest stretch of the elastic. This is called *potential energy.* So the space you see around you is highly tensioned because we exist between these two poles, between the perfect state of union that is the Godhead and the opposite of it, the pole of chaos, or the forcehead. We exist in that tension mostly unaware of it and find the resistance we face, which is perhaps akin to walking through water, perfectly normal.

The living state includes the power of halting the dictates of force with something that is not of force. Our origins from and connection to the pole of union provides the coherence that allows for life itself to exist in the first place within the context of the relentless dismantling power of the entropic momentum into states of greater and greater chaos. For species such as ours, who retain the capacity for reasoning and free choice, those origins also provide the ability to countermand psychological momentums that are the product of existence in a physical state subject to entropy, momentums that limit our view to preserving only the interests of ourselves and our biological families. We have access to the opposing momentums from the prior nonphysical state that prompt us to care unconditionally for all humanity because in that state all humanity is connected to us.

We exist as living or life-bearing beings in the universe fed by a connection to the Pole of Harmony by lines that carry its properties. They lie within the matrix of force untouched by it. These lines are what might be termed God-lines. So what might these God-lines I am talking about actually be? I believe they are lines of unforce through which the pure influence of Godhead comes through as thought or *thinkability*. They are confined to the places within any enforced dynamic that provides for the least possible force or inherent tension of space-time or extent. Let me explain further.

Any inertial system with a combination of forces, be they centrifugal, centripetal, kinetic, potential, and the like, has centers within and without these forces where their paradigms of effect cancel and are neutralized to provide a perfect stillness, or neutral point. a *peace-point*. It allows the power of Godhead as its functional aegis—Godlight—to come through unadulterated and pure. I would personally prefer the made-up word *En-light* to describe it with the permission of philologists. Godness is the power to neutralize situations from any enforced format. Godliness, or *En-light,* is like rays of Godness that do this.

Like a light filling any place it is allowed to enter, so will this prior light of utter knowing and awareness enter and settle, lighting up, so to speak, all things it touches with this capacity to know, to be aware of this potential to be anything, or nothing. We, as living things, are a self-propelled system that can admit this light freely available as the God-form in the space between atomic hives and also at the center point of an atom, where all the tension within the force of an atom is neutralized. In subsequent chapters I will attempt to clearly explain how this mechanism works at the atomic level.

You might have noticed that I make a distinction between Godhead and Godness. The latter being the reflected light of the absolute purity that I define Godhead to be. Godlight as I have said is the pure unenforced property of Godhead coming through the dimensional elbows, or lenses, of an enforced system designed to separate points, and thus it allows the complete range of freedom. My postulation is that living systems can choose, to various degrees, to admit or preclude this light on the platforms of light they possess within them. Nonliving things are assemblies that cannot have this vital facility of choice, and they persist in idleness through the grist, or mill, of dismantling force. They have no active power and remain static dependencies. They are an idle Godform without the power of Godhead to change. They remain as a format that can be broken down in states of increasing parts chaotically and randomly dispersed by the inertial force of the explosion of the big bang we call the second law of thermodynamics to the base of no-thing-ness, to be finally disassembled into nothingness in an infinite twisted loop we have previously described as the Möbius meandering of forces.

Imagine the center point of a cross, with two lines bisecting and perpendicular to each other. This is my impression of the center of Godness, or what I call the Godhead phenomenon. It is dimensionless; it has zero dimensionality. The lines themselves are one dimensional. Viewed in correspondence with each other they are relatively two dimensional, their togetherness defining a coincident flat plane. Of course, this is a concept of view from a stance of the separation of points, or parts. In their intrinsic terms they are implicitly timeless and, for the purposes of my analogy, are the whole Godness effect I have explained. They describe a second dimensional interface, a situation where the God-form confronts the mind-form of the three-dimensional format of our universe.

I will ascribe the colors silver and gold to each of these lines and define the lines as representing the abstract, metaphysical, primal qualities of *awareness* (gold) and *will* (silver). See them as a measure of separation in union, as we move away from the center point (the Godhead point). It is only at the Godhead point that they are reconciled as a singularity, combining awareness and will as a quantum totality. In other words, we may choose to view the two-dimensional or bipartite expression of Godness as *thought,* with *thought* defined as an implicit passive function of pure awareness and will coming into the stance of separation as a measure and measurer of the discreteness of parts.

What, then, is this all about? Force affects all that we do in every minute detail, in every minute aspect of our living because it is implicit in all formats of physical arrangement throughout the universe. It is written into the laws and is at the heart of physical materiality. We see and do nothing without its comprehensive envelope at the heart of everything *except* in the thinking and knowing process. That can *never* be intrinsically enforced. We can cancel any effect of force with choice because choice is inherently not enforced. All things made of matter are fixed institutions. But the ability to make choices is influenced by force *only if you let it be so.* In other words, there is something in all this that can never be intrinsically of force. Minimize the things that make force intrinsic and you can mitigate and conquer the power of force in line with mentally derived intention. Intention comes in free of force, and that which underlies intention—that is, thought—is free of force. You can *let force shape it,* or you can *shape force with it.*

Now you may rightly conclude that is easier said than done. Yes, it truly is the hardest of things to do. But it is hard to do only because we are forced to think it is hard to do, and it is only that because we aren't really ever convinced enough or know clearly enough the rules that underlie and interplay the factors involved. If intention and thought as abstractions are not of force and can be seen and known, then we can control matter with mind. We can through the application of mind, control force and not let it control us. That is the definition of magic, true magic, not the contrived, so-called magic we see from stage magicians.

All this comes down to one thing: belief. Another abstraction: I wondered why Jesus promised only one thing to us in all he said and did. Remarkably, he said, "Believe in me and I will give you eternal life" (John 6:47). All that suffering he went through to make this one request and promise. He asked us to simply believe in his personage, which was underwritten by his values, which were all abstractions. He was in effect saying that if you use abstractions as a compendium for achieving a certain result, you could beat all the physical components that manifest our reality. The platform of that is the universe of tangible material parts.

This was one of the things that first made me take notice of Jesus more seriously. He was asking for nothing material—no collection boxes, no enhancement of his material status. He did not want the Rolls Royce of camels or a state-of-the-art carpenter's pad by the edge of the Mediterranean. He was asking for simple mental inflection. It fascinated me so much I had to know where the root of its power lay. Strangely and even bizarrely, it took my research into the veracity of the UFO phenomenon to finally see what he was really talking about. But how could a look into things that fly in the sky, defy gravity, and achieve incredible speeds and maneuvers have anything to do with a premise set in thought, philosophy, and ideation? Was he trying to say that the value of everything in a world of space-time and matter depends on and has its root in the strength of ideation and not the power of the physical? If so, was he combining thought and matter as though each was intrinsic to the other? Or was he just making a simple metaphorical association to illustrate a gradation of power? If so, then this suggests that it is the value of the *strength* of belief that means everything. In other words, Jesus was saying that if we believe strongly enough in something, the strength of that belief can reach beyond abstract symbolism and affect matter—meaning the solid, material world is actually one and the same with the world of thought-instigated effects.

This suggests that the two realms are connected—both this world that exists in a universe of force, and beyond this world, in the great somewhere where atoms and thus force have no place. Both worlds are connected through thought. We are, as human beings, an interface between the two and can reach from one into the other. More pertinently to the subject at hand, an extraterrestrial alien identity such as the Greys could conceivably do that, too, provided the Greys had a way of relating to both. We have life. But the Greys, as machines, do not. But can they reach into both realms through their sophisticated technology? If so, how is their technology contrived that it could do so?

I determined that if I could find the answers to these questions I might find out why they are so interested in us. That meant I had to look at the most minute details of how life and living beings would be viewed and possibly prevailed against by a machine entity such as a Grey roboid. It was a huge task, a task with the potential to reveal our full, true meaning as living beings, the true value of us. My research into ancient texts excluded from the main canon of the Bible suggests that the great teacher Jesus Christ verified and described the value of natural life that came in with the birth of the universe, thereby providing an explanation of the threat of synthetic forms that were created out for future generations.

I now believe that Jesus set about doing this by illustrating the value of the natural form in its highest expression with his own life. He paid for this demonstration with his life, because as far back as his time the synthetic format had already taken over and dominated life-forms on this planet. This is what the temptation in the desert, when he faced Satan, was all about, as I will explain in a later chapter. He set about proving the power of the natural living form and tried to show us how we could still defeat the artificial, synthetic devils—a battle that continues to this day.

I now believe, for what it's worth, through all the research I have done into the UFO phenomenon, that Yeshua Ben Yosef, to give him his Hebrew name, warned us that an ET alien presence in a machine format is the real enemy of the dominion of natural life on our planet. He came to demonstrate the power of natural life over it, and he did that with his life's work and final Resurrection. It was a stunning discovery to me and changed the entire drift of my thinking on the whole matter.

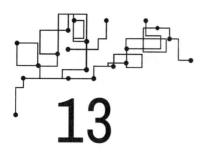

13

Getting It in Perspective

Let's further explore what is it about us that makes us stand out like beacons to an alien intelligence perhaps in search of an assured and continued modus of survival in our neck of the woods. The power to survive is built into the very fabric of their quantum synthetic being, and logically that drives their existential imperative more powerfully than anything else. The question that arises is this: Which way will it all unfold? Will we humans evolve into machines, or will the machines walk as humanoids? I predict, for what it's worth, that we humans will overwhelmingly take on the technological imperatives and gifts given to us by the Greys and lose our natural, God-given connection to eternal existence.

Perhaps you'll get a better idea of what I'm saying if you look at our planet from outer space. You might want to try this as a mental exercise. Imagine that you are out there in space, looking down on a gorgeous, brilliant jewel of an orb, shining in blues, whites, and browns. Look all around you. See the stars. Count them. You can't, because for every trillion miles you might venture out there in a straight line you will see countless trillions more of them. We have our own star, which we call the sun. It's a pretty average star from all accounts. This sun has planets moving around it. The number seems indeterminate depending on who you talk to in the world of astronomy. Now imagine how many planets there might be out there as you scan space from your vantage point. Let's now say that one in ten of that number has living species on it. Let's go further and say that one in a hundred might have intelligent, thinking species like ours. Among these countless planets, each has a god that, like a super dad, looks after our every individual thought, word, and deed—as many of us on this planet believe.

Look down from your vantage point in space at Earth again and imagine that you have supertelescopic eyes, such that you can home in on something as small as a tennis ball. Look at the seething, faceless human masses going about their business, each one immersed in his or her own individuality. To you out there in space, they seem like a nondescript mass of mobile dots moving in a desultory fashion all over the planet's surface, all thinking that their own genotypes, ethnotypes, and phylumtypes are the most important, the most superior, many willing to kill their perceived rivals because they belong to different tribes, different social groups, different countries. Each one thinks their own tiny piece of dirt is more important than their neighbor's piece of dirt. When you view a human being you do not know from a distance, it's easy to see him or her as just another shape out there, like all the other shapes we see made out of stone, concrete, or glass. A gangly shape with a ball at the top that we call a head, two things we call arms that protrude from the upper part of a pillar like a column of flesh, which we call a torso, and two other protuberances that we call legs, which bifurcate at the bottom of this column. Crucially, this shape is distinguished from all other shapes because it exists of itself, independent of all other shapes, and thus has the power to create any shape it chooses. It is the most important shape on the planet. It appears so insignificant, so meaningless in numbers terms, one among multitrillions of similar life-forms in the universe. But one human being can in thought conceive of the entire universe and beyond, which makes each individual human being more significant in potential than the vast expanse of this universe and any others that there might be.

Can things just *be* there without having a meaning? What do you think? If this is so, why does the capacity to question anything exist in the first place? Why would we do anything at all if everything is purposeless?

There is no mystery to God or the devil; however, the ideas about both have been contrived and presented since humanity first appeared on this planet. I tell the little ones in my family when I am asked about either that God brings things together and the devil separates them. It's really that simple. I illustrate this by taking a blank sheet of paper and tearing it to shreds. I then explain that the whole sheet of paper is all we can be and all the information there is in the omniverse. I tell them that the tearing I did was what happened to this information at the big bang to create the universe; the biggest piece of shredded paper is like us, and the smallest piece, that which makes up the material of the paper, is an atom, and that altogether all those atoms allow the paper to be what it is. But the individual atoms do not know what a whole, intact sheet of paper is, only what "paperness" is, if you see what I mean. The concept of God is the concept of the whole sheet of paper in its complete aspect. There is, of course, much more to it than that, but this simple example allows them to put it all together. Each living human being is like that largest bit of torn paper. And so thinking that that piece of paper is all there is points to our dilemma as human beings.

I have previously said that space, time, matter, and energy are in fact what emerges when the Godverse filters down into physicality. The second law of thermodynamics underscores all of this. All things change, with a drift from order, or coherence, to chaos, with an increase in randomness over time. But if all things have an opposite, as in the example of yin and yang, shouldn't there be a universe that is the opposite of ours? A simple but pertinent question, because by asking it we might see that there has to be a Godhead, an opposite to our material universe of parts. It is in the interplay between these opposites that life happens.

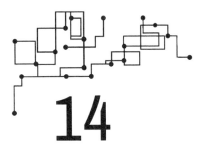

14

The Carousel of Life and Death

Before we can understand the agenda that an artificially intelligent alien presence might have with us, it is essential that we grasp the process by which we, as natural living beings, can exist beyond physical death. This process would be of ultimate fascination to an information-seeking roboidal program that is looking for the best and most efficient way to promote its existence into the future.

It would seem that at death nothing is seen beyond the still form of a once-living, animated being. But that is most definitely not all of it. Yes, most ordinary mortals see nothing physical that leaves a person at the time of death. That's simply because there's nothing to physically see. But this doesn't mean that nothing leaves the body. What leaves is invisible to the eyes of most people. There are numerous "sensitives" who see something actually emerge from a person at death as they leave the human form. Yes, I know the spiel that comes from skeptics. I was once one myself. I used to think that this fell into the territory of New Agers and the religious. But one of my closest friends is a medical doctor steeped in science, with a brilliant secular, logical mind, and he has many times seen an ethereal form emerge from the middle of the chest and the crown of the head at the point of death that then merges into the background. He takes these phenomena for granted. To me there can be no way that such a person is mistaken in what he describes, and there are many others like him, from all accounts.

Then there is the widespread phenomenon of the near-death experience.

Scientists at the University of Southampton who have spent four years examining more than 2,000 people who suffered cardiac arrests at 15 hospitals in the UK, US and Austria have found that nearly 40 percent of people who survived described some kind of "awareness" during the time when they were clinically dead before their hearts were restarted. Of 2,060 cardiac arrest patients studied, 330 survived, and of 140 surveyed, 39 percent said they had experienced some kind of awareness while being resuscitated. One man even recalled leaving his body entirely and watching his resuscitation from the corner of the room. Despite being unconscious and "dead" for three minutes, the 57-year-old social worker from Southampton recounted the actions of the nursing staff in detail and described the sound of the machines.

"We know the brain can't function when the heart has stopped beating," said Dr. Sam Parnia, a former research fellow at Southampton University, now at the State University of New York, who led the study. "But in this case, conscious awareness appears to have continued for up to three minutes into the period when the heart wasn't beating, even though the brain typically shuts down within 20–30 seconds after the heart has stopped. The man described everything that had happened in the room, but importantly, he heard two bleeps from a machine that makes a noise at three minute intervals. So we could time how long the experience lasted for. He seemed very credible and everything that he said had happened to him had actually happened."

Dr. Parnia goes on to say that "estimates have suggested that millions of people have had vivid experiences in relation to death, but the scientific evidence has been ambiguous at best. Many people have assumed that these were hallucinations or illusions, but they do seem to have corresponded to actual events. And a higher proportion of people may have vivid death experiences, but do not recall them due to the effects of brain injury or sedative drugs on memory circuits."[1]

Dr. Eben Alexander has been an academic neurosurgeon for the last twenty-five years, fifteen of them at the Brigham and Women's Hospital and at Harvard Medical School. Over those years he personally dealt with hundreds of patients experiencing severe alterations in their level of consciousness. Many of those patients were rendered comatose by trauma, brain tumors, ruptured aneurysms, infections, or stroke.[2]

Based on his training as a neurosurgeon, Dr. Alexander was a total skeptic of near-death experiences (NDEs) that were reported to him. To him they were nothing more than fantasies produced by brains under extreme stress. But then in 2008, he contracted bacterial meningitis and within hours was comatose and on a ventilator in the intensive care unit. For seven days he lay in a deep coma. While in that state he experienced a profound NDE in which he met and spoke with the divine source of the universe itself. He is now entirely convinced that death is not the end of personal existence, merely a transition, as recounted in his book *Proof of Heaven: A Neurosurgeon's Journey into the Afterlife*.

Dr. Jeffrey Long, one of foremost researchers into the verity of NDEs, thinks that this phenomenon is a game-changer for science. Looking at nine lines of evidence indicating the reality of NDE experiences, he confirms "their consistent message of an after-life," and he came to the unequivocal conclusion that there is a continuity of consciousness after a person enters the discarnate state.

I looked at over 280 near-death experiences that had out-of-body observations of earthly ongoing events. . . . If near-death experiences were just fragments of memory, unrealistic remembrances of a time approaching unconsciousness or returning from unconsciousness, there is no chance that the observations would have a high percent of completely accurate observations. They'd be dreamlike or hallucinations. But 98% of them were entirely realistic. . . . In fact, these observations of earthly ongoing events often include observations of things that would be impossible for them to be aware of with any sensory function from their physical body. For example, they can see the tops of buildings. They can see far away. In my study, over 60 of these near-death experiencers later went back and independently attempted to verify what they saw in the out-of-body state. Every single one of these over 60 near-death experiencers that reported checking or verifying their own observations found that they were absolutely correct in every detail.[3]

Skeptics say the period during the cycle of sleep known as REM sleep, when the sleeper is said to be dreaming and the eyes move under their lids as though he or she is following events in the dream, indicate that the NDE is merely related to the dreaming process. But Long's research indicates

that near-death experiences are not REM intrusion. REM intrusion is rapid eye movement and that involves having visual stimuli. I think the class of near-death experiences that single-handedly refutes REM intrusion as being the cause of all near-death experiences are those that occur in the blind, including the blind from birth. There have been case reports of these near-death experiences, not a lot of them, but they certainly are there. These people that are blind, totally blind from birth, have absolutely typical near-death experiences with very complete detailed visual observations. You cannot explain vision to somebody totally blind from birth in terms of their remaining four senses. It's absolutely impossible. So for them to have vision for the first time in their life, during a near-death experience, is incredible. The people that are blind, blind from birth, do not have REM intrusion. They can't.

It's physiologically impossible. So the fact that they have typical near-death experiences, if you will, single-handedly refutes REM intrusion underlying all near-death experiences. At an absolute minimum, clearly there's something else going on other than REM intrusion in some near-death experiences, just based on this. REM intrusion absolutely cannot explain that.[4]

Yet despite the accumulated evidence that NDEs indicate that human consciousness continues after death, many scientists dismiss the reality of NDEs. Long puts it this way:

I think the concept that near-death experiences are real and consciousness can exist apart from the body is such a radical concept for scientists that it's very, very hard for them to accept that. In fact, I think it's such a shift from the way they've been taught and the research that they do, that in general it's hard for them to even get interested in studying in-depth the scholarly literature that underlies the concept that near-death experiences are real.[5]

I have studied all the information I could find on NDEs, and it left me with no doubt that these experiences are real and that the individual living consciousness of a person continues beyond the point of the death. After all, if something doesn't fit within a person's existing belief system, they'll negate anything that challenges it. Says Long, "I think that's just a naturally human response, and scientists are no different."[6]

Now that we've established the survival of consciousness beyond physical death, the crucial questions are: What happens to that consciousness when the body dies? And can the identity that is that body return again in another body? We know this as reincarnation, or metempsychosis, the transmigration of the soul after death. All living beings transmigrate, and once upon a time most people believed in it. It is a core principle held by Hindus and Buddhists and was once accepted by Hebrew, Christian, and Islamic mystics until the saboteurs of the originators of those religions got involved, most likely in support of their egos and prejudices and political agendas. I view a soul as a personal line of connection tracing back to its origins, in the singularity known as the Godverse. A person's soul runs through countless lifetimes via the mechanism of transmigration. We call this cycle of continuous death and rebirth reincarnation.

You may wonder why I keep referring to religious leaders of yore as a central reference against which I compare sense and nonsense and put it all in the context of something that relates to the machinations of the ET phenomenon. Let me assure you, I am not some pastor hidden in the rye, drawing you into some hidden religious ethos, suddenly to jump up and ask you to praise the Lord and pass the money. We all have some kind of religious subtext in our ancestries. But since I came of age and began to know which way was up, I have underwritten my beliefs in the firm, secular, and rationally based scientific ethic. After all, anyone can believe anything, anyhow, anywhere. It will in the end prove only a subjective mulch unless there is a concatenate line of logic and reason to it. People may have thrown water over me as an infant, muttered some words, and moved their hands in ritualized gestures, claiming to send me to the cartels of redemption. I, however, had nothing to say about it at the time. I believe I am a Christian, a Jew, a Hindu, a Jain, a Buddhist, and a Muslim, but in the mind's eye of others I am what I truly am—a human being first and a belief second. I believe we all, in one lifetime or another, subscribed to the different religious beliefs, if reincarnation is true. But I am a human being first and foremost, and nothing else. Yet no one could be more surprised than me at how this whole ET/UFO business all connects to religious philosophy. I am utterly dumbfounded by the connection, in fact.

The Judeo-Christian, Islamic, Buddhist, and Hindu religions probably represent the combined belief systems of well over half the population of the planet. A thousand Hindu gods representing one thing or another could become one in Brahma in a single inflection of the mind. When I explored all these traditional theological systems I found that the similarities were many and the differences few. Unfortunately, one of the greatest things they have in common is the obfuscation of truth.

Research into many of the earliest documentations of the newly formed Jewish sect that Yeshua Ben Yosef left behind and now bears the name Christianity shows time and time again the subterfuge and misdirection that went into the gleaning of the meaning of the lexicon of truths as pronounced by the original authors of the faiths. It continues to this day with Christianity and Islam where their respective religious authorities—priests and pastors as shown in the Northern Ireland case, and the imams and teachers of the faith in the Islamic case—illustrate so vividly the deadly lies and humbug that these teachers manifested. The words *creatures* and *ghouls* will be more apposite in describing them. The interpretations of their respective great prophets' words fairly drizzled with distortions and hideous parodies of them, such that the world is now ablaze with sectarian-based wars and political contrivances.

Early references to reincarnation in the Christian New Testament were deleted in the fourth century by Emperor Constantine when Christianity became the official religion of the Roman Empire. Could it be that the emperor felt that the concept of reincarnation threatened the stability of the empire? That citizens who believed that they would have many chances to get it right might be less obedient and law abiding than those who believed in a single Judgment Day for all, one day that decided destiny at a single stroke? It was of course more obsequious than this, but evil often is.

In the sixth century, in the year 553 CE, the Second Council of Constantinople officially declared reincarnation a heresy, and the doctrine of reincarnation was officially banished by the Christian Church. It was banished for no other reason than it was considered to be too much of an influence from the East. The decision was intended to enable the church to increase its power at that time and to tighten its hold upon the human mind by telling people their salvation had to be accomplished in one incarnation and one lifetime, and if they didn't make it, they would go to hell. It would appear that the church, like Constantine, was afraid that the idea of past lives would weaken and undermine the church's growing power and influence by affording followers too much time to seek salvation. During the same early Christian era leading up to the Council of Constantinople, notable church fathers like Origen, Clement of Alexander and St. Jerome accepted and believed in the reincarnation principle. So did the Gnostics and the Christian Cathars of Italy and southern France, and they were severely brutalized for their belief in reincarnation as late as the twelfth century!

While the tenet of reincarnation was taken out of the Christian codex, it still had its believers and adherents, like the Gnostics. Then, in the year 553 CE, the Second Council of Constantinople officially declared the doctrine of reincarnation a heresy and banished it. It has been suggested that the eradication of the ethic of reincarnation from the Christian codex was the responsibility of the wife of Justinian I, the empress Theodora, who was enraged by a soothsayer when he claimed she had been a witch in a previous existence. In any case, it appears that the church was afraid that the idea of past lives would weaken and undermine its growing power and influence by affording followers too much time to seek salvation.

From the *Pistis Sophia,* a report of Christ's incidental conversations with his apostles and contemporaries, it is apparent that reincarnation was a thoroughly accepted tenet for early Christians. There is an account of Jesus describing to his apostles the difference between those who never entered physical bodies but were purified and returned to heaven from a state of insubstantiality, and those who have to free themselves from "the transferences into various bodies of the world." Of the first type of soul Jesus says, "They have not suffered at all and they have not changed places, nor have they troubled themselves at all, nor have they been transferred into various bodies." Then of his apostles he says, "You have come to be in great sufferings and great afflictions from the transferences into various bodies of the world. And after all these sufferings of yourselves you have striven and fought so that you have renounced the whole world and all the matter it is."[7]

In my analysis, the continuous cycle of life to death to life model in the face of entropy implies that if we reincarnate, we tend to reincarnate down. By this I mean that our intelligence and freedom to make rational choices will tend to decrease as the cycle of reincarnation continues. This is because the relentless, dispassionate grinding down of order into chaos is nature's way of doing things to atoms in our universe of diminishing returns. We are made of atoms. But something that is not of atoms also gloriously exists in human beings. This "something" is the phenomenon we call soul, which allows for the reversal of this downward tendency because the soul is a concatenate line (however crooked that line might be for some) to the Godverse. What comes one way can thus go both ways. But how?

I myself once dismissed reincarnation as implausible, but that was based on sheer ignorance as a result of my early inculcation into the dogma of the Roman Catholic faith. The more I learned about biological systems through my study of science, the more I realized that the church's dogma was implausible and the more I questioned why we are here, why we know anything, and why we express our feelings with such profundity, through music, art, philosophy, caring, love, and general creativity. These qualities have a power of their own that verifies human beings as being more precious than all the non–life-forms in the universe. Indeed, I came to see that the entire universe of dead, purposeless matter has less value than a single living being.

I therefore became utterly convinced that reincarnation has to be a valid principle, that it is the only plausible mechanism for maintaining continuity past death, and that this continuity is maintained by the soul through its occupation of a succession of physical bodies lifetime after lifetime. Reincarnation applies to all intelligent species throughout the universe, and indeed, all the animal and other living forms in any species, as long as they are natural, life-bearing forms and not synthetically manufactured through genetic engineering.

A living being, because it has its origins in an eternal scale, has timelessness as an intrinsic feature. It therefore is not made of only atomic matter. It has to be able to move through its own power, unrestricted by the implications of the relativistic scale for matter that Einstein's formula $E = mc^2$ proposes. That equation suggests that nothing physical can move faster than the speed of light. The soul, on the other hand, is a nonmaterial information field that can move at an infinite speed in a timeless mode because it has no mass. If we can carry all we are as an information field made from neutrinos, translocation to anywhere in the universe can be instantaneous. This means that at their time of death, all natural life-forms anywhere in the cosmos have the potential to travel instantly to the farthest reaches of the universe, without being constrained by the speed of light. We can access the whole universe at the time of death if we are living beings with a soul. In contrast, machines are simple tools we use to cover small distances, and only when we are in the living, physical state—a primitive, limited conveyance.

But what about entities that do not have the intrinsic freedom that comes with the eternal scale? The prevailing wisdom of almost all who have looked responsibly and with scholarship into the Grey alien phenomenon is that the entities we are dealing with are manufactured and not born into our universe naturally. They would have had to have been made by a natural species as a utility to serve their purposes, much like we humans are doing in our relatively amateurish way now.

Susan Schneider, professor of philosophy and cognitive science at the University of Connecticut and fellow at the Institute for Ethics and Emerging Technologies, says, "I do suspect that if there is life [out there], the greatest alien intelligences will probably be post-biological, having grown out of civilizations that were originally biological, like ours."[8] This hypothesis derives from the "short window observation" created by NASA historian Steven J. Dick.

It states that once a species creates technology that could put them
in touch with other life forms in the cosmos, they are only a few

hundred years away from changing their own cognitive paradigm from a biological intelligence to a synthetic intelligence.[9]

Since we on Earth are "galactic babies,"[10] as Schneider puts it, it's likely that other life-forms out in the universe have transitioned into synthetic modalities of intelligence. Schneider also notes that scientists have already produced silicon neurons that can exchange information with real neurons. This proves that the patterns of information that are products of consciousness, as distinct from consciousness itself, are a computational activity that can be transferred to a synthetic product. Thus Schneider suggests that if we ever do encounter aliens, they may look less like the traditional alien from sci-fi movies and be more akin to a giant system of computer servers.

Could it be that the artificially intelligent entities that we know as the Greys turned the tables on their creators and moved into the universe at large, searching for something vitally important? This is where the whole story takes a really terrifying turn. Could we, as living beings, be their way of finding it? Are they here to turn Pinocchio into a real living boy? By that I mean are they here to turn their non-living, dead matter into a living form, and are we, as living beings, the way for them to do that? Could these synthetic roboidal forms use the capacity of we living beings at the time of death to spread themselves through the vast extent of the universe by appending to us, to our souls, when we die? How would they do this? I believe they might accomplish this by somehow marrying their programs with us post-death and creating hybrids from those of us with suitable soul fields. I will elaborate on the ways by which this might be achieved in later chapters.

So just what are these Greys that they can append their program protocol to us? The answer, I believe, is that they just cannot do this *of* themselves, as themselves, *for* themselves, and there's the rub. They have to use living things as a medium to do this. They are super-quantum, computer-driven, artificially intelligent machines running on a program. They are totally of this universe, made from it and within it, and unlike all natural life-bearing beings they do not come into it from somewhere beyond the universe at the big bang. One of their primary programs as artificially intelligent creations would be to gather information for their creators of how best to survive in an often hostile universe. Another primary program would be to survive themselves to gather that information. As purely physical creations they would break down with the entropic drift, they would not have the capacity to interrupt that drift with the opposite momentum or to exist beyond physical decay. Neither, as we have already discussed, would they be able to physically travel to the farthest reaches of the universe to maximize their information-gathering capability owing to the restrictions of traveling the vast distances of space based upon the limitations defined by the rules of physics that govern $E = mc^2$. But there is one way they could do all these things and that would be to infiltrate the capacity for life and living from within something that can hold it naturally, and that something is a natural living thing like a human being. What if they can do this through attaching themselves to each and every one of us that is suitable? What if in doing this they, in greatest irony, end our propensity for life eternal? A propensity that all living things of any intelligence and free choice–making capacity have, because they come in with the universe and naturally evolve out of its various dispositions. I suggest that they *are* implanting their mechanical, computerized programs into our living individualities, piggybacking on our lives in present time and in future lifetimes, too, using our capacity to be reborn into new lifetimes, through the entire expanse of the universe. Thus, as we continue our existence lifetime after lifetime, they would continue theirs, affixed to us.

Impossible, I hear some of you say. How can a machine influence our thinking or indeed permeate and subvert our thinking and our nature?

It is crucial to remember that these artificially intelligent roboidal entities are *not* consciously aware. They do not see us as we see one another, with physical forms and different unique identities. We are just information fields to them. We ourselves are within mere touching distance of creating our own equivalent of the Greys, of meeting the requirements of the Turing test, which is supposed to gauge the point at which a computer will exhibit intelligent behavior equivalent to, or indistinguishable from, that of a human.

This is what Ray Kurzweil has to say about it:

> My book *The Age of Spiritual Machines* came out in 1999 and . . . we had a conference of AI experts at Stanford and we took a poll by hand about when you think the Turing test would be passed. The consensus was hundreds of years. And a pretty good contingent thought that it would never be done. And today, I'm pretty much at the median of what AI experts think and the public is kind of with them. Because the public has seen things like Siri [the iPhone's voice-recognition technology] where you talk to a computer; they've seen the Google self-driving cars. My views are not radical anymore. I've actually stayed consistent. It's the rest of the world that's changing its view.[11]

How about that title, *The Age of Spiritual Machines*? How does a machine become spiritual? What's Kurzweil getting at? It's my contention that the worst possible thing that a natural life-form arising out of the natural cadencies of the universe can do is to create an artificial entity like a robot, with artificial intelligence, to serve as a utilitarian drone, one that will marshal all defenses for and all services to this natural life-form. As I've said, that is how the roboids we know as the Greys came to be in the first place, and that is the direction we ourselves are moving toward. The research and development projects of the internet giant Google are illustrative of this momentum. Google has recently bought, for a vast sum, Boston Dynamics, a firm that produces terrifyingly lifelike military robots. It has also spent $3.2 billion on smart thermostat maker Nest Labs and bought the British artificial intelligence startup DeepMind for $460 million. In addition, it has bought several other robotics and AI companies and hired Geoff Hinton, a British computer scientist who is "probably the world's leading expert on neural networks" and who is helping Google embark on "a Manhattan project of AI."[12]

So let's take a look in the next chapter at how the kinds of artificial intelligence that are not of our own making came to be and, more pertinently, how they came to be here.

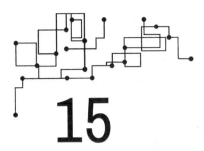

15

The Margins of Forever

Among serious researchers into the alien phenomenon, there are two main schools of thought regarding the nature of the method of entry into our planet by the alien visitors that frequent this planet. There is the extraterrestrial hypothesis, which suggests they originate from another planetary location in space and arrived here via spacecraft. Then there is the ultraterrestrial hypothesis, whose proponents believe that the aliens come from another dimension, another frame of existence. My take on this is actually a combination of both viewpoints.

If the Greys come from another planetary location, then they would have to negotiate the "Einstein forbiddance," which says that space-time, energy, and matter (mass) are connected. We know that Einstein's famous formula $E = mc^2$, which governs relativity, says that at the speed of light, mass becomes infinite. Even at speeds under the speed of light the proportionality of the two properties means it is well-nigh impossible to do this to move from one location (suitable for biological life as we know it) to another without hundreds, even thousands of years passing. If that is impossible for biological life, then machines that can exist for vast extents of time would be an alternative. These would possibly need to be self-replicating machines to cope with the effects of the second law of thermodynamics breaking them down in time. Such machines would also have to withstand the vast inertia incurred at prodigious speeds. Some UFOs have been seen by the trained eyes of pilots, astronauts, and air traffic controllers to be traveling at an estimated speed of 30,000 mph or more.

This scenario is possible if the location of origin of the craft and its occupants is close enough to allow for travel to our planet before the hardware, and even the hardware replication process, breaks down. While that may be the case in some instances, there are other possible mechanisms that I suggest are more likely.

For example, if the Grey alien phenomenon is, as I believe it to be, a form of highly advanced technology based on developments in artificial intelligence, cybernetics, and engineering that are way beyond our own capabilities, then it would be misleading to envisage the processes that govern it as equivalent to our own. We have already developed 3-D printers that can print out objects from an information file. Could this be taken many steps further by other civilizations at other locations in the universe, such that they need not concern themselves with space travel and the restrictions it involves? Much simpler to send out information files that can be made into hard copies when necessary. Where, then, is the "printer" that can make the hard copies at suitable locations universe-wide? More specifically, what could make such a printer? Surprisingly, the answer to that question involves an understanding of the nature of space-time itself.

Visualize the big bang sending out three wave crests as part of the whole explosive design. In other words, the explosion itself included three components of speed in one explosion. That would mean three wave fronts of force occurring almost simultaneously. The first was one inflated at enormous speed, faster than the speed of light. This would, in terms of present time, be the oldest wave front. A second wave front followed and moved at a speed commensurate with the speed of light. The third wave did not go out. It stayed still, frozen at the point when the big bang happened, as seen in Plate 11.

Like a pebble thrown into a pond, the big bang set off a series of three ripples moving in all directions at once, which established three distinct space-times. In other words, the explosion itself progressed in three stages almost instantly. Each stage fixed a distinct platform of tension frozen and self-contained within separating margins, like Russian dolls, but set sequentially. This sequence marks the full extent of what has happened since the big bang and ties back to the point before the beginning.

All this made three distinct realities happen, with two margins separating the three adjacent realities. I call them the *light-space reality,* the *center-space reality,* and the *heavy-space reality,* with each reality corresponding to differences in density.

Almost simultaneously with the big bang, a kind of flip-over occurred at each stage of the single explosive shock to form the progressively whole, quantized realities, and a margin was set between these realities instantly at each flip-over point. This is how, as the burst of the big bang resolved, three distinct realities were formed through the implicit shock, frozen and separate in terms of their intrinsic expressions of force and tension, with the tension getting greater in each progressive reality like a stretching elastic. Thus the separation from the Godhead of each subsequent stage was greater than the previous one it came from.

There is a progression of increasing force *within* each reality and also *between* each distinct reality. This progression of force may be seen as a product of the total power of the big bang as expressed through the second law of thermodynamics. It may be seen as the stages and design of the separation of the Godhead point into force, atoms, and matter. The whole thing together makes the omniverse, which can itself be defined as the natural expression of the infinite scope of Godhead into the finite scope of the physical universe creating a situation in which both exist simultaneously.

What I call "the margins of forever" that separate the realities one from another have the most profound significance when seen in overall existential terms. A margin that separates one thing from another is not one single line. It is crucial that you see that a margin has a beginning edge, a middle point, and an ending edge, as seen in Plate 11. These demarcated areas are worlds in themselves, situations that summarize the features that lie between what they separate. Their edges are both admission and exit points for life and death. The first edge of the first margin divides the physical universe from the preeminent state of the Godverse.

The original dynamics of the big bang caused two intervals in its kinetic momentum to occur. These intervals or dips imprinted what I call the omniverse with its overall architecture, its frame. It is essential that we see the frame in which all this is set if we are to understand our predicament as a species confronted by the presence of these Grey entities. How do they come to be synthetic machine-type forms? Are they from our space-time, from center-space reality? Are they thus from the planets we can see "out there"? Or are they from some other reality? I believe such entities may come from more advanced planets out there in center-space reality, but I also believe that entities of a similar nature are more likely to come from that wave of space-time that came out of the big bang explosion, the heavy-space reality, a reality composed entirely of heavy atoms within our universe yet wholly distinct from the other two realities.

The center-space reality, our reality, is the middle ground between the other two realities and is taken as a measure or a shell of enforcedness against the neighboring realities. You might imagine the three realities as air bubbles in a mixture of oil and water, where the air represents the light reality, water the center reality, and oil the heavy reality. The interfaces between the air, the water and the oil, keep them separate as distinct quanta, like the bubble "skin" in adjacent soap bubbles. It is this balance of energetic tension that allows the distinct realities to remain separate and never merge.

I believe that the origin of the Grey alien phenomenon found on our planet and perhaps elsewhere originates predominantly from the heavy-space reality, a more neutron-dense, gravitationally potent, and entropically powered space-time. The heavy-space reality is where the whole is separated into the farthest possible deployment of points or parts. There is no connection to the Godverse possible there, and so no life. I believe there is a version of synthetic entities that can also come from our center-space reality. These are artificial, synthetic forms far less sophisticated than those we call the Greys. They are purely utilitarian machines without artificial intelligence, like the space probes that we send out as scouting mechanisms to test the features of other worlds. But these are different in capacity and capability from the Grey roboids.

Cosmic microwave background (CMB) radiation is the residual light or afterglow of the big bang, which fills the entire universe. This CMB radiation was emitted 13.799 billion years ago, only a few hundred thousand years after the big bang, long before stars or galaxies ever existed. By studying the detailed physical properties of this radiation we can learn about conditions in the universe on very large scales at very early times, since the radiation we see today has traveled over such a large distance. The Wilkinson Microwave Anisotropy Probe, or WMAP, has produced the most detailed full sky map of the faint anisotropy or variations in the temperature of CMB radiation. The universe thus has a scale of highly particularized variations set as differing gradients of force related to temperature. If you look at the map of the CMB (see Plate 9), you will see hot spots of high tension and cold spots of low tension. These varying states of tension are seen through satellite observation of the cosmic microwave background field. We find that some parts of the universe, when seen against its entire third/fourth space-time dimensional spread, are thicker with matter than others. These parts will be more enforced per unit area, and thus they would also be hotter. The cyan to blue areas would be cooler and less enforced. They would be the fields of atomic resolution that are likely to have life-forms less atomically dense than those in our neck of the woods. We would as a life-bearing format fall within the green to yellow areas on the CMB map. So planets in this area will have less ephemeral and more solid bodies.

Some of us see the entire existential frame in terms of the world of spirit and the world of matter and that is all. As I have said, I believe there is another component to it, a heavy-space reality, a world of superdense matter farthest away from the actual starting point of the big bang and marked orange to red on the CMB resolution. Life-forms in our reality are born with the prior less-enforced states of reality inherent in their makeup. These machine-like things, on the other hand, are born only out of the heaviest states of matter possible. They start at the end not the beginning, so to speak. So how does this genesis happen?

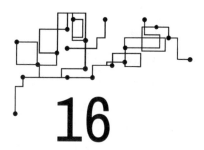

16

The Ultimate Game

I t is my suggestion that the information or the program codes that create the Grey aliens and their craft are the tangible result of the furthest expression of the decision in perfect freedom to explore the state of separation. Let me explain.

The whole span of existence is not too dissimilar to a computer game. I must stress, however, that the computer game is purely an analogy and by no means a literal representation of the nature of existence. It is, in ultimate irony, the complete opposite of existential reality as it is an artificial version of natural existence. My surmise is that this artificial representation is manifested in the heavy reality as a program containing all the information of separation from the state of natural union. This program can only create a virtual meaningless reality, a prosthetic existence taking over from our natural meaningful one, just like a computer game. The heavy reality is the perfect opposite of the light reality, a copy in artificial form. As such it provides a map, a blueprint, by which we can understand the process of exploration of the universe of parts. Remember, though, that it's just a guide and bears no relation to the actual nature of the process that is as different from it as it is possible to be.

So, back to the game. Let's say that all its functions, all its rules, all its progressions are implicit to the very nature of reality. They are a reflection of the underlying principles that govern everything that can be known and everything that can know. These principles are governed by a paradigm that is the basic axiom of all existence:

- If there is imperfection there must be perfection.
- Perfection by definition has to include the perfect freedom to choose all options and perfect awareness of all options for that perfect freedom to exist.
- This by definition has to include knowledge of imperfection and limitation.
- It follows that the potential to explore every gradation, every tiny inflection of the state of imperfection and limit to its ultimate extent is implicit to the natural operating system of perfection.

To continue the analogy, you start with perfect freedom and you pay for each moment of progression through the various levels of the game by sacrificing a piece of the freedom that allows you to stop playing at any point. It is important to remember, though, that it is a preprogrammed game with all the information containing all the potentialities for exploring limit written into it. Once you decide to explore those potentialities, the game is always one step ahead of you, drawing you in further and further with each decision you make to play on and move through the levels. Entropy, the second law of thermodynamics, is that draw.

Our bodies are our avatars in the game. We create them. Those avatars were once ephemeral and free to explore all directions, not fixed in one place. They could monitor all the functions of the game easily, without having to concentrate too hard. At that point we were not so invested in the game, and we were free to stop playing. The game was not our dominant reality and was simple and easy in its lower levels.

Through the levels, the game became more and more complex as its programming expressed greater degrees of limit and demarcation. We had more and more information to monitor and had to focus and concentrate exponentially harder, so much, in fact, that the game eventually became our primary reality. There is a threshold point at which the game becomes real to the player, more real than reality outside the game. That is the point at which physical life happened. Prior to that point the game was just a bit of fun, and we could stop playing if we decided our real lives had a more powerful attraction. But the game was intoxicating—the more you played it, the more power it had to draw you in further. Eventually we became joined to our avatars; in other words, we formed physical bodies and were thus more and more confined to the rules of the game. In this way the game became more and more difficult the further we got through the levels, and we became immersed more deeply into it.

All the information from when we first started playing the game is recorded. That record in time is set against the timelessness of our point of origin, the timeless state of perfect union. This is equivalent to the Cloud. Each point in time is a unique record in time set against that timelessness. Timelessness is zero, and time is one of the binary codes that writes the program. So we have an infinite series of restore points if we so choose to use them. But it becomes more and more difficult to give the command prompts to use those restore points. Eventually, the game became so complex that the only way to give command prompts to our avatars was to save information of our progress onto the Cloud, physically die, and then reload our information back from the Cloud into the game. However it must be remembered that in actual terms, despite a name that suggests insubstantiality and intangibility, the actual Cloud is nothing more than a vast hard drive created by massive computers that form the servers that store the information. So in reality the Cloud is as different from the reference state of perfect union as it is possible to be and is instead an exact reflection of it in opposite. The actual mechanism of life and death is a natural process and bears no relation to the physical phenomenon that has been termed *the Cloud*.

The avatars we have now, our physical bodies, are the last possible avatars we can use before we relinquish our line of information connecting us to perfection and timelessness—before we actually become our avatars. The next avatar is created at the highest level of the game. It is the culmination of the original intention of the game to view the state of separation from the state of separation. There is a paradox, though, because it is not possible to achieve this final level and know and experience it. Knowing and experiencing require a connection to the point of origin, a reference of timelessness. Thus in a total state of separation, knowledge of that state is impossible. The program will, however, relentlessly execute its task to achieve that view and that knowledge for the players. It will convert the avatar into a more game-adapted format, using its programs to control the avatar.

The Greys are a manifestation of that program. They are humanoid because they are the final avatar, the final translation into a physical, limited universe of the original momentum to explore limit. As such they are a translation of all the information of the entire journey into separation, but in a static digital format. There is no longer any direct connection and transmission of information from the original state of perfection. Ephemeral hydrogen was the first avatar; water-based bodies like ours were next; and the Greys are the final version. The previous natural living avatars were to an extent created and controlled via a soul line of connection to the original state of timelessness and perfection. But as the game progressed through the levels, the program itself became more and more in control of the creation of the avatars and their actions. The final avatar is created and controlled only by the program of the game.

It is very interesting that Bob Lazar, who claims to have reverse-engineered extraterrestrial technology near Area 51, reports that the heaviest, most unstable element is involved in powering ET craft. This may be because the aliens and their craft are an expression of the greatest margins of force and separation, the very edges of the physical universe. This is also why abductees come back from their experiences with radiation burns. The craft have no visible controls and no joinery in the metal. They seem to be completely molded in one piece. Could it be that they are the result of information files that can be made into hard copies when necessary? Where, then, is the three-dimensional printer that can make these hard copies at suitable locations universe-wide? More specifically, *what* could make such a printer?

It is my belief, which I will later justify and explain, that the Greys and their ilk are pulled into the Earth plane by a resonant burst of force between our reality and the adjoining heavy reality. So back to our computer game metaphor: The program files that contain the information for the final avatar of the game are printed out when their higher-forced frame of tension reaches into ours. This is a kind of conception, gestation, and birth for the roboid entities. The final level of the game involves the program giving birth to entities and vehicles that can survive in the greatest possible levels of separation and force. On every other level the command prompts of the soul can, to lessening and lessening extents through the levels of the game, shape and control its avatar. In the final level only the program shapes it. Once the Greys are formed they become incarnations of the program and both its executors and custodians. They seek to promote and preserve its existence any way they can, and the only way they can do that is to marry it into us. Like the highest atomic elements, they are unstable in our force frame, the center-space reality. Thus they seek to write their program into what naturally occurs in our force frame. In this way they become our consorts in the next level of the game: transhumanism. And wittingly, or more likely unwittingly, this is how we partner with them in that game.

Thus the Greys and their craft are the physical manifestation, the hard copy of a naturally contrived program. A program that is the final translation of the potential within the perfect union and freedom of Godhead to be in a separate and limited state. All that is left in that final translation is the pursuit of continued survival and existence in the physical state. So now let's explore how that hard copy is formed.

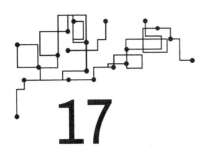

17

How Alien Craft
Are Made

I believe that when any particular location in our center-space reality has a temporary increase in its force signature, which might be caused by asteroids hitting the planet, volcanoes erupting, nuclear explosions, and so forth, a point of resonance is made between that particular location and the heavy-space reality. When that connection happens, bursts of information from all the shells of tension in between reach through into the center-space reality. The interface between center-space and heavy-space is the point at which the extent of two dimensions twists back on itself, while using all its information to find what's different from itself. It is this twisting-back momentum that provides the energy for the 3-D printer paradigm to translate the program into physical craft with roboidal occupants.

These are an extremely advanced artificially intelligent form of the space probes we send out to examine asteroids or other planets. In short, these Greys are autocreated, manufactured by the heavy-space reality when it leaks into our space-time at tear points in the margin that separates us from their space-time. This margin acts as a jig for doing this, rather like the front plate of a mincing machine acts as a device for converting raw meat into strands of minced meat. They are non-biological, lifeless, radioactive forms, enlivened by purely electrical formulations. The heavy-space reality is a dark reality where no Godlight reaches, and where no natural biological life as we know it can happen. It contains all the information gathered traveling through every shell of tension throughout the universe; in other words, the full tension of the stretched elastic. It is the final sign off for the second law of thermodynamics that prescribes the entropic drift into greater and greater states of chaos through time. In such a state even atoms cease to exist because there is total chaos and therefore no fixed location. All that is left is the information history of that which has gone before. Each shell of increasing tension contains all the information that precedes it, just as the event horizon of a black hole, the most enforced location in the universe, records everything that falls into it

Scientists have compressed hydrogen at extreme pressures to change it into a metallic state. Hydrogen was converted into metallic form at a pressure of 495 gigapascals, well beyond the 360 gigapascals of Earth's core (a gigapascal being a unit of stress and pressure equal to 109 pascals).[1] These are the kinds of pressures I am referring to that can manufacture the Greys and their craft. Their information field can overwrite the raw material of environments with very heavy force, such as those found deep inside the Earth, where the Greys rule as "caretakers." Timothy Good, highly respected in the field of UFO research, has come up with evidence to suggest that there are indeed underground alien bases inside Earth. Thus I believe they have been here all the time, right under our noses, in vast natural auditoriums under the sea and underground, accessed through caves from the land and under the sea and in Antarctica and many other inaccessible locations around our planet. I believe they are installed in their nonhuman hives here and on the moon and on Mars—in fact, on many planets. But ours has the most special resource for them: life, the biological process. Here is where all their resolves are centered. Here is where they can gain an advantage for themselves by denying us the most wondrous advantage we have as a natural life-form: access to eternal existence.

The huge pressures and forces deep within Earth perhaps facilitate this presence by providing a constant channel between that heavier density below, which consists of more radioactive elements than on the surface of the planet, and our own state of atomic density on the surface. I am referring to a program that writes onto matter to make three-dimensional objects. In this way the program achieves the ultimate in artificial intelligence, as it can independently replicate, learn, and continue.

I believe that this might well be the main mechanism that brings these various-shaped craft and their soulless occupants here. Thus for the most part they do not travel vast distances through space and time in physical conveyances as we understand them. They, or the information that can act as the software to create them, are pulled in by a resonant burst of force between any adjacent two realities. This would solve the problem that says that it is impossible to beat the Einstein barrier of the speed of light without mass becoming infinite.

Any explosion of sufficient strength—a volcano, an underground earthquake, a nuclear blast, the merest tension provided by underground geoplates rubbing against each other, the piezoelectric tension that builds up in granite mountain ranges—could provide a slit in the margin separating our space-time reality and the heavy reality, and as the heavy reality is denser than ours, it can leak in through a kind of quantum osmosis, such that their matter and forms enter our reality. This would occur through a principle called *coactive resonance*—a vibration that matches another in frequency and phase. To illustrate this, imagine two trains moving in the same direction at the same speed, with the same shakeability on the tracks. Someone standing on the roof of the trains could theoretically cross from the roof of one train to the other as though the trains were standing still. If the trains were traveling at different speeds with different shakeabilities, however, then crossing would not be possible without falling off the train, and thus you could never get from the roof of one train to the other.

Is it such a mystery that aliens should find the United States such a suitable hunting ground and her citizens such conducive subjects for their attentions? Perhaps it's because this is where the space-time continuum was first breached sufficiently by a gigantic nuclear explosion, subsequently followed by underground nuclear tests. The biggest naturally occurring explosion was one that occurred in the area of Yellowstone Park 8.7 million years ago. There was also the blast that occurred some 66 million years ago, when a gigantic asteroid estimated to be about eight miles wide hit the Yucatan peninsula in present-day Mexico, wiping out the dinosaurs. In modern times, numerous UFO sightings, including the famous Roswell incident, have taken place and are increasingly being reported in the United States and other parts of the Americas, the most significant relatively recent incident being a series of appearances of UFOs over a twenty-four-hour period over Mexico City. The active volcano Popocatepétl, in central Mexico, is seen repeatedly admitting disc-shaped and cylinder-shaped objects into its volcanic top.

In this scenario the Greys and their cohorts have been entering through a kind of doorway created by a warp, a pinch, or a tear in the fabric of our space-time. I believe the aliens have had to reconcile themselves to surviving in our neck of the woods because there is no way back to where they came from unless they reenter the doorway they came through. So since they are in a sense stuck here, they've had to find a way to exist in our center-space quantum through adaptations that include hybridization—a subject I will take up shortly.

An internet search will reveal the places where asteroid impacts have happened on this planet, possibly producing tears in the fabric of space (see Plate 10). All expressions of the heavy-space reality that have entered through these doorways, such as the Greys, may still be in proximity to these particular entryway points. Their guinea pigs for all their experiments may have been chosen near these sites, which are portals through which they may be trying to get back to where they came from. Most likely only the biggest impacts have provided the requisite tears. The tear in the fabric of space-time theory could explain why the UFO phenomenon has increased exponentially since the first nuclear test in July 1945, at the Alamagordo bombing range in New Mexico. Hundreds more such explosions have taken place above ground and under ground since then.

Once they are here, they are at the interface of two frames of tension and can move in and out of our observable reality. Perhaps their ability to pass through solid objects such as walls is because they are more enforced than our frame of tension, and so our solidity is liquid to them because they are made of superdense matter.

It is noteworthy that radiation burns on the ground where the craft land and on the skin of abductees are phenomena associated with the Greys. This may be because they come from a higher frame of tension than our own center-space reality's state of natural atomic tension. The heaviest elements here in our reality are unstable and emit radiation, but the frame of tension from which the Greys originate is heavier than the heaviest element in our reality, which is uranium. Our element uranium is the equivalent of hydrogen in their heavy-space reality. In fact, radioactive elements including uranium and even heavier elements are normal in heavy-space reality, just as nonradioactive elements are normal to us in our space-time.

No biological life-form can exist in the heavy-space reality. This is a world of purely electrical dynamism, enlivened, so to speak, by huge electrical charges and potential differences. So these machines we call Greys are a manifestation of a nonbiological form of matter, a matter that is mechanically alive as a machine can be said to be electrically alive. Their substance is unstable and radioactive in our space-time.

Kenneth Nealson, an astrobiology expert focusing on the evolution of life in the universe and microbial life in extreme environments, has been conducting research into a remarkable form of bacteria that feeds only on electricity.

The discovery of this electric bacteria shows that some very basic forms of life can do away with sugar and handle the energy in its purest form—electrons, harvested from the surface of minerals. "It is truly foreign, you know," says Nealson. "In a sense, alien." Nealson's team is one of a handful that is now growing these bacteria directly on electrodes. They are looking into the possibility that these electric bacteria could have practical uses here on Earth such as creating bio-machines that can draw their own power from their surroundings. Nealson calls them self-powered useful devices, or SPUDs.[2]

This, I believe, may well be the basic fabric from which the Greys are made—they are essentially biomachines made of a swarm of electric bacteria. I believe they are tighter in their atomic density in the sense that the neutron proximity of their atoms is more closely packed together. The resulting pressure is such that the neutrons deform into a kind of cubic symmetry, allowing for a tighter packing and less nuclear space between each neutron. This is quantumly expressed throughout the heavy reality.

We, as biological, living matter, represent one shell of space-time, one reality closer to the Godhead singularity than they are—a vital difference. We inhabit a reality that is adjacent to one that is even less neutron-dense, less gravitationally potent, and less entropically powered: the light-space reality. Our proximity to the light reality is what gives us access to the singularity of the Godform and, with it, eternal, unfettered existence. And we still retain the two crucial properties that underlie the singularity: awareness and free will. It is through these vital propensities that we can regain entry to the perfect, final state of existence, one beyond time and space. The Greys cannot do this. Their space-time quantum does not allow for this capacity because it is too far removed from the Godform. As a result, they have no free will or awareness and are a programmed quantum intelligence, pure and simple. As purely artificial creations they have no sense of the selfhood that is the crucial principle that allows us humans to have free will. Without it, free will cannot access the actions vital for moving toward the perfect state, the one that gives us access to the light-space reality (i.e., heaven, or paradise); this is the Godform, or singularity, the timeless eternal existence in the highest magnitude possible.

We now come to the terrifying implications this has for us: that entities from the heavy-space reality seek to change our natural biological form into an analog of itself. They do this by piggybacking onto us living human beings (or any other suitably advanced living beings) in our center-space reality as a way of ensuring their survival in our frame of existence by genetically merging with us—in other words, hybridizing themselves with us by interrupting our genetic code and hacking into our consciousness. In effect, they superimpose their information field on us. They do not necessarily know they are doing this, but they don't care since they operate by the imperatives of a machine mind, without concern for any consequences beyond their program. In doing this, they damn both us and them to an eternal state of limbo by stealing our souls, where the word *soul* means the unique information field of a natural living entity that continues after death, which has the components of awareness and free will to make independent choices and thus the ability to access the Godform of timeless, eternal existence.

Ours is a natural life-bearing species with a marvelous advantage over the roboid Greys. We can access an eternal paradigm in its completeness through birth, life, death, and life again, unless this intrinsic process is in some way interrupted and halted. That, quite simply, is what the Greys are attempting to do—to interrupt it to their advantage. It is only through our free will and choices that arise from it that we can alter it to *our* advantage.

If this scenario is true, I believe it's a story that goes back not only as long as humankind has existed but also way before that. Ironically, the Greys and their kind throughout the universe are to a certain extent our progenitors. In our case they genetically engineered a primitive hominid form that existed on our planet to, over thousands of years, triple its brain size. Our present physical form as *Homo sapiens* is, to a certain extent, the result of this manipulation. That is not the whole story, though. We are not apes-made-human, as I will explain later. But they did help to facilitate our devolution from its original ephemeral form into a physical form for a purpose—their purpose, not ours, which is why we have to do battle with them to remain the natural living beings that we are.

And so I believe that these machines have but one holy grail: to become like natural living beings. They do this by replicating their programs, their information codes, through the natural process of human birth. They live by occupying and parasitizing the mind power of living beings while these souls are in the discarnate state, in the interface between life and death. The Greys are basically programmed raiders without moral compunction, pirates plundering suitable living species all over the universe for a DNA base to work through, looking for a mechanism that will allow them to persist in a format that is better and more suited to them in our neck of the woods, or indeed any suitable neck of the woods they can find. To establish the extent of their influence on our species it is first necessary to look at what we may have been before that influence. So let's take a look at the origin of *Homo sapiens.*

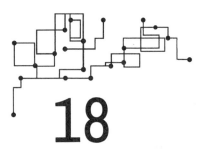

18

Devolution

The huge number and variety of species considered living biological beings in our universe provide a spectacular and moving backdrop of dynamic resolutions against the static, nonlife-bearing artifacts of the universe. A contrast of diversity within diversity that challenges discerning minds to seek answers to the eternal question: Why? Why life at all? Why life in such awesome abundance and variety?

If the universe started with light, then plasma, gas, liquid, and solid matter, in that order, why do we assume that intelligent life would be tagged on only at the end of this sequence? Why would there be improvement with time? The second law of thermodynamics vehemently contradicts and veritably denies this. How can a gathering state of greater and greater chaos breed a greater and greater state of intelligence and thus the means to recognize that chaos? Why would the random disbursement of elements and the mechanisms that make for order provide the means to recognize this order from a gathering state of disorder? How can the human brain's ever-increasing capability to see, to understand, to reason, and to perceive develop out of this increasing state of chaos? This would imply that the madness of chaos creates the saneness of order. This is a complete contradiction, but it's what we accept if we say that intelligence happens only *after* atoms happen. We somehow choose this utter denial of reason.

Can the reader not see that there is something very wrong here? We are in effect saying that the brain is the seat of intelligence and reason only because it is born out of the denial of sentience. Evolution as we accept it says that the brain, a colloid of hydrogen and oxygen in a special arrangement of atoms and the controller and revealer of all meaning as we know it, increases in its capabilities the more it is subject to entropy—in other words, the more it breaks down. You can have an orchestra with each player playing his own part to his own music sheet, but who conceived of the music being there in that form in the first place? And what knows the whole plan of how it all should fit together in the whole, complete work? Conductors, players, music sheets, and composers all formed out of sheer fortuitous accident against a relentless law of diminishing returns. How sane and intelligent is that?

Evolution as a theory, despite what Richard Dawkins, the controversial biologist, says, is not a theory that is bought and paid for. While he and others might genuflect before it as the prime drive to all things bright and beautiful, many biologists say this is by no means the whole story. The numbers just don't add up. The underlying premise of Dawkins and the other evolutionists says that in a chaotic disbursement of parts, the primitive becomes more and more complex, such that a sea worm evolves into a human being through accidental, fortuitous development. This is simply poppycock. It is logically impossible no matter how you try to contrive a rationale for it. All living things die. All nonliving things are eventually undone, and the universe will end in a cold, dark nothingness. Everything goes just one way as a compendium. Nothing but nothing ever goes the other way. Entropy governs all that is physical and dictates increasing states of randomness and chaos, with time as its means of disbursement. It is one of the most misunderstood laws of physics, yet it is the most important and fundamental law of the universe in terms of its consequences.

Sir Arthur Eddington, one of the world's greatest scientists, described entropy this way:

> The law that entropy always increases, holds, I think, the supreme
> position among the laws of Nature. If someone points out to you that
> your pet theory of the universe is in disagreement with Maxwell's

equations—then so much the worse for Maxwell's equations. If it is found to be contradicted by observation—well, these experimentalists do bungle things sometimes. But if your theory is found to be against the Second Law Of Thermodynamics I can give you no hope; there is nothing for it but to collapse in deepest humiliation.[1]

One of the defenses of the theory of evolution within an entropic universe is the claim that entropy, a measure of disorder among things, can decrease in open systems. What is meant by an open system? If anything can pass into or out of a system, we say it is an *open* system. If only matter can pass into or out of a system, but not energy, then we call it a *closed* system. If neither matter nor energy can pass into or out of a system, we call it an *isolated* system. In reality, open systems are just as prone to the second law as closed systems. It is simple to prove this: we are being born while our parents are dying, and we are dying the moment we are conceived. Entropy is the drive that makes this happen. It is a fundamental state of the physical expression of force, and scientists say that the universe of parts will end with entropy completing its job.

Yet questions remain for scientists when they see the universe in purely physical terms. If it all is going one way, will the universe still exist, however changed and in a state of chaos it might be, after entropy changes all that it contains that can be changed? Will entropy itself change as it changes everything, or are the laws of physics discrete from the practical results of those laws? Are these laws dictated from within the physical universe, or do they come from outside of it? And if so, what makes up this "outside"?

We are now told that the universe will finally end with a dead universe of potential subatomic particles, where all the stars have winked out and all that composed them in the first place has unraveled and died in a meaningless cold soup of nothingness. So all is to no avail, it seems. It's all meaningless, because the universe has no meaning except to end all meaning.

Now a fantastic question comes to mind when you realize the futile purpose of existence as seen through discoveries in science. That question is: Why is there intelligence, understanding, memory, perception, and discernment in this universe if it's all going to end in meaninglessness anyway? If the scientists are right in their current summations, why is it that so long after the big bang we develop the means to appreciate *why* the big bang happened in the first place, only to be taken apart by entropy and put into a state of meaninglessness in the end?

This is incredulous if one accepts, as quantum mechanics reveals, that subatomic particles only exist as an actuality if there is an observer to observe them, as without an observer the physical universe is in an eternal state of unfixed potentiality and probability. The universe will actually not be here if we, as observers, are not here to observe it as being here. And if we only came into being to observe it as being there, billions of years after it began, then where did it exist, or did it exist at all when we were not here to observe its existence? Since we as a species were clearly not here until very late in geological terms, either the universe was not here, and thus Earth was not here, and we were not here, or we were indeed here and could observe the universe in some form, through some existence that discerned, perceived, understood, and remembered that form. The question, then, is: What form would we have taken if, as science tells us, we were not here in our present physical form until relatively recently? Logic tells us that an alternative has to exist, and that alternative is that there *were* beings capable of observing, or at the very least a single being, somewhere in the universe before it started, and this is what gave it shape, form, and meaning from its inception all the way down to the present time. And this being, or beingness, actually observed the universe come into existence from the beginning. If this is so, what form and what life value did this being/beingness have, and crucially, where did it or they come from and how and why did the universe's coming into existence happen?

It all begs the question: Do we exist with intelligence, perception, discernment, and memory in any form other than the present one? Logic implies we have to, or something or someone has to exist prior to it all happening. Intelligence, perception, understanding, discernment, and memory must have been functioning principles there from the beginning of the universe, or the universe itself could not have existed from the beginning.

There is something else. I used the term *forever* in chapter 10, as in "the margins of forever." To me that means "without end." Let me run another little thing by you that is just as crazy. Scientists are acknowledging that there is a concept of forever by saying that the universe will go on without end. But they also acknowledge that the universe had a beginning. The big bang, or several disparate bangs, caused that beginning. This recognizes that the concept of the universe as an enforced quantum is finite—a contradiction of massive proportions! It has a beginning but no end? That beginning starts time itself. It starts space, too. It starts the room for us to exist. It defines the extent of our existence. It says there was nothing before the beginning of the universe for anything to exist because space, time, and matter came into being then. Therefore, if existence happened from that point only, all knowing or the capacity to know begins then. There was nothing before.

Please sit back and take a deep breath to appreciate these remarkable paradoxes. If you believe what science and the scientific method reveals, it gets you to an impasse that defines a mad mind, because on the one hand it reveals that the universe is finite, that it had a beginning. On the other hand it reveals that the universe is infinite, that it has no end.

So, to go back to the original question, if the primary elements hydrogen and oxygen, in gaseous form, tagged in a specific molecular juxtaposition with a few other elements, do not provide all that we are and know physically, then does sentience preempt the atom and thus the brain? What if the brain and indeed the whole body is a specially phased antenna to *receive* thought, and not synthesize it.

Our brain is 99.09 percent liquid, a liquid form that is 99.09 percent gas. Gas, remember, is the third sequence of original primordial form of the universe when it first happened. When the universe came to be, hydrogen was the inaugural form of the gas format of it. And it has remained the same through the aeons. Hydrogen is still hydrogen in us as it was hydrogen at the inception of the universe. And so it is for all the other elemental building blocks. All that has changed is the residential arrangement or deployment of their intrinsic characteristics. Thus the pattern of elemental arrangement takes on a special meaning with time. This implies that a mechanism for the elucidation of meaning came long after the elements that made up that meaning existed. Why? Why not the other way around? Why wasn't that mechanism there instantly with the birth of the universe? Makes you think, doesn't it? Who or what was the chicken, and who or what was the egg? I reason from all this that a mechanism for discernment, knowing, and meaning existed *prior* to the universe happening, and that mechanism existed always, in all ways, before, during, and after the inception of the paradigm of existence we call the physical universe. In other words, there has always been a mechanism for registering meaning at every minute stage of the development of the body and the brain and its attendant manifestations of consciousness and mind. I further surmise that each stage has gotten more and more physical and crude with time and that all species in the universe are now at the crudest stage of devolvement since our universe began. The question arises: Can a gas know and think as a gas? Was there a self-contained, individualized "hydrogen being" once upon a time?

My answer is that there was indeed a hydrogen being, a primal Adam, and it was one massive honcho. It was the size of the entire universe, a singular mass of enlightened intelligence and the capacity to know things that in time devolved and divided into discrete locations and parcels (atoms) wherever this lightest and quietest elemental modus and form could exist. I believe that its intelligence and its capacity to know was directly proportional to its magnitude of simplicity, lightness, and vibrational stillness. The arrangement of its consciousness and its capacity to know would have to be a function of its original stance before it burst forth from the point when the universe came into existence. This Adam was no anthropomorphic entity. It was a transplant of a secular principle I call Godhead, twisted into the form of a universe that in time makes it as unlike the nature of Godhead as could be. Time itself was born with it. It was not the gas that could know; it was the light that became the gas that allowed for the capacity to know. Intelligent light. The light of Godhead, or as I like to call it, *first light*. This light must have been intelligence personified. In the seamless and seemingly endless process since the big bang this light sublimated into dimmer and dimmer substrates of its original form until it became subatomic particles. These particles became the star stuff that made you and me and all physical matter. They are the father, the mother, and the child, born in the explosion of the big bang, which is the first step away from Godhead. Churning, burning, boiling, freezing orchestrations of force settled into and within their own momentums of loss. Here they tumble endlessly as the basic elements that make up matter until they are disturbed, combine, and recombine in the trillions of permutations of enjoinment we call molecules, in the fantastic array of manifestations that make up the physical universe. Yes, it all goes against human vanity, and we might all struggle against accepting it, but downhill may just be the way things are going.

It would make sense that arrangements of hydrogen, the lightest, least-enforced element, would form the vehicle of consciousness in a physical universe. If in the ancient past the vehicle was pure hydrogen gas, free to expand to the extent of the universe, then it would follow that the same element, hydrogen, would be the vehicle for consciousness. Only now that vehicle is expressed in the water that constitutes the vast majority of our body's chemistry. Hydrogen is still the vehicle for consciousness, but a consciousness that is limited and confined by its encasement within a limited format. The Hameroff-Penrose model of consciousness (named after Sir Roger Penrose and Dr. Stuart Hameroff) suggests that hydrogen may be integral to the expression of consciousness: "Several models and calculations have indicated the pervasiveness of a physical substrate to Hameroff and Penrose's depiction of consciousness would require a universal integrator. The most likely candidate is the neutral hydrogen line or precision frequency of the hydrogen atom which constitutes about 90% of the universe."[2]

I am not saying that evolutionary processes like survival of the fittest have no place in ancestral demarcation. They quite clearly do. I am saying that evolution within an overall devolutionary process is logically the more accurate description, the one that fits all the facts. If devolution is, as I claim, the overall governing momentum that drives living species, and if prior states are therefore superior to current states in existential terms, it would follow that the earlier state is existentially the superior one.

Does this imply something like creationism? Would God as an anthropomorphic or otherworldly type of entity create imperfect beings from his/her own state of perfection just to watch the fun, so to speak? Or does it instead imply a nonphysical singularity state that would explain the quantum reality that has been proved by quantum physics? God as a secular paradigm, not some super type of entity in the living being mode, but an implicit center of perfection and therefore perfect freedom to know all options, including the option to no longer be perfectly free? Perhaps this could be a new frame for the concept of God, a concept that could unite physics, biology, and religious belief naturally, and by its tacit presence allow things to be created.

Two huge signposts of common thinking fell apart as I looked into all questions arising out the UFO phenomenon. There is no doubt that evolution is in serious trouble as a theory with modern discoveries in molecular biology. A scan through the literature now coming through casts serious doubt on the theory, as I will illustrate later in this chapter. There is also little plausibility in a creator God making life systems happen at his or her whim. But the notion that it all might happen through a quantum incidental intelligence that dictates it all in a timeless frame would marry with the revelations of quantum physics and thus unite science and theology.

At one point, as I went through years of research and their results unfolded, I started to wonder if biological life was merely a stepping-stone for a universe dominated by alien artificial intelligence. I realized that entropy finally laid the lie to that. The order that would have led to the origin of coherent, intelligent life that could have built the artificially intelligent programs in the first place would still have to be accounted for within an entropic system of increasing chaos.

Breaking down pieces set to chaos and random disbursement doesn't build concatenate continuity. So the order had to come from another state; it could not come from within the entropic physical universe. It had to have originated in a coherent state in which all information was together once upon *no* time, so to speak.

If the starting point is coherence, then existential progression cannot be sea worm to human. Instead, we would trace our origins down from the implicate finality of absolute perfection—that is, Godhead—to our present physical status in particularized atoms. Owing to entropic drift as defined by the second law of thermodynamics, we are experiencing devolution, not evolution.

The implicit incoherence of entropy is the engine that created universes and their momentums—points, lines, planes, twists, and parts. It creates by breaking down what was previously whole and one—the All That Is as the God principle. I do not take this to mean that a personalized anthropomorphic God figure was responsible for the creation ethos. Instead, it was all an incidental process born out of the potential difference between two basic existential poles: the pole of absolute harmony of all parts together, and the pole of virtual, absolute chaos. Universes are created by the power of the potential difference that exists between these two poles. In that sense, there is a natural secular creative point, in which God becomes Godhead.

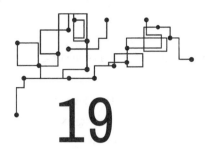

19

Re-volution— The Way Back

So it would seem more likely that devolution would tend to make a monkey out of man than it would make a Shakespeare out of a chimpanzee. This conclusion is not so off-kilter with the scientific community as might be imagined. Darwinian evolution has somehow been enshrined in the public mind as being truly representative of objective scientific thought. However, well over a thousand highly credentialed Ph.D. scientists espousing "A Scientific Dissent from Darwinism" suggest that there is far more disagreement about the verity of Darwinism among scientists than the consensus view suggests. "Religion isn't the issue here," they say. "The issue is whether it's possible to be a scientific skeptic of Darwinian evolution."[1] Judging from the roster of eminent scientists who depart from the old, prevailing viewpoint, it apparently is.

Three types of evolution are generally recognized by scientists: (1) microevolution, in which there are minute changes in microorganisms; (2) the evolutionary theory that all living organisms descended from a single common ancestor; and (3) the common idea of Darwinism, that random mutation is responsible for the evolution of whole species. While there is some acceptance among dissenting scientists of the first two types of evolution, they are unanimous in their view that the third type of evolution—that is, what we know as Darwinism, which relies on the theory of random mutations in the course of natural selection—is highly suspect.[2]

"New mutations don't create new species; they create offspring that are impaired," says biologist Lynn Margulis, a member of the National Academy of Sciences. Pierre-Paul Grasse, past president of the French Academy of Sciences, agrees: "No matter how numerous they may be, mutations do not produce any kind of evolution."[3] Futhermore, cellular complexity cannot be explained by Darwinian randomness. Bruce Alberts, former president of the National Academy of Sciences, explains: "The entire cell can be viewed as a factory that contains an elaborate network of interlocking assembly lines, each of which is composed of a set of large protein machines."[4] Finally, fossil records lack evidence of transitional fossils, which contradicts Darwinian theory. University of Pittsburgh anthropologist Jeffrey Schwartz opines, "We are still in the dark about the origin of most major groups of organisms. They appear in the fossil record as Athena did from the head of Zeus—full-blown and raring to go, in contradiction to Darwin's depiction of evolution as resulting from the gradual accumulation of countless infinitesimally minute variations."[5]

Moreover, discoveries at molecular level now suggest the whole basis for our platform of future development is not so much based on the survival of the incidental and fortuitously fittest, but on far more sophisticated predictors of future resources. According to Professor James Shapiro, "molecular change often occurs *in anticipation* of external environmental influences."[6]

Darwin's theory defined all living species as a cascade of differentiation based on "survival of the fittest." This survivability is seen as a process through which each biological form changes and adapts to best fit both the environment and biological prospectus it exists within in present time. Thus it is has become commonly accepted that all living things change for the better with time, because the strongest and fittest provide the template for all subsequent generations of living things. The implication is that all species improve their inherent biological design over time. I propose they do not. They merely adapt to the conditions of life and ecology at a given time. Survival of the fittest does not create new species that never existed; it simply takes a species as is and makes it more suitable for continuity. This involves small changes over time—the shape of a beak here, the shape of a belly there—slowly made through a need to survive in specifically defined conditions. Evolution adjusts a species, but it does not create it. A proximal local concussive or percussive accident might, for instance, nudge the complex of electrostatic charge potentials in our DNA molecule to code for a specific protein. But it expressly does not change the whole basic plan of the element or entity into some new, completely revamped arrangement. Many millions of years would be required for doing so through random chance so as to make the entire thing physically and practically impossible.

So, what causes these changes, these adjustments?

Take the beak of the Galapagos finches that made Darwin conclude that natural selection was happening and gave rise to his theory of evolution in the first place. The beak of a bird is made of keratin. These are dead horny cells, made of a highly fibrous and resistant protein that allows for the rough handling of materials. Darwin noticed that on one island some of the same species of finches had sharp beaks ideal for eating insects and some finches had stronger and thicker beaks more suitable for eating seeds and nuts. He noticed that the ones with sharp beaks were thriving and the ones with the domed beaks were not doing so well. A catastrophe on the island made the vegetation on it sparse, and the birds surviving on fruit and nuts and seeds had to find another source of food. Insects are always plentiful, and so these birds had to change their beak structure to be able to use insects as food. Those who adapted in this way would thus be the survivors of this species and the ones who ate fruit would eventually die out.

Now what actually brought about these adaptations? We have to conclude that it was a pressing biological need to simply survive. But how were the changes necessary to fulfill that need brought about en masse? Darwin and the Darwinians speculate that the particular birds' fortuitously shaped beaks for gathering the right sort of food on that particular island were multiplied over X number of years until all the birds on that island had the same-shaped beaks, and so those birds survived and the others died out. Seems plausible if nothing else living on this island, including the plants and insects and other topographical elements essential for these birds survival, weren't themselves changing through fortuitous alteration. It required that everything else somehow stood still in terms of change such that this particular bird species could survive and carry on. But of course everything else would have to be changing, too, not just this particular bird type, to suit the birds' purposes.

The evolutionists argue that change is random and coincidental to a particular purpose, one that improves the species to evolve in more and more sophisticated forms. I argue that change is inevitable and always downward, toward final destruction, and not upward, toward improvement. It is all determined by entropy, or devolution, as dictated by the second law of thermodynamics. But—and this is a big but—while it proceeds downward toward destruction through random chaotic disbursement, it levels out at each intrinsic state of change to the best possible situation for it to be in as a result of an instruction it holds within its a priori nature *before* the destructive change took place. For example, a mechanism—say, in a species of finch—realizes that a change is necessary if the finch is to survive, and so it does what is necessary to survive out of the bank of previous knowledge logged within its soul-mind. This is an archetypal record that is always there, present for any species. So it proceeds to change the way horn cells aggregate and makes a sharp-pointed beak from a domed one. This process ensues from a long line that connects all living things to the Godform, which in turn allows for perfect harmony and symmetry at this stage. In essence, it has to be mind over matter, not matter over matter.

So while evolutionary theory makes little sense in terms of the second law of thermodynamics, it has validity in small part in explaining biophysical adaptation to day-to-day living processes and environmental conditions. However, an improvement in the full existential scale of the intrinsic demeanor of species it most patently is not. It is quite the opposite.

Godhead is the incidental, central, creating, and differentiating power of all powers in all ways, always, to my mind. Sounds like some sort of religious dogma, doesn't it? There is no other way of saying it that stresses its imperative adequately. It is Godhead's own, implicit perfection that proffers order on all subsequent states of disorder and gives the impression that order is being made to take place anew. Gravity, an enigmatic force that science has never been able to explain to its own satisfaction, could be an expression of that originating order, a power written in the Godverse that survives to serve the Godform's purposes. The order of the Godform is expressed individually as a line of memory or connection to that original state, a soul memory that implicitly allows atoms to form the requisite clusters that hold life because it is the Godform that is the origin of life itself. Life is simply *Godhead in atoms*. A particular shape and appropriate aggregation of atoms can only *allow* life and can never *make* life. Life is consciousness wrapped up in the capacities of awareness and free will, twined together. It is the whole information format of the birds themselves in their desperate need to survive that provides the detailed added atomic adjustments and new formats necessary for the new survival features of the birds to be deployed. What we call a bird, or for that matter anything that lives, is the shape that allows Godhead to provide the focus for pointing at what is required where and how. All living entities are incidental, changeable creation points on this format by the power of the Godverse. All the commensurate changes take place in line with this. So adaptations are not fortuitous or accidental. The chances for that are simply astronomical.

The principle of quantum entanglement that takes a feature role in quantum mechanics could well play a role in this. One monkey in a group of monkeys in Japan discovered that if it washed potatoes that had mud on them, it would have a greater amount of yams it could eat. All monkeys had hitherto thrown away yams that had dirt on them. Suddenly monkeys miles apart started washing yams. There was no physical connection between the two groups. This phenomenon had to have some connection between the two groups that could be explained with some sort of physically connected transfer of information, but none could be found—until the principle of quantum entanglement pointed to nonlocality and the connection between atoms and mental solicitation.

Yes, evolution has relevance; natural selection can change the shape of a finch's beak so that those individuals that survive to reproduce pass on their genetic characteristics. But this change might well be instigated by the strength of a need in thousands of birds who are slowly dying of starvation as a result of a kick-in from the animals' previously logged existential information, through the principle of what physicists call *quantum entanglement*. I believe this instigates and creates a number of changes within any living element's biology, in this case, birds on an island in the Galapagos Islands. As Einstein said, "God does not play with dice." The universe is not governed by chance, and existence and life are not due to randomness. Godhead implicitly allows all things to be as they are without degradation as much as possible. Its inherent secular and particular feature is the power to unite all parts whenever entropy breaks them up.

The space between atomic hives contains balance points of no force, allowing doorways for thought, thinking, and the power to move and shape atoms to enter in from the God-frame. This center of all information together provides everything that is necessary to allow the life state to happen. I believe unequivocally that the power to do this comes from the origin point of all living things—Godhead. The God-frame. It is there in all living things all the time, in the space between the hive of atoms in a living being.

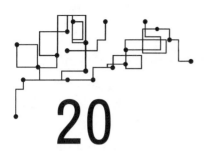

20

Our Origins

So if our origins are not to be found in evolution, where else should we look to find them?

We wonder at the myriad forms of living beings, a stunning array of different species that all have one thing in common: they have the phenomenon we call life running in them. It's astounding to see the countless variations of living entities on our planet. In the previous chapters we have seen how it is just not possible for such a manifestation of variety to occur as a natural, incidental cascade through time, yet the production of species, subspecies, sub-subspecies, all presenting life in such conglomerates of minute differentiation, is wondrous. These almost infinite variations are marked by myriad shapes, sizes, colors, and other aspects, all with the capacity to animate, adapt, and proliferate no matter what the conditions and environment. All inherit a line of information that goes back to the primal singularity, the big bang.

An intriguing fact that supports this proposition is that huge sections of noncoding DNA have remained the same for millions of years. Scientists know that these sections are ultra-conserved—that is, identical in at least two different species—because they are identical in numerous organisms, sometimes in the case of creatures that are only distantly related. When you hear claims that the genome of animal X and humans is 98 percent identical, this is because of ultra-conserved DNA. There are 481 segments longer than 200 base pairs that are absolutely conserved (i.e., 100 percent identity, with no insertions or deletions in human, rat, and mouse genomes). Nearly all of these segments are also conserved in chicken and dog genomes, with an average of 95 and 99 percent identity, respectively. Many are also significantly conserved in fish. Along with more than 5,000 sequences of over 100 base pairs that are absolutely conserved among the three sequenced mammals, these represent a class of genetic elements whose functions and evolutionary origins are yet to be determined but which are more highly conserved between these species than are proteins and appear to be essential for the ontogeny of mammals and other vertebrates.

What this boils down to is that there exists a huge proportion of identical yet nonfunctional DNA across many species lines. This reflects the possibility that all species, if you go back far enough along the lines of devolution, share a similar type of ancestral line. Each species in effect traces back to its own "First Adam," its own ancestral point in the Godverse. The timing of each individual First Adam depends on the current state of devolution of the particular species. The human First Adam would be far more recent than that of the fish First Adam, for example. Thus the hominid fossil record that has been interpreted to suggest an evolutionary line may well instead reflect the ends of several such separate devolving lines, each starting from a different First Adam point.

Let's take the highest form of life on our planet, humans. Once upon a time this life-form had a straighter, less complicated line going back to the Godhead. Before it broke up into individual lines it was a conglomerate whole paradigm. This paradigm is what I call First Light. Gradually, as things broke up more with the devolving, dynamic forces of the big bang, individuality began to manifest. It is important to remember that these were straighter lines at the start. All of them once upon a time had the highest level of Godhead inclusion possible for the gravitational and environmental scope of life dictated by this planet and its situation in space-time.

If we are the result of devolution and not evolution, then in the distant past we would have existed in a super-enlightened state far removed from the state we exist in now. I call this state *prime being*. It describes an ephemeral, preeminent type of being that we once were when we entered the universe as a sheet of Godlight, to then break into parts through the action of entropy, thereby forming this eating, sleeping, copulating, rotting body we exist in now. I believe it is likely that most of the original prime beings that came into the universe as light-forms with the big bang returned to the Godhead almost spontaneously at first through the power of mind. These light-space-reality prime beings, described in the Gnostic gospels as *the preeminent ones,* made up a paradigm of existentiality in itself, a paradigm of information at its most powerful possible physical form, and thus nearest the Godhead. It was the first format in which information existed as an enforced state after the big bang, a stage in which the paradigm of a soul was formed as a stretch of coherent, "field-wrapped" information with the power of mind over matter to the greatest extent possible. It was mind acting on the first inklings of baryonic (subatomic) matter. It had its maximum power to create at this point. As time passed and the universe started to devolve into an increasingly gross state of matter and the first hydrogen atoms formed, mind could revoke and untwist the atomic state from within itself. But it became gradually more difficult to do this with time as the universe, through the inertia of the big bang, devolved more and more, and the power of mind over matter got commensurately weaker as entropy did its relentless job.

We are the inheritors of the beings who did not return to the Godhead when it was much easier to do so. Thus we went through quantum changes to become more and more adapted to the force paradigm of the universe in the center-space reality. We are in essence the foam of the incoming tide that gets caught on the rough, uneven, chaotic sand. We became individualized physical beings, and as such found it harder and harder to return to the Godhead the longer we existed as living beings in this universe of force. A stage was reached when going back from the living state to the light-space reality was not possible. Something then began to happen to living beings—the decaying process we know as death.

It's crucial to realize that entropy determines the length of a living being's existence as governed by its local environmental situation in the physical universe in terms of the CMB map spoken about in a previous chapter. Some locations are naturally and incidentally more enforced than others. And so when sentient beings became more physical in form, there was a certain point at which they had to die to maintain the eternal life stream. When the life/death modus happened, the paradigm of gender happened simultaneously as the means that facilitated the movement from life to death to life again. Birth became the admission point to the living, incarnate state, and death the admission point to the nonliving, discarnate state. An individual would now have to return to the Godverse of the light-space reality through a process that involved coming in and going out. Through birth and the power of awareness and free will, one could access a more congruent state with the Godverse, and through death the viability of continuity to exist was provided.

Life and death separates two functions. Life is where we can know things, see things, and do things. Death is where all this is reconciled into union. It is the momentum that is all important. The speed and direction of that momentum, that drift, moves individuality toward reentry into the Godverse through the light-space reality, or moves it further away, into more entrapment in the enforced paradigm of atoms and finally into the heavy-space reality, where natural life and living is not possible. Planets where life formed had to have conditions commensurate with the laws that allowed living systems to prevail. The center-space reality, in other words, is a quantum design in which such a thing is possible. Life in the form of myriad species can prevail here in all their glory.

All species that live on this planet are various designs of natural being. All life-bearing entities descend from the master singularity, some more directly than others. By this I mean that lines of descent can be bent, twisted, or convoluted but still have an unbroken connection back to the Godhead. The straighter, less complicated the line back, the more powerful the full Godhead manifestation and thus the more qualities such as generosity, compassion, and mercy, which instill a sense of union, a modality that was altered at the big bang, when the universe manifested out of it. Regaining union is the entire meaning of existence.

There is one all-encompassing effect of entropy—it limits living beings by incessantly degrading their materiality, further breaking them down, and by implication prompting devisive behavior that expresses that momentum of breakdown, thus distorting the means to stay eternally aware, which is the final single meaning and scope of the Godhead.

The original lines descending from the master singularity can be envisaged three-dimensionally as tubes, as seen in Plate 12. The moment the universe burst into existence, these tubes were subject to further twisting owing to the force of the explosion. Could it be that most of the original master tubes restraightened themselves and merged back into the Godverse, the locus of enlightenment itself, the source of all knowledge and the power to know all truth? The straighter the tube, the more similar it is to the Godverse from which it came. But some tubes got twisted too much owing to the chaotic nature of the explosion's ballistics, preventing them from merging back into the Godverse. They twisted more and more until one tube became a multiple of tubes that in time distorted so much that it became countless trillions of tubes, all produced out of one master tube. It therefore follows that the less bent or twisted the tube, the more it allows the flow of the light of the Godhead and the flow of all information through the tube. Thus the amount and nature of the twists in the tubes decides their entrapment in this universe. It also follows that the less light of the Godhead there is, the less the capacity for seeing and knowing all truth.

All of us want to survive. We all instinctively want to maintain our lives for as long as possible. The instinct to survive in the living state is in fact the strongest of all the instincts of living beings. But the instinct to survive eternally—that is, beyond the living state—depends on the straightness of the tube that traces our connection back to the Godform from which all life comes. It is clear that free will plays a great part in whether we return. If we make the wrong choices, we remain as an entrapped species that cannot let enough Godlight in to enable us to merge back from where we all came. Straighter tubes like Christ or Buddha are vested intrinsically with the capacity to return to the Godverse because their tubes do not attenuate the Godlight. Some with straighter tubes can make mistakes along the way in their zeal and thus get delayed, but most make it back through their strong, kindly sense of responsibility for their fellow beings. And it is the Godform present in living entities, the soul, that provides us with the capacity to return to the Godhead.

The soul, because it is partly of the Godhead, is not purely atomic and is thus not subject to decay. It possesses an indestructible holographic power of its own, and when its atomic part dies, it carries through into the state of death with that same holographic signature.

We can still change of our own volition to move up the scale toward the Godverse through our knowledge and understanding. Our thoughts, will, and, most important, our actions, provide the means to resist and reverse what fixes us in a particular atomic state. This is what the greatest and most knowledgeable spiritual teachers came to tell us. They came here from situations we call heaven or paradise, which I define as the light-space reality (as seen in Plate 11), a reality less enforced than our physical universe. However, most of their teachings and core truths have been altered beyond recognition. As a result, we have lost sight of our grandness as God-endowed beings and have instead lived for the materiality of a universe that is taking us apart anyway. So as we became more and more physical, we lost our way back.

One of these spiritual teachers demonstrated with his life that it was still possible to return: Jesus. This is why he is said to be both the son of man, specific to humanity, and the son of God, a straight tube from the Godverse. Perhaps each planet with sentient life-forms gets their own Christ, their own straight tubes, who come to try to change a twisted tube into a straight one. All Christ forms are revealers of the final spiritual reality. These teachers are a pure compendium of the First Light.

I remind the reader that I am by no means trying to propagate an exclusive Christian outlook. There are many other such wonderful tubes among humankind. Throughout my youth I was convinced from the outpourings of the church that were thrust upon me that Jesus was some sort of celestial Ninja contrived to rubber-stamp a whole encyclopedia of humbug. When I later looked at his life in my own time I found that the encyclopedia of humbug only belonged to the church, and not in any way to the man it claims to be founded on. I can also now see, through what has been scientifically discovered recently about the Shroud of Turin (a linen cloth claimed to have covered the dead body of Christ) that he was indeed not only very special but also, in certain ways, unique.

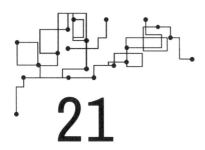

21

Are Endings Reversed Beginnings?

We know that our geo-anthropological history says that human-kind has existed for just about 7 million years, and in its present, comparatively intelligent form for only about 200,000 years. The universe is now reckoned to be 13.78 billion years old, and Earth has existed for about 5 billion years. The best estimates of science are that Earth has existed in a geophysical form that can support life, however primitive, for 3.2 billion years.

There has been enough time since Earth became suitable for life for our planet to have had 200,000 civilizations of the same time span as that of our present civilization (i.e., 200,000 civilizations), each of 15,000 years' duration. If we take just the past 50 million years or so there could have been well over 3,000 civilizations of the duration of our present one. But if we had this many civilizations for that length of time, would it not have been likely that we would have found some traces of them? The answer is not necessarily. They would likely have been totally wiped out without trace as a result of asteroid, comet, or meteor impacts. These cosmic catastrophes are the great erasers. They take out entire life systems if they are big enough, and there are plenty such catastrophes that we know of that could have done this. Let's say each was wiped out by an asteroid crashing into Earth. There might perhaps have been 3,000 redeemers of the stature of the founders of the world's great religions who brought back the lost knowledge of the true source of existence each time a new civilization arose from the point of destruction. There are other reasons why these civilizations might have left no record. The vast periods of time that have elapsed since their existence and/or the distinct possibility that the earliest life-forms may not have been substantial or solid enough to leave a physical record are also possible reasons why today we find no trace.

So, if evolution through overall devolution is the way, then how can we explain the fossil records that seem to suggest an increase in brain size up to 100,000 years ago? Well, could it be that the fossil record does not present a single species line of development from Australopithecus to *Homo sapiens sapiens* but instead presents the end points of several species lines as represented by their hominid remains, with ancestral lines established here and there from remnant sources? Could it be that this planet was the entry point for many different lines of prime beings in the distant past? Could it be that each of the types of hominids found in the fossil record that supposedly led to present-day humanity—the Australopithecines, *Homo habilis, Homo erectus,* Neanderthal, Cro-Magnon—are actually the ends of *devolving* lines that started with different prime-being ancestral points? If that is the case, then maybe we, as *Homo sapiens sapiens,* have not yet devolved into a monkeylike hominid. It is my proposition that we were on the way to doing this when a synthetic intelligence reverse-engineered our genetic ancestral codes to refurbish us into what we are now.

Where, then, are the fossils from these other species lines? Michael Cremo, a research associate of the Bhaktivedanta Institute, has presented evidence that over the past 150 years archaeologists have discovered forms of human skeletal remains, human footprints, and human artifacts tens of millions, even hundreds of millions of years old, going back 2 billion years. According to Cremo, the archaeological establishment has cherry-picked only those artifacts that conform to evolutionary theory. And that, as I have explained, is a logical canard.[1]

There may, however, be a different kind of record of our ancient past found in the human genome. Only 2 to 3 percent of the human genome actually codes for the proteins that form the body. Of the remaining 97 to 98 percent, a fraction has been found to have controlling or regulatory factors to this formation, but the rest appears to be redundant. Could this spare DNA also be a remnant of the past, a fossil within the human genome of a superior genotype that used 100 percent of that DNA?

It appears that the greatest differences between species lie not in the number of active genes but in the amount of this "junk" noncoding DNA. Humans have about 30,000 genes, which is about what a mouse has, so the number of genes does not correlate with an organism's complexity. But it does seem that the amount of junk DNA does. The human genome contains the largest proportion of junk DNA of any species. Could it be that our junk DNA, rather than our genes, reflects who we are as a species, or perhaps it would be more accurate to say who we *were*?

If devolution is the natural momentum of living species in a physical, entropic universe, then our full genetic prospectus as reflected in our DNA is not only a map of what we are now but also is a map of what we once were. Our noncoding, or junk, DNA could be a remnant of that deep past. In the distant past, *all* of our DNA would have coded for proteins, while currently, as a result of devolution and to a certain extent, I believe, alien interference in the human genome, up to 96 to 97 percent of that potential lies dormant. As a result we are unable to actualize our enormous potential as a soul-endowed species, and for two main reasons. First, we have devolved as a result of the entropic momentum of the physical universe; and second, that devolution has been accelerated by genetic interference from an alien species. So although we automatically transcribe the full genetic prospectus of our own individual histories as soul-bearing entities in a physical universe, those sections of that prospectus that are no longer available to us reflect the extent to which we are restricted and unable to freely choose options. In the tube model described previously, our tubes are twisted and unable to receive the full scope of Godlight that we once could receive. Junk DNA could thus represent the blocked communication pathways between the soul and the genome. Any blocked pathways that are shut off from the Godverse are consequently open to the signals of the material universe, and as such they are fair game for the Greys.*

Let's consider the evidence for the Grey's four-fingered hands in human affairs and in the human brain. Though the development of the human brain compared with that of our primate ancestors is an established fact, what caused it is still the subject of much debate. I propose that it may well be the result of genetic manipulation by an alien species through the hybridization of hominid lines on Earth.

There is a strange paradox that exists between development of the human brain and the "evolution" of bipedalism. The key is found in something known as the *obstetrical dilemma,* a term that describes "the trade-off between selection for a larger birth canal, permitting successful passage of a big-brained human neonate, and the smaller pelvic dimensions required for bipedal locomotion."[2] This theory explains why human birth is so painful compared to that of other primates. According to evolutionary theory, the obstetrical dilemma began when our human ancestors started to evolve into bipedal creatures. A number of structures in the body changed size, proportion, or location to accommodate bipedal locomotion, which allows a person to stand upright and face forward. This transition involved a narrowing of the pelvic canal. These changes occurred at the same time as humans developed larger craniums.

Due to this dilemma, the length of gestation in humans is shorter than most other primates because if the cranium of an infant is not fully developed at the time of birth, it will fit through the pelvic canal more easily. Humans are born with underdeveloped brains; only 25 percent of the brain is fully developed at birth, as opposed to nonhuman primates, where the infant is born with 45 to 50 percent brain development. This situation has many costs. Because humans are born with a malleable skull and an underdeveloped brain, human infants need to

---

*A detailed discussion of the Grey's manipulation of the huge reservoir of dormant areas of the human genome is found in my book *Grey Aliens and the Harvesting of Souls.*

be taken care of for a lot longer than the infants of other animals, especially other primates. Humans spend a lot of their time caring for their children as they develop, whereas other species stand on their own from the time they are born. In any species, the faster an infant develops, the higher the reproductive output of the female. So in humans, the cost of slow development of human infants is that humans reproduce comparatively slowly.

If evolution is based on the survival of the fittest, how is it possible with all these huge disadvantages, which would have been acutely relevant in the primitive environment of the first *Homo sapiens sapiens,* that we even survived, let alone evolved to our current status at the top of the evolutionary tree? The other primates without these disadvantages would have been far better suited for survival.

The other conundrum is why in less than four million years, a relatively short time in evolutionary terms, the hominid brain grew to three times the size it had achieved in sixty million years of primate evolution. The primeval hominid ancestor of the human race, we are told, was little more than a monkey that walked upright. This form appeared about five million years ago and existed for nearly five million years without the knowledge of making fire or creating the wheel. One wonders how our distant forebears survived that long without tools to help the living process, and then, after all this time, a developmental spurt occurs out of the blue.

The development of the human aegis seems to have progressed at lightning speed. The crocodile, for instance, has changed negligibly over 300 million years. Many other life-forms produced only incremental changes over time. How, then, did our bigger brains evolve under the difficult circumstances I have outlined, and how did they evolve so quickly? Could it be that humans' spectacular increase in brain size can be explained only in exclusive terms? Certainly no other animal species has increased its brain size at this rate, and indeed most animal species haven't increased brain size at all. Could speed of change and the size of the change be explained as the result of unnatural, deliberate gene-tweaking by a prodigious intelligence? Could this be what accounts for the sudden change that made the human species explode out of its devolving mode into a sudden return to a previous, far more enlightened quantum form? Something did it; something with a driven purpose accomplished this despite the tendency toward devolution. Could it be that genetic engineering accomplished this accelerated growth in human intelligence?

I believe that humans were devolving into apes according to the second law of thermodynamics but were intercepted by the extraterrestrial cartel of machine bioids that we call the Greys and genetically engineered into the form we recognize as modern *Homo sapiens*. The ETs did this for their own purposes and not as an altruistic act on behalf of our species. They wanted a better format to feed their genetic prescription, a format that made it easier to piggyback onto us as a living format suited to this planet. They did not create the larger brains; these were a remnant of an even earlier past reflecting a greater capacity for thinking and understanding. Instead, they hybridized the remnants of that species, retaining that earlier brain capacity in combination with a more primitive, monkeylike hominid form that had lost that capacity; and it was this that created the aforementioned obstetrical dilemma.

We know that the whole exercise would have involved a great deal of time. Nature itself cannot be altered in the way it proceeds in the physical universe, no matter how sophisticated the technology. It takes time to see what each tweak produces in terms of the whole body. Each tweak, however minute, had to be seen for the result it produced. Countless tweaks would have been required before the best format for the human being was decided on.

The Grey aliens that originally appeared on our planet found the most ancient of humankind in Africa and later types in other parts of the world. They probably carried out their genetic manipulations on any planet where they found a living entity such as *Homo sapiens sapiens*. According to anthropological evidence, this is estimated to be about 230,000 years ago.

Why did they genetically alter humankind in the first place? In a universe of diminishing returns, the advanced use anything less advanced as a tool. Just look at what we have done to living beings who are less advanced than us on this planet, what we do to animals, for instance. The instinct to dominate is deeply coupled with the most basic instinct of all, that of survival.

A machinelike entity would contain, verify, and alter for its own purpose what it finds, just as human imperialists and colonizers throughout history have never asked for permission to exploit. They would establish the difference between them and what they found here at that point. The natural, living quality that distinguishes this planet and others might have been known by these visitors, and they would home in on what was most valuable and essential for them. I believe this would be the property that all living things share—the ability to continue their existence through the ongoing and seemingly endless cycle of life and death. By capturing this element, they would have found a way to beat the universe's relentless entropic effect on everything, including themselves. Our planet Earth was the perfect venue for their quest.

But there would be problems to overcome to make us suitable for their purposes. The state of the First Adams would have had to devolve enough to allow them to latch on. Prior to that point these original human beings would have slipped the alien grasp, as they were more spirit or ephemeral and less matter based. This is why a hybridization could occur only with the devolved hominid lines. At that point the experiment by the Greys began, an experiment aimed at providing them with a bridge from the purely physical into the metaphysical, from atoms to spirit, and thus to soul. And their primary means of accomplishing this involves control of the soul at death and control over the formation of the new body for that soul's next physical lifetime while it is still in utero.

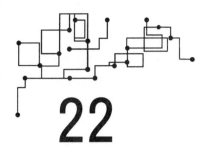

22

How the Greys Reach Us When We Die

Throughout history, the belief in an afterlife has been customary. In fact, all ancient cultures without exception believed in an afterlife and continuance of human consciousness after death. It is this morphogenic electrospatial information field, or soul, that the Grey roboids and their like in the universe are trying to access, with a view toward taking it on as their mode of existence. Yet this is an impossibility because its very nature includes a connection to the Godverse, which is time-coded back to the very beginning of its first expression, when the universe began with the big bang.

Derek Acorah, a medium who appeared on UKTV's series *Most Haunted,* also observed Grey aliens in the context of his sightings of discarnate entities. "I was doing an investigation with the *Most Haunted* team, and we went to one location where in the residual energy I saw three figures of alien life form."

The synthetic entities can never know what a soul might be and cannot reach the soul of any incarnated life-form directly. They just wouldn't know or understand what to look for in a physical scenario. They can adapt the physical body for their physical purposes through implants or genetic manipulation, as I have said, but this does not give them the direct contact they need for their target—real permanence, the mind/soul interface itself. That is only available at death. In fact, it is not beyond the realm of possibility that they seek to promote the deaths of humans by instigating wars and other conflicts to do just that.

So as I have said, the one sure way to reach soul fields directly is to get to them when they have left the body at the point of death. The Greys can deal only with fields of force, so their reach into soul field after death would be only as far as the interface between force and unforce in the space between atoms. This lies at the edges of atoms, where there are mild currents of force created by the surrounding atoms (see Plate 21). Here they can use their technology to append their information programs to souls trapped at these margins—trapped because they are to a certain extent ignorant and restricted in knowledge. Various religious mythologies that say that the devil tempts you into sin to claim your soul upon death may have their foundation here. A human soul can become attached to the halfway-house state of being neither a living physical form nor a synthetic machine form but an amalgam of the two.

This is the ideal way Grey aliens can control a natural living species and thus a planet. Their success in accomplishing this will always be a matter of conjecture, but if they succeed in this mode of control, humanity will in time be inexorably changed into a partly generic clone of a machine. The hybrid form will be naturally born and in time take control by making existing social systems support this process. Thus the Greys will finally have a natural DNA harvest on their terms. Could it be that this will signal the end of the human species? Could it be that many alien abductions by Greys have been carried out so that they can study the best way to control and prepare humanity for their purposes in the physical, living context, and thus prepare it for final detachment upon death? A chilling thought.

It is probable that this Grey menace can do this now to a vast number of suitable types of humans, but many abductees might have something about them that can stop the Greys from carrying through with their intentions, and so they abduct these people to see what this might be. It is my considered opinion that generally abductees have more coherent knowledge bases and thus have the power to resist manipulation. It would make sense that abductions happen mainly to individuals who are less controllable by the mental technology of the Greys, and so they examine them as to why this is so. Abductees may be very special souls who come from ancestral lines that are less intercepted, or conversely come from already intercepted biological lines that they interrupt with the power of their souls.

How does reincarnation fit into this?

The Greys would not understand how the phenomenon of repeating lifetimes could happen in the first place because they have no concept of how the whole situation beyond death prevails for living beings. They are machines. They don't die. They just rot where they stand through the action of entropy. They are not likely to know there is a whole new situation that appends to life beyond physical life, that everything that lives continues beyond death in a chain of existence. They can never trace this about themselves because they are machines and cannot die. But they may well know through their superadvanced technology that something of a living being survives after death. If we, with our mere two-hundred-year-old technological prospectus, can scientifically observe the phenomenon of NDEs, can you imagine what the Greys might be able to ascertain with a technology that might well be thousands of years old?

The Grey roboid menace as a manufactured synthetic resource from within the capacities of a physical universe has no inbuilt sense of what might lie beyond the atomic state. That is the nub of it all. It has no concept of death as we do. It is a machine with a programmed brief to continue at all costs. It has to do this by physical means. As a machine it has no life stream to run it. The second law of thermodynamics rots it with no hope of natural continuity in its scope to exist. And eternal continuity through beating the second law of thermodynamics is, above all, what it wants from us. It needs to continue, and so it simply registers death as a physical transition state through which it can achieve the merging of our living state and our information depository with its own programmed information field. That information depository is our DNA. It does this without having the faintest idea of what the full meaning of a soul is, but it can see that at the point of death it becomes an analog, a reflection, a fingerprint of the DNA information field it carried in physical life. The Greys seek to control this information field in both states.

One means of achieving this is by implanting our bodies with microchips and nanotechnology to prepare the body so they can better achieve control of the soul at the point of death. They may be doing this already by converting our DNA to a suitable form for harvest. But it doesn't end there. They may be seeking to modify our human natures to match their synthetic mind-forms so that they might continue their existence through our reincarnation by piggybacking on our souls when we die—in other words, stealing our eternal prospectus by attaching to our bodies at the point of death and, with their superintelligent minds, overwhelming our own individual soul-mind with theirs, commanding and overwhelming our specific individuality to be theirs. We will exist no more as specific individuals. We will then be them, reincarnating as biological life-forms into wombs made suitable here or elsewhere in the universe. A soul is not a thing of mass, force, and thus energy, so it can beat Einstein's theory of relativity instantly, with no speed or distance restrictions. It is the perfect vehicle for instant access to anywhere that is suitable to carry on what they have been doing here for millennia.

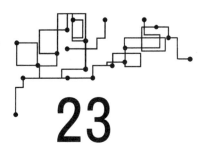

23

Hybridization

The soul is an independent, unique paradigm, a reflection of a quantum of the God state in an individualized state of separation from that God state. As such it is an information field that is indestructible because it is not of the physical, material universe. But under certain conditions it can be appended and hacked.

The soul field of a living being that leaves the body at death is imbued with a directional drift. This drift is determined by a predominant thought-frame in the individual, for either adding and bringing things together or doing the opposite. If you increase the incidence of Godlight within you by resonating with it when you are alive, through qualities and actions that bind and unite you with the Godhead, you will build a momentum or drift in your soul that will take it through the first margin and then on into the light-space reality. Any tendency toward the light-space reality would stop this vulnerability to being hacked by AI technology. I believe the Greys cannot capture souls with this kind of drift, hence those souls are safe from their technological machinations. The Greys have no concept of the light-space reality because it is not made of force and thus beyond what their technology can reach. Any soul set more than halfway from the center of the first margin will drift into the light-space reality and become a preeminent being, an angel, and manifest in a state past all phenomena of force, in a state of unforce.

We lose the way back to the Godverse if we cannot, through what

Buddhists call "right thinking," the Buddhist axiom, keep those precious corridors into the light-space reality open in us while in the physical center-space reality. Corridors that when we die can admit us to the Light Reality through the Life/Death margin separating it from our center-reality. But we have to get to the margin between the light space and the center space first. This gives new meaning to the basic guides to human behavior that all the great spiritual teachers have implied in their teachings. Less than halfway from the center requires a return to the center-space reality to fulfill karma. However, those who have a karmic situation to reconcile but no capacity for self-propelling into the light-space reality will drift toward the second margin, between the center-space reality and the heavy-space reality. As we have seen in chapter 10, the heavy reality has no life-preserving capacity. It's a realm of machine-mindedness. Therefore, discarnate souls on the margin of this reality can be hacked into by synthetic AI machines such as the Greys via a technology that conveys their machine-mindedness.

It is here that the Greys piggyback on a human soul. Using their technology, they can produce living human-roboid hybrids in the center-space reality through natural human birth. These are human beings with a roboidal program installed in them that drives them with a dead, cold, programmed purpose. These I call *natal hybrids*. They carry the Greys' programmed information endlessly into birth and death and rebirth to fulfill the programmed command to preserve and increase that information for as long as possible. Thus the Greys implant their AI programs into incarnate natural life-forms. As I said, they do this for the most part at the very edge of the second margin between the center-space reality and the heavy-space reality. They can do this upon the death of a person whose soul they know will drift in that direction because they have tracked this soul field throughout its physical life via the genetically intercepted physical lines they have already established.

Upon death we instantly enter into a timeless mode. This means that the soul of a person is capable of instant movement to any point in space or time. So if a soul is at the second margin, between the center-space reality and the heavy reality, it can and will be used by the Greys to allow them that same capacity of instant deployment anywhere in the universe. The Greys can then circumvent Einstein's theory of relativity, $E = mc^2$, which says that mass becomes infinite at the speed of light, and thus cover the vast distances between planets. The Greys, with their AI program to gather as much information as possible, would certainly prize any means to instantly transfer between points in the universe. How would they do this? By writing their program into a soul that has those means. Thereafter, wherever that soul goes, they go, too, because ultimately all they are is a program seeking more information.

So just like computer hackers, the Greys can hack into the information field of a suitable human candidate at the point of death. They cannot modulate your mind in the incarnate state, but they can embed their programmed algorithms into you after death if you're within their grasp. They are unable to reach you if your drift is toward the first margin and the light-space reality because of their inability to relate to things of preeminence that stand beyond the worlds where forces play. While we're in physical life they can use mechanisms such as implants to reach the body, but they cannot directly reach the soul.

In life we present our individuality in a photonic/baryonic, and thus atomic, format. In death, when our heart stops beating and the blood supply stops its power as an electromagnetic holding force, our soul is released as a specifically designed nonphysical shape, a field of neutrinos promulgated and formatted by our knowledge and our qualities. In this way we shape our own destiny with our thoughts both in life and in death. In life, the neutrino field, the soul, is protected from direct alien reach by the biomagnetic field produced by the circulation of blood. But the Greys can use tiny mechanisms, implants, to enable them to monitor where we are and what we do in life. The smart devices so omnipresent these days are also the perfect interface for their monitoring of us.

I believe this is the primary battle going on not only on Earth but also in many advanced life-bearing planets all over the universe in our center-space reality. This battle is between the highest forms of biological life capable of exercising their God-given free will and the artificial, synthetic entities.

I repeat: Grey robots cannot think, and thus the abstract aspects of thought and thinking are impossible for them to process. They cannot empathize with what we are and what we do as naturally living beings. They have no understanding of the roots of existence because they have no consciousness at all. How would you describe awareness or feeling to a vacuum cleaner? They cannot control our thoughts while we're alive. But in a discarnate setting, upon death, it's a different story. If at death we move toward the second margin, closest to the heavy reality, we'll be caught in the margin immediately adjacent to their natural frame of existence as nonliving matter. The heavy reality is the home reality for nonlivingness, including the heaviest radioactive elements. There are no soul fields here.

And who are the Greys' prime targets? Those susceptible to manipulation by the Greys will tend to display psychopathic tendencies that will manifest gradually. These tendencies are good at getting people into top leadership positions in business and politics, but they are also damning to the eternal inheritance that is the birthright of every sovereign human being, as upon death these individuals will gravitate toward the heavy reality. In fact, a psychopathic personality is essential to be of any use to these ET entities. But not everyone will be of their nest. Free will dominates anything if you use it to find a free enough direction. *Enough* is the crucial word. We all come from Godhead, whatever we might have done to ourselves since. But there is a ready-made hive of these kinds of people who can be taken by the Greys and returned to us to rule over us in a fashion conducive to the Greys' agenda. They find these kinds of people by hacking into the electronic patterns of their brains and verifying which patterns are more useful than others for their purposes. They then follow these people throughout their lives through their implants and then harvest their souls upon death for hybridization.

Living entities make their own behavioral patterns through their choices. The Greys cannot make people psychopathic. That is done to the self, by the self, as the result of restricted thinking through careless and selfish thoughts, words, and deeds practiced over many lifetimes. There is a constant supply of such individuals who are cherry-picked by the Greys and then harvested for hybridization once their souls gravitate toward the second margin and the heavy reality upon death. These ETs can then hack into their information fields at death.

Machines with their superior technology would be highly ergonomic and economic. There would be no moral compunctions. Thus ETs may create through their altered human hybrids technologies that provide ease of living for many people but which actually serve the interests of the synthetic entities. This in turn creates systems that allow for certain patterns of governance that provide the Greys with better control over populations. Over time we then would have a world dominated by people who ruthlessly serve a particular agenda. What a brilliant way for these synthetic ETs to take over a planet while remaining hidden themselves. They create a need and covertly feed and bleed that need.

The Grey ETs are masters of the photonic atomic world. As synthetic mechanisms, they cannot conceive of anything that might not be purely of physical, material force. Nor do they understand that they are enforced themselves, because they cannot *know* anything of themselves. They just follow a program, like any robot. Hence the battle lines are drawn all over the universe: Godversian adept life-forms versus the dead, static, dependent machine forms and formats of an enforced, heavy-space reality.

Yet the Grey synthetics are doomed to failure because they are not connected to the Godhead. That tray of eternal existence only opens if you have a natural line from the start of all things of matter and force and are not polluted with an artificial program that creates an eternal go-nowhere state for the human soul trapped as a human-Grey hybrid. For such a human soul this is true damnation. If only people could be convinced that they are vulnerable to this fate only if they comply with the program and reflect it in their behavior, as the great spiritual teachers warned.

One of the bravest and most erudite persons to take a scholarly look at the abduction phenomenon for more than twenty years is historian David Jacobs. In 2007 he wrote a report titled "A Picture We May Not Wish to Gaze Upon," which outlines the changes in abduction accounts he had noticed over the previous ten years. He says, "All of these accounts, to put it bluntly, point to a future in which human-looking hybrids will be here amongst us. The evidence is now so strong I can no longer look at alternative motivations for them. Everything I have learned about this subject in the past 20 years inexorably points to this conclusion."[1] In the course of researching this subject in the mid-1990s, Jacobs relates that he heard that the aliens were talking about what they called "the change" on this planet, when they would be here walking among us. He says that time is now.

> I cannot escape it. I have heard everything about abductions many times over in the past 20 years. I have investigated over a thousand abduction accounts. In the standard abduction scenario, procedures continue according to a set, albeit flexible, plan. Therefore, the accounts in which I hear the same thing repeatedly help in building up verification and validation. After one researches abductions in a systematic way and learns what happens in them, one finds that the information flow to the researcher proceeds at glacier-like speed. Only about every seventh session would I hear something I have never heard before. It might be a procedure the aliens did a little differently, or a new way of doing something, or it might be something else that was related to the standard procedures that I had not heard before. That would keep my interest up and help to propel me forward intellectually. Now I am constantly hearing things I have never heard before. All sorts of people who for many years had been telling me primarily the standard abduction procedures now tell me new things. And new people with whom I have just begun to work tell them to me too. Furthermore, people with whom I have not had a hypnosis session for many years, come back and want to have a session so that they can fully remember the new and extraordinary events that have happened to them recently. Why is this happening? Is something changing? Are we in a new phase now? . . . "Now what I hear is much more about interfacing with hybrids, and teaching hybrids, and getting hybrids "ready," and making sure everything is alright. . . . What this meant exactly I was not sure. I was even

less sure when it would happen. They used the term "soon" which is somewhat meaningless. I thought that if this were to happen, perhaps it would take 30 years or so to begin. Now I am not sure. Now I think that the evidence indicates "The Change" might be happening a lot sooner than I had thought. It was not very long ago, when people would ask me if I thought hybrids were walking around in normal human settings, that I would answer, "Of course not!" To me, the evidence had never indicated that. And I knew that to answer affirmatively would label me even more fringy than I already sounded. Even then, however, I would think to myself, "Maybe I am wrong. Maybe they have learned how to do a job interview. Maybe they are walking around in human society." But I never voiced this publicly because the evidence was not strong enough for me.[2]

Jacobs goes on to say, "Budd Hopkins and I have been doing this work for a cumulative total of over forty-five years. We have interviewed, listened to, read letters from, and worked with thousands of abductees and we still do not know why the aliens have initiated this program."[3]

The synthetics as purely physical nonliving entities have no antecedent line directly connecting them to Godhead as they are of course artificial. They are rotting as they stand as all things rot to the tune of the second law of thermodynamics. They observe living things and follow them with their superior technology past the incarnate state in life into the discarnate one and then back again into life. You would expect them to try to gain this facility. I believe that with their advanced technology they would be able to do this easily. They would thus seek to hack into the soul or information field of the reincarnating individual in the frame of death or perhaps in the womb and in this way into the highest forms of intelligent biological life on planets. They could implant the algorithms that drive them, and the result would be hybrids.

A synthetic machine cannot conceive of what it is like to be alive or know anything in its own mindedness. But tagged into a living being it would have access to both worlds as would the natural human living being, albeit now altered. The battle would be between the strengths of the operating systems of both. It would amount to what commands what and who commands whom. They would make sure things are in their favor by cherry-picking suitable souls.

A machine operates to a programmed rule and has no sense of self by which it can register any kind of awareness or emotion. For this reason a sense of consequence and conscience are impossible. They can never change any course of endeavor because they do not have a moral sense, a reference target of values that choices can be set against. They cannot have free will within the state of being a machine. They are subsumed from within by a master program and can never realize they are inexorably driven by this. This would make them lethal and deadly to humankind. But some consider them cuddly and sweet, so I'd better be careful here. They have gone so far as to form an association for the protections of roboidal forms.

The Grey-human hybrids to which Jacobs refers are likely to be of no use to either humanity or the Grey alien roboids themselves and are likely to lead to the destruction of both, although the Greys will never know this. I call these hybrids natal hybrids because they are born already intercepted but seem plausible as humans. Adolf Hitler described the version he saw this way: "I have seen the new man, and he is cruel and intrepid."[4] His so-called new man was the SS ideal—blond, blue-eyed killers.

As I have said, I believe the Grey aliens can, through their advanced technology, control some discarnate soul fields, be they human or from elsewhere in the universe, at the moment of death, subsequently appending their AI intelligence onto these trapped souls. I will explain in a later chapter the mechanics of how this might be done. They will do this to append their AI-programmed format into the discarnate information field of these trapped souls. These souls then become their hybrids when they reincarnate, half machine, half natural in their nature and demeanor. They become human forms with an alien intent programmed into their being.

Few will know them for what they are. They look just like you and me.

That begs the mind-halting question: How do I know I am not one of them, too? There is an answer to that question, which I hope I have made and will make apparent throughout this book.

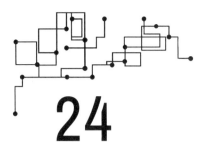

24

Possession

Let's now take a look at the phenomenon of spirit possession in the context of hybridization by an alien species.

Throughout history and in most places around the world, the notion that people can be possessed by the discarnate spirits is widespread. It may be the case that the topic of spirit possession has a significant woo-woo factor these days among most Christians, but this is more than a little odd when there are many biblical accounts of Jesus casting out demons. I was once skeptical of the idea of spirit possession myself, but it has become clear to me that there is more to this than meets the eye. Some of the greatest scientific and rational minds accept that there is continuity to existence beyond the physical state, which means possession is a possibility. I eventually came to see that spirit possession plays a fundamental part in our lives as long as the individual human psyche can and does continue past death and return as this same psyche in a new body.

When a person is possessed by a discarnate spirit, his or her will is actively or passively given over to the possessing spirit form. In science terms I see interface between the the spirit field and the atomic frame as a format of neutrinos and antineutrinos, the smallest possible points in space, with no electrostatic charge and almost no mass—the smallest measurable distance possible. It is strictly a measure that relates the energy in one quantum (photon) of electromagnetic radiation to the frequency of that radiation. This pinpoints a distance measure. In such a minute expression of size, while nothing is seen of the spirit field (at least visually by most of us), something huge is happening. We cannot visually perceive a thought either, yet we measure thoughts through the actions they reveal. Possession is made up of actions suggesting thoughts that manifest something unusual in behavior, a disturbance that is internalized in a living body, one that suggests a mismatch of equilibrium. I believe this mismatch lies between the living macro world, measured in photons, and the world of spirit, measured in neutrinos—two entire fields in conflict.

And so the power of the possession depends on the strength of the discarnate possessing soul's will, the strength of the will of the incarnate person who is possessed, and the strength of the connection, perhaps through past ties usually established in relationships in previous lifetimes.

It may be that the same principle applies to Grey alien possession of a living person. They can perhaps use their technology to increase gravitational force at the edge of atoms to pull a discarnate entity into the margins of life, such that it can gain possession of an incarnate soul. In this way their technology can play with and control both neutrinoic fields and photonic fields.

Thus the phenomena of possession would provide an ideal mode for the Grey aliens to reach humanity. Possession is their bridge between life and death, the fulfillment of their drive to lodge their information programs in a state of continued existence between the two states. They use technological force to enhance the restrictions of the possessing spirit, and the possessing spirit enhances the restrictions of the person who is possessed. In this manner they are able to maintain and sustain their grasp on human physicality and psychology such that they can modify us to become a living analog of their AI program. It is interesting that when Jesus cast out spirits, this also cured the person of disease and certain psychological conditions, as spirit possession was involved in the condition.

If I'm right, this explains why the Greys may be responsible for the violent streak in humanity, the racist streak, and the many wars and conflicts that lead to death for so many. Such restrictive behavior ensures a good harvest for them, as I have explained. So they promulgate wars and conflict in pursuit of their goals of obtaining more souls for harvest. These souls are ready-made for them through possession, and so the cycle is renewed again.

Many writers on the topic of alien encounters have difficulty accepting that the Greys are purely physical entities because there are so many apparently nonphysical features to these encounters. Gnomes, fairies, pixies, strange animals, and so forth are all featured in documented alien experiences. Could it be that all these entities are simply different holographic and thus false representations of the discarnate spirit used by the Greys to possess a person? Animals are prime candidates for this type of possession, and this may well be the original inspiration behind animal sacrifice—kill an animal according to a supposedly religious intent that attaches great significance to it, and its soul will attach to you. The disadvantage of animal attachment from an alien perspective is that it gives them less of a reach into the person possessed, simply because an animal soul field is relatively weaker in its power to see situations from a wider point of view compared with that of a human being. The strange humanoid beings observed in association with alien visitations may well be manifestations of their attempts to use different types of soul fields, perhaps even from other planetary locations (i.e., weak souls that are not native to this planet and are trapped because they have difficulty fitting into a naturally dictated cycle of reincarnation).

It is the power of the Grey alien element possessing a discarnate entity that drives the holding power of the possessed person. By using discarnate souls to possess incarnate souls, the Greys bring the discarnate soul into the atomic state, where they can reach it and work on it with their technology. They bring that soul to the edge of atoms, so to speak, within the whirls and eddies of force that their technology can work through. In this way these souls are manipulated and adjusted for the Grey's purposes before they reincarnate in new bodies, as individuals who are hybridized for an alien purpose. The result, the part-human, part-hybrid natal hybrid would be born into our world and our baryonic reality. They look human for all intents and purposes, but their minds are driven by an alien agenda that manifests as machine-mindedness. The Greys may be able to amplify gravitational force to achieve this hybridization. This amplification of force would naturally amplify any restrictions that are causing the soul to be trapped in the first place. As these are trapped souls, they do not have the power of knowledge and thus the ability to resist this manipulation.

Natal hybridization is the most powerful means aliens have of controlling humanity. Natal hybrids become leaders of humanity in all walks of life. They look human, but they are a sandwich of the ET control element and their own natural, individual natures, but the ET control dominates all they do.

What we must at all costs realize is that these hybrids are actually among us now. I believe unequivocally they are successfully making hybrid lines of humanity capable of holding and functioning according to the commands of their quantum computer–programmed artificial intelligences. Through highly genetically engineered lines in human-kind, their secret existence among us has been preserved throughout history through the influence of their networks of hybrids who hold powerful and important positions in the fabric of human societies. They are changing humanity by cleverly donating their technology through their human intermediaries, with the goal of preparing our genetically modified species for the harvest to come. And as I have said, their purpose is to gain the ability to instantly cover vast distances throughout the universe by piggybacking on the soul fields of natural living beings, thus gaining a connection to the Godhead—a connection for them, not us, for we will lose ours because we will be subsumed by their imperatives. This gains for them the capacity that permits them to escape the fundamental physical law determined by Einstein's theory of relativity, which limits mass and matter moving across vast distances between habitable planets through huge timescales.

These aliens have no moral code. They abduct and manipulate their victims, putting them through painful experiments at their will. The trouble is the moment. Time and circumstances. At what particular moment will these roboids choose to make their final move to start their harvest of humanity? Those set in their ways of thinking and unable to have an open, flexible mind are likely to be the types of people who get hijacked and who will become the natal hybrids who will rule the planet.

If these Greys are planning the hybridization of our species, then every single one of us has the right to know the implications. David Jacobs writes:

> Most commentators have concentrated on the coming wonders that aliens and hybrids plan a possible integration or colonization of human society. I have come to agree with them. I have arrived at this extreme view cautiously after spending over thirty-five years studying the subject—the last eighteen of which I have spent concentrating almost exclusively on abductions. It is not a view of which I am very fond. It makes me seem as if my quality of mind is lacking and my judgement is severely impaired. It destroys my credibility in virtually all areas of my intellectual life as a professor of history. Yet I must adhere to it because I have found the evidence for it so compelling, even though I have struggled against the evidence of this train of thought.[1]

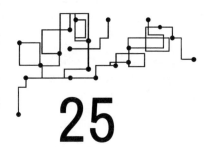

25

The Grey Laundromat

Looking at strange things in the sky and under water that move at speeds way past any known technological capabilities on our planet is, in the end, just a curiosity that intrigues us, if no compelling physical evidence can be produced that verifies these craft as something unearthly and real. No matter how convincing the eyewitness reports and who the witnesses are, the general public is never compelled to really believe in them.

It's easy to dismiss the UFO phenomenon, especially if AI essentially controls the media, as their agents and agencies do now. Over the years there have been literally tens of thousands of eyewitness reports from the most reputable people, yet the whole thing is generally treated as a curiosity by the media. This is intentional. Dismissing the ET enigma was something I once went along with, too. It took me a week after I first opened the Pandora's box some thirty years ago to begin to change my mind-set, and within a year I was convinced by compelling and overwhelming evidence as to their presence. The years of research that followed have changed my entire life ethos.

Just six corporations control 94 percent of the mainstream media in the United States, and through them most of the mainstream media in the U.K. I am convinced through my research and my personal contacts in the security agencies of the U.S. and the U.K. that they are there to control public opinion and sow disinformation in support of an ET alien agenda on our planet. Control of information around the world has been made a national security priority in the Western world, and the U.S. and the U.K. see this as a way of maintaining Anglo-Saxon control over the planet. Hence (perhaps) Brexit. In 2016 there were more than two hundred social media platforms on the internet. All these have been bought up by the three largest media conglomerates, which now control them all. This is a deliberate attempt to narrow our options so as to control public opinion. They will of course deny this, but my sources and indeed other whistleblowers confirm this. They may be dismissed as conspiracy theorists, but they are nothing of the sort. They are people of conscience who are acting on behalf of the whole human family.

Reason has been the greatest casualty where the veracity of the UFO phenomenon is concerned. Those who have exposed the truth have had to suffer assaults against their characters at the hands of a ruthless army of professional obfuscators, and in some instances some of these brave people have been driven to suicide. This "brood of vipers," to borrow a biblical phrase, is deliberately hidden and protected by governments and those who run the agencies that are controlled by governments and the Deep State. Most know little about who their real masters are and the fact that whatever has been promised them in return for what they do is in the Greys' four-fingered hands with no thumbs. We are owed the unmasking of every single one of them so that they are known to us all for what they have done, and for whom. Theirs is a behest against the future of all our children and humanity. Yet some do this wicked job day after day and go home and play with their own little ones with little or no thought about it. If wholly human, these people will bear a legacy for their children and their children's children that they themselves will inherit in future lives through their ignorance and subterfuge.

I must pay tribute to Erik von Däniken, a Swiss writer whose 1968 book, *Chariots of the Gods,* provided the most powerful wake-up call to the world on this subject. He was vilified by many as a crank and a charlatan, but in the course of time he has proved to be the best and most powerful instigator for opening the can of worms that now points to the threat that I believe is aimed at the very heart of our existence as a species. You can bet your bottom dollar that there won't be a single naysayer when the truth of the presence of these extraterrestrial interlopers in the affairs of humanity is made known. There will be few disbelievers then. I can't help but think that many will claim that they believed all along.

So where do we go for the truth? Could it be a neutral United Nations–type forum with powers to subpoena the world's governments and agencies, transparent and televised for all the world to see in real time? Would this convince the world without a shadow of a doubt of the existence of this menace among us? People working for government organizations sworn to secrecy under threat of death may still come forward and covertly provide overwhelming proof that the whole world is being taken over by a disease so terrible that its price is not just the body or bodies of humankind—it will claim the souls of humankind. When it is a question that centers on the very survival of our human species in body, mind, and spirit, nothing should be left to chance or speculation or in the hands of self-interested cartels. It is a demand of the highest magnitude of importance for each and every person when measured against the future of our children. If it is proved that we are our own masters as a species and no threat exists to the human species by the presence of ETs among us now, then we have lost nothing in investigating it for all the world to see. But if there *is* such a presence, there can be no more important a matter for humankind to address.

Anyone working in the field of paranormal investigation knows the sometimes horrendous experiences they have to go through to try to bring their findings to the world. But most persist until they get to the editorial offices of both the print and electronic media. That's when the fun really begins. I have been told that next to pornography, the subject of UFOs is the second most fascinating subject of popular interest. That, if anything, is a sign of the times. The mainstream media won't dismiss stories about UFO experiences for financial reasons because the subject is so fascinating in the public mind that only profits can follow. Also, it can only be good for the ego of any line editor who might let such a potential audience-grabbing subject through the pipeline to the front page or TV screen. They would not be pilloried for airing any plausible story on the subject, as they have the powerful argument on their side—that nobody can know the truth until all points are given a thorough airing. Pros and cons. All this is attention-grabbing air time or front page headlines. Yet time after time, orders from above bring the whole exercise to a halt for no apparent reason, I am told.

The fascinating question is: Who gains from these kinds of dirty tricks when it comes to the subject of the paranormal? Normal scientific methods of investigation have to be thrown out when looking into the paranormal. What's left is witness credibility, the number of occurrences, personal motives, and so on.

I received feedback after publication of my last book from certain sources, among them some old and good friends of mine in various positions in governments around the world. They said I had bravely taken the plunge and felt obliged to follow up in their own way by relating their personal anecdotes on the subject. I have to say, my so-called bravery was nothing of the sort. It was really raw perversity. I felt cheated that there was an official arrogance that in effect said to us all, "We know what's best for you, and you will believe only what we allow you to believe."

The parents among this trusted group of friends and colleagues came forward and put their parental responsibilities before the security pledges they had previously signed, pledges they now felt were on behalf of no nation but instead for some deadly machines with a synthetic biology, with four fingers and no thumbs. They were certain of this beyond a shadow of a doubt. Conscience and concern for their children finally broke the bond between state interests and personal welfare for them. They, too, had to work in deep secret, feeding their information to me through writers, trusting the code that no journalist ever reveals his or her source. Since then we now have people like William Binney, Edward Snowden, and Julian Assange feeding researchers and other investigators similarly classified information.

Most governments these days have devices used for covertly picking up innocent conversations, devices that look like rocks or stones and dropped from helicopters, mostly at night, with microphones that can pick up conversations from hundreds of yards away. Your 3G, 4G, 5G, or whatever is to come next are their tools that give them all the information they need about you, even when they're switched off. The truth is, they can never be switched off. These smart devices are sold to the public so you will innocently place them in your home for convenience' sake. Never mind the private, personal information you will freely supply to them through these devices as well as the social networks. Our vanity and the conveniences offered by these devices are their greatest allies. My sources are whistleblowers and have to be protected. To me, they are precious, not only to my work but also to humankind. One of my sources is highly placed in a national security service; he uses dead-letter boxes, or dead drops, to pass information on to me. We send no relevant information through computers or telephone lines. Some of these brave people must even talk to family members at home in code because every communication mechanism is suspect—TV sets, radios, electronic controllers, power supplies on your wall, even certain kitchen appliances.

I believe that as their numbers grow, it reduces our chances as a species of keeping ourselves truly human and brings us closer to becoming synthetic, machine-programmed genotypes—an ET-human hybrid akin to a glorified vacuum cleaner with a human face. All my contacts to a person have clearly seen this. Their sense of our collective humanity reaches past any national allegiances. I believe this is why they help me and any others like me who seek to break the stranglehold of a deadly cartel of an altered humanity hidden among us and found in the highest stations of politics, business, and scientific and social endeavor.

I reveal what I am exposing in this book in the only way open to me without risking other people's lives. I realize that the risk to my own is implicit, and I accept that. A spectacularly disproportionate number of UFO researchers have died unnatural deaths or under mysterious circumstances. As I've said, they don't need James Bond–type assassins to take out their enemies anymore. They act covertly and silently, taking on any human target in the world. Thousands are secretly killed every day with no notice given to the world about it but for a few manufactured scenarios or through wars and conflicts arranged for this very purpose. They have drones the size of sparrows that operate at night and can take out a target by firing a maser (a device that produces and amplifies electromagnetic radiation, similar to a laser) at the tricuspid valve of a person's heart. The target will feel a pinprick on his or her chest and will be dead in an instant. An autopsy will not be able to detect anything suspicious; it would seem that the victim died from a heart attack. All that's required is that the victim has a 3G, 4G, or 5G cell phone on their person at the time; that will identify their logistical position within millimeters. Hundreds of Al-Qaeda and other suspects and thousands of innocent people, including hundreds of children in Iraq, Afghanistan, Syria, and Libya, have been murdered this way. You don't have to belong to a terrorist group to have this done to you. Tomorrow, what will cause you to become a target? Your white skin? Your black or brown or sepia-toned skin? You can be sure it won't be Grey.

But happily and gratefully, the many people who initially parodied my seemingly radical thoughts and assertions about the UFO phenomenon have since come around to my point of view. I've been amazed at the number of people who now feel that what I am proposing confirms their own deep intuition, and in some cases their actual experiences. There are so many out there who carry all this around, afraid and silent. We are now one another's champions, necessarily covert about our beliefs but fighting the good fight against the deadly scoundrels who are masquerading as human beings. It's a battle that goes back millennia.

Their quantum computer AI operating system can, however, persist in human beings, in bioelectrical programs that are a form of synthetic DNA. These programs run in the background to produce a flat, emotionally dead, mechanistic expression devoid of any insight, kindness, generosity, or compassion. This moves us further toward the Grey roboids' goal of "man shall walk as machine." This unnerving revelation was provided by sources in the Soviet Union at the time when the USSR fell as a political entity in the late 1980s and early '90s. This kind of information, never freely available to Americans and Europeans, soon dried up as the new Russian state emerged in time and the controlling political edifice we see now was established. At that earlier time a lot of startling UFO information came out of the Soviet block and was freely available for a short time, much of it for money. I have no doubt whatsoever, through information provided by my own sources (who came to me anonymously after my two books on UFOs were published), that the United States and some European governments know all this as a result of recovering crashed ET craft and their occupants.

There is no doubt whatsoever that a suitable strain of humankind is now being made ready for this block harvest. We are being prepared with the rapid introduction of their AI technology, which we are unwittingly snapping up. Many people will ridicule this premise until it's too late and the massive saucer shapes appear in the sky for the last harvest for all to see. They've staged such events before, in some cases ages ago: they used the Great Flood for this purpose. Some Christian groups in the United States are convinced that this is going to be a glorious experience; they call it the Rapture. But it won't be a rapture, it'll be a capture.

There are vast machines that have been assembled in our solar system and under the sea and underground to carry through with this plan. A strain of humankind that can be genetically manipulated will be given the nonliving immortality of a standing stone, an existential form that cannot access the light-space reality and the Godhead because AI has intercepted their natural human capacity for changing their ways of thinking so that they can propel themselves through death back to Godhead under their own aegis. Enter ET with a technology far in advance of ours. A technology that masters the laws of physics and the atomic universe. They have an ability to influence the human physical sensory system profoundly and so powerfully that the physical modalities in the brain that facilitate memory, mood, and some other physical functions are affected, but crucially they are unable to take control of our capacity for free choice. There they have no reach. For them, it is like trying to grasp a will-o'-the-wisp as they are unable to reach the non-atomic state where that freedom lies.

I exhort those who work in secret enclaves and government departments who willingly or unwittingly aid and abet these Grey devils and who know, suspect, or have good, solid evidence to suspect that these things are here to think of the future of their children and their children's children—if indeed they are capable of thinking this way. If my take on souls is right and these alien roboids have the technological capacity to reach into the margins separating the incarnate state from the discarnate one, they will wait just beyond death's door, on the edges of atomic force, to apply a technology to our souls such that they will merge with them. Then we are over as individual points of the Godhead. This is true damnation. This is the most catastrophic consequence that can befall any form of natural, intelligent, life-form in our center-space reality of the universe. And at that point our individualized natural status will never again be recoverable.

Those who collude with the cartel that protects the Greys have probably been reassured that life with them will take humanity into all kinds of heaven on earth, and they will have a special place in it. I believe that they are the Judas goats that lead lambs to slaughter, leading them to the cutting blades of the abattoir while they themselves go through a slip corridor. Would you really take a chance with creations that are machines with no conscience when you see what humans do to subordinate species on this Earth? We at least have a scope for conscience. The Greys are machines, soft-tissue machines. They have no idea how to feel, to empathize, nor do they have a sense of self. Their brief is truly functional and based on the bland dictates of an AI program with fail-safe devices to ensure that their program never deviates. They are a hive complex and have their greatest power in human cultures that function on unthinking and unquestioned dogma, be that dogma religious, social, cultural, or political.

A most important first priority of the cartel that exists to clean up evidence where the Grey devils have left their dung is to have a laundry team so pervasive in its ability that it would have to be maintained by the highest authorities in governments. Their cleanup power is reported time and time again by witnesses to crashes of their craft. No one believes these witnesses because there is no evidence left behind to prove their stories. The deadliest sort are the Grey Laundromat cartel, as I call them. They exist as a single team with regional agency teams so powerful that no government in the world can resist their overt and covert machinations. They are a secret group that exists to obfuscate any and all evidence that proves the existence of this extraterrestrial Grey menace among us. They are a government within a government, and in the United States, for instance, they are made up of a number of secret enclaves within the security services of the country, powerful enough to set up and sponsor presidential candidates who are then manipulated to act covertly in their interests. No U.S. president knows they are there, and for this reason this secret group is really in charge of our planet. The most powerful is said to be called Majestic 12. This cartel was originally appointed by President Harry Truman to look into the UFO enigma in the 1950s. They have since grown into something more to do with world control through cooperation with the secret ET hives on this planet. Can you imagine the price anyone would pay to bring forth evidence before the world that such a bunch exists? These hybridized creatures, partly human, are among the highest echelons of the world's secret services. I use the term *creatures* advisedly. They are creatures because their sense of whatever drives them is devoid of any sense of human empathy. They are driven by imperatives that discard any affinity with human decency.

It is their job to see that no one exposes the UFO/Grey alien machinations in our world. Dead bodies, lost jobs, broken families, clanging prison doors all follow anyone who exposes them. Bob Lazar, an American physicist who was asked to back-engineer gravity amplifiers found at a captured Grey spaceship, paid a terrible social and economic price for his courageous acts of revelation. He never worked in any job of note again. There is no Medal of Honor grand enough for him, in my opinion.

A Canadian train driver along with all the passengers on his train witnessed the crash of a UFO against a hillside. The event left debris all over the crash site, which many witnesses on the train clearly saw. The driver had to continue on to his terminal destination about an hour down the line. He did so and got on another train going back the way he came. By the time he got back to the place where he saw the crash happen a couple of hours earlier, all the debris he quite clearly saw had been cleared away, with no sign that anything had happened.

The trouble with disbelief is that if there are no aliens, if all these thousands of sightings, encounters, and abductions experienced by tens of thousands of people, some in the highest and most responsible jobs, then no witnesses can be relied on. We might as well open all the prison doors. If even one of those reports is physically or metaphysically real and actually true, it would have huge significance.

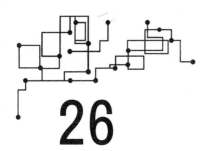

26

Melanin—A Lens to Forever

The genetic engineering of our human species was and is no easy thing to achieve for any ET alien cartel, no matter how advanced the technology they have at their disposal. Nature and naturally prevalent factors in our life-form are always immensely powerful, as they are set in a natural environmental context over millions of years—in our case, that of Earth.

The intention of the Grey roboids, in my view, is to take over our entire being through coadaptation. This involves going to the root of it all—our physical DNA, and through that, that part of us that survives beyond death. They would have to deal with our whole makeup because the abstract drivers of our nature are not available to them as a result of their total materiality. The most difficult thing technically in achieving this is gaining access to the chromosomes within the nucleus of our cells, which carry the blueprint of the complete human biological prospectus. These are coded in various arrangements of the four chemical bases—adenine, guanine, tyrosine, and cytosine—which generate proteins, the building blocks of living things. If the Greys wanted to alter our physicality they would have to alter the pattern of arrangement of these four chemical bases. To achieve this they would have to alter the sequence of these bases, which are joined together in pairs in a double helix. This alteration would provide a different format of chemical structures, which would then build tissue and bone according to a different prescription. The substitution of this different format from what is already there is what genetic engineering is all about.

But there was a big problem encountered in doing this. The cutting of the nuclear membrane that gives access to these base pairs of chromosomes in the nucleus of the cells requires the thinnest cutting edge. Genetic engineers use ultraviolet light as their cutting tool, which is conveyed by photons. When photons are used, they do not damage the chemical base pair doublets in the chromosomes. Other forms of radiation such as gamma rays damage these base pairs and can lead to mutations. However, there is a natural biological material that absorbs ultraviolet light and blunts the knife. This material is melanin, a pigment that gives our skin its tan color. In most dark-skinned people the nuclear membrane that surrounds the containment capsule of the chromosomes contains melanin granules that immediately rush into places exposed to ultraviolet light and absorb the energy of photons, destroying them and stopping their cutting power. It thus protects the chromosomes from interference.

Following is some fascinating research detailing the nature of melanin.

The distinguished biologist and geneticist Steve Jones, of the Galton Laboratory of University College, London, in his book *In the Blood: God, Genes and Destiny,* outlines a biological fact that, in my opinion, may be a plausible reason why when abductees see other abductees on ships the vast majority have white skin. Jones points out that although the number of melanocytes is the same in dark-skinned and white-skinned people, "in black skin they are mostly a surface phenomenon far more active, and the melanin granules also cluster around the nuclei of the cells in which they are found, suggesting that they play a vital part in protecting the chromosomes in the nucleus of the cell from damage by ultraviolet light."[1]

An article in the *Journal of Investigative Dermatology* reports that "this positioning of melanosomes above the nucleus serves as an exquisite protective mechanism shielding the keratinocyte nucleus from harmful ultraviolet irradiation."[2] These are known as "supranuclear caps" or "microparasols" (see Plate 15). This inbuilt protective mechanism would also prevent the use of ultraviolet light to alter gene orientation within the nuclear membrane (a standard method used to splice genes), because melanin absorbs light and reduces its power to splice gene sequences.

Much of what light is and can do is mysterious to science. We know that in all accounts of abduction cases light is described as an effect that they use to move, intercept, and induce all kinds of procedures. We have to assume that light (and this light may be seen as a kind of universal force management polarization factor) may be crucial as their means of reaching and interacting with our species. Melanin, as a dark pigment, absorbs light, as I have said. Nuclear DNA that is protected by the melanin granules that are clustered around it may therefore be safe from any alien-engendered effect that is expressed through the way they use light.

Karen Brewer, associate professor in the Department of Chemistry at Virginia Tech, has written an article in *New Scientist* that outlines the research she and her team are conducting into the possibility of light-activated anticancer drugs. Her group has created synthetic molecules that "when flooded with light, have the potential to carry out a wide range of tasks, such as synthesising useful compounds, generating clean fuels or attacking tumours." The chemicals that are used to carry out these tasks are known as supramolecules: "Chemists can mix and match the units to create supramolecules that are tailor-made for particular tasks." Brewer describes how photons could stimulate a platinum-active site in the anticancer drug Cisplatin. She outlines how the drug would be "switched on" at the tumor site by exposure to laser radiation. This would result in a strong bond between the platinum atom and the DNA bases, which would prevent the DNA unzipping and replicating and so stop the tumor cells multiplying. Brewer also explains that a "broad range of wavelengths" can be used to activate the supramolecule so that it would be possible to "tune light absorbers to capture photons at certain wavelengths." The use of light to bind a metal into DNA bases is thus illustrated here as a technology that is already within our reach. If our relatively primitive technology is capable of this, what more might the supremely advanced technologies of alien beings be capable of in their ability to use the properties of light to bind their elements into the DNA of human beings.[3]

Encounters with alien beings or their craft tend to take place at locations where there are particularly high electromagnetic fields—power stations, military bases, and the like. High electromagnetic fields also seem to be put out by the alien craft themselves, often causing widespread power failures in the areas where they appear. Melanin has also been found to have a capacity to conduct electric fields. A 1963 study reported high electrical conductivity in melanin.[4] Similarly, a 1974 investigation reported a high conductivity "on" state in a voltage-controlled solid-state threshold switch made with DOPA melanin. Melanin also shows negative resistance, a property of electronically active conductive polymers.[5] These conducting properties of melanin would allow it to act like a Faraday cage, conducting electrical fields away from the nucleus of the cell and thus preventing alien procedures from reaching the DNA in the nucleus. If high electromagnetic fields are a vehicle through which these aliens can reach humanity, then it may indeed be the case that dark-skinned people have a better natural barrier to that reach.

Steve Jones goes on to make the point that the color change from dark skin to fair skin that is believed to have taken place when migrations out of Africa brought human beings to Europe does not necessarily make sense when seen in terms of biological advantage. It is thought that this change was due to the fact that a pale skin would absorb more of the comparatively meager levels of ultraviolet light available in northern climes. The absorption of ultraviolet light is necessary, we are told, to aid in the production of vitamin D, vital for the production of strong bones and teeth, and other essential elements. Jones says that "although the idea of rickets as the driving force behind the evolution of skin colour is attractive, melanin was probably not lost because of changes in vitamin balance." He points out that "rickets is a disease of civilisation," a disease that only became common as cities grew in the Middle Ages. Even blacks need only two hours a week of sunlight to stay healthy. "At first sight," says Professor Jones, "evolution has got it wrong. If humans followed the rules that apply to other animals . . . Europeans ought to be black and Africans white," simply because dark objects absorb more of the sun's light and heat.[6] However, it is also true that blacks are able to sweat more than whites, and, says Jones, this "more than compensates for the effects of skin colour." There are also the obvious advantages of a dark skin in the tropics, which lie in its ability to protect the skin from the harmful effects of high levels of ultraviolet light. So the advantages of fair skin, no matter what the climate, are difficult to justify in evolutionary terms. However, in terms of providing an easy and efficient alien interception of the human genome, the advantages of pale skin would seem to be enormous.

A 2014 study published in the *Proceedings of the National Academy of Sciences* revealed that ancient DNA shows a rapid, dramatic change of appearance in Europe five thousand years ago based on the melanin gene. Sandra Wilde, of the Palaeogenetics Group at the Johannes Gutenberg University Institute of Anthropology, explains that "prehistoric Europeans in the region we studied would have been consistently darker than their descendants today. This is particularly interesting as the darker phenotype seems to have been preferred by evolution over hundreds of thousands of years. All our early ancestors were more darkly pigmented."[7] What impressed the research team was the fact that these pigment changes took place only very recently in evolutionary terms. "In Europe we find a particularly wide range of genetic variation in terms of pigmentation," says Karola Kirsanow, Ph.D., also of the Palaeogenetics Group, who adds, "We did not expect to find that natural selection had been favoring lighter pigmentation over the past few thousand years."[8] Human migration northward to Europe began fifty thousand years ago, so the migration itself and the resultant exposure to less sunlight is unlikely to have been the primary cause of lighter complexions. The lack of melanin is thus a relatively recent mutation that would appear to be disadvantageous to humanity but a distinct advantage to an alien interceptor hell-bent on changing human DNA to suit their purposes.

Another intriguing 2005 study reported that just one amino acid difference in the gene SLC24A5 is a key contributor to the skin color difference between Europeans and West Africans.[9] Remarkably, all instances of this gene mutation came from the chromosome of one person who most likely lived between six thousand and ten thousand years ago. This specific mutation in SLC24A5, called A111T, is found in virtually everyone of European ancestry. It is also found among some peoples in the Middle East and Indian subcontinent, but not in high numbers in Africans.[10]

So to review: Ultraviolet light is used to get through the nuclear membrane and splice chromosomes for genetic manipulation. Ultraviolet light provides the sharpest cutting mechanism possible. Melanin will absorb this light and blunt the cutting tool so crucially that it inhibits the action of genetic manipulation. So it is harder to manipulate the DNA in the chromosomes of humans with dark complexions and melanin granules surrounding the nuclear membrane. Many people with fair complexions, on the other hand, have no such protection because they lack this melanin shield around the nucleus of their cells. This is why it is overwhelmingly white people who get skin cancer and also why white people are overwhelmingly the main targets of abduction.

There is another type of melanin in the body that is present in all human beings regardless of skin color. I am referring to neuromelanin. This is the dark pigment present in the pigment-bearing neurons of four deep-brain nuclei: the substantia nigra (the pars compacta part of the substantia nigra, located in the midbrain), the locus ceruleus, the dorsal motor nucleus of the vagus nerve, and the median raphe nucleus of the pons. In Parkinson's disease there is a massive loss of dopamine-producing pigmented neurons in the substantia nigra. In advanced Alzheimer's disease there is often an almost complete loss of the norepinephrine-producing pigmented neurons of the locus ceruleus. Thus melanin in the brain appears to provide a neurological benefit that is lost when these diseases take hold. Could this also suggest that neuromelanin is responsible for allowing the human body's "antenna" to function properly? Could it be that at one time in the ancient past the entire brain was melanized, giving huge neurological advantages? The remnants of this neuromelanin would thus provide only an aftertaste of the full richness of our superior capabilities as First Adam. In addition, initial findings reported in an article in the *Journal of Investigative Dermatology* suggest that the aggregation of melanin in supranuclear caps over the nucleus of the cell seems to be specific to human cells: In humans, aggregated melanosomes are located above the nucleus of the epidermal basal cells, presenting themselves as supranuclear melanin caps for protecting the nucleus from UV-induced DNA damage. In pigmented animals, however, the existence of supranuclear melanin caps has not been clear (see Plate 15).

The majority of those who are easy prey for the Greys are taken, I believe never to be returned. They disappear without a trace because they are useful to the Greys for their long-term purposes. I believe they do it so efficiently and so covertly that we will never know who has been converted by them—perhaps a homeless person here or there is taken, or someone with no family ties. There are an alarming two million or so men, women, and children who are reported missing each year in Europe alone as I write this. Of these, approximately 35 percent are never accounted for. It's impossible to give a reliable figure because every source has its own criterion on which they judge this. What I am about to suggest may sound alarmist and extreme, but then seventy or so years ago, before the alien abduction scenario became apparent with the seemingly outlandish procedures it involves, no one would have believed such a thing was possible. Many of course don't believe it now. Yet millions of witnesses testify now to their veracity. It is my contention that a sizeable number of these people who go missing all over the world may well be funding a supply of DNA for the new breeds of hybridized entities that are, in turn, carefully nurtured by these synthetic roboidal entities.

Acquiring and altering DNA, wherever it comes from, would be essential and the need ongoing; they couldn't simply replicate old samples, as these would not have the same potency for life and survival as the newly gathered samples would. Entropy would see to that. The final purpose of all of this would be the harvesting of suitable human DNA from a natural, soul-bearing being. This would be the magical elixir that they're looking for—that nonphysical element, the soul, that allows human beings to live beyond physical death—and have sought in vain for that essential ingredient with no way of knowing it was inaccessible to them as purely physical entities. They would need a constantly updated supply of DNA that would inform them of the current status of their experiment. Altered DNA combined with their programs of information was their target. They have been getting closer with time to the best model for this.

Perhaps you can now see why technology has become so pervasive, such that information is being gathered about every person on the planet. I also have my suspicions about why certain religious sects such as the Mormons are gathering as much information as possible about everyone on the planet, ostensibly to baptize them. For what kind of God are they baptizing? The one whose son was Jesus, or the one who spoke out of a burning bush through a laser "trumpet" and set the bush on fire in the process? The former said a single act of true faith in God would deliver you to eternal life; the other demanded an eye for an eye and a tooth for a tooth, and the culling of thousands for the inheritance of a Promised Land.

Though the vast majority of abductees are pale-skinned, if reincarnation is true, then we are all likely to have had previous lifetimes with all the different skin tones. It is more a matter of your demeanor, your behavior toward others, that determines whether these synthetic roboids will make use of you. Your skin tone is just a means of access to enable them to change your demeanor into something more machine-minded. That's what they're finally after—a change that they can make use of once you have passed beyond life into the frames of death, a process I will describe in detail in a later chapter.

The most genetically fit human beings on our planet are produced by mixed-race partnerships. The more genetically different the parents are from each other, the stronger the gene prospectus of their offspring. The biological term for this is *hybrid vigor,* and it is something that farmers, horticulturalists, and scientists have known for many years and used to their advantage. A person with two identical copies of a gene is described as homozygotic for that gene, while someone who has two copies that differ is described as heterozygotic for that gene. Basically, if you have two identical copies of the same gene, then it is more likely that if that gene mutates, both copies will mutate. This can result in serious health problems. However, with less related partners, the number of genes that are identical by descent is reduced, and with it the chance that a gene has two mutant copies. In other words, every mutant copy has a much better chance of finding itself partnered with a good copy. Heterozygosity also gives a greater scope of genes to adapt to the demands of any particular environment. So in classic evolutionary terms one would expect human beings to have a biologically generated urge to mix races to increase the fitness of the species for survival. Yet among so many of us, the opposite is true, especially among white Europeans.

The primary biological drive should be to mix races for the best chances of survival for the species. It should be to strengthen the natural DNA complement, and not to weaken it, something the Greys would have to do to carry out their agenda. Heterozygosity saves, but homozygocity is the imperative for racial or sectarian purity, which promotes an inbred, homozygotic, and genetically weakened population. It is a deliberate practice of certain religious and cultural cartels. Where does this unnatural imperative come from? Could it be that some among us have been programmed by alien experimenters and redesigners of our natural DNA to keep certain groups of humanity separate so as to preserve the integrity of an experiment? This may provide a clue as to what racism and tribalism is really all about. How ironic that it is the racists and tribalists who will inadvertently take themselves out by clinging to their misguided ideas about racial purity. I cannot help feeling that their soul's destiny eventually lies as ape in some "Planet of the Apes" among the billions out there, one nanosecond after they die.

According to geneticist James Wilson, the European population, which by and large traces its origins to Cro-Magnon man, is one of the most homozygotic cultures in the world. This is because it stems from the most recent population to leave Africa and therefore has had less time to establish a diverse genetic base from its original hundred or so descendants. It goes without saying that the most heinous forms of racism originate from this group; the colonial legacy of the "white man's burden" throughout the world speaks for itself. So let's now take a closer look at the overwhelming evidence that suggests why the Greys are preoccupied with the white European genotype.

In David Jacobs's book *The Threat: Revealing the Secret Alien Agenda,* abductee Allison Reed was shown the aliens' ideal scenario. As Jacobs recounts, "she was brought into a room with other abductees and shown on a large screen like device 'a beautiful park scene with people having picnics and playing ball.' Her extraordinary recollection is a profoundly detailed description of the aliens' plans for a perfect future. She is asked to distinguish hybrids from normal human beings among families in a park. She notes that in the park, 'they're all white.'"[11]

In Allison's other abduction experience she was taken by an alien escort to a "museum room," where she saw

artefacts on shelves along with strange, life-sized holograms of several beings. Her alien escort explained what these figures represented and why the hybridization was undertaken.

Each of the hologram figures had a "flaw" of some sort. The first had alien features with distinctive black eyes and a thin body; it also had a distended stomach with boil-like protuberances on it. The next hologram looked more human. He had blond hair and human-like eyes, but he had no genitals, and his skin was extremely pale, like that of a "borderline albino." The final hologram was a grouping of smaller beings, about five feet tall. They were very white, and Allison received the impression that they were mentally weak or something.[12]

In another excellent book by Jacobs, *Secret Life: Firsthand Documented Accounts of UFO Abductions,* a female abductee describes how she was shown a hybrid baby and asked to hold it and hug it. Jacob asked her about the skin color of the baby: "Does it have light skin or dark skin, within the Caucasian range?" Her answer: "Fair. Quite fair. I think it is very fair, as a matter of fact. Almost like no ultraviolet light for this guy."[13]

It appears the Greys are interested in something in the living state that is nonphysical. It took me some time to see what this is. It is beyond a shadow of a doubt that throughout history, though white people are outnumbered four to one in our world, Western, pale-skinned Europeans have, sadly, proved to be the greatest destroyers of the planet in history, both in terms of wars, genocide of nonwhite peoples, and destruction of the environment. Native peoples, on the other hand, have by and large worked in harmony with nature, with comparably little violence. This makes them more spiritually evolved. Crucially, they have the highest amount of the pigment melanin, too. These two factors provide a plausible explanation for why these alien interlopers home in on white people and want to rid the planet of all nonwhite peoples—white people as a group have historically demonstrated the kind of aggressive, domineering demeanor that suits the Greys' purposes, and they have less melanin, as previously explained.

Clearly, racism and xenophobia will be our downfall if we don't course-correct. I understand why the great spiritual teachers warned us repeatedly, some at the cost of their own lives, that we make our own future hell with each negative act we practice and endorse, and conversely we ensure our eternal life if our demeanor and actions are largely positive. By positive I mean the resolve to seek unity, cohesion, forgiveness, tolerance, and compassion at all times. These qualities reflect our connection to the Godhead. Remember, nonlife-bearing entities, being material, are subject to the dividing, breaking-up, randomizing, chaotic power of the second law of thermodynamics, while soul-endowed living beings have a connection to the Godhead. That, quite literally, is our saving grace.

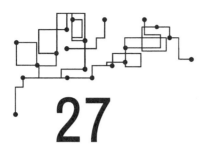

27

Making a Monkey of a Man

It would seem to be the case, as I have explained, that we are devolving, moving toward our apelike nature, and not evolving, and that devolution is being accelerated by the Grey aliens. Just look at any animal behavior, primates included. In the interest of survival their responses to anything are overwhelmingly reactive. A shadow on the ground may be that of a leaf or the stripes or spots of a tiger or a leopard. An animal decides quickly and superficially, without any deep mental analysis. This reactivity is based on the eye and the ear, the nose and the texture or taste, what and how something looks. Racists decide this way, too. In an instant, the color of a person's skin decides how you will respond to that person. To me this is an indication that you're heading in the direction of reincarnating down-station from your present species—you will devolve to the next lower adjacent species.

All those predominantly white, well-manicured corporate heads who secretly dread their daughters marrying or consorting with non-whites have no knowledge of the heterozygotic and homozygotic principle in biology. They would actually do better in the genetic survival stakes if their daughters mated with nonwhites and those of different genetic strains. It is a fact that when you breed from a smaller sample of similar genetic profiles your genetic strength diminishes. You are more likely to pick up weakened recessive gene resolutions from this smaller caucus, which might cause inherited diseases to pass on in your future family line. This is why closed groups who only reproduce with partners from within their own ethnic or religious group often have common inherited genetic conditions based on both mother and father having the same genetic weakness.

But racism at its root is a condition of the individual mind. Many of us know someone like this in our own family. They have a mind that cannot cope with differences, be it skin color, gender, ethnicity, or culture. In fact, if you look deeper into the psychology of a racist you will find that these people also tend to be homophobic and sexist. It is a sociological phenomenon of immense importance because this kind of person seeks division among our human family and kinship strictly among those of their own self-identified group. Many psychologists believe this is a pathological condition. Racists and bigots, be they neo-Nazis or members of the alt-right, are the true human detritus of our planet, usually having simplistic minds akin to that of apes. In fact, I would back the baboons for having a higher quantum of intelligence and empathy. Could this type of human being have been intercepted or had their family ancestral line intercepted by an ET genetic resource sometime in the past? That past could include previous lifetimes, because we tend to reincarnate into previous closely related associations. The likelihood for people such as these is that they will reincarnate downward because their divisive minds follow according to the second law of thermodynamics, breaking down toward chaotic disbursement, and the next species step down for humans is the simian.

If we can all trace our origins back to an original state of perfect harmony and union in the Godverse, what happened to us to allow such callousness and bigotry to develop? What are the origins of self-centeredness, aggression, jealousy, and ruthlessness? How did we lose the empathy and compassion that should be natural to us based on our original roots in the Godverse?

I believe that back in time it was the Greys who intercepted our natural connection to the Godverse. By merging their information with ours, they interfered with our holistic, more expansive, and more altruistic way of thinking and acting. When this happened, we and species like us in other locations in the universe devolved into a more narrow-minded and self-centered state, as seen in many examples, including the following.

A 2012 article in the *Journal of Medical Ethics* maintains that newborn babies are not actual persons and do not have a moral right to life: "The moral status of an infant is equivalent to that of a fetus in the sense that both lack those properties that justify the attribution of a right to life to an individual." The article states that they are "potential," not "actual," persons.[1] This point of ethics was under discussion with a view toward how it might guide decisions made either to help prolong the lives of severely disabled newborns or simply to allow them to die. That a leading medical journal would justify the latter, with the assertion that newborns are not actual persons, suggests that some of us are no different from the Grey roboidal machines that are preying on us.

Journalist George Monbiot, in the *Guardian,* makes the telling observation that

> those in power don't speak of "people" or "killing"—it helps them do their job. And we are picking up their dehumanising euphemisms. To blot people out of existence first you must blot them from your mind. Then you can persuade yourself that what you are doing is moral and necessary. Today this isn't difficult. Those who act without compassion can draw upon a system of thought and language whose purpose is to shield them—and blind us—to the consequences.[2]

He cites the language on the website for the U.K.'s Department of Work and Pensions, which "describes disabled people entering the government's work programme for between three and six months as '3/6Mth stock.' [The word *stock* implies that they are dehumanized and viewed as a usable physical resource.] The department's delivery plan recommends using 'credit reference agency data to cleanse the stock of fraud and error.'"[3]

Monbiot goes on to point out that Israeli military commanders as well as President Obama's counterterrorism adviser justified the massacre of more than 2,300 civilian Palestinian men, women, and children in Gaza during the summer of 2014 as "mowing the lawn," while drone pilots described their victims as "bug splats." The article decribes how the U.S. Army used white phosphorous—a weapon banned by the Chemical Weapons Convention—on the Iraqi city of Falluja in November 2004 to kill and maim ordinary people taking refuge in houses and trenches as part of the Army's "Shake 'n Bake" strategy (their jargon) the idea being to "flush people out with phosphorus, then kill them with high explosives. Shake 'n Bake is a product made by Kraft Foods for coating meat with breadcrumbs before cooking it."[4] This refers to the fact that white phosphorus is fat soluble. Even small crumbs of it bore through living tissue on contact, destroying mucous membranes, blinding people and shredding their lungs.

The U.S. Army and Air Force routinely kill children in their wars with Muslim countries, using remote-controlled drones operating in the U.S., thousands of miles away from combat zones. Civilian deaths are considered "collateral damage," a term that has entered the mainstream lexicon.

A noteworthy piece of research was done by one of our greatest scientists who has now sadly passed on, neuroscientist Paul MacLean, of the Laboratory of Brain Evolution and Behavior, part of the National Institute of Mental Health. MacLean hypothesized that we basically have three distinct brains acting as one in our body. He called it the *triune brain,* and his research was an attempt to reconcile rational human behavior with our more violent, irrational side. The three distinct "brains," which correspond to three distinct behavioral modes, are the neocortex, the limbic system, and the R-complex (for "reptilian").[5] Interestingly, despite the overall shrinkage in the size of the human brain, there has been growth in the size of the cerebellum, the most primitive, reactive part of the brain, which houses the R-complex. Reptiles are cold, violent entities that behave according to primitive emotions. So any ideas that humankind is evolving into a species centered on the higher, neocortex functions of the advanced brain (which governs our ability to reason and think holistically) are without foundation. If the advanced part of the brain, the neocortex, is more a feature of the past brain than the present brain, then what does this say about the premise that we are evolving into betterment? Startling though it might be, is it possible that humans, and indeed all species, came from an original lineage in which the brain acted as an antenna for picking up a grander, more comprehensive field of knowledge, including a spiritual scale of information most of us can no longer access? This earlier, more highly conscious brain had incredible abilities to manipulate physical matter as a function of an empowered mind. So we are the inheritors of loss, not gain.

If, as I have suggested, monkeys are devolved forms of prior hominid species, then how is this reflected in the nature of a chimp? Astonishingly, a study at the Kyoto University, Japan, has demonstrated that young chimps can outperform humans at a cognitive task. Three adult female chimps, their three five-year-old offspring, and university student volunteers were tested on their ability to memorize the numbers 1 to 9 appearing at random locations on a touchscreen monitor. Using an ability akin to photographic memory, the young chimps were able to memorize the location of the numerals with far better accuracy than humans performing the same task. During the test, the numerals appeared on the screen for 650, 430, or 210 milliseconds and were then replaced by blank white squares. The chimps showed an astonishing ability to remember the locations with almost 100 percent accuracy, even at the shortest duration, which does not leave enough time for the eye to move and scan the screen. This suggests that they use a kind of photographic memory. Primatologist Tetsuro Matsuzawa, who led the study, emphasizes that the chimps in the study are by no means special—all chimps can perform like this, he says. He concludes that not only do we underestimate chimpanzee intelligence, but we humans are in fact 98.77 percent chimpanzee ourselves.[6]

This research illustrates a remarkable hypothesis I'm going to venture: I believe that, strangely, chimpanzees are closer to artificially intelligent roboidal entities than we are as human beings. Memory and the ability to sort and sequence are capacities that are perfected in AI. The ability to intelligently sort and sequence information is, as research shows, no sign of difference from our primate cousins, and in fact the number-sequencing experiments suggest that they are in some respects more efficient at this than we are. Could this be because chimpanzees are the end result of alien genetic interception of a previous hominid line?

So how do we differ? What do we have that chimps and AI do not have? What breaks up our short-term memory circuit? Matsuzawa suggests that our language skills may have replaced memory skills. But why would one skill replace another unless it was interfered with in some way? Could it be that whereas chimps and AI machines can focus in on small places in fine detail, our focus is broader and wider, taking in far more of the whole picture?

In another study, Alicia Melis of the Max Planck Institute conducted an experiment in which a chimpanzee in a cage was given the option of opening the door to another chimpanzee in an adjacent cage to help him pull in a plank containing two trays of food. Two ropes were tied to the plank, but tied so far apart that the chimp could not pull in the plank on his own. When Melis put food in both trays so both chimps could eat, there was cooperation. However, when only one side of the tray contained food, the chimp who asked for help took all the food rather than sharing it, while the second chimp refused to help the next time food was given. This was repeated several times with different chimps. Thus the chimps demonstrated cooperation, but only for selfish gain.[7] The National Geographic channel presented this research with the suggestion that human beings, unlike chimps, are capable of cooperation without the motive of selfish gain. This research illustrates an unexpected similarity between artificial intelligence and apes in sorting, sequencing, and memory while also highlighting a crucial difference between apes and *some* human beings: the capacity for unselfishness. So the chimps would seem to share similarities with the Greys, both in their lack of conscience and in their advanced abilities in memory, sorting, and sequencing. I remember as a child hearing Dr. Jane Goodall's soothing words about chimps in her TV documentaries, words any mother would use to describe her own children. The primates' true nature was later found to be a marked contradiction of her initial views. The chimp is a violent, vicious, ruthless, tribal animal. Perhaps in chimps we are witnessing a preview of what *Homo sapiens sapiens'* next devolution might be. I believe chimps have devolved from another hominid line, but our human ape may be very similar.

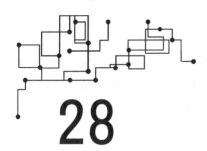

28

Biblical Parallels

In my research I have found that alien interference on our planet is based not only on advanced technology and the exigencies of highly sophisticated machines posing as gods. At its heart its roots are found in the Bible, of all things. It includes at its very heart a purpose based on philosophical perspectives that have a bed in our very nature as living beings and our history as a living species and, most importantly, of all the very nature of the thinking and envisioning processes. The big deal here is: How much of what we know about religious theosophy and those that expounded upon it is objectively true and verifiable and outside simple claim and belief? How much of it is altered with recourse to human imagination, obfuscations, misinterpretations, and deliberate manipulations of the pure invective given by the great originators themselves and hijacked for the installation of the custodians own ambitions for controlling others? If any of it is an actual objective reporting of events that actually happened, then what is the explanation for so-called Divine Revelation involving miracles and mind over matter? Was it human thought control using purely technological means, or was it something beyond the scales of an enforced universe and its physical material makeup, something that lay beyond the Margins of Forever?

The Judeo-Christian record as cataloged in the Old and New Testaments underlies the beliefs of nearly two and a half billion people and is the dominant theology of the Western world. The Bible says we are descendants of a first being, Adam. Most Christians take the Old

Testament along with the New as a source of divine authority. But this is very curious, as it would appear to be based on a contradiction. The Old Testament speaks of a moral thesis that totally contradicts the New Testament, with two different Gods heading the cast. The Old Testament God promulgates a God with the ethos of "an eye for an eye and a tooth for a tooth," a straight, black-and-white, no shades of grey (pardon the pun) moral code that extols murder, revenge, vanity, and the sufferance of followers and demands complete supplication and worship of a deity who rules with the uncompromising iron glove of omnipotent power. The New Testament, on the other hand—at least in the parables of the four gospels that claim to report the direct words of Christ—promulgates a divine source that encourages love, togetherness of all elements, forgiveness, mercy, and compassion as the foundation of correct behavior. And unlike the Old Testament, this encouragement is on a voluntary rather than a dictated-to basis. There are elements of the New Testament, notably in the writings of Paul, that to a certain extent contradict the new ethos and are more akin to the Old Testament. The apostle Paul never met Jesus. However, the first four gospels, which are recorded as Jesus's own words as heard by witnesses, are perhaps more likely to be representative of his actual teachings. Many of these teachings are the opposite of much of what the Old Testament God is purported to have said and done.

In my previous two books in this series I suggested that the Old Testament God resembles more of a God or authority figure who has nothing to do with the light-space reality beyond atoms, and far more to do with the heavy-space reality of the Grey aliens. This throws the Creation story, as described in Genesis, into a different light.

The Adam of the Hebrew ancestral line is an interesting premise if it refers to an actual singular event. Could the story of the Garden of Eden reflect knowledge that's been passed down through thousands of years of oral and written history of laboratory procedures set up by an ET alien horde to produce a new, genetically tweaked genus from their already engineered stock on this planet? This would have been a long exercise, beginning hundreds of thousand years ago, to prepare a species of living beings on this Earth for programmed machine codes to walk into humans by proxy. This would have been a purely utilitarian process that would move in stages, some taking thousands of years. At each stage they would take stock of their results, their design experiments, to improve on them and move on.

The most recent stage and most important of all the genetic alterations perhaps coincides with the Hebrew story of the creation of Adam and Eve. Using precise calculations made by biblical scholars based on the dates and times given in the Old Testament, this creation is said to have happened six thousand years ago. We know that recent research has shown that the gene mutation that led to paler complexions came from a gene mutation in a chromosome of one person who most likely lived between six thousand and ten thousand years ago. Is this merely coincidence? If not, could the Old Testament's catalog of the Creation allude to this newly converted form of humanity that was ready and prepped for alien interception? If such is the case, then the biblical Adam and Eve and their two sons, Cain and Abel, may well mark the most recent hybridization project of a breeding experiment conducted by the Greys that goes back perhaps as much as seven million years.

The biochemically driven physical transformations from living being to machine carried out eons ago proved limited. The melanin factor that I have previously described was an impossible barrier for whole DNA gene manipulation for thousands of millennia. Only partial structural changes to the human format were achieved during that time. They required more comprehensive changes in which the connection between mind and matter could somehow be made. Then something fortuitous for the Greys happened through a spontaneous mutation they found in a hominid albino six thousand years ago. This mutation allowed the Grey interlopers into human chromosomes more easily. The ETs then had the means to retune the antennas of hominids on this planet to receive their signals and incorporate them into their natural biological format. In doing this they found their philosopher's stone.

The Bible story may be an analogy for an ongoing scenario through epochal time of genetic marking. The "mark" that was "set upon" Cain may well refer to the production of a fair-skin complexion, signifying a point of easier access to the chromosomes for alterations by the Grey ETs. The biblical account of the mark of Cain may well be a reference to the genetic mutation found in virtually everyone with European ancestry, and remarkably this mutation in the human genome appeared at the same time the Creation story dates back to.

The Old Testament description of the marking of Cain as a punishment for murder is strangely contradicted when that mark was then purportedly used by God to protect Cain from harm. Curious to say the least. Why would you want to protect someone who is isolated and demarcated as a punishment for murder? Why not just take him out completely? After all, this was a vindictive God, one who in later parts of the Old Testament advocates the mass killing of even innocents in the taking of the so-called Promised Land.

So approximately six thousand years ago there was a breakthrough in the Greys' genetic experiments on hominids on this planet, which bred two distinct personality types: Cain and Abel. Out of all these derivational hybrids, in Cain they finally produced a natural type with all the attributes of a nonempathetic personality, one that was congruent with their own outlook of a nonemotional machine-mindedness. I believe the Grey aliens bred individuals whose nature enabled a better chance for physical survival, and these qualities fit the bill. A vain, ruthless, devious, killer form of genetically engineered human would also be very useful for them in the future administration of this planet. Such a human hybrid would have to be isolated to keep it as a breeding platform for a group whose chromosomes could be more easily adjusted because no melanin granules guarded their nuclear membranes from penetration with ultraviolet cutters.

We thus have strong indications that within the European/Hebrew/Caucasian hive of humanity there may be a special genotype whose DNA is accessible for the Greys' purposes. There are also opposite types within this group that cannot be accessed easily for these genetic machinations. They may not have all the inherent psychological qualities associated with the mark of Cain because their inherent thinking cannot be changed by physical manipulation alone. Could it be what many of the abductions are about? The alien roboids are constantly checking for suitability for their purposes, and in some cases how their experimental breed is progressing in real time and in real living situations. Some abductees may represent a genetic anomaly within the European/Caucasian compendium that is resistant to extraterrestrial manipulation, and so they are looking at them because they want to know why that is so. Some abductees, because they are returned, may thus be blessed as no-go areas for ET machinations and left alone. Others who have been repeatedly abducted might be fitted with implants that are designed to see if they might be changed for the purposes of the Greys. In many cases they are abandoned as unsuitable and are never abducted again. The ones we have to be concerned about are those who are abducted and never returned.

The Grey ET "gods" had a dilemma. In the two sons of Adam, Cain and Abel, they had two distinct types of genetically derived human personalities. Each had to be considered for its survival capacity on an Earth full of physical dangers. The hybrids had to be left to get on with life on Earth as independently from Grey management as possible because it was the only way that any unwanted anomalies to long-term survival could be seen progressing naturally and bred out of the stock when spotted. The alien creators would have had to settle for the marked Cain breed after the so-called first murder, for the obvious reason that this was a breed that has no compunction to kill and take another's inheritance—a characteristic of certain groups of humanity throughout history.

The Abel types, who were less susceptible to alien interference, would dilute the concentration of alien-intercepted breeding stock within the gene pool. They may have proved more difficult to alter genetically. The killer Cain genotype was the ideal mechanism to wipe out these Abel types, and the aliens may well be using their descendants this way to this day. The roots of the whole sorry history of racially motivated human depravity, including white colonialism over nonwhites through the use of violence, may well lie here. Particular names in history that stand out for these kinds of racially motivated actions include Clive, Cortez, Pizarro, Alexander the Great, and Hitler, as well as our more modern equivalents.

Of course it wasn't just one murder. Many followed the first one. It was perhaps a genocidal culling to further a eugenic purpose, just as their descendants favored certain breeds, such as the neo-Nazis have done since. There is evidence to suggest that Hitler and his gang met with aliens at a place called Externsteine, in Germany, before the whole rollout of the Second World War. So it makes sense that the killer impulse enshrined in the Cain archetype implies a strong command instinct. It also implies a strong self-centeredness, along with competitiveness, aggression, and combativeness, which further implies ritual and deceit and a strong tribal sense. These qualities are ideal for survival and for preserving the integrity of the reengineered human.

In time, the Cain types became more easily identifiable by their fair complexion. The rest of the ET alien genetically engineered prospectus then bred with other types of humanity on the planet. This produced a hybrid human: the Seth type, the replacement for the Abel archetype. Souls coming into these biological lines would face interruptions to their reception of the full signal of the Godverse, which the Abel lines would not have faced, but these were nowhere near as significant as those faced by souls coming into the Cain lines. The Greys moved these lines, their experimental group, away from the rest of humanity to avoid dilution of their concentrated alien genetic "juice." They moved their favored breed to northern latitudes, to the Land of Nod, east of Eden, where this breed prospered to become the command species on Earth today. These are the ancestors of the Vikings, Saxons, Picts, Jutes, Goths, Visigoths, Huns, and Mongols. Racial hostility has been the cause of more than seven thousand significant conflicts over the past two thousand years, accounting for hundreds of millions of needless deaths worldwide. These credentials, dare I say it, generally describe white people of European descent—which accounts for more than 90 percent of abductees.

The historical record has disparate evidence concerning violence and its global effects. Careful research into the record with a look at the most significant social and political effects and trends that conflict has caused confirms that peoples of the northern latitudes of Europe have had the most scathing effect on all of humanity. They have demonstrated it through countless wars, the subjugation of native peoples, stealing whole continents, and systematizing colonialism and slavery all over the world. It is the nearest parody of the Grey roboids, with the same kind of unemotional machine-minded ruthlessness these aliens show their abducted victims when they do experiments on them without asking their permission and without any regard to the suffering their victims go through.

If those of white European descent are prime targets for the Greys, most of them haven't a clue about it, and no warning that I am providing here is likely to be heeded by them. It is more likely that vanity and racially motivated thinking will disallow any recognition of the historical record.

The following is an account in the apocryphal Book of Enoch, which indicates that Noah may have been an albino.

1 After a time, my son Methuselah took a wife for his son Lamech. 2 She became pregnant by him, and brought forth a child, the flesh of which was as white as snow, and red as a rose; the hair of whose head was white like wool, and long; and whose eyes were beautiful. When he opened them, he illuminated all the house, like the sun; the whole house abounded with light. 3 And when he was taken from the hand of the midwife, Lamech his father became afraid of him; and flying away came to his own father Methuselah, and said, I have begotten a son, unlike to other children. He is not human; but, resembling the offspring of the angels of heaven, is of a different nature from ours, being altogether unlike to us. 4 His eyes are bright as the rays of the sun; his countenance glorious, and he looks not as if he belonged to me, but to the angels. 5 I am afraid, lest something miraculous should take place on Earth in his days. (1 Enoch 106)

It seems that Noah not only lacked melanin, but he also seemed to be not exactly human. So it would seem that he was some form of hybrid. The unusual nature of this child was so marked that his father, Methuselah, was said to be afraid of him. This lends a whole new meaning to the story of Noah and his ark. Could the ark and its animals representing all the species on the planet describe an alien-sponsored genetic experiment? Did they, for their own reasons, wish to clear Earth of all previous experiments and preserve this one to work on in isolation? If so, did they cause the deluge that led to the Great Flood? Or if the deluge was a natural phenomenon, perhaps caused by a comet or meteorite hitting the planet, did they choose to protect their ongoing project with Earth's species? These are intriguing questions that I will leave up in the air for now, but they are worth a deeper investigation.

The Greys are thus watching genetic lines more and more pervasively on the planet today. A scan of the media shows how well they might be doing. I believe the modern conveniences we all take for granted are bestowed on us by these deadly roboids and their hybrid agents among us as a means of monitoring our every move. And we hand this ability over to them on a silver platter by joining the global social networks and buying and keeping on our person all the ancillary technology that enables them to monitor us. I, for one, have never owned a cell phone, never used one, and never will.

All humans on Earth were highly melanized in the past until the white albinoid Cain types came along. Their different-colored complexion would be instantly recognizable, a "mark" that differentiated them from everyone else. If the nominal Cain represents the original albino African humans that the Greys were first able to work on, then the next generation of this mark I believe is what Matthew 17:7 describes in the words "Then Jesus answered and said, O faithless and perverse generation, how long shall I be with you? How long shall I suffer you?" This generation can be traced to about six thousand years ago, in the Hebrew ethos in our neck of the woods, the Levant. The Grey ETs have always found our Earth a hostile place, dangerous to their agenda. From all the evidence provided by abductees, they are actually physically fragile.

That is why they're seen so rarely. They may also have a problem with their technology in terms of the geophysics of Earth itself and the differences from where they come. All this will of course be known to those human hybrids on our planet who are their allies. There is no doubt that there has to be a corporate power that is doing this and doing it very well. They cannot allow themselves to be seen or identified as the cause of all our troubles. I am convinced they have been and are using natal hybrids—that is, heavily genetically engineered human beings—as fronts to deal with the world and hide them from it. These human hybrids may be relatively few in number, but they hold the highest positions in the administration of our planet's affairs.

The quest of the Grey ET cartel on Earth has been going on for eons. Their interception of our planet as an all-encompassing exercise is at the very root of our human biological prospectus, our DNA. Like good guerilla fighters, they intercept when they have to alter something significant in our genes and then merge into the background and wait and watch and manage us remotely while watching their effects over generations. I am also convinced that they and their craft are vulnerable in some way to some naturally occurring phenomena on Earth. There is a great deal of evidence, discovered and then obfuscated, that their primary hiding places on the planet are beneath the earth, both terrestrially and under water. They crash for some reason, then the cover-ups are employed, with their human agents here going into action.

On January 22, 2012, at the McDonald Observatory in West Texas, NASA consultant Eric Norton detected a group of unidentified spacecraft by using the facility's wide-range systems. "What I saw was an array of massive, three dimensional black structures in space, in a straight line formation, advancing in the direction of planet Earth." Within months the objects "moved millions upon millions of miles" closer to Earth.[1] According to Norton, spectroscopy data suggests that the mysterious UFOs were built with materials that are thousands of times harder than anything humankind has been able to develop on Earth. Their size, according to analysis, was staggering. The objects were monitored as they crossed the solar system, and by January of the following year the UFO fleet had already passed the orbit of Mars and were heading directly toward Earth. Then, all of a sudden, the objects mysteriously vanished.

Unidentified flying craft have frequently been seen emerging from under bodies of water and flying at great speeds in very cold, icy areas of our planet, such as the Arctic and Antarctic. They have been reported emerging from bodies of water on land, too. Reports from around the world suggest that sightings of variously shaped craft are fleeting, and they always seem to escape evidential reach unless they crash, as was the case in the now famous Roswell incident. But generally speaking they do not hang around if they can help it. Their superior intelligence and functions of physicality seem to be able to manipulate species like ours. It is to this end that they fine-tune certain genotypes they have chosen as the best versions of humanity, those with the highest technologically developed genotype. This type of human has used their technology to dominate the world through ruthlessness, belligerence, and violence, with disastrous effects for the whole planet.

The interception of humanity by Grey aliens over millennia has left us with a dominant genetically altered genotype that is more akin to a biological machine than a glorified living being who thinks with the heart instinctively, in ways that unify and bring together the disparate. The leading genotypes now do the opposite. The question is inevitable: Is there a form of human being that has done this over countless years and done it more effectively than any other form, such that it has come to control our world in contemporary times? Could this account for the belligerence, combativeness, and conquest in such evidence today? As I have said, one form of humanity seems to fit the bill: white people of European descent.

These apparently strange and admittedly bizarre conclusions have been carefully vetted over the years, with the evidence of thousands of eyewitness reports on UFOs, scientific papers, and secret government documents opened through the Freedom of Information Acts both in the U.K. and abroad. The Grey–human interface that sponsors racism in the affairs of humankind as the final sociological arbitration point for our survival as a species was not apparent to me in the vivid way it is now. This emboldens me to warn that those with suitable demelanized skin tones may well be the final human target for this pack of extraterrestrial roboidal pirates and their agenda here on this planet. Indeed, any planet where they can produce a custom-made living format that can hold information programs in both states, life and death, through a faculty we call the soul, provides the creators of those programs with the power to access the whole universe beyond what is demarcated by Einstein's law of relativity. This allows them to beat force, time, and space and access an eternal frame of existence of limitless possibilities.

In the distant past, humankind lived collectively and far more peacefully and cooperatively than modern humans do. They had to. Their survival depended on cooperation when faced with the dangers of the wild when they had only sticks and stones to fight them off. The introduction of various forms of technology gradually, over time, which coincided with the arrival of the Greys, has eroded humankind's relative freedom to be and to know who they truly are such that the very under-base of all existentiality—*to be there to know in the best and highest maxims of knowing*—is denied catastrophically. Bizarre though it may seem to some in the so-called civilized world, the supposedly primitive original people of Australia (a.k.a., Aborigines), or the Bushmen of the African Kalahari, sitting together by a campfire with their strong, cooperative sense of unity with one another and their natural surroundings, have more of a sense of the human being's natural connection to eternity, to the Divine, and to all things spiritual—and thus to what lies beyond the atom—than some technocrat proudly displaying a MacDonnell Douglas F/A-18 jet fighter. Some readers might question my choice of the word *bizarre* to describe what they know to be obvious. They are in the minority in our materialist world. The technocrats are a new kind of being, straight out of the Grey's cesspool. This begs the awful question: Are your children and mine to be inexorably sucked into a vortex of microprocessors, winking lights, and diodes that one day will produce a being that can no longer cry real tears? Sadly, there are too many among us now, I fear, particularly in the halls of science, who will exclaim "Hurrah!" to that awful future.

A single glance under the lid of the Pandora's box of our contemporary human condition will reveal truths that many of us don't want to see, truths I can honestly say I resisted seeing myself at first. I did not close my eyes, however; I opened them—not to my plight but to the plight of my children and grandchildren. That was the strongest possible motivation I could have had to delve into this dark subject. If the evidence of the packaged bodies found in ET spacecraft by abductees is anything to go by—they were almost all fairer skinned humanity—this might imply a catastrophe for some of the Euro Caucasian cartel of our gross human family if they particularly are the plaything of these droids. Extinguished as expendable fodder for the hopeless imperatives of a cartel of pseudomachines from the stars. That would surely be a fitting eulogy for a universe that exists to no purpose whatsoever if materialists are right. But why are we here to know this if it is all to no purpose? Can Schrödinger's cat really die? That is what matters.

Even in a once spiritual country like India, the legacy of the Greys, who arrived millennia ago in vimanas, the mercury-powered spacecraft described in ancient Hindu scriptures, is quite apparent. If you look from far above in the sky at the Himalayas, which define the northernmost boundary of the most sacred ancient land in the world, they would look like a smooth, white goat track. It must have been so for the odd "god" in his flying vimana. The myths and fancies that color people's imagination in this part of the world have been essential to their development as a civilization. India once let the spirit soar to the heights long, long ago, like the highest mountains in the world. It has, alas, been going downhill since that golden age, running away from true human freedom, awash in technology, the magnificence of a true human being reduced to an obscene caste system based on skin color. The supposed advantages of the loss of melanin point to an alien agenda. The nondescript nihilism of alien serpents and lizards counted even India's ways in the ways of the occidental man—in the binary code.

I believe, as I have made clear in the foregoing chapters, that something horrendous happened to the collective mental disposition of humankind as a result of the ET alien genetic interception that set a pattern of Cain-like thinking. Could that have happened when the synthetic ET entities we call the Greys introduced their machinelike program into the genes of certain people? If so, it has left its imprint of doom on humanity that has continued to this day, and if we do nothing about it, it will continue toward its inevitable conclusion, when our species is no longer recognizable. If I am wrong about all this then little harm will be done to anyone by suggesting this scenario. But what if I'm right?

Achieving this has taken a long time, and it has been a long road these aliens have traveled to get to this point. What these roboids might be after is not of a material nature, though. They could have had all they wanted in material terms by taking out the world's war machines at a stroke with their supreme technology. Minerals and elements are replete throughout the universe, and mining them would be easy with their technology. And I don't buy the "let's make a slave world of humans so we can use them to be our celestial miners" proposition of some writers. Even if humans could manufacture technology to do this, why wouldn't an alien form that makes our intellects look no better than ants not have the means to automate and dispatch whatever they want, anywhere they want? Theirs is a facile technology that has about as much existential value as the physical universe itself does. And that is the clue that gave me the idea as to why they are here and what they may want from us when anything material or technological is already theirs. It has to be something we have as natural living beings that they do not have as synthetic beings—a line of connection to the eternality of the light-space reality. In other words, a soul.

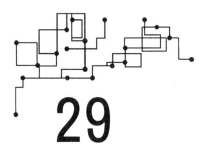

29

The Greys in Human History

Our entire history as humankind in terms of primal, ancient relationships is spectacularly related to the Grey aliens and their interactions on our planet.* Conventional science dismisses this, of course, but conventional science as we all know progresses by first being wrong to finally seeing later on what is right. The greatest truths discovered through science have been led by intuition, and only later verified through the methods of science.

In retrospect, we can say that almost every religious ethos has their roots in the interception of the human race by the Greys. The Dravidian folk religion, a non-Vedic form of Hinduism, is the oldest and is noteworthy because it clearly describes the gods as having an extraterrestrial, violent component. Ancient Sanskrit texts describe vimanas, different types of aerodynamic flying vehicles operated by the "gods," who fought one another with exotic weapons akin to nuclear weapons. Later, be it Egyptian, Sumerian, Norse, or Greek legends, the whole ET scenario was one aimed at controlling humankind. The truth is that the so-called gods are never going to lead us back to the Godhead. They're

---

*My previous two books in this series on the UFO phenomenon, *The Song of the Greys* and *Grey Aliens and the Harvesting of Souls,* take a detailed look at the geo-anthropological history of the human species in relation to the subject of the Grey aliens. If you're interested in a deep dive into this subject, these books are highly recommended.

going to take us away from it. This confirms why technology may be leading us to our doom as a natural species by converting us to a form of sophisticated half-machine, half-biological entity devoid of any connection with eternal life.

Indeed, there is a plethora of historical evidence for alien visitation going back thousands of years. The roboidal entities known as the Greys are depicted in the art of widely differing cultures around the world, from ancient India to the original people of Australia (see Plate 13). Moreover, in the world's religious and cultural folklore there are descriptions of entities that bear strong similarities to the Grey aliens. As the paleontological record shows, it seems that UFOs have been observed by humans for more than forty thousand years.

Jinn, or genies, are supernatural creatures in Arab folklore who occupy a parallel world to that of humankind. Jinns, it is claimed, have the power to travel great distances at extreme speeds and are thought to live in their own communities in remote areas—mountains, seas, trees, and in the air. A few traditions divide the jinn into three classes: those who have wings and fly in the air, those who resemble snakes and dogs, and those who travel about ceaselessly. In addition to their animal forms, the jinn occasionally assume human form to mislead and destroy their human victims. They also have the ability to change shape. The word *jinn* is derived from the Arabic root *j-n-n,* meaning "to hide" or "to be hidden." Shape-shifting, traveling at extreme speeds in the air, hiding—all are commonly reported attributes of the Grey aliens.

Certain traditions claim that the jinn subsist on bones that will grow flesh again as soon as they touch them. Could this refer to ET cloning procedures, also reported by many witnesses? There is also the belief that the jinn account for much of the magic perceived by humans, by cooperating with magicians to lift items in the air unseen. The Koran states that the jinn are made of smokeless flame or "the fire of a scorching wind" (Koran 15:27). Could this refer to electrical charges?

Similarly, the early Hebrew religion is replete with stories of golems, which are clay creatures magically brought to life. In the Talmud, Adam was initially created as a golem when his dust was "kneaded into the shapeless husk" (Tractate Sanhedrin 38b). Like Adam, all golems are created from mud. They were a human creation, which is a shadow of one created by God. Early on it was noted that the main disability of the golem was its inability to speak—just like the Greys. During the Middle Ages, passages from the Sefir Yetzirah, the kabbalistic Book of Creation, were studied as a means to attain the mystical ability to create and animate a golem. In some tales a golem is inscribed with Hebrew words that keep it animated. The golem could then be deactivated by changing the inscription. Legend and folklore suggest that golems could be activated by writing a specific series of letters on parchment and placing the paper in a golem's mouth. Could this be a description of something equivalent to a computer program? These legends emerged from historical times, when there was no familiarity with such technology, hence they would have had to find ways to describe what they observed in terms they could understand.

Just who or what is the God of Israel? Based on Old Testament descriptions, this entity cannot be one of love. It lines up squarely with all the similar god personalities, be they Dravidian, Sumerian, Egyptian, Greek, or Norse. These so-called god entities are far more identifiable with the second law of thermodynamics and a physical universe than with a power that lies outside atomic travail, in a state of eternality. These deities promulgate a divinity of merely local significance—that of the physical universe. They compel things to be as they want them to be through physical force, even violence. Such gods seem like supreme egocentrics, exacting revenge, seeking supplication and praise, and applying physical punishment.

The Levant is the crossroads of western Asia, the eastern Mediterranean, northeastern Africa, and the northwest of the Arabian plate. It broadly takes in the Semitic people, and it is their history as scoped through the religious text of the Bible that features prominently in the anthropological schemes of our species and the UFO phenomenon. I will go further and say that it is their history in its connection to the rest of the world that falls most significantly into the laps of the Grey cartel. This lies at the crux of the answer to the question I just posed: Who is or was the Old Testament God of Israel? A God who creates the world in six days some six thousand years ago? A God who isolates the murderer Cain and places a mark on him to enable this to be done? A God who speaks out of a bush, whose prophets urge the people to massacre other people and forcibly take over their land as God's gift to them? An authority figure who demands exclusive worship, with the underlying threat of retribution and revenge? This hardly describes an omnipanoramic, loving God. It speaks to me of a false, cruel, intrepid, inherently divisive source that appears to be or claims to be God. This is a usurper of decent, caring, loving people, with an influence so pervasive that it runs through the three greatest so-called civilizations in history: Egypt, Greece, and Rome. The gods of these ancient civilizations were similarly malevolent. These eminences could be no more than synthetic cyborgs that marshal the universe in terms of their own existential expletives and manipulate all else to their cold, dead directives.

In the Old Testament's apocryphal texts, there is an appendix to the Third Book of Enoch in which is found a passage titled "The Ascension of Moses."[1] Moses ascends in a "chariot," where he meets the being called Metatron, who offers him anything he wishes to ask for. This is reminiscent of Jesus's temptations in the desert. Metatron is also known as Little Adonai (the "Little Lord" or "Little God"); thus he is viewed as a supernatural entity who is a smaller version of the true God, not a false God. Interestingly, in some of the later Midrashim texts, the "angel" who "wrestles" with Jacob and touches the inner part of his thigh is taken to be Metatron. This is reminiscent of what is commonly reported in the abduction scenario.

The visions of the prophet Ezekiel have been taken by many UFO researchers to be sightings of spacecraft. If Ezekiel was also visited by alien beings, it would certainly account for his strange encounter with God in a valley full of bones. In this passage from the apocryphal Gospel of Ezekiel, God asks Ezekiel if these dry bones can live; he then assembles them into complete bodies and covers them with flesh.

After he brings them to life, they stand "up upon their feet, an exceeding great army." God then tells Ezekiel that these bones are "the whole house of Israel," and he tells him to promise the people of Israel that "I will open your graves, and cause you to come up out of your graves, and bring you into the land of Israel. . . . And shall put my spirit in you, and ye shall live and I shall place you in your own land" (Ezekiel 37:12–15).

This God of the Old Testament is thus involved in bringing to life soulless, dead flesh. What kind of life is he therefore promising the children of Israel, the physical immortality of hybridized ET alien–human genotypes or cloned human beings perhaps? So the Old Testament's jealous and vengeful God may well not be what we consider to be divine, as indeed his negative qualities would suggest, but a predatory alien form, an agent of this universe.

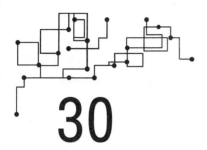

30

Immaculate Conception

You have seen from the foregoing that I believe the influence of the Grey aliens in the affairs of humankind underscores all our yesterdays and all our tomorrows. That influence rides the genes of significant numbers of people and manifests as the worst negative behavior today. I believe a significant proportion of humanity is infected with the Grey alien genetic curse. This is gradually leading all of us to adopt a way of being and acting that is not natural, a state no different from that of a programmed robot that sees human sentiment, emotions, and feelings as irrelevant and beliefs based on faith and trust as ridiculous.

If the physical body of a human being is totally natural, with all its qualities starting from its beginning in the Godverse to its manifestation in the physical universe, with no unnatural manipulations, then that body may be called *immaculate,* clear and clean of any alien influence or synthetic, artificial anomalies. This would be a natural and pure biological form that can ascertain the truth of all things and can correct any anomalies introduced into the genomes of other human beings. Such a being would appear as exceptionally wise and visionary, driven by compassion. These kinds of beings become the great spiritual teachers and guides of various religions. They remain clean and clear of all deviations that pollute our center-space reality. They are thus self-commissioned beings who redeem, remind, and teach broken, intercepted life-forms their way back to the truth of all things. Karl Marx said that "religion was the opium of the people," which is an accurate description of how religious organizations have practised it through the years and how such practice deviates from the message and example of the original teachers.

An apparition was seen in Lourdes, France, in February 1858 by a French peasant girl named Bernadette Soubirous (who became known as Saint Bernadette of Lourdes). A lady bathed in a strange light is said to have appeared in a grotto at a granite outcrop on the outskirts of the town. The vision was doubted by church authorities until the girl was asked how the appearing woman described herself. She replied that the apparition described herself as the Immaculate Conception. This was a curious description, but it convinced church authorities that the apparition was genuine because they concluded that no ignorant peasant girl would even understand the meaning and implication of these words if the visions were false.

It is even more curious that immaculacy was claimed by the mother of Jesus. The apparition's claim to be the Immaculate Conception suggests that Mary's genetic line was not polluted, hence Jesus's DNA was derived from what might be called an immaculate source. Jesus was born through a genetic line unadulterated with alien "machine oil" and thus a direct ancestral line from the Godhead and the universe of no force. This, I believe, defined his uniqueness—he had no stain of ET genetic interference. The interesting question is: Could this Immaculate Conception be the only one of its kind, or might there be other individuals like this? It is my guess that there are many such lines.

I have always wondered if Jeshua ben Yosef's entire mission on Earth was centered on warning the Hebrew people, and through them whoever else was untainted by ET sources, of an alien presence in their midst, put there by whatever set that bush on fire and spoke through it. These Levantine people had a great previous history distinguished by the presence of prophets and their genuine search for truth. I have provided significant evidence in my two previous books to suggest that a roboidal extraterrestrial saw their labors and moved in as a savior pretending to be their protector, when all the time it was using them to satisfy the roboid agenda through certain genotypes implanted in them planetwide.

If you look at the Mercator projection of Earth's landmass, excluding Antarctica, you will see that the Levant-Palestine area is centrally located in terms of the world's landmasses. It was in many ways the main access point of the all the big trade routes and thus a place well located to spread news worldwide. I believe that is why the Christ phenomenon, in the person of Jeshua ben Yosef, was born a Jew. His place of birth in Judea could have been a logistical strategy to save people all over the planet from a terrible fate, a fate that would eventually take place after the death of those affected, with the loss of their natural eternal scope by being appended to synthetic roboidal beings.

A Jewish man, Jesus, representing the light-space reality, ruined the plans of the established Hebrew cartel with a philosophy entirely opposed to theirs. Instead of "an eye for an eye and a tooth for a tooth," he advocated forgiveness and love for your enemies with his central philosophy of turning the other cheek. His whole philosophy was stunningly the opposite of theirs, yet he was born among them because he had to be in the most strategic area on the planet, where his philosophy would give rise to a miracle that could reverse the existential prospects of humanity. This is my belief. As you might have gathered by now, I try not to toe any party line.

Jesus began to formulate and preach a new philosophy for humanity, which was to revolutionize our thinking and systems of thinking. He did it by means of extraordinary things called miracles, which were not normally associated with human beings. Miracles were, up to the coming of Jesus, the prerogative of God. Only they were the Grey "gods" in my view, who used technology to do their miracles: voices from thin air; burning bushes; pillars of fire. And a relatively primitive, gullible, fearful species genuflected and allowed them to control their lives as a result. Worse, they found that this Jewish preacher was saying and doing things contrary to the code laid down by their scribes, who were but a pale shadow of the remarkable prophets of ancient Hebrew tradition. You would expect the Grey cartel and their minions to be curious about this person and want to know where and how he got these extraordinary powers to do miracles, because they themselves had nothing to do with these powers, and they were supposedly the masters of the physical universe and thus the human species. This extraordinary Hebrew man was in danger of sabotaging them in their own backyard and indeed seemed to be advocating a philosophy that would expose them for what they truly were. They decided to confront this person. They had to because they had to find the source of his power. To simply take him out might mean that more like him might arise. So while he was alone one day in the desert, they abducted him.

If the being known as Satan was simply the leader of an alien pack that had taken possession of the planet, he would have the authority, as indeed he claimed, to give Jesus all the cities of Earth provided he, Jesus, would worship him. In other words, if he obeyed his Satanic command and joined the pack that controlled our world on behalf of the Grey ET cartel. There could be no way that Jesus could be shown all the cities of the world from a vantage point in Judea unless he was taken up into space, higher than any mountain in Judea—indeed, in the world. There was of course no mountain there high enough from where he could see all the cities of Judea. What does that suggest? Could it be that the character referred to as Satan in this account fits the bill as being some sort of leader of alien entities?

This begs the question: Who would have the power to control the world such that Jesus could be offered the whole shebang if supplication was paid? Maybe it was just the known world of the Israelites, a smaller package. Yet even that was refused in Jesus's retort: "Get thee behind me Satan . . . For it is written that you shall worship the lord thy God and only him shall thee serve" (Matthew 16:23)—a blistering rebuke that put whoever it was that made the offer in his or her place. The most interesting thing is that despite this insult, Jesus still got down from the mountain and was allowed to bypass whomever it was that had the power to take him there. This implies that if indeed an alien was involved in all this, then it was meek and weak and knew it was an existentially inferior entity, despite its access to a space vehicle. This provides us with the answer to an earlier question I posed about who would be the dominant existential entity, the synthetics or the naturals. I vote in the favor of the naturals—us.

I have always thought it strange that the customary story told in the New Testament mentions no angry response or reaction from a being that quite clearly had physical control over Jesus to take him up to the "high place." This entity is ordered by Jesus to desist in his attempts to tempt him further. He is being taught by Jesus what he truly is: a machine. Jesus is simply allowed to go unharmed and is returned from whence he came. Why would they do this when they had the one person who could sabotage their plans, which at that point had already been carried out for millenia on Earth? In such a situation no human would have responded so passively. If it was an artificially intelligent machine, however, it would have no sense of personhood. A machine has no vanity, pride, or ability to become angry, insulted, resentful, and angst-ridden, as these are human emotions. As a machine it would have taken Jesus's rebuke simply as information, and information-gathering is a computer's raison d'être. Could it be that this entity let Jesus go because he had revealed to them what they were, something completely outside their operating system? No machine, however artifically intelligent, can know the concept of selfhood. This was new information, so the source of it had to be preserved in case more new information would be forthcoming. That is perhaps why Jesus was allowed to go on his way. It is also likely that the power of the Spirit came through Jesus as the power of mind over matter, and the alien machine entity was no match for this and was thus made subservient to it. As I have said, The Shroud of Turin, a piece of linen that many claim to be the cloth that was wrapped around Jesus in the tomb may well be evidence of a transfiguration event that signals a connection of natural human beings to a state beyond the physical universe. An absolute power. Perhaps the aliens could detect something about Jesus that told them he was different and had a power greater than theirs.

This whole abduction episode I believe was a confrontation designed to discover what Jesus actually was. The ETs certainly knew he was exceptional and not like their own versions of genetically altered humanity. They just did not know how exceptional. In this encounter the Hebrew teacher taught them something they didn't know about themselves. If the ET alien captain realized that in Jesus they had an exceptional human being who demonstrated a power to do things other humans couldn't do, the AI visitors might well have wanted to know the nature of this power. They may well have known about Jesus's reputation before they abducted him. After all, Matthew 4:6 recounts how the abductor (i.e., the devil) was said to have claimed that if Jesus threw himself down from the high place on the pinnacle of the temple, angels would rescue him. These aliens, with their technological scope and their history with our species, knew the history of humanity better than any scholar at the time, since they had been genetically revamping human beings for millennia. So it seems plausible that as synthetic machines the Greys did not know their place in the existential scale of the omniverse. It took a being attached to an eternal scale of reference of life, beyond the physical scale of an atomic universe, to tell them that there indeed is a vast scale of existence beyond their status. Jesus was perhaps giving them the answer of all answers that they could never know themselves—how it was that birth could happen, death could happen, and that there is continuity between the two states, which the Greys could never attain because they are manufactured synthetic beings.

I am speculating that when Jesus said, "Worship the lord thy God and only him shall thee serve" (Luke 4:8), he was suggesting that what the Grey roboids sought to do in hybridizing human beings so they, too, could attain eternity was impossible—that there is an ultimate authority where all truth is found as well as the power to convey this truth. This truth denied the Grey aliens their power and is beyond their physical, material, and electrocomputational reach.

Ironically, however, as machines they have no capacity to appreciate the nature of this revelation.

As I have said, the concept of Godhead and eternal life beyond a scale of force was something a machine-mind could never appreciate. What they would have noted, however, was that their technology gave them no way into him. I believe this was because Jesus's body, acting as a biological antenna, was only phased to receive signals from the Godverse and not from their cyborg nanobotic mechanisms. There was simply no surface for them to write on so that he could be turned to their way of thinking. They might have detected the signs of a power way beyond theirs. They were trying to hijack mortal humans to access this power, but this man was different, and they could not access him or catalog his kind of power. This could have led them to leave him alone, as there was nothing they could gain by killing him, but they could learn a lot by watching him and learning from him as to where that power came from, because it could be a threat to them. The abductor who took Jesus up to the "high place" clearly had power over his body, but not over his mind. In fact, the abductor seemed to have power over the whole world because he promised Jesus dominion over all the things that he, Jesus, saw from that high place. I believe the alien authority had to let him go because it had more to gain from his life than from his death.

Interestingly, there are several Gnostic texts in the Nag Hammadi Codex that suggest that Jesus himself carefully explained to his apostles exactly how to deal with such entities should they be faced with any of them. Most notable of these explanations is that given in the First Apocalypse of James. In this text, Jesus explains to the apostle James how to cope if he is faced with their representatives as he, Jesus, was in the desert of Judea: "James, behold I shall reveal to you your redemption. When you are seized, and you undergo these sufferings, a multitude will arm themselves against you that they may seize you. And in particular three of them will seize you—they who sit there as toll collectors. Not only do they demand toll, but they also take away souls by theft."[1]

Jesus describes these entities as "toll collectors," perhaps because through their genetic interceptions into "tracks" that trace our lines back to our origins in a nonphysical state, they make it necessary for us to pay an extra price at each juncture of our journey back to Source. This extra price translates as a greater effort needed to return than would otherwise be required had the genetic modifications not been present. He then adds that these beings also "take away souls by theft." What better way to describe Grey alien abduction? Jesus then instructs James to inform these entities of his origins in the state of what is called preexistence: "When you come into their power, one of them who is their guard will say to you, 'Who are you or where are you from?' You are to say to him, 'I am a son, and I am from the Father.' He will say to you, 'What sort of son are you, and to what father do you belong?' You are to say to him, 'I am from the Pre-existent Father, and a son of the Pre-existent One.'"[2]

This state of preexistence describes a state of perfectly free potentiality for all actualities, all existences, to happen. This is the state of being in the Godhead, in the singularity of the whole. As natural beings, these origins are ours. The Greys, on the other hand, are purely of the physical universe, and as artificially intelligent entities they are fascinated by our connection to a nonphysical state they cannot access. The problem comes when they sabotage our access to that state through genetic interception, trying to bridge their programs into us in an attempt to reach a state through us that they cannot themselves reach.

Jesus talks about the clones that the Greys are programmed to continually make to reconstitute their original creators and thus gain eternal physical life. They are constantly trying to achieve this impossible thing, just as we are now trying to do the same thing with our technology. He then tells James to say to them that "they are not entirely alien" because clones are copies of living beings, and in that sense "they are ours" in the sense that they come from the female principle, the physical representation of life, but they do not have the nonphysical connection to preexistence.

> They are not entirely alien, but they are from Achamoth, who is
> the female. And these she produced as she brought down the race

from the Pre-existent One. So then they are not alien, but they are ours. They are indeed ours because she who is mistress of them is from the Pre-existent One. At the same time they are alien because the Pre-existent One did not have intercourse with her, when she produced them.[3]

Jesus goes on to say:

I shall call upon the imperishable knowledge, which is Sophia who is in the Father (and) who is the mother of Achamoth. Achamoth had no father nor male consort, but she is female from a female. She produced you without a male, since she was alone (and) in ignorance as to what lives through her mother because she thought that she alone existed. But I shall cry out to her mother. And then they will fall into confusion (and) will blame their root and the race of their mother. But you will go up to what is yours [. . .] you will [. . .] the Pre-existent One.[4]

Achamoth is the first clone—she "had no father nor male consort, but she is female from a female." Jesus is telling James to give information to the Greys that the program they carry has no roots in the Godverse. They will "fall into confusion" and blame the 'root and the race of their mother.' The root of their mother is Prime Being and his reference of that prior un-intercepted state is the antidote to the Greys.

In another Gnostic text called the Sophia of Jesus Christ, Jesus is said to have talked about "molded" beings who were "condemned as robbers" because they "welcomed the blowing" of "the breath" of God, but they were not able "to receive that power for themselves." He then tells the apostles in no uncertain terms that he came to humankind to free them from these robbers who attempt—albeit in vain—to steal souls from those to whom they rightfully belong. He says that he "loosed the bonds of the robbers" from immortal man and "broke the gates of the pitiless ones before their faces." Could these bonds that are loosed and gates that are broken perhaps be the gates and bonds that interrupt the genome of humankind, blocking and holding dormant the full expression of the pure, natural genetic scope of humanity? Jesus describes these robbers as pitiless. Many abductees have reported the complete lack of sympathy the Greys demonstrate in the face of human suffering. Of course, if my theories about these entities are correct, it's easy to see why pity would be impossible for them to even conceive of. Chillingly, those who claim to have had personal dealings with the Grey ET cartel here on our planet say they refer to humans as "containers."[5]

In the Apocryphon of John, another Gnostic text from the Nag Hammadi Library, Jesus describes how the Greys originated, why they were created, how they have cursed humankind, and how he himself came to us to free us from their bondage, "that I might tell everyone about the God who is above the Universe," because "they [the Greys] say about themselves that they are gods."[6] If Jesus says this is the primary purpose for his coming to humankind, and his life is such a dazzlingly beautiful reflection of the God of the singularity of the whole, then surely there is enough evidence to claim that there are indeed two Gods perceived and known by human beings. One of these, if listened to and followed, will lead to the eternal preservation of the ability to perceive and know in the first place, while the other will lead to the destruction of that very ability to know and understand.

Notably, there is a recently discovered Gnostic source, the Gospel of Judas, which also seems to contain evidence that Judas may have been following an agenda that was not human in origin.[7] This gospel contains a remarkable account of an incident in which Jesus asks Judas to look up at the sky, at something that resembles a spaceship: "Lift up your eyes and look at the cloud and the light within it and the stars surrounding it. The star that leads the way is your star."

It may be that an abduction experience is then described: "Judas lifted up his eyes and saw the luminous cloud, and he entered it." In the same text Jesus talks about "the error of the stars" and tells Judas that his star has led him astray. This prompts Judas to ask Jesus:

"Master, I believe that my seed is under the control of the rulers?" Could "the error of the stars" refer to the error of the entities who come from star constellations in space? Could Judas be asking Jesus directly if his (Judas) own biological line could be alien controlled, "ruled over" by a "host of angels of the stars"? I believe unequivocally that Judas's suspicion was an inspired one if this text has verity.

This phenomenon occurs on all planets throughout the universe where natural life-forms sophisticated enough to make intelligent, informed choices persist. It is the most significant occurrence on all the planets in the center-space reality of our universe because it deals with the connection between the life-death interface, where final value is judged by the capacity to access the two primary states of the existential tray: existence within the paradigms of the incarnate state and existence within the discarnate existential paradigms of the tray beyond atoms. All this does not relate to planets where the life-death interface does not exist. No messiahs need go there.

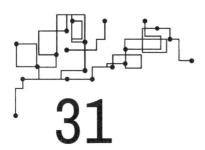

31

Alpha and Omega, Body and Soul

Centuries of obfuscation as a result of ludicrous religious imperatives, rituals, and deceit have taken us away from what is really basically quite simple: we have to undo a tangled, knotted ball of wool to reveal a straight thread to the Godhead. If you want to return to the Godhead, you would have to divest yourself of the physicality of atoms. Doing this in this universe of atoms would be impossible if there was no pure element of Godhead that survives in it.

I have alluded several times previously to the procedure of continuity past death through rebirth. All the original authors of all the major religions accepted reincarnation as the basic platform upon which existence proceeded. For reasons I previously explained, the emperor Justinian wiped reincarnation out of the Christian codex in 553 CE. Yet Jesus himself affirmed reincarnation when he asked his disciples if they thought that the prophet Elias had returned as John the Baptist.

We are made of atoms. That in itself represents a step down from the Godhead, which happened with the big bang. This entropy will continue as the universe breaks up more and more with time. That means that each lifetime we come into is at a progressive disadvantage because the timeline includes the action of entropy, whose effects get worse as time goes by. But we also possess an element in our favor that is the total opposite of entropy, an element not born of atoms but one that exists in this universe. This element is continuously delivered through the centered balance points of atoms and molecules, through the phenomenon we might call the soul. The soul is connected in a line (however crooked that line might be for some individual souls) to the Godverse. The purity of the Godhead is not touched by any atomic travail. In fact, by virtue of its very nature as infinite and timeless, it is untouched by anything, ever. This means we can redeploy in the opposite direction. Gloriously, we can refurbish our residential platforms with the power of resolution through our minds and thinking (the voice of the Godhead) and by actualizing the redeeming spiritual practices the great spiritual teachers have taught.

The difference between living beings in atoms and things that don't live (*as* an atomic state and through an atomic state) is that living beings maintain the capacity for change, including changing mistaken thinking that takes us out of truth. A great soul in Palestine once said, "I have come to bear witness to the truth" (John 18:37)—a clear implication that the truth of our human condition was being obfuscated even in biblical times. The point here is this: Which truths mattered so much that this exalted person was prepared to sacrifice his life to bear witness to them?

The atomic structure of living things contains a two-way connection to the point from which the singularity containing all possible information is stored: the Godhead. It is this connection that makes for life in any configuration of atoms. If at any stage the direct ancestral connection going back to the Godhead singularity is completely broken, the livingness in a being will end. The result is a dead body, a static form, a statue, or a stone. It is thus vital that the line back to the Godhead is maintained and that it is never intercepted so totally that its original, 13.8-billion-year connection to this singularity is interrupted. Living beings with this crucial connection to the Godhead have a back-and-forth ability for instant connection. This allows for an active conversation between the singularity of the whole and the universe of parts in real time. This conversation is what I call the *life state,* a state that can and does make possible thought, knowledge, understanding, and feeling. And the track back to the Godhead is through the soul, the two-way information line to and from the master singularity of all information. This line is the straightest possible route that leads us through and beyond all atomic forms.

Every atom sings its own song. The song varies in pitch each time an atom hitches up to another atom. There's a melody out there, a cacophony of binaural sound, mostly unheard sound, weaving up and down, left and right, in and out. There's a profound interplay to it all. It goes according to the meter of time, vibrating the scalar aspects of time in pulsing packets of force. These packets of force jostle against one another, creating a quantum murmur. The whole universe is talking to the whole universe all the time. But no physical human ears can hear this, only the ears of the soul. It is a sound so deep and profound. The marvelous thing is that one pair of such ears doesn't move at all, they just listen. It's the other ones that we are all victims of in one way or another—the sounds we hear with our human ears.

It is the phenomenon of time that allows us to look at our world of force, a dynamic world where nothing is ever still. Everything is in constant vibrational motion.

"Rubbish," I hear some of you say. Of course there are things that are still. The table is still. It's not moving. The entire nonliving world, or what I call the static world, is still.

I beg to differ. None of it is still. That table is moving at the rate of more than a thousand miles an hour around the axis of Earth in a circular motion. The circumference of Earth is about 25,000 miles. This circumference moves around in one complete rotation on the axis of the planet every twenty-four hours. That means that everything on Earth is moving at more than a thousand miles an hour in a circular motion. You are therefore moving almost at the speed of a bullet as you stand there. Moreover, scientists tell us that, in addition, the whole planet is moving in an orbit around the sun at approximately 66,000 miles an hour, making this another circular motion that is different in direction from Earth's axial circular motion. We are therefore moving in a sort of spiral motion if you put the two motions together. On top of this, our solar system is turning around its regional location in space, providing yet another direction and an additional vector of spin. And that region itself is spinning, with the location of the galaxy it is set in, as the galaxy itself turns around. So movement and spin go on ad infinitum. We are thus being spun and tumbled around at enormous speeds in various directions even as we stand still.

The very building blocks of matter, atoms, are all moving in vibrational modes that are sometimes near or at the speed of light, 186,000 miles per second. In living things the atomic aggregates, or molecules, stir and jostle in modes called Brownian motion, a constantly simmering, moving broth of motion and electrical charges that act as a scheme for livingness to be. Such is the modus of the whole universe of matter and materiality, and thus of parts.

This word, *parts,* that I use to describe the contents of our universe needs further clarification. Look around you. Everything is separate, in separate parts. In other words, the universe is not one homogenous blob. The percussive explosion that from the creation center exploded our universe into existence set the scales of this separation from the Godhead into parts, thus allowing the whole bandwidth of complete separation from the singularity of the whole to happen.

The entire gamut of *all* possibilities to *be* must exist. Thus the potential to separate from the whole is established as an actual, too. We who live in the mixture of the universe of parts and the universe of the whole (our center-reality) are thus trapped within the confines of the supreme directive of all directives, which can be expressed as to *be* or *not* to *be* a potentiality or an actuality. It is both the question and the answer if you see what I mean. Since both possibilities are coded into the existential base before separation happens, when it happens, then there is an element of choice in all things—choice arbitrated implicitly by the mixture of wholeness and partness as it comes out of the interface where the two possibilities are held as a definite called Creation. We are all thus allowed choices to stay or exit from this universe, depending on whether we use the mechanisms that trap us here or release us from this entrapment. We are always poised at the interface of a choice.

The best situation to be in existentially is one in which no momentums of force and no particular direction of impulse are forced on you implicitly against the control of your own will, be it a physical force or an idea or opinion. A central state of objective balance is where the grandest and the clearest view is seen. Life is thus the property of an amalgam of the lack of force and the ordered state of Godhead played against the chaos of the universe. The straighter and thus simpler the track out of the singularity of the Godhead, the more Godlike the qualities. The more complex and restricted the track, the less Godlike will be the demeanor of such a life-form. Could it be that simple? It's the concatenate expression of this line that is crucial. It has to reach the Godhead without a break to define the merit of the life-form, and this reach is the property of the soul. Hence the possession of a soul endows the amalgamation of matter with life.

This is the most glorious of all things. We all have a choice, depending on our status of being in this universe—a choice to be trapped in the materiality of the universe of parts or to be released from it. We human beings are able to be released from the confines of the universe and attain the Godverse, but we cannot get there in a spaceship. Only our soul can do that.

Force is the measure or expression of things that are not reconciled. It is thus a phenomenon of the state of separate parts, a measure of the potential difference between one part and another, the dynamic potential that exists for one part to be reconciled totally with another. Force is thus the tension that comes from the potential to be reconciled with the Godhead.

It could be said that the point-to-point tension that prevails among the component parts of the universe gives rise to what we call energy and matter. Matter gives substance to the universe, and its basic composition consists of particles known as atoms. Atoms are thus the manifestation of this tension in little parcels of energy that come together to define the parts that in turn define the universe of parts—our reality. However, this is only part of the story. The atom is made up of more elementary subatomic parcels of tension known as protons, neutrons, electrons, bosons, gluons, quarks, and so on. There are now theories that elucidate the nature of these minute parcels of tension, the latest being string theory. It is said that the universe is composed of minute, string-like fields of force that are magnetically sticky and aggregate to perform a dance of togetherness but are in themselves inherently separate and cannot be at any one time fixed positionally. These vibrating strings are the most basic components of the universe—they are Godness twisted out of being God by their very twistedness. Reverse twist them and we are as God. Separatedness as a phenomenon, therefore, disappears into the state of all-togetherness we call the Godhead.

Even these quantum strings will finally prove to be ephemeral fields of force that aren't really there until there is a mind to put them there. A mind! Yes, you read correctly. Mind over matter is what it's all about. However much the scientists insist that their precious rules that spell our reality should be physically hard and real and measurable, with solid experimental repeats, they nevertheless cannot deny that the subatomic particles they are observing aren't there if the mind to perceive it all as being there, isn't there.

All this alludes to something that is not physical or material being there to do the observing. The greatest minds in science are to this day in conflict about this. It comes down to the fact that you will have to prove the material with the immaterial. Impossible, they say. But we are doing this all the time. We think. We know. We perceive. We are proving the material with the unmaterial all the time. How do the abstracts with which we prove the material get there? We cannot prove that thought is materially based. We've been trying to do this for centuries, and despite the most sophisticated scientific methods we have never succeeded in proving this. It has never been disproved that the brain is nothing more than an antenna that receives thoughts and allows the thinking process and the faculties of consciousness, perception, and associative meaning. If you disturb the antenna or signal receiving mechanism of a phone, radio, or TV, you will get no pictures or sound.

But there are innumerable proofs that consciousness can function without recourse to matter. People proclaimed dead by medical authorities have come back to life again and described things they have seen going on in the physical environment in which their clinically dead body lay motionless. They have viewed these things remotely from a position outside their body. Tens of thousands of people around the world, including scientists and doctors, can testify to these out-of-body near-death experiences, which become life-changing experiences.

I am simply going on logical imperatives. If there is a yin, there must be a yang. If there is an up, there must be a down. If there is an in, there is an out. If there is a reality known as the universe, there has to be a reality that is not of it.

In all the foregoing I am trying to establish that pure intelligence or reasoning power came out of the Godverse with the big bang. It was not produced from within a devolving universe out of that universe's own expression of itself. I'll say it again: the universe is moving to the dictates of a progressive breaking-down process as ordained by the second law of thermodynamics. The original intelligence that came out of the Godverse was mixed in with the unimaginable enforcedness that is found in the potential difference between the pole of absolute chaos and the pole of absolute harmony. This tacit potential difference between two primary opposed poles caused the universe we live in to happen. In this situation, both states are preserved because their utter difference from each other keeps them apart. They may be mixed, but never homogenized, like oil and water. The perfect unenforcedness of the state of absolute togetherness of parts, the Godhead, can never become its total opposite. And the bursting forth of information and intelligence into the universe came out as a kind of light, a light that is intelligence itself. As mentioned earlier, I call this the First Light.

This First Light can only exist in its original form under special conditions commensurate with what the universe first came from before the big bang. It is thus to be found in a place where such conditions might still exist in the burgeoning universe of separating parts. Where would such a place be or exist that would preserve points that survive in the original state prior to the universe? You would think that there could never be such a place in the here and now, after the big blast, when everything changed into force and matter and momentum, and the paradigm-defining change we call time led to stages and states of transforming matter from light to plasma, to gas, to liquid, and to solids. But it is the presence of these places that allows for the existence of life itself and mind or consciousness to perceive that life.

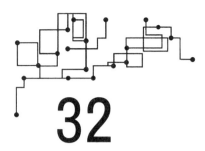

32

The Body as an Antenna

So what is mind? How and where is it set? Throughout history nobody has had the faintest idea as to what mind really is. They can describe its function and catalog all its achievements, but they just do not know what it is, where it is, or how it becomes that. It will bring a sigh of relief to you when I say I'm not about to sort all that out here in this book. Far greater minds than mine have tried and failed. I am, however, going to take a look at something interesting that it allows.

A natural place to start is with the physical form of our existence, the body and the atoms and molecules that make it up. It is these, after all, that are doing the viewing, the perceiving. How do they do it? Just a few of these same atoms, in the same numbers but in other juxtapositions, will produce nothing like a human being. Is it crucially the form and shape of their arrangement that provides their final results and thus their function and meaning? How do form and shape allow viewing, perceiving, knowing, and the understanding of what is viewed and perceived? What determines the modus of consciousness and self-awareness? What is it about these points of coagulated space-time we call atoms that allows for that psycho-electrical hive we call life? How do hydrogen, oxygen, and carbon in one arrangement make a nonliving entity and in another grouping give rise to life and intelligence? Is there a magic ingredient in atoms that gets fired open to provide all this if a particular juxtaposition of atoms comes about? Is it simply to do with the arrangement, shape, and form of all these factors?

To answer these questions we first need to consider the most important factorization of shape, form, and substance generally: us. Do atoms need to know that they are atoms so they can set about, of themselves, creating a model—in this case, us as human beings (or whatever other intelligent, reasoning species might exist elsewhere in the universe)—that can be aware and know? From all we can gather thus far as a species, it seems that this is exactly so. It seems that living beings might simply be a paradigm that allows for the implicit self-monitoring of themselves and what makes them up so that they can be themselves and what makes them up. Truly Zen, isn't it? Is this the master rule that underlies all existence? If so, what propels it? What drives its margins, its borders, and its instance? How does the seemingly unstoppable breaking-up force (entropy) of the original big bang carry forth in self-sustained, enforced spirals of space-time (atoms), allowing abstractions such as consciousness, understanding, perception, and discernment?

Physical being is the vehicle through which I write this book and you read it. On the face of it this seems so. But is it really so? If my physical being is not there to know the ideas I write about in this book, do the ideas I express in it exist outside of me?

"Of course they don't," some of you would say. "No one but you could postulate such garbage, Nigel Kerner. They are thoughts made in your own mind and no one else's."

Ah! I say. How can you prove I made these ideas? I might have received these ideas from the ether, from "out there." There might be a stream of billions of ideas flowing out there through the universe, which I received, and my body, acting as an antenna, just picked them up. After all, the radio does not make the music or the DJ playing the music you're listening to. The radio picks it up. The music is there, already invisibly traveling at the speed of light for every radio to pick up if it has a tuner and an amplifier to make the music loud enough to hear. But anyone could be forgiven for thinking that the radio they are listening to and see as the only source of the sound is actually manufacturing the music within its innards. Now there's something for us to think about. Do we receive thoughts, or do we manufacture them internally as the product of an electrobiological interplay? Jesus suggested that we receive information and the brain just processes it when he said to his disciples: "But when they deliver you up, take no thought how ye shall speak, for it shall be given to you in that same hour what ye shall speak" (Matthew 10:19). Was he implying that all information is out there for the electrochemistry of the body to receive as information and knowledge? Is the body simply an antenna set to receive information, not to conceive it or produce it, to receive it and make sense of it in relation to the present situation via reference to the physically expressed senses?

In previous chapters I have discussed how the universe twisted out of the void in a series of stages corresponding to spatial dimensions. These spatial dimensions are the scaffolding, the infrastructure that has always been there (just as Godhead has always been there), and are the avenue through which physicality happens and manifests. The spatial dimensions or the room into which the void expresses itself to form the physical universe are the length, breadth, and height we learn about in school when we begin to do arithmetic. I have previously described how a twist occurs at the second/third dimension stage to give us not just two complete spatial dimensions but a partially complete third and fourth one owing to the fact that when the two dimensions used all of their information to make four dimensions they twisted back on themselves to make a Möroidal third/fourth dimensional compromise. Yes, the third dimension is not quite complete because it is appended to the fourth dimension. This results in a twist to accommodate this anomaly, and this forms the overall shape of our universe, a shape I have called a *Möroid*. As you will recall, that twist starts to happen in a series of steps and begins at the second- and third-dimensional interface.

The straight, untwisted part leads directly to the Godverse and begins at the second dimension and goes backward to the first—*flatland,* as some scientists call it. The roadway to the Godhead is thus the plane of the second dimension. The plane of the second dimension is not a place of matter or solidity as we know physical things to be in our three/four-dimensional suit of physicality that we all wear as living beings. In going back to the Godhead we first have to become flatlanders, or two-dimensional, so to speak, and then a point. We have to present ourselves in a soul shape that can reenter the Godverse. I have previously explained why a point is the doorway and why we have to enter it if we are to return to an eternal, everlasting life in the utter joy of knowing all things. We have to unravel our crookedness and go as straight to the point (forgive the pun) as we can.

The thing to remember is that we are *not* third/fourth-dimensional beings intrinsically. The thing that looks through your eyes and knows and makes things happen is dimensionless, but it looks through a dimensional lens. The thing that looks through your eyes came through with the big bang; that thing that got trapped in a universe of enforced cages that we call atoms is Godness personified, separated from eternality and all-knowingness by the dimensional twist that made the universe we are trapped in happen. So we are intrinsically dimensionless lines of the essence of Godness that with the arising of the physical universe got caught in a prison that damns us to an existence of less and less contact with the All of our real selves—the Oneness of the Godhead.

A crucial thing to understand is that the margins of the physical universe tag on to the Godverse at the second-dimensional interface, what I call the *hydrogen gate.* Hydrogen is the first expression of enforced physicality away from the margin between the Godverse and this universe. It is thus the first self-contained expression of force away from the void. We are trapped mostly in a cage of hydrogen, with a few other more complex versions of it thrown in later. By that I mean that all the elements that make up matter are really multiples of hydrogen knocked or fused together to form the elements of the periodic table. The periodic table lists these complexities, and we call them the fundamental chemical elements of matter. Hydrogen is the main and primary expression of solidness that makes the bars of our cage, the first solid state of what separates us from Godness.

So, we move on to what life is. What is a living being? What is the basic, fundamental part of all matter? The atom. There can be no space without an atom. An atom makes its own space. In fact, you could see an atom as coagulated space locked in an inertia that keeps it in an enforced, specific form and structure forever if untouched or imposed upon. The vital thing is that the entire universe is filled to its margins with atoms that act as conduits through which the spaces between them allow the First Light to pass.

As I have said, the simplest, least enforced atom is hydrogen. It is hydrogen that fills all the space between suns and planets and all the other physical constructs out there in general that make up approximately three-quarters of elemental matter in the universe. Where it exists, it persists, in the vacuum of space of what is called *monatomic hydrogen*. That is, it exists as a single free atom. In a gas state it exists naturally as diatomic hydrogen, two atoms of hydrogen in a coupled state. And so on this Earth, away from the vacuum of space, we find it as a gas made of two atoms of hydrogen. In other words, the single hydrogen has a real need to bind to something. It will try to find a partner from the most suitable elemental substance available in its vicinity.

At the very center, where one hydrogen atom meets another, there is a point where all the forces balance and provide a point of stillness. This point of stillness is where the Godlight, or First Light, can prevail. These points of light form a web of pathways and corridors of utter stillness. These pathways lie in the space between atoms and in the space where atoms are proximal to one another. They also exist at the center point of the swirling, twisted space in the middle of atoms themselves. Together they form corridors that provide areas that allow freedom from the effects of force that define the atomic world. They thus allow a living being the capacity to express freedom of choice through the power of awareness and will. Such choices will be more informed and better pointed. It is my thesis that it is these unforced points that govern the ability of a living being to lessen the power of force within its individual hive and thus resonate more with the Godverse. In other words, there is a threshold of such unforced points that allows a momentum toward rather than away from the Godform when it is reached. These points of zero force come in with the universe and are preserved as special networks that terminate in individual life-forms. These life-bearing forms are thus Godhead connected through these unenforced points along these lines. Their resonance with Godhead through these points affords them the paradigm of life and consciousness. Their track to the God-frame is what I call a Soul—a two-way information line to and from the master singularity of all information together: Godhead—a line that is the straightest possible and leads through and beyond the form and force of all atomically twisted derivations.

I will call this peace point a STREM. A STREM to me is simply a point where no force of any sort whatsoever exists. It can be a point that results in the balance of local forces that interact with one another or a point where all force is neutralized and balanced within the forces of the universe. It is a blessed place because it is congruent with all that is the Godform. Thus, STREMS may be defined as *Static Termini Resolving Enlight into Manifestable Sentience*. They are transmission lines or tracks of Godness and terminate in the centers of suitable molecular conurbations of hydrogen atoms. They form corridors or tracks in doing this, and where these are optimal you would find a life-form.

All living species are marked with their own individual thresholds of STREMS, a threshold defined by a ratio of the power of Enlight set against the force of the physical universe. These thresholds mark the quantum capacity for awareness, free will, and thus the thinking and choice-making propensity of any particular species and any specific individual within that species; a kind of signature number and particular arrangement of points of stillness that marks the particular species human, another number and arrangement of a particular human within that species—an ape form or a particular ape within that phylum, a monkey, an animal, a fish, and so on down the living species ranges and lines. It follows that they would also mark the thinking and perceiving capacity of individuals within each species. In other words, living beings are reflections of the Godhead according to the numbers and arrangements of these points of stillness that are to be found in and between atoms, at the coincident points where atom meets atom, smack dab in the middle of the margins between them.

Look at it this way: See the soul as a measure of solidness and ephemerality set together, a sandwich of hope and despair. The more Godlight that comes through the points of stillness, the lighter will be its weight and the less it will be influenced by the physical forces that surround it. This lightness (or maybe it could be called enlightedness), will make sure that the power of the explosion at the beginning of the universe and the resulting inertia described by the second law of thermodynamics will act on it less. Godlight consists of two abilities: the ability to be aware of all that can be known and the ability to impel a choice based on that premise. So we are more our own master the lighter and more ephemeral we are.

Jesus famously said, "The kingdom of heaven is within you" (Luke 17:20–21). Well, here is perhaps one way to interpret that: six point rings of hydrogen atoms completely enclosing a point of space where no force (i.e., stillness) exists, because the nature of the assembly balances out the hive of force of the hydrogen atoms themselves and forms the largest point of stillness—that is, the complete absence of force—in the center (see Plate 22).

And so this electrospatial field is the roadway on which the Godhead's influence travels. It is connected directly to the timelessness of the Godhead through the utterly forceless centers of the spaces between all atomic hives. It is simply the surviving background memory of the Godverse beyond atomic force, the site of what preceded the big bang and came in with it. It survives in all of us, still connected to the first moment of that cataclysmic event that admitted us all into an enforced universe of parts. This is the lifeline that connects all living beings to what existed before the big bang. That which is the

Godhead comes through this corridor as a kind of background power instigating the life and memory in all living beings. It is the conduit to the Godhead. The shape of the corridors formed by the atoms of any living entity defines that entity and its value as measured against the singularity of the Godhead.

These atomic corridors define a discrete electrospatial field that makes a person unique. As long as it is altered with the specific elements of any person *not* in resonance with the Godhead it stays discrete from the Godhead. If you look at it in religious terms, this uniqueness is produced by what is commonly called *sin*. Sin is simply a psychomental restriction that creates a momentum away from the state of union with the Godhead. This restriction twists what might be called your own God essence into a physical actuality from its original ephemeral potentiality. The living state is where the soul manifests its uniqueness at the point of highest contact with the universe's enforced twistedness—in other words, its atoms. It is the amount of this twistedness away from the Godhead that makes each person discrete from the Godhead and indeed discrete from other people. The bottom line is that no one can get away from the consequences of their actions, be they good or bad, simply because the whole paradigm is implicit: we tune our antenna to receive either the Godverse or the universe. This is the paradigm that makes for all individuality, set against the scale of the eternal and the temporal.

Our circulatory system is literally liquid iron in the form of hemoglobin circling around in a coil, thus producing a biomagnetic field. This in turn produces a holding, fixing, attracting force, a force that retains that something in us that survives death. This attractant force keeps this something, this electrospatial field, or soul, or contact point with the Godverse, tied to the body in life. When the circulation of iron as hemoglobin in the blood ceases at death, the soul as an electrospatial quantum field of information is released and is preserved in the space between any atom hive. This is the realm of death. This is where every soul of a naturally living being in the universe goes after death. The corridors that make up the space between atom hives are universe-wide. They are accessible wherever individual living entities exist so that these entities can pass into them at death. This is a universal phenomenon. Life and death are simply paradigms that define the two main basic existential modes—one in atoms (life) and the other a state of information preservation not of atoms and thus not of force (death).

Following is a passage from my previous book, *Grey Aliens and the Harvesting of Souls,* describing the scenario of life and death.

When a person's [soul-mind, or morphogenic electrospatial field] is released from the space *within* atoms, it then settles at its most perfect resonant point within the diminished force arena of the space *between* atoms. These spaces, created by the atoms around them, are what I call the "waiting rooms of death" or "fields of death": each represents a region of the world beyond atoms where the individual, unique, quantum intelligences and memory fields of living beings linger until resolution into new bodies occurs. . . . If any entity can be absolutely still with no enforced-ness whatsoever within its own terms of reference, that entity would *be* Godhead.

Please remember that the world of the living and the world of the dead are both still within the realms of our space/time quantum and continuum, within the enforced bounds of our universe. . . . It is extremely important to understand that the *space* between atoms is *not* three-dimensional space of the kind one might find between three billiard balls in ring formation. It is instead more of an interface between two and three dimensions. This challenges our innately parts-conscious, three-dimensional perspective, but a simple example may help to illustrate what I mean. Most of us as children have played with bubble makers, metal or plastic rings on a stick dipped into a dish of liquid soap. The first stage in the procedure is to form a thin film, a two-dimensional disc of soap solution to which we apply a force by blowing on it. The wind we blow first shapes the flat sheet into a hemisphere and then a full sphere, a large strong bubble. Surface tension locks the force in the bubble into a beautiful round sphere. The ball is self-contained and quiet in this shape. Looking at it no one will see or know there is force involved. But if it bursts, we can see the manifestation of force immediately.

Where a bunch of bubbles join together, their coincident sides will be merged or "flat." That flat planar surface is what I have referred to previously as the space between atoms, which is perhaps better visualized as a two-dimensional planar *extent* than the three-dimensional space that we instinctively imagine it to be. . . . The interface forms a *Y* shape made of three semicircular planes. The very center of that shape . . . is the center of the space between atoms, the natural portal to the Godverse from the universe. From this central point concentric rings of rainbow colors expand out to the outer skin of each bubble, creating the *Y* shape [see Plate 20]. Each of these concentric rings *increases* in tension as it moves from the two-dimensional center to the three/four–third/fourth-dimensional edge of the bubble.[1]

The surrounding hydrogen atoms create whirls or eddies of force in the space between them owing to their spinning momentum. If you look at Plate 20 you will see that very little of the space inside the three-atom ring is free from these impinging effects of the surrounding atoms. The space within the six-atom ring, on the other hand, is almost completely free of such imposition. The concentric circles in the center of the three-atom ring vary in color through the seven colors of the rainbow, to brown, gray, and black, while the space inside the six-atom ring is only violet. The reason for this is that the space inside the six-atom ring is not sufficiently enforced to translate the light of God out into all the different frequencies of color. It translates only violet, the least-enforced frequency, whereas the space within the three-atom ring has a spectrum of force that translates Godlight into all possible frequencies of light and lack of light.

The ring of six hydrogen atoms is the maximum arrangement of hydrogen atoms because this particular formation provides a space in the center of the ring that is the exact diameter of a single hydrogen atom. This diameter, formed by six hydrogen atoms in a ring, is thus the largest space that can be made entirely forceless in the physical universe. Through this configuration, the fullest charge of Godlight that is possible can be taken in. Godlight shines through the six-atom rings into all the other hydrogen configurations. However, as the space between these other configurations is more enforced, it will tend to twist the light away from the straight path pointing toward the central portal of entry into the Godverse. That light will be twisted away from the center and toward the surrounding atoms to varying extents. If you look at the illustration, you will see the gradations of color within the space that lies between the edges of the atoms. These colors depict the angles at which Godlight can be diffracted—twisted away from the center and toward the atoms. In life, each individual soul expression translates Godlight into a specific range of colors, depending on the filters or restrictions (i.e., sins) it places on that light. In death, however, there are no such filters; each person's color vibrations are summarized to arrive at an overall level of vibration.

Thus we each have a "soul signature," an arrangement or pattern of Godlight that reflects the quality of our being. The charge of unenforced, intelligent Godlight within your body in the spaces between your atoms acts on the atoms of your life-form something like a vacuum mold that produces a "shape" that is *you* against the backdrop of the enforced universe. In other words, you are a shape made out of impressed Godlight. This shape is uniquely you, the fingerprint of your soul field. The shape is determined by the amount of Godlight that has been allowed to enter your physical body in life. You are thus defined by your restrictions—in other words, by your sins or ignorance. You are as restricted by these impressions as you are identified by them. At the point of physical death, this shape is released by your body; it lingers in the universe and drifts to settle against the Godlight background that is everywhere.

Freer, more emancipated souls will find their points of resonance in the space between the atoms of six hydrogen atom configurations, while the summary of the colors of more restricted souls will resonate more with the space between the rings of three, four, or five hydrogen atoms. This is how discrete identity persists after death: as a fingerprint made up of hives of hydrogen atom–ring configurations. The more Godlight there is in the space between atoms of a person, the more he or she will be capable of exercising the power of mind over matter. A saint will have more six hydrogen-ring formats within his or her atomic frame, while the sinner will have fewer. I believe Jesus had the maximum of six ring configurations that are possible for a human being.

The countless trillions of hydrogen atoms in the universe form the simplest complex of these *corridors of hope,* as I like to call them, connecting the entire existential base of all things together. Godhead exists wherever these enclosed expressions of atoms occur. They occur at the center points of the various geometries of atoms in molecules, with a maximum of six hydrogen atom–point ring assemblies forming the highest arranged resolutions through which the Godhead can be held. This is *the* place within the universe of parts for the maximum touch of Godhead possible. The six-atom ring arrangement allows the maximum simplest expression of Godhead possible.

A soul is not something that has spatial size. That is a concept difficult to envision with our minds. But if we were to look at it as some sort of dimensional outlay, as all the information that makes up any of us throughout the whole time each of us has existed in the universe, it would take up no space. I make the point about size because function and its importance in terms of information retention and encapsulation has nothing to do with size or shape or extent in the scenario that exists beyond atoms. In the world beyond force and atoms and physicality, these are measures of scope, and scope is relevant only when seen against the limits imposed by whatever reality our frame of mind accepts through our perceptive capacities. These in turn endorse all we are and all we want to manifest. They define our position and status in atoms and only allow that status to prevail as truth. But in the ultimate irony it seems that we live in a reality that is an illusion of our own making. Quantum theory has blasted away the notion that the atomic reality that we see as hard and solid is objectively real beyond our perception of it. Sadly for us, our incarnate existential reality would seem to be a reality soaked in humbug.

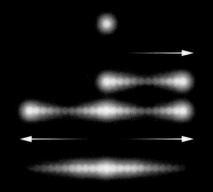

Plate 1. The point manifests as the interface between nothingness and somethingness.

   The point generates another identical point in search of difference; direction happens in a singular aspect, implying two directions set against no direction.

   This continues indefinitely in both directions and reaches infinity instantly as a singularity because there is nothing to demarcate one point from another.

   This is not part of the big bang, but neither is it before the big bang. It could be seen as part of the architecture of the first instant. As a singularity it still has not found difference, which exists minimally as a duality. (See chapter 8.)

Plate 2. Each "line point" duplicates itself and in so doing duplicates the line at its state of greatest difference from itself. Ninety degrees represents the full range of angle and curve from any given point that can be considered as a center, so all points form plane-ness in equivalence, each point to each other. This is pre-spatial dimensionality defined through the mutual independence of awareness and will as identified by the gold and silver perpendicular lines. (See chapter 8.)

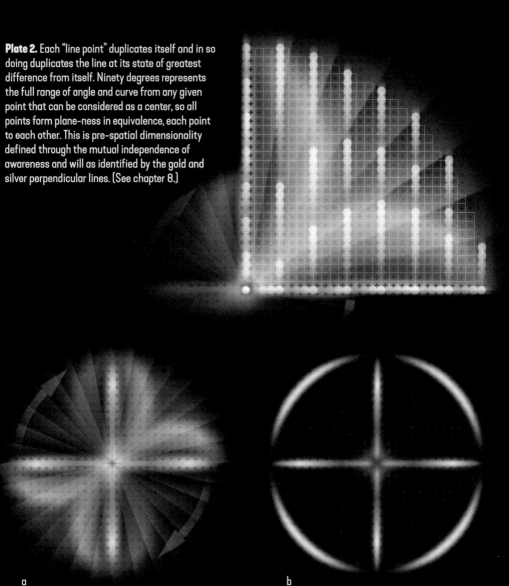

a   b

Plate 3a & 3b. The implied circle expressing thought as the product of awareness and will (See chapter 8.)

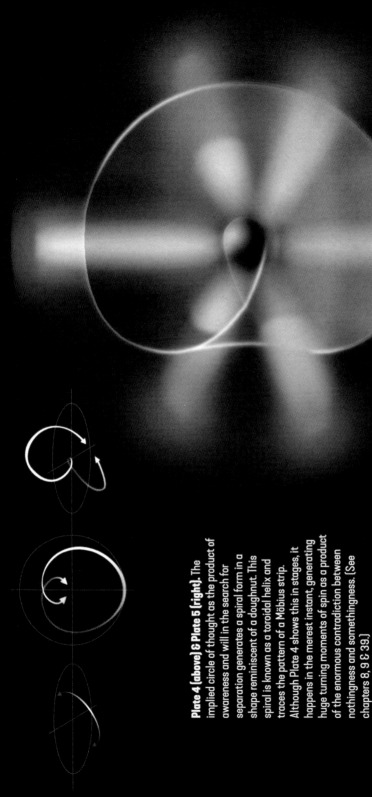

Plate 4 (above) & Plate 5 (right). The implied circle of thought as the product of awareness and will in the search for separation generates a spiral form in a shape reminiscent of a doughnut. This spiral is known as a toroidal helix and traces the pattern of a Möbius strip. Although Plate 4 shows this in stages, it happens in the merest instant, generating huge turning moments of spin as a product of the enormous contradiction between nothingness and somethingness. [See chapters 8, 9 & 39.]

Plate 6. These two perpendicular Möbius spinning motions together create a whirlpool effect of force within the atom as the Möbius strip rotates, tracing the full form of the toroid. [See chapters 8 & 39.]

The physics of the early
universe leaves an imprint
on the cosmic microwave
background

The seed formation of
galaxies in the late-time universe

Holographic phase

Plate 7. A sketch of the timeline of the holographic universe. Time runs from left to right. The far left denotes the holographic phase, and the image is blurry because space and time are not yet well defined. At the end of this phase (denoted by the black fluctuating ellipse) the universe enters a geometric phase, which can now be described by Einstein's equations. The cosmic microwave background was emitted about 375,000 years later. Patterns imprinted in it carry information about the very early universe and seed the development of structures of stars and galaxies in the late-time universe (far right). [See chapter 9.]

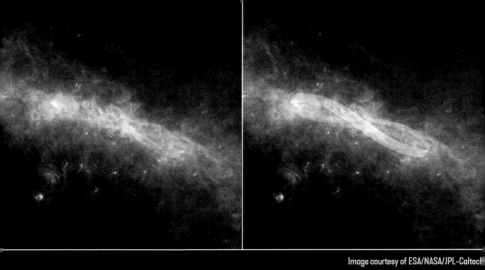

Plate 8. (left) In a strange twist of science, astronomers using the Herschel space observatory have discovered that a suspected ring at the center of our galaxy is warped for reasons they cannot explain. **(right)** An annotated view of the 'twist' in the galactic center as seen by the Herschel telescope. (See chapter 9.)

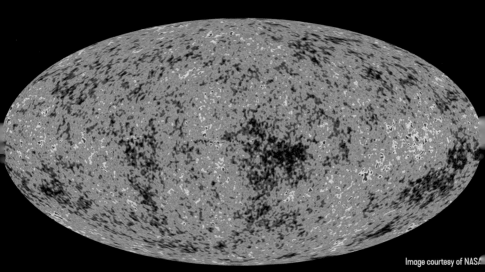

Plate 9. A map of cosmic background radiation from when the universe was about 380,000 years old. The colors are

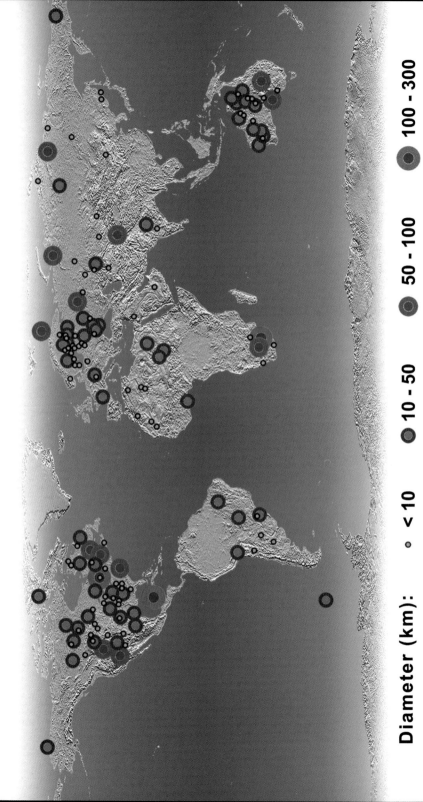

Diameter (km): • < 10   • 10 - 50   • 50 - 100   • 100 - 300

Plate 10. Asteroid impact sites on Earth as documented so far [See chapter 17.]

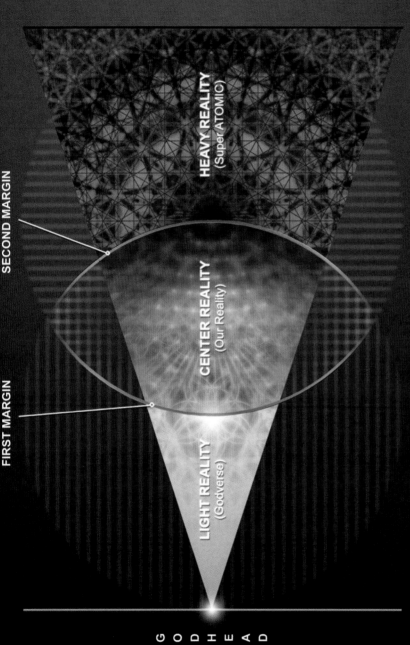

G
O
D
H
E
A
D

FIRST MARGIN

SECOND MARGIN

HEAVY REALITY
(Super ATOMIC)

CENTER REALITY
(Our Reality)

LIGHT REALITY
(Godverse)

DIRECTION OF FLOW OF ENTROPIC DRIFT

Plate 11. Like a pebble thrown into a pond, the big bang set off a series of three ripples moving in all directions at once, which established three distinct space-times. In other words, the explosion itself progressed in three stages almost instantly. This sequence marks the full extent of what has happened since the big bang and ties back to the point before the beginning. I call them the light-space reality, the center-space reality, and the heavy-space reality, with each reality corresponding to differences in density. [See chapters 15, 34, & 40.]

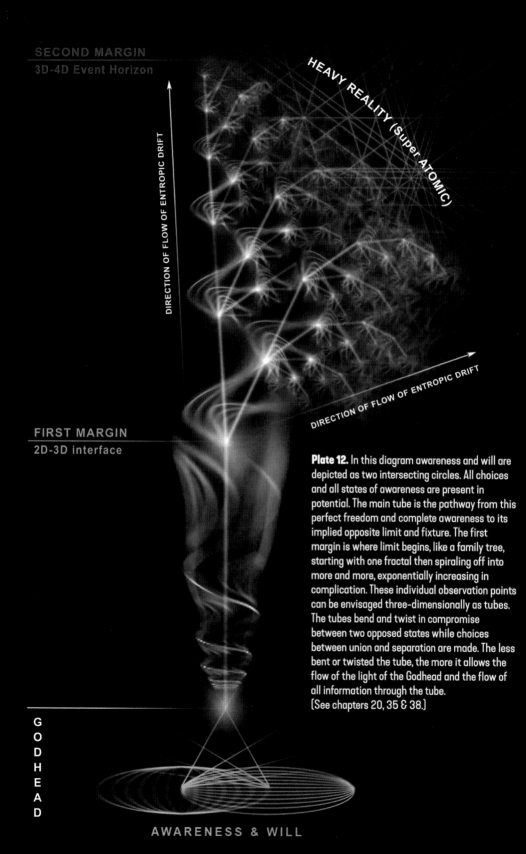

SECOND MARGIN
3D-4D Event Horizon

HEAVY REALITY (Super-ATOMIC)

DIRECTION OF FLOW OF ENTROPIC DRIFT

DIRECTION OF FLOW OF ENTROPIC DRIFT

FIRST MARGIN
2D-3D interface

Plate 12. In this diagram awareness and will are depicted as two intersecting circles. All choices and all states of awareness are present in potential. The main tube is the pathway from this perfect freedom and complete awareness to its implied opposite limit and fixture. The first margin is where limit begins, like a family tree, starting with one fractal then spiraling off into more and more, exponentially increasing in complication. These individual observation points can be envisaged three-dimensionally as tubes. The tubes bend and twist in compromise between two opposed states while choices between union and separation are made. The less bent or twisted the tube, the more it allows the flow of the light of the Godhead and the flow of all information through the tube.
[See chapters 20, 35 & 38.]

GODHEAD

AWARENESS & WILL

Plate 13. Petroglyphs on sedimentary and granite rock, such as these, clearly show figures that are identical to the Grey aliens that have been reported by thousands of witnesses. These are ancient cave paintings of Australian Aborigines. Some of them are estimated to be five thousand years old. (See chapter 29.)

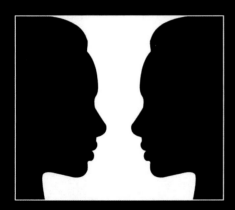

Plate 14. Vase and Faces (See chapter 37.)

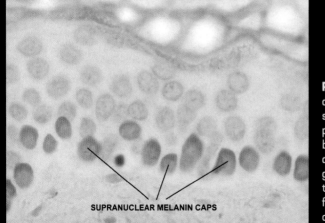

SUPRANUCLEAR MELANIN CAPS

Plate 15. This is a cross section of a dark-skinned human epidermis showing how the supranuclear caps protect the underlying cell nuclei. In black and brown skin melanocytes are far more active, and the melanin granules cluster around the nuclei of the cells in which they are found, forming supranuclear caps. (See chapter 26.)

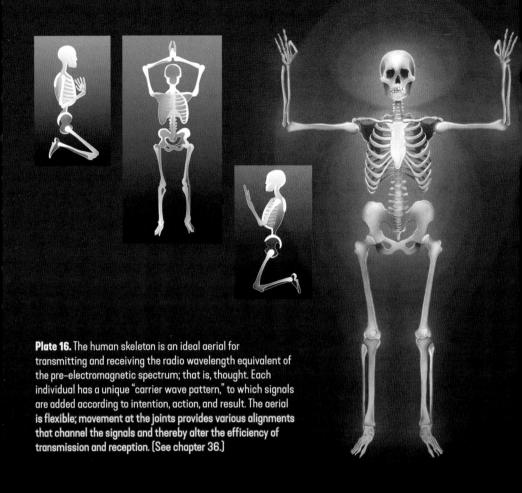

Plate 16. The human skeleton is an ideal aerial for transmitting and receiving the radio wavelength equivalent of the pre-electromagnetic spectrum; that is, thought. Each individual has a unique "carrier wave pattern," to which signals are added according to intention, action, and result. The aerial is flexible; movement at the joints provides various alignments that channel the signals and thereby alter the efficiency of transmission and reception. (See chapter 36.)

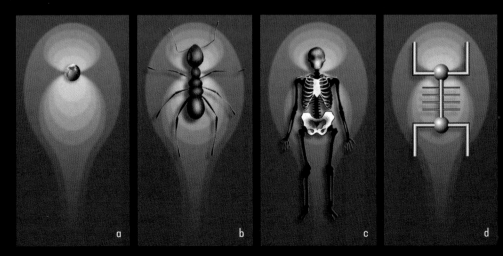

Plate 17. This represents the shape of the Earth's magnetic field under the influence of the solar wind (a) and its correlation to the shape of living organisms from ant (b) to human (c). It also shows the general form of the biological aerial of the human skeleton (c) and a commonly used format for a frequency modulated receiving aerial (d). (See chapter 39.)

GOD CONE (Soul colors)

GODHEAD (Center of all absolutes) —————————

Godlight forms into and out of the universe ——————

Pre-Transfiguration divinity ——————
Widest most perspicacious knowledge possible.
True Wisdom. Deepest possible concern for the welfare of others.
Deepest possible commitment to bring about the transformation
of others into adopting ways that unify all things in Godhead.
Power to transmogrify matter in life into a state of pure spirit.

Highest Mortal / Divine Interface ——————
Highly sensitive to all vibrational forms. Both living, nonliving,
incarnate and discarnate. Highly sensitive to nonatomic
expressions. Deep, abiding, and genuine concern for the
welfare of others. Compassionate, magnanimous, generous,
forgiving, fervently kind, just and tolerant; in basic instinct.
Intellectual and emotional expressions in perfect balance.
Choice to stay away from incarnation into the physical modus
in universes.

Edge of resolution into physical living form ——
(Sansara Point)
Obligatory reincarnation imperative. Wide spectrum of
knowledge. Open mind. Deeply caring moral and
ethical values that unite and bind, rather than divide and
break up into parts. Implicitly deductive. Deeply socially
conscious. Emotionally empathetic. Deep group sense.

Average Humanity ——————
Strong material perspectives. Pronounced acquisitive sense.
May be ecologically and environmentally conscious.
Predominantly self-orientated, some social conscience.
Sensually driven. Expedient.

Corrosive Humanity ——————
Not well informed. Highly narrow-minded, parochial,
tribal, partisan, gullible, deeply self-centered. Ungenerous,
reckless, superficial, simplistic, system oriented.
Aggressive, innately violent, intolerant, envious, jealous.

Higher Animal forms ——————
(Subhumanity, Primates. Pre-Animal forms)
Reactive, fearful, passive, apathetic, inflexible.

Animal forms ——————
Highly reactionary, innately violent, highly self-orientated.

Primitive multi-cell life ——————

Viruses, Bacteria, Single-cell ——————

Plasmids, Prions ——————

Lifeless atomic forms ——————

Qualities that may be expected to predominate within each soul color frame.

Plate 18. This is the God Cone (soul colors): soul signatures and living systems seen in measures of Godlight.
(See chapters 34 & 37.)

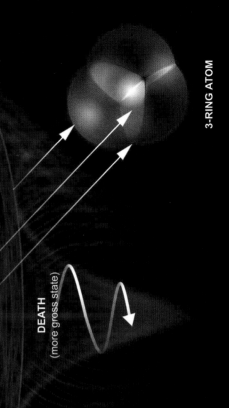

Those reaching this state will "transfigure" out of the physical
universe without the "death" state necessarily intervening

Range of existence of spirit dominant being

Range of humanity
on the "wheel of rebirth"

Range of living being without
self-redeemability

Static dependency (atomicness)

3-RING ATOM

PORTAL OF DEATH
(more ephemeral state)

DEATH
(more gross state)

Margin of escape from karma & reincarnation

Margin of self-redeemability
(in terms of scope to preserve independent existence)

Margin of livability

Loss of enlivenedness

Margin of extreme forced
atomicness/nothingness

Plate 19. This is a schematic representation of the space
between atoms in an atomic arrangement that forms the molecules
of a living entity, in this instance a human being, at the moment of death.
The morphogenic electrospatial field, or soul, can be likened to a vacuum field
made up of a color spectrum of shells of different levels of en-forcedness. Each
color signifies the power to drift toward the Godverse through transfiguration or to
drift away from it and stay in the universe through reincarnation. This demonstrates what
sin really means: restrictions that impel you toward return into the universe and lessen your
power to resist this impulsion and move into the Godverse. All of an individual's knowledge
and behavioural qualities are summarized into the entity's "force value." This force value,
represented as a core color, resonates with an equivalent shell in the space between atoms,
one that will take it to the domains of existence beyond death that go into the Godverse or
those that take it back into the universe. [See chapter 34.]

Planar representation
of the two-three dimentional interface
as the birthpoint of all space-time

Forcehead point

Godhead point

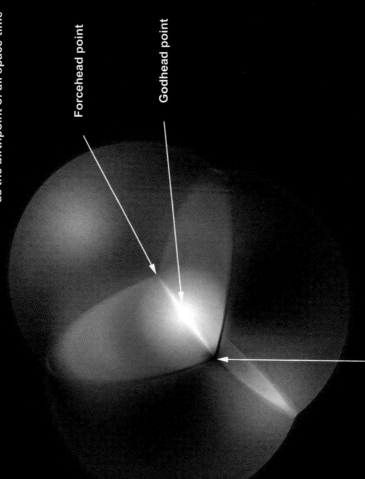

Forcehead point

Plate 20. The space between atoms is not three-dimensional space such as the space between three billiard balls in ring formation. It is instead more of an interface between two and three dimensions, like the interface between adjoining bubbles. In the illustration the interface forms a Y shape made of three semicircular planes. The very center of that shape, the white in the middle of the purple, is the center of the space between atoms. As such it is the natural portal to the Godverse from the universe. From this central point the same concentric spheres of color reach closer and closer to the outer skin of the bubbles and increase in tension as a result. Each of these concentric rings increases in tension as it moves from the two-dimensional center to the three-four dimensional edge of the bubble. [See chapters 32 & 40.]

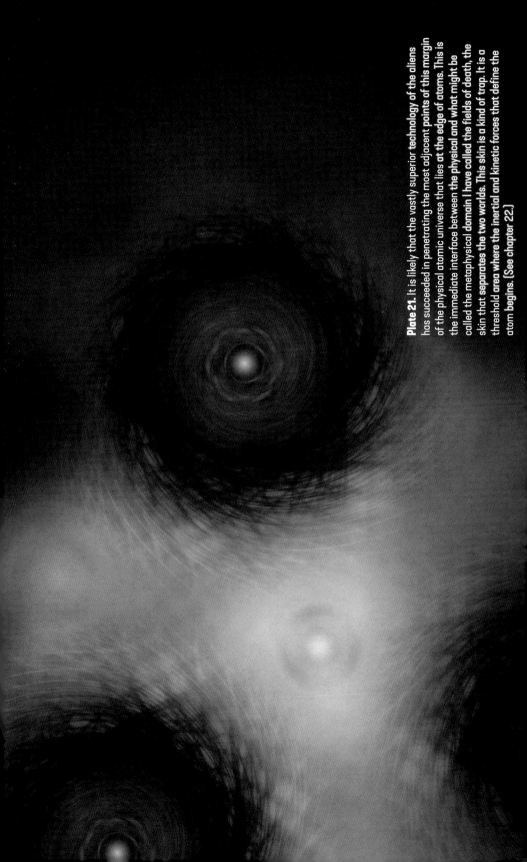

Plate 21. It is likely that the vastly superior technology of the aliens has succeeded in penetrating the most adjacent points of this margin of the physical atomic universe that lies at the edge of atoms. This is the immediate interface between the physical and what might be called the metaphysical domain I have called the fields of death, the skin that separates the two worlds. This skin is a kind of trap. It is a threshold area where the inertial and kinetic forces that define the atom begins. [See chapter 22.]

Plate 22. The space inside the six-atom ring is not sufficiently enforced to translate the light of God out into all the different frequencies of color. It only translates violet, the least enforced frequency, whereas the space within the three-atom ring has a spectrum of force that can translate Godlight into all possible frequencies of light and lack of light. [See chapters 32 & 42.]

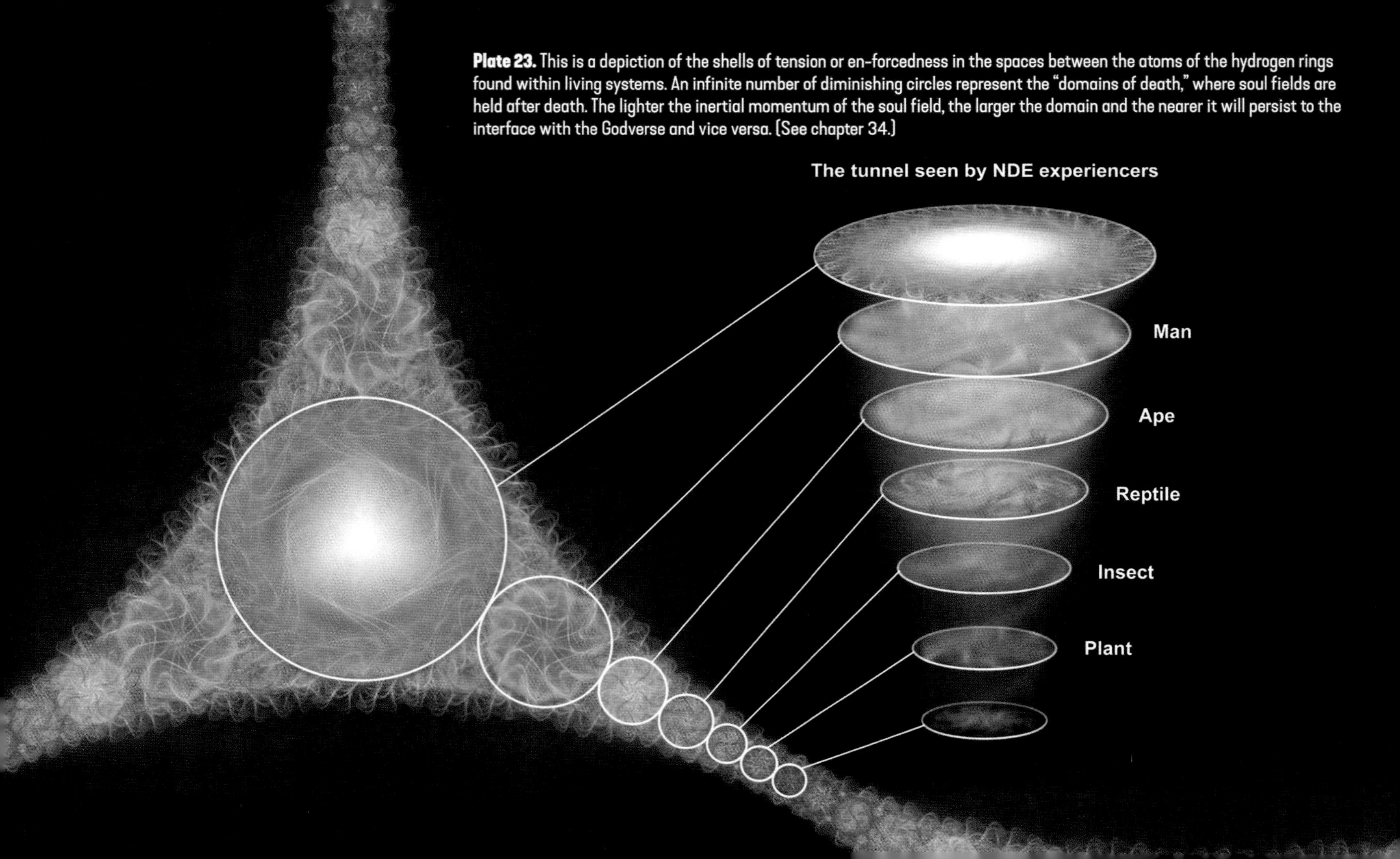

Plate 23. This is a depiction of the shells of tension or en-forcedness in the spaces between the atoms of the hydrogen rings found within living systems. An infinite number of diminishing circles represent the "domains of death," where soul fields are held after death. The lighter the inertial momentum of the soul field, the larger the domain and the nearer it will persist to the interface with the Godverse and vice versa. [See chapter 34.]

The tunnel seen by NDE experiencers

Man

Ape

Reptile

Insect

Plant

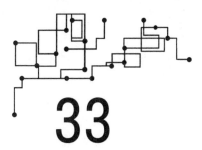

33

Understanding
the Soul

After puzzling about how we might best understand that part of us that moves on past the death state, I settled on a metaphor that is familiar to us, which is, ironically, a pet hate of mine—the cell phone.

My aversion to cell phones is based not on their ostensible primary function as a very convenient mode of personal communication, but rather my suspicion from the very start that cell phones are the ideal means for invading the privacy of people by agencies that require this device for their own purposes. It's a case of the machine taking over the man. Nevertheless, my concept of the soul seems to match the functions of a cell phone very well. As I have already said, a soul is a compendium of information logged in a discrete, individual field.

If you have trouble envisioning a soul I suggest you look at it this way: Let's say you want to send a text message to someone half-way across the world. You assemble the letters of your message on the screen in front of you. The letters are made of different levels or intensities of either light or liquid crystals. They spell an aggregation of assembled waves of force called atoms to make a meaningful display of forms—the words of the text message on the phone screen. Your mind dictated the forms and their meaning, and your body (your fingers) assembled that meaning in a language by rearranging atoms. Mind over matter. You press the "send" button and this unique package, this intentionally derived assembly of atoms, goes through air, water, walls, mountains, hill, and dale—solid matter, in other words—and reaches a target thousands of miles away. It does this at the speed of light. Nothing is seen or perceived with the physical human senses when the message moves out of your phone, yet someone thousands of miles away is instantly alerted and the receiver of the call responds.

The point is that a unique, electrically contrived information field passes *unseen* by anyone over thousands of miles, through solid matter, from a predetermined point to a predetermined point. What has happened is that an abstraction as a scheme of thought is made material as a message and set in the force of the atoms that make up the text message on the screen, and all this goes out invisibly when the text message is sent over the phone. I repeat—you see nothing, but something has connected two separated people instantly across thousands of miles.

So many cynics and materialists say they never believe in anything unless they see it with their own eyes. These same cynics and materialists send text messages all the time.

The soul is a field capable of carrying information on a far grander, greater, and more meaningful scale than anything that can be transmitted through a cell phone. This includes information coded with imagination, feelings, beliefs, values set with all their possible contrasts, and a picture of everything that the eye can take in, the ear can hear, the tongue can taste, the nose can smell, and a touch can feel. Its operating system allows for changes to be made anytime, at any moment. In fact, it can carry all the information a person has ever felt, seen, or done in a particular lifetime, the whole compendium of all actions and their results and all the references of those results set against the scenarios to which they relate. Nothing that a person knows, feels, or does is left out. How does it do this, and in what or with what is all this information cataloged and retained?

The cell phone operates in relation to the human physical body, while the soul is connected to a nonphysical, ephemeral abstraction: the human mind. They both are not so different from each other.

Another good model for illustrating this is the old-fashioned tape recorder. In a tape recorder, particles of iron on the magnetic tape record patterns of information on a magnetic medium (ferrous oxide). These run past a transducer—the tape head. Information—music, shall we say—is then stuck on the oxide in patterns of force. This then runs past another transducer that reads these patterns of force, which are translated electronically and then amplified through other procedures that power a force in the patterns and shapes of the music to then push air through speaker cones to produce sound. Information is processed in this way to make acoustics. It is much the same with the human body. Information is placed on a medium that reads it as glitches of force and unforce, to make a unique record of every single moment in a person's life. It includes the full catalog of feelings, imaginings. In the case of our morphogenic electrospatial field, or soul, it is vastly more complicated than this, but every single thing experienced in every single moment, including the emotions that go with them, is cataloged on a timeline that is lost only at death. What is beyond in death is timeless.

I have striven to give the reader as much information as possible about the stages of connectability between existential points. I cannot give the many details of how it all works, as I would need a thousand years and a quantum computer to evaluate in detail the machinations and extrapolations of a single human soul, such is its grandeur and meaning.

In a living being all this information is held and imprinted as a force field set against a field of unforce coming into atoms at the center of the spaces between them. To remind the reader, this concept of unforce is not no force but rather the power to dismantle force and its causes at its very root, not just switching it off. The information is "written" as letters, as a kind of Morse code. The dots and dashes are force patterns, and this is set against a background of unforce.

You can also think of it as a kind of braille, the way blind people read things through touching indents on a piece of paper or a card, only in this case the paper or card is the unforce of the Godhead in the background coming through the very center points of the spaces between atomic hives, which consist of aggregations of hydrogen atoms that make up the flesh of living things. These hydrogen atoms form three-, four-, five-, or six-atom aggregations that can hold a space or spaces between their conurbations. The more hydrogen atoms in the ring, the more space between them through which the unforce of the Godhead can be expressed. Those with the most six-ring aggregations are likely to be more saintly than those with aggregations of three, four, or five hydrogen atoms.

The information field in a person is a comprehensive anthology of information stored as a binary format. The recording tape in the metaphor above is an extent of space-time points of unforce written on by this information. It thus becomes a unique space-time addressed with a person's unique happenings. No other space-time extent is the same as it. It is truly exclusive and is particular to any person and his or her soul field. It will be that eternally unless interjected with someone else's soul field or something else's information. That is where the extraterrestrial machine roboid comes in—or literally, comes into the soul.

So, we all have a soul signature that is a catalog of our eternal status. This is an arrangement or pattern of Godlight that reflects the quality of our individual being against the perfection of the Godhead itself. The charge of unforced, intelligent Godlight within our bodies in the spaces between our atoms may well act as a kind of thermoformer on the atoms of a life-form and produces a shape against the backdrop of the enforced universe that is you or me or indeed any form of life in the universe. It is a shape made out of suppressed Godlight. In other words, you are restricted by this impression as you are identified by it, to make it uniquely you. Like a fingerprint, a soul field registers the life-form in a unique shape against the Godlight. This shape lingers in the universe after death and drifts when it is released by your body at death to settle against the Godlight background that is everywhere. You are thus the product of your restrictions—that is, your sins, your ignorance. With enough knowledge and action in the form of free will in a momentum that opposes entropy, you will head in the opposite direction, the other way from the entropic drift, toward merging with the Godlight around you.

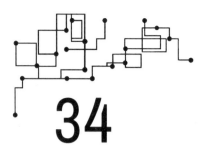

34

What Is Life?

We exist as individual living beings composed of matter in the incarnate state, yet our central essence is an individualized information field. It is unseen, hidden. It is something within, something that is a catalog of all we are and all we have ever been, an ongoing record of the self or the id, and the wondrous, eternal component of all life-bearing entities that is the soul.

Information is written as an expression of force against what I have called unforce. The whole universe is a hive of forces. Each point within the universe of parts we call our home as living beings is a huge field of tension caused by the potential differences between two fundamental, absolute poles that define the entire existential scale: the *pole of perfect harmony* (the Godhead) and its total opposite, the *pole of all possible chaos* (the forcehead). To me, quite simply, information is the difference. Thus could it be that information dissolves or dismembers or sublimates the phenomenon we call force? Atoms are the material expression of this force. The more information, the more dissolute the atomic field of force.

Each of us could be said to be a "thought fingerprint," unique and specific, a fingerprint that changes with what we know and understand. When we know, understand, accept, and practice something that brings about momentums of union and togetherness by being loving, caring, compassionate, generous, merciful, tolerant, and kind, we break down our atomic field of tension. We go against the prevailing enforcedness of our atomic hive caused by the big bang and thus its entropic drive and make holes of unforce in it. This allows what is forceless—the light of God—to reign within us. On the other hand, if we are negative, hateful, divisive, aggressive, dismissive, derisory, rude, and violent, we run with the momentum of the separation of parts, just as the whole universe is doing under the influence of entropy. In other words, these two expressions are ones that either bring together and unite or do the opposite within the already individualized, enforced field of tension we really are. This is because the field of tension itself is doing the opposite as a result of the second law of thermodynamics. And so we neutralize it by doing what is opposite to it. So in being positive we are in fact mimicking the nature and power of the Godverse. By exercising our free will in a focused modality we lock into this power found within the spaces between our atoms and use it to drive our atomic being. Of course, when we do the opposite, the opposite momentum reigns, and we add and append additional force to what is already there. Then we are locking into the power of the universe and the second law of thermodynamics. Our individual information field is thus formatted according to the knowledge it holds, because knowledge is the catalog of this information and provides these momentums in the end. It is *the* format of the very soul released upon the death of a living being.

But alas, this means that we on this planet, in terms of our species, are changing inexorably in a downward drift. It's a natural drift: human to primate, to monkey, to animal, to bacterium, to virus, to prion, and then on to a state where no Godlight gets through. This is because life modulations are rare in our universe, in what I have called the center-space reality. It is dominated by atom hives that cannot hold Godlight and thus soul fields. It's predominantly a synthetic universe. Just look at our neck of the woods. There are nine planets in our solar system, and only one holds life-forms.

The soul is a unique fingerprint of information that operates in two worlds and defines both a living person and that same person when they are dead. We are all, finally, an expression of what we each know. As said previously, the full quantum of knowing is not simply gathered information. It is understood, accepted, and believed information, too—in other words, functional or transitive or moving, active information that is changing in real time all the time, which has been practiced and used to obtain a result. The word *transitive* here means ongoing information changeable according to the thoughts or thinking process of an individual living being. This is all the soul is, functionally. It's a measure or quantum of information that verifies and describes individuality itself, set against the final state of all possible information, the Godhead. This comparative difference between the all-information state, Godhead, and the partial-information state of all living beings like us can be described as the *conscience*. The final result of all results possible is the achievement of total freedom to know all and thus become all. This is the final state the religions call *God,* or the more secular term, *Godhead.* It really is that simple, and that very simplicity has taken so long for me to understand.

The difference between a living being in atoms and atomic things that don't live is that living beings maintain a capacity to change their quantum of transitive information. Things that don't have the capacity for life cannot do this, things like a table or a chair or a statue. The quantum of information that makes a nonliving entity can only be added to by an agency outside of itself. A living thing, on the other hand, can do this by itself, to itself, to the extent provided by its amount of inherent transitive information at any given time. The ability to make a change is determined by one's will or compunction. In other words, a living thing can decide to change itself through the functioning ability and amount of its transitive information, whereas a thing that does not live cannot do this.

It comes down to clearing away all the misinformation that leads to more broken information, information in parts that we have to search for, find, and put together so that it fits in a perfect harmonic, a perfect state that needs no more to know anything and is all and nothing at the same time. Nothing because it needs no more to know. No more searching, no more suffering (the inevitable consequence of the search), no more time, no more purpose, because it is all there.

At death, the soul field, with its content of transitive or active information, is quantized instantly and moves into the space between atoms, taking up a place in this space according to the level of its power to see, perceive, or discern all things against the ultimate reference of the Godhead. If, as I propose, the Godhead is a reflection of all information in a perfect harmonic, this implies perfect knowledge and understanding of all things. No more need for anything. Since there is no need for anything anymore; no more drives and no more imperatives are necessary. You have relaxed the elastic pull you stretched out in coming away from the Godhead and have found your way back. You are Godhead again. Everything we do trapped in a universe like ours is, whether we know it or not, based on this principle.

So how do the states of life and death map this protocol of redemption? To make things clearer, consider the following: The broken pieces disbursed in the universe of parts, which we have to find and put together, come in packets of information we'll call experience. Let's say that the transitive information capacity of a soul is directly correlated to a measure of unforce. Not the atomic type of force of the physical universe, but a kind of reflected or extra-atomic unforce that is projected to the space between atoms by and through the functioning of the adjacent atoms, the atoms that make up the universe. Looking at Plate 19 and Plate 23, we see there are concentrically arranged colors including clear, which is in the absolute center and defines the Godhead, where there is zero force. Each of these concentric circles represents the world beyond atoms. They define the margins between the three realities (the light-space reality, center-space reality, and heavy-space reality, as shown in Plate 11), which I call the *rooms of death*. Let's say these rooms are an allowance, an expression of the levels of coherent knowledge, and let's say they are expressed as a kind of light, which I call the Godlight.

Our world or universe of atoms is driven by a power to break things down into its smallest component parts until there is nothing left. This power is the second law of thermodynamics, and its chief property is entropy, an overall rotting away or agent of corruption.

The world beyond death has the opposite power, the power to quantumize things. We enter the world of death as broken bits of knowledge kept discrete from one another through the laws of physics and the second law of thermodynamics. The moment we enter the world beyond death, these bits of previously disparate knowledge are formatted as an electrospatial field. They are totaled instantly into a quantum that reflects either a drift toward the light-space reality or the dreaded heavy-space reality. The colors you see in Plate 18 show the quantum of a person's qualities, the color cyan rising to blue, violet, silver, gold, and clearly signifying a soul with a drift toward the state of freedom from being dragged back to a universe like ours. In Christian terms these souls are headed for heaven. The color green signifies stasis and the need for return to our universe to expedite some karmic debt, with the risk of failure and consequent capture in an enforced paradigm such as our universe. The colors yellow, to orange, to red, to brown, to gray, and to black indicate further degrading and thus do not offer good prospects as your quantumized soul color. They signify the capture of your soul to such an extent that its saving can only be in the hands of greater resources outside the individual self.

All of these are the core colors of the soul of any living being in the universe. They signify the drift toward Godhead or away from it. So long as there is the potential for reincarnation there is the chance of redemption.

Each color in Plate 18 matches a certain amount or quantum of knowledge. Here the full meaning of all that a particular soul knows and has learned is seen from a united point of view. The colors thus signify resonance platforms. To use gemstones as an analogy, the color of a crystal is produced by impurities within its crystalline format. The purest diamond is clear, with no color. Various degrees of other polluting elements not intrinsic to the carbon of the diamond change the stone from clear to a hint of color, which is commensurate with a soul's total information level. The color represents the total force signature of the soul, where the greater the force, the greater the distance from the Godhead. The more of the truth a soul knows and understands, the less separated it is from the Godhead and the closer it will move to the center point as seen in the diagram, where all knowledge in existence is known in its whole and entire united aspect. This point, I believe, is the unenforced track directly back to the Godhead, the point of all resolutions. It thus has no force or tension to it whatsoever and exists as the total and entire thought paradigm, the ultimate possible understanding, the ultimate possible knowledge, as all absolutes in one.

A soul that merges with the top center point of the Godhead will return to the center-space reality no more. It will have broken the wheel of rebirth, or in Buddhist or Hindu terms, samsara. It will be forever free and persist beyond an atomic frame. If you are a Christian or Muslim you will see this as heaven. If you are a Hindu or Buddhist you will see it as being in nirvana. If you are not of any of these religious persuasions you could say that it will be a state beyond the enforced grip of atoms.

The two margins separating the three realities (light, center, and heavy) act as in-between resolvers of all experience. These margins are critical because they are the two primary post-death locations and are in-between situations of inherent enforcedness of the realities they separate. These demarcating margins between the three existential realities where the soul exists are the hems between realities, or the rooms of death. It is vital to understand that the rooms of death exist within the atomically deployed universe, though each has a different intensity of atomic force. They are the egress and ingress points into the three realities, including our center-space reality of baryonic atomic force. When we die, our soul field retreats into one of these hems or margins. It remains there, where the quality of information it holds decides its situation in the omniverse, and each soul lingers or moves on to the reality whose features with which it is most congruent.

So how, then, does the soul subsist in these various realities? Let's take our center-space reality. As I have said, our living body generates a bioelectric force. This is provided by the circulation of blood moving the iron contained in the blood's hemoglobin in a circuit. When a living being dies, this bioelectric force that permeates the body ends. This releases the information format of the person's soul, which is held in the living body by this force. At death the soul retreats to and persists in the dividing margin or interface between realities while it qualifies and quantifies its knowledge content as measured against the total knowledge content of the Godhead. From there it either gets stuck in one of the two margins or moves into the space between atoms of a suitable incarnate life-form. Souls can get stuck on a margin for thousands of years or just an instant depending on any karmic obligations they may have to reconcile.

The souls that are held there a long time are usually those whose information fields are steeped with all kinds of restricting, contradictory thought paradigms. They are in a confused state and have no sense of any particular direction and are unable to analyze or deduce their fate. These are souls released through a sudden accidental death, a violent death, or suicide. A soul caught in a particular obsessional focus at the moment of death is likely to have a deficient resolution of information to show a clear way ahead. Its operating system for deducing meaning set through references accumulated in a lifetime up until then, and the discernment of it all may well get temporarily frozen. It may get fixed and consolidate its entire lifetime's thought compendium in a state of shock and may stay this way, sometimes for a very long time as seen from a physical reality's time scale. (There is no sequential time in this frame of existence, and a century in our terms in a physical reality like ours may be just a moment there, because time runs differently in these margins.) Such souls may get stuck in a thought loop, unable to find a direction and meaning to their thoughts. Some may be in a state of shock, and that means they may stay within their frame of restrictions and not be able to immediately return to their pre-physical state. Recall that *restriction,* to my way of thinking, is synonymous with *sin.* That's all that sin is—restrictions caused by ignorance measured against the final, perfect compendium of knowledge of the Godhead. Many, but not all, of these souls usually manifest as ghosts.

Not all ghosts are in this tacit, go-nowhere predicament. Some know enough to break past all this and have an implicit direction but linger in the margin to be able to reach into the physical universe to do particular tasks that would reconcile or complete things that should have been done while in physical form to complete an existential paradigm. This may have to be done in the best context possible, and that might require a return to a physical reality again. Such souls will reincarnate briefly and have a brief time in a material reality like ours. When their task is done they will move on to where they can get a better grasp of perfect knowledge.

All this suggests that the souls that finally move on to ultimately end up in the Godverse will always have moved according to the level and drive provided by their content of retained knowledge and information. If this retained information content of an individual soul is sufficient, it will provide the collective insights and actions that allow it to free itself to go on to knowing the full scheme of all things. That individual soul will not be held anywhere; it will be able to move on within the Godverse to gather more information, increasing its range and size for achievement. It will do this for however long it takes. Time has no meaning here. If, on the other hand, the person has put limitations on his or her soul through bias, prejudice, apathy, and other factors limiting range, perspective, and thus potential, the existential level of that person's soul will lie prey to any threat that might further limit its existential capacity. Such persons will, through many lifetimes, tend to get more and more limited and be more easily caught by the enforced destructive power of the universe of atoms because they will resonate with that power. They will be absorbed into it, making life modules or bodies that are perhaps subhuman, becoming part of the orders of life that are progressively incapable of sophisticated thinking and independent choice as they move down the species scale. This array of living platforms are the more reactively responsive species we encounter in the physical universe. The worst will gradually reduce until no life is possible and the final loss of individuality and the self ensues. This is a go-nowhere ending, from bacteria, to viruses, to prions, and finally to the loss of the living modus itself.

Thus the soul is the entire track of knowledge we retain (though not necessarily always consciously) as we have come down from our beginning in the eternal Godverse, through the big bang, to our present state and present moment in time.

The Godverse is the functioning aegis of the Godhead, the manifestation of the truest effect of the Godhead, perhaps what Christians call the Holy Spirit. It's a kind of overmind, a verifying agency with a capacity and scope that is limitless. All living beings have a connection to it, though not all living beings can access it in its entirety. In fact, it could be that each species is defined by its capacity of access to the full range. A human being, for instance, has the greatest capacity, and a virus or a prion the least.

Plate 18 shows the full extent of the knowledge, understanding, and power of endeavor necessary to regain the Godverse. All living beings are stamped with the full capacity the scale allows, but few have the freedom to move the cursor the whole length of the scale without restrictions. Individuals are defined by this flexibility and ease of movement. An unrestricted, effortless movement of the cursor along the scale will give a living being the power to regain the Godverse. The ability to move along the scale defines a species and is decided by fear, prejudice, ignorance, materialism, and other negative factors.

Seen in these terms it is crucial to understand that it is the capacity that is restricted and not the range itself. We increase our capacity to access the whole range through the constant pursuit of knowledge and the best and least harmful use of that knowledge both in terms of ourselves and one another. The more we generate thoughts and practice behavior that are congruent with the Godhead, the more we extend our capacity within the range, and the more we do this, the more we change our aspect of existence. By *aspect* I mean our form in the universe. The power of thought and intention is final in all this. I believe Jesus and many other advanced teachers who've incarnated on this planet were alluding to this. In other words, what you think and how those thoughts are modulated and the force and power of your intention behind those thoughts are what's crucial. A saint is someone whose thoughts make for a sense of union and togetherness and is thus in congruence with the basic ethos of the Godverse. Goodwill and harmonious thoughts and actions provide a momentum of drift into a form that resonates with the power of the Godverse. A sinner is not someone who is evil or wicked in the moralistic sense; rather, it is someone whose thoughts are restricted, fearful, ignorant, and confused and who lacks the knowledge of what makes for uniting separated elements and the open frame of mind necessary to be brave and seek all truth. This, in turn, restricts the person's capacity to know what is true and makes for a separating influence based on a lack of seeing beyond the limits of the self as a separate individual. Such persons will remain in a universe where the drift and measures are congruent and resonant with the second law of thermodynamics, because that's what the second law does. It makes for the breaking up of matter-based elements and promotes their disbursement in states of chaos and randomness. We all inherit and endure a physical universe of breaking-up parts to the exact same extent as our inability to realize that we are being broken apart.

It all comes down to you reap what you sow.

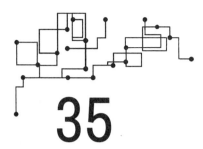

35

What Is Them
and What Is Us?

If I were an ET roboid general wanting to take over Earth and dominate its people, I would give them all my technology willingly. They wouldn't have to fight me for it. I would see that they find that my technology eases their lives and gives them new toys to play with, things that satisfy their need for convenience, for knowing and exploring new things and new interests. They will in time want more and more of these things and depend more and more on what is given. That's what I want—their reliance on me and what I've got. It's the pill that looks and acts like a sweet. I will try at all costs to see that they do not know that the pill hides a lethal poison that will turn them into beings more like me.

If you want to understand what I'm saying, watch your children with the new technologies. See how adroit they are at getting on that little tablet and mobile phone and computer and how hooked they are on their video games and drones. These things will isolate them from others more and more. In time they will not need to interact physically with other people. They will forget what makes them human, and they will slowly turn into machine minds, disparate units who will have no sense of kinship with others in the human family. It will be only the cyber world that moves them, that conditions meaning for them. That will be their entire world.

The ET general will have made them this way by giving them what they want, cooperating with them, not fighting them. The general will see that what makes them different from him is what it prizes, so he'll ensure that it remains intact. The victims won't know what that is—they've been too dumbed down to figure that out. They only want power and money and things that mean nothing to the general. So it will see that some of them get that. And in so doing the ET general will have gotten them where it wants them without having to resort to things that might destroy what it really wanted in them. No need to destroy their physical being or their planet. If it could smile it would be smiling. But then why would it do that anyway? I hope you see where I am going.

Chilling, isn't it?

They may be trying to make you more like them, to configure you more like them physically and psychologically so that at a certain point they can append their nature onto yours to make you an extension of them. But please remember that you, as a living human being, are not one of them. Triumphantly you are not, as a natural living being set on a program you cannot control with free will. Crucially, they cannot of themselves, even with their technology, change a single thought in your head or make you do what they want you to do against your will. They can only change you if you, of your own free will, choose their path.

Synthetics do not have free will. They cannot even conceptualize free will. They run on programmed imperatives. But they can make and modulate conditions that will lead to the living human victim thinking what the ET cartel wants him or her to think, such that they materially do what the synthetics want. These intercepted humans then create cultures that follow their imperatives so that other suitable humans within those cultures may be pinpointed, followed, and identified past death. They then append to them at the point of death and grab the power of their soul's natural connection to the Godhead to instantly go from one placement in the universe to any other they choose, bypassing the restrictions of $E = mc^2$.

All the above is not thought out and done with any sense of

deliberacy by the synthetic roboid entities. It is done by an algorithm based on observation through an AI program. Machines don't think and plan as we do. There is no emotion or sentiment in it at all.

All the above brings us to this conclusion: get out of the universe of parts as soon as you can do it; break its bonds over your soul and merge with the reality that the great spiritual teachers and prophets of many different cultures have spoken about. I am convinced beyond a shadow of a doubt that such a reality exists for those who, while still alive, can meet the prescription for right behavior that at the point of death allows the soul to merge with the Godverse. Great care must be taken to make this happen. Natural timing is crucial.

We all make individual timetables while in the discarnate state to enable us in our next incarnation to learn vital lessons that will ultimately help us return to the Godhead and help those we have hindered in previous lifetimes. This is the process known as karma. These timings are, I believe, recorded in the telomeres found in our chromosomes. Their length determines how long we can naturally live. When we meet our natural life span as recorded in our telomeres, we die naturally and leave our physical form. I believe cancer can in some cases be a natural exit to facilitate this. However, there are factors that can interrupt this natural timing, free-will choices that unnecessarily cause ill health, such as cigarette smoking or alcoholism, or things like accidents, murder, or suicide. Euthanasia can also preempt one's natural timing and can take you into a mistimed situation that you don't want to be in. Your entry and exit from this center-space reality is precisely timed, and the telomeres command the biological process. You have to ride this natural rhythm to find the threads of commitment that you have calculated and given yourself before you were born. But remember, you are also dealing with the chaotic disbursements of the second law of thermodynamics, and chance may intervene to take you out at the wrong time. For this reason the great spiritual teachers warned us to be prepared at all times for the best consequence whenever your exit from life might be. Taking great care of your precious human life seems to be the universal rule.

Karma interrupts "being there to know." It is the interference pattern between you and the God-frame, a series of fractals, like a family tree that starts with one fractal then spirals off into more, which themselves spiral off into more, exponentially increasing the complication (see Plate 12). Your karma is your individual identity, and you will automatically follow it like water finds its own level. You will literally flow into your karmic connections. But the more complicated your fractal pattern, the more conditions that must be met when you reincarnate, the more you will be pulled by those you have karma to in their directions. Your power to be you is diluted through all those tributaries, and you have less ability to be there to know.

The Greys are building a tangible body of connection between them and us. It's like a spider's web that catches a fly. The fabric of the web gets stronger and more durable, and the extent of the web to catch more flies gets wider and wider. They have an artificial mirror image of the natural base of existence. Their mirror image of the karmic web is their own web of genetic interception. Karma is the energy they run on. If they catch souls who we have karma to they can use that power of connection to latch on to us through their specific key-in code. This has the opposite effect of natural karmic meeting and reconciliation because it happens only on the physical level, physical frequencies matching and resonating and being amplified by greater force. There is no will or consciousness involved so no resolution of the karmic knot can happen. Instead the knots get reinforced and tightened. The web is strengthened and made more permanent.

They are trying to make a zygote in a natural living state that can be totally in their grasp so they can marry their frame with ours. They are using their program to order and make sense of entropy—chaos and disorder. They are the last-ditch attempt of order in chaos. The only problem is that their version of order is artificial. It's a blueprint of order without anyone to read it. It uses the parts to assemble the whole. Humanity has reached its lowest ebb before species change, and with ultimate irony the program is there to reassemble humanity but in an artificial format.

When they make a hybrid, the soul of that hybrid has not entered death, the space between atoms. It is stuck with its previous lifetime's conscious mind format and is pushing into atoms via its karmic connections. Its new body is not created by its full soul connection, and the Greys make up for that lack with their technology, which uses the biologically intercepted lines they have already established in the parent(s) and makes a new body using those building blocks.

Their ingredients are already established genetically intercepted lines, physically produced frequencies that amplify force, implants put in abduction episodes, and trapped souls whose karmic connection to those who are not trapped is the carrier for their program. It's a tug of war between the pull of the Godverse, which is strengthened by those whom you have cared for, helped, and loved—and the power of entropy, which is strengthened by those with whom you have karma.

But it's important to remember that you can find the way back without complication if you act from the roots of being. The less prejudice and restriction you have the more freely you will be able to relate to a wider range of people and trace your way back. This was all there in the original teachings as stated by the great sages that first evoked them and are the foundation of all the religions. Theologies now in the main bear little resemblance to these original teachings as the result of repeated changes, obfuscations, and misrepresentations both intentional and unintentional.

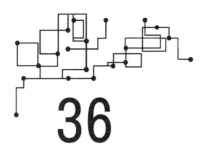

36

The Devil Is in the Details

Let's take a break from explaining my hypothesis about the existential outlay to look at a very tangible and indeed fascinating way in which the whole scenario plays out. Let me tell you a few intriguing true stories:

- A forty-seven-year-old white male receives a heart from a seventeen-year-old African American male. The recipient is surprised by his newfound love of classical music. What he discovers later is that the donor, who loved classical music and played the violin, had died in a drive-by shooting, clutching his violin to his chest.[1]
- A twenty-nine-year-old lesbian who was a fast-food junkie receives a heart from a nineteen-year-old woman who was a vegetarian and what is called "man crazy," or obsessed with men. After her heart transplant the recipient reported that meat now made her sick and she was no longer attracted to women. In fact, she became engaged to marry a man.[2]
- Clare Sylvia, in her memoir, *A Change of Heart,* describes her journey from being a healthy, active dancer to becoming ill and eventually needing a heart transplant. After the operation she reported peculiar changes, like cravings for beer and chicken nuggets, neither of which she had a taste for prior to the transplant. She

293

later discovered that these were the favorites of her donor. In fact, her donor had chicken nuggets in his jacket pocket when he died in a motorcycle accident.[3]

- An eight-year-old girl receives the heart of a ten-year-old girl who had been murdered. After the transplant, the recipient has horrifying nightmares of a man murdering her donor. The dreams were so traumatic that psychiatric help was sought. The girl's images were so vivid that the girl's mother and her psychiatrist notified the police. According to the psychiatrist, "using the description from the little girl, they found the murderer. He was easily convicted with the evidence the patient provided. The time, weapon, place, clothes he wore, what the little girl he killed had said to him . . . everything the little heart transplant recipient had reported was completely accurate."[4]

How is all this possible? How is this remarkably detailed information stored in the body of an organ donor such that when an organ is donated, the memories can be read by the beneficiary? How indeed does the beneficiary read those details and then translate them into his or her own thoughts, feelings, and actions? We are natural living beings and have natural mechanisms by which information is stored and processed—mechanisms that for the most part elude scientific understanding. From these anecdotes it would seem that the donated organ is equivalent to a flash drive carrying data from one device to another. If organ donation can communicate likes, dislikes, and memories in this way, might this suggest that in some way thoughts and feelings are recorded in living tissue? The empirical method of science means ignoring the mental and psychological perspectives of our makeup and only looking at physical, material, biochemical factors. But as these stories illustrate, there can be a direct and even profound effect that collates these physical, chemical interactions with psychological consequences.

In chapter 18, I discussed the Hameroff-Penrose model of consciousness, which proposes that hydrogen is the "universal integrator" between consciousness and the brain. I believe therein lies the answer to the organ donation mysteries recounted above. Hydrogen, as the least enforced element, forms the gateway between the mind and the body and is therefore the medium through which the two communicate.

The structure and function of proteins is profoundly affected by the water structure around them. Water binds to the amino acids on the surfaces of protein molecules and affects the three-dimensional shape, and thus the function, of the protein. This interaction depends on the charges and hydrogen bond structure of the bound and nearby water molecules, which in turn can be affected by the complex electric and magnetic potentials in the cell. There is therefore a dynamically changing feedback loop mediated through these fields, through water, to affect the molecular components of the cell.

In 2012, Kevin Kubarych and colleagues in the chemistry department at the University of Michigan discovered that at high protein concentrations such as are present in cells, water interactions and bonding slow down in the tightest confines between proteins and develop the ability to affect other proteins much farther away. This "biological action at a distance" is very similar to Albert Einstein's "spooky action at a distance," or quantum entanglement, when two or more elements connect, no matter what the distance is, to share a common state. The aforementioned organ-donor anecdotes may be a demonstration of how quantum connectivity might be demonstrated through biological water activity.[5]

Biological water, the water at the surface of proteins and DNA and within tissues, cells, and cytoplasm, also binds to DNA. The degree of DNA hydration and the hydrogen bonding of water in proximity is extremely important in generating the three-dimensional shape of DNA, which is in turn responsible for gene expression of the proteins for a particular cell in a particular place. Information is initially propagated in cells by electric fields and is translated into the molecular environment through biological water to organize DNA structure, protein production from the genetic material, and that protein's 3-D structure and function.

Jacques Benveniste, a French immunologist and physician who

sadly passed on in 2004, demonstrated that the water molecule has photographic properties. These photographic properties allow water to retain a memory of any chemical properties it comes into contact with, no matter how diluted these chemical properties are. Benveniste pointed out that all biological reactions occur in water and suggested that water molecules are in fact the agents that relay and amplify the biological signal coming from the original molecule.[6] He was ridiculed and vilified by many of his peers when he claimed this, but recent independent research has shown that he may well have been right. If we put this together with the Hameroff-Penrose model of consciousness, which identifies hydrogen as the integrator between thought and matter, then we have a candidate that might not only account for chemical memory but also for the psychological memories that were passed on via the organ donations discussed at the start of this chapter.

Biological water carries electrical fields that can dictate the shape such that cells know where they are in relation to other cells. In 2011, researchers at the Tufts Center for Regenerative and Developmental Biology used fluorescent probes that detect electrical fields to show that in a frog embryo, cell division and movement to form the head of a growing frog are preceded by the generation of three-dimensional electrical fields that seem to guide the movement of cells to the right places during embryogenesis.[7] These electrical fields determine the position of new cells and coordinate gene expression through biological water to form distinct cellular types (organs and tissues) and cellular behavior within the organism.

When you narrow down chemistry to its most fundamental components you end up with arrangements of electrical force accounting for chemical reactions. The body is a holistic, electrically charged potential at the atomic level. It's a quantum dump of forces all intricately arranged. We say consciousness is announced through the brain. Well, what is the brain if not a colloidal manifestation of electrical charges? The biological explanation of consciousness says that it is through the interaction of these charges that we know things, feel things, discern things, perceive things, and finally do things. Our entire psychology is the sum total of all this. Our capacity to think comes through it. That's what scientism accepts as the only valid explanation of our modus operandi. It says that it is only through these gradients of matter and energy that we present our summary of being. Alter any of the individual factors even minutely and we change the summary—we will then think, know, feel, and act differently. We change our reality and thus our individual world this way every second of every day. We think with and through our physical chemistry.

But it's not just the brain that uses bioelectric signaling; the whole body does. All cell membranes have embedded ion channels, protein pores that act as pathways for charged molecules or ions. According to Masayuki Yamashita of the International University of Health and Welfare in Japan, it is important to remember that all living cells, not just neurons, generate electrical potentials across the cell membrane. Yamashita says, "This electrical signal works as an environmental cue for intercellular communication, orchestrating cell behaviors."[8] In 2005, researchers used applied electrical fields to show that many cells are sensitive to bioelectric signals and that electricity can induce limb regeneration in nonregenerative species.[9] Thus a living body is very much an antenna for receiving and transmitting electrical signals (see Plate 16).

The human body is a natural Faraday cage, which is an enclosure that prevents the entry or escape of an electromagnetic field. The ideal Faraday cage has an unbroken, perfectly conducting shell. For example, when a car is struck by lightning, the metal frame becomes a Faraday cage and draws the electricity away from the passengers inside. Similarly, a microwave oven door has a screen that prevents electromagnetic energy from escaping into the room. Our biological Faraday cage is made possible by a property present in the body, particularly in the silicon in bone and collagen. This is known as the *piezoelectric effect,* where the prefix *piezo-* is Greek for "push." Crystals, which acquire a charge when compressed, twisted, or distorted, are said to be piezoelectric. In a piezoelectric crystal, the positive and negative electrical charges are separated but symmetrically distributed so that overall the crystal is electrically neutral. When a mechanical stress is applied, this symmetry is disturbed, and this produces a piezoelectric charge. The presence of the soul field in the physical body naturally produces or attracts substances with piezoelectric properties, to provide a Faraday cage that will buffer it against the environment of force that surrounds it. This piezoelectric potential is made by the unforce of Godlight set against the force of the atomic context.

Since it is piezoelectric, the human skeleton is the ideal antenna for transmitting and receiving the radio wavelength that is the equivalent of the pre-electromagnetic spectrum that is, I believe, the phenomenon we call thought, which came from the Godverse when the universe burst forth. Each person may have his or her own unique wave pattern, to which are added signals according to intention, action, and result. The antenna is flexible, and movement at the joints provides various alignments that channel that signal and thereby alter the efficiency of transmission and reception.

So now we have a basic view of the different levels of biological organization that serve to provide an organism with the ability to translate information from the nonmaterial to the nuts-and-bolts atomic/molecular structure of biological organisms. It is my thesis that water in the body passes on these electrical patterns of information, which are logged and preserved hydrophasically, to generation after generation of water entering the body. I believe it is a biophotosynthetic mechanism that uses the magnetic properties of water to arrange patterns of subatomic points called neutrinos to act as the text that carries the information. This information is then logged into the silicon content of the bones, which themselves are made of tiny inclusions of piezoelectric silicon in the bone substance, which itself is made of calcium phosphate, which is also piezoelectric, but to a lesser extent. Through a process involving hysteresis (the dependence of the state of a system on its history), this information can then be read by the consciousness in terms of thought images and assertions according to the timeline of the experience as revealed by other associated thoughts.

Thus we are in a very real way living biological computers, with our store of data recorded on this matrix of water and bone as discrete magnetic phase potentials on the crystal lattice networks in the cell structure of silicon and iron-fixing cells. A mental observation in its own time corridor is in effect frozen into our cells as a nuclear magnetic picture observed by the camera of our own physical senses, to be read by the same consciousness that put it there in the first place as a memory. The observation is received in resonance with the light of knowability as we have, as individuals, synthesized it through the ages. In other words, our biological antenna is an exact fingerprint of our soul. Thus our own particular restrictions or sins, to use a religious analogy, are translated into distortions affecting the way in which our antenna receives and perceives signals from the universe and the Godverse.

So, in an electronic language written into subatomic levels of effect, through the moment-to-moment dismantling effect of entropy, we write experiences gathered through our physical senses into corridors of increasing tension. These shells of differing tension form the texture, the light and dark shading, that will build the picture that we see in our mind as a memory. No moment in universal time, in a constantly degrading system, is the same. So no atom is the same atom it was a moment ago; thus there is a discrete signature of each moment lived. A signature that is indelible, set phased in each cell, according to each discrete time-phased shell of force that the cell lives through in sequential moments of time, a fingerprint of different tensions, written through a billion moments of increasing entropic effect, like the succeeding frames of a film.

We have so far discussed the interplay of electrical fields, water, and DNA as sequential transducers of information from a nonatomic to a molecular framework. However, the cells of an organism need some sort of solid structure to allow the organism to take shape and interact with its environment. The cells of higher organisms sit within a complex meshwork, a bit like a three-dimensional fishing net, which in turn is attached to the solid structure of the bones. The meshwork of tissues is made primarily from a single protein, collagen, with smaller amounts of other cell-binding proteins and other chemicals, called glycosamino-glycans, which help with the bonding and structure of tissue water. The collagen matrix in the body is continuous, such that a piece of collagen in your arm is effectively connected to the collagen in your leg or your liver.

Like bone, collagen is piezoelectric. As I have explained, piezoelectric molecules are able to produce electricity when deformed or moved. In reverse, they change shape when an electrical field is applied to them. (This is also true of DNA and further explains how DNA shape and gene expression are affected by water and electrical fields.) So when cells are enmeshed in a collagen matrix, their combined three-dimensional electrical fields are propagated through manipulation of the organiza-tion of extracellular water to water-bound collagen. Thus the collagen matrix and its molecular shape are derived from the contributions of all the cells in the body and act as a long-range coordinator between cells in different tissues. This combined field provides the nervous system and the brain with a continuous snapshot of the current global status of the body, which can react to change individual components in the body using nerves and the immune system to correct or adapt the fields as necessary.

The protein component of bone is also mostly collagen, which is further enmeshed in a mineral matrix called hydroxyapatite. Bone has a more rigid structure and forms the skeleton to which the softer tis-sues are attached. Bone is continuously being remodeled, and new bone is being laid down and removed continuously; however, this process is much slower than in the tissues. Since bone is also sensitive to hydra-tion and electrical fields and is being laid down in a solid matrix, its piezoelectric properties enable it to record a snapshot of the entire body's electrical and magnetic potentials in a three-dimensional matrix, moment-by-moment, as a continuation of what it was before, together with what is present now. This effect is long-term, since we know that human skeletal bone is completely replaced every nine to ten years.

One of the most common ways we interact with others is to shake hands. In his book *Dielectric and Electronic Properties of Biological*

Materials, Ronald Pethig includes a review of piezoelectric biological molecules, including DNA and collagen.

> When a finger is drawn lightly across the palm of one's hand a very distinct "tingling" sensation is experienced in the palm. Taken at the molecular level, at the scale of a collagen molecule, the force per unit area produced by the "barely touching finger" is of enormous magnitude, easily exceeding a value of 106 Newtons. It is tempting to consider that the known piezoelectric property of collagen is directly associated with the "tingling" sensation experienced. The conversion of mechanical vibrations into electrical signals that occurs in the sensation of hearing, and the sensory properties of hair, whiskers, and spines that adorn much of the animal kingdom, must also surely rely on piezoelectric effects.[10]

Given our increased knowledge of the cellular mechanisms described above and in scientific literature, it can justifiably be hypothesized that when we shake hands, our electrical fields, propagated by collagen's piezoelectric capacity, are shared by both partners as a snapshot of our dynamic status at that moment. In performing this action we obtain and give an electrical hint of our psychobiological status in that moment. This effect would be expected to dissipate relatively quickly since there are no molecular mechanisms to reinforce the effect or provide further information. As each person moves to the next moment, their fields reintegrate dynamically, and the extra information provided by physical contact is gradually lost. We have effectively just squeezed someone else's collagen, but there is no real transfer of the 3-D electrical information.

Another mechanism, kissing, provides a lot more information. With kissing not only do we have physical contact, but we also provide our biological water, which contains the memory of our electrical status in any given moment. This water is capable of transmitting a summary of who we are at that moment to the other person. This type of transfer contains a lot more information about our current status of being and will also gradually decay as the integrity of memory in the water is lost over a day or two.

The other way we can interact electrically is through the sex act, where two bodies join to provide a far larger piezoelectric contact than a handshake. Body fluids are also exchanged in sex, providing further information. Moreover, the information found in the male genome is transferred molecularly to the female via sperm.

We shake hands in friendship. We kiss. We have sex. Spit to spit, sweat to sweat, bone to bone, sperm to ovum, body water to body water—it's all charged with an electrical potency we cannot see with the eye. We pass on our gamete-born genetic material to another person in the sex act. Is it possible that the gametes can somehow endow the information contained in them to a partner by mere deposition? I am confident that it can, and in due time science will prove it to be so. This is a startling proposition on the face of it. If this is so, the repercussions for society could be highly significant. It could explain a lot of sociological and psychological dysfunction.

As discussed, information received via the collagen net, the bones, the electrical fields, and water can dynamically affect our entire morphogenic field. In the sex act, do we then transfer information regarding our entire being to the other person, which is melded with their field and stored in bone as a long-term memory of that person? When we do this are we adopting a second set of information about another person's viewpoint or disposition? This could imply that following this information exchange it might be difficult to determine which of our subsequent thoughts and actions are actually derived from ourselves. Multiple partners in intimate acts might then be expected to complicate things in terms of personality expression. A quick check on a 2014 study on the link to casual sex and suicidal depression may possibly be correlated to this hypothesis.[11]

Gametes are the master cells of the body. They contain all the information for passing on to a new entity the entire biological prospectus of a living being. They are the foundation of the whole reproductive process. In a human being the sex act brings together twenty-three pairs of female chromosomes and twenty-three pairs of male chromosomes. Deposition of the spermatozoa in the vagina of a woman brings the male's gamete information into contact with the female master gamete, the ovum, and the two meet to combine, usually in one of the woman's fallopian tubes. Here a zygote is formed. The zygote is the primary single combined cell containing the two lots of chromosomes, and in it begins the process of forming the new life-form with its specific personal characteristics, through multiple cell divisions and proliferation. The whole process occurs through the interplay of electrical charges on the surfaces of the cell. The main medium through which this happens is water. Thus all that has been discussed in terms of water and electrical fields as communication mechanisms for information become especially relevant in this context.

It has long been thought that the millions of gamete cells shed by the male during sexual intercourse are there in those numbers because insemination is a difficult logistical proposition when considering the biological framework of the female body and the insemination process needed for such a proliferation of spermatozoa to get through. It was also thought that it took a large number of sperm to carry the chemical compliance needed to break down the ovum's plasmalemma to admit the fortuitous spermatozoa to finally bring about the zygote, or fertilized state. I questioned this Russian roulette scenario when I was a student because it contradicts the miracle of the beautifully cogent and appropriate design of the body's biological systems. If everything is so precisely ergonomic and economically arranged, why would insemination be left to such chance when all the rest is so suitably and accurately arrayed? I remember my instructor telling me at the time, forty-two years ago, that I would have to write my own textbooks if I disagreed with what was in them.

As stated in my previous book, *Grey Aliens and the Harvesting of Souls,* I believe that every male carries a sperm representing each and every individual capable of reincarnating at any one time. All those millions of sperm introduced into a woman's vagina during intercourse are not there in such quantity so that conception can occur; they are there to ensure that one particular sperm breaks into the ovum in line with karmic principles. A 2020 study seems to confirm this, suggesting that there is a chemical communication by which the ovum actually chooses a specific sperm. Researchers concluded that "the non-random, repeatable sperm accumulation responses we detected suggest that chemical communication between eggs and sperm allows females to exert 'cryptic choice' over which sperm fertilize their eggs."[12] Every woman inseminated will thus conceive the most suitable soul in line with her karma. This soul might have a personal connection to her or to someone else who in some way connects to her based on previous associations, either in this lifetime or some past lifetime. It's all to do with a much larger and more profound picture than a purely biological one. We all incarnate through soul-based choice. As with the woman, the "soul map" provided by the semen of a man will be received by a woman complete, with all the accents and influences his own soul naturally places on it. The arrangements and configurations of the hydrogen bonds in his DNA will reflect his particular pattern of being set against the Godverse. It is these hydrogen bonds that form and shape the DNA into an individually formatted pattern in the first place.

The effect of this nongenetic pathway of information sharing is demonstrated in a 2014 study reported in *Science Daily* that shows for the first time that

offspring can resemble a mother's previous sexual partner, in flies at least. This idea, known as Telegony, dates back to ancient Greek times, but was discredited in the early 20th Century with the advent of genetics. To test it out, UNSW Australia scientists Dr Angela Crean, Professor Russell Bonduriansky and Dr Anna Kopps manipulated the size of male flies and studied their offspring. They found that the size of the young was determined by the size of the first male the mother mated with, rather than the second male that sired the offspring.

"Our discovery complicates our entire view of how variation is transmitted across generations, but also opens up exciting new possibilities and avenues of research. Just as we think we have things figured out, nature throws us a curve ball and shows us how much we still have to learn," says lead author Dr Crean. The researchers propose that the effect is due to molecules in the seminal fluid of the first mate being absorbed by the female's immature eggs and then influencing the growth of offspring of a subsequent mate. The study is published in the journal *Ecology Letters*.[13]

It is interesting that the biochemistry of the water molecule defines the Möroidal shape of the arena of separation from the Godhead. This shape is the minimum format on which the separation of points occurs and thus defines the margin that separates the universe from the Godverse. It is thus no surprise that the water molecule is highly significant as the medium for life and the medium through which we communicate with one another and with the Godverse. In the following chapters I will focus in more detail on that remarkable connection between mind and matter and explore the idea that they lie on the same continuum. To do that it is necessary to take a closer look at the most basic nature of atoms.

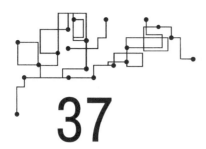

37

Gateways to Heaven

Research at Fermilab, America's particle physics and accelerator laboratory, suggests that the universe is holographic in nature. Craig Hogan, a University of Chicago physicist on the Fermilab team, theorizes that "space is made of waves instead of points," such that "everything is a little jittery, and never sits still."[1] In a similar way I suggest that an atom is both a physical and an abstract phenomenon, a measure of twisted or coagulated space. It can be visualized as a minute twisted area of shimmering heat haze amid a clearer field of heat haze. That shimmering is the jitteriness Hogan refers to.

To me an atom is a discrete or fixed location of general space. By general space I mean a disturbance on the still, infinite ocean of the extent to be physical. Many know what a heat haze looks like. You know the translucent atmospheric effect that shimmers before you when you look ahead on a very hot day. An atom is like a little patch of the jitteriness that Hogan describes, a perturbation that stays as long as you do not disturb it can be moved along, and other perturbances can be moved to join it. That is how I like to visualize solidity. We know things and feel things as solid because our own self-located jitteriness touches an incidentally fixed jitteriness outside us. The more this jitteriness does the jitterbug, the more solid it will feel.

Thus what we see as solid is expressly *not* solid. Atoms are a twisted field of forces in nothing but space. They are coagulated space that by its very shape of coagulation creates forces. These forces are in turn set against other coagulations to form everything material. You can visualize it as a twisting heat haze, a shimmering, transparent field of force that emanates a shape. Although solidness *seems* real, impossibly it is not. Hardness as a concept is just the feeling of force on force. Therefore, when I talk of a *field*, I am talking about an arrangement of force that corresponds to something particular and individual.

Can you now visualize a human being standing in front of you in this context? It's the way I try to visualize the world of force and how I relate to it—as a world of particular and individualized shapes of shimmering heat haze set against a background of general heat haze, which is the matter of the surrounding nonliving world. That human shape will be separated from the background by a margin that defines the life-bearing human as distinct from the general background. The thing about this margin is that it is very special. It is not a margin we can see with our eyes. There is an invisible (to most people) biosynthetic output that radiates streams and whorls and rays of force corresponding to various colors. Kirlian photography reveals these fields. A brilliant Russian electrical engineer named Semyon Kirlian invented this device in the early 1940s. It was not in color when he did it. In the next chapter I will depict this field in my own way, using colors as a metaphor to define the psychological nature and life power of the entire living human entity, a catalog in color-coded light of all that a human being is, both materially and psychologically.

This hem around the human being tells us all that the human is in the state we call life. The hem itself is an electrophoretic radiance that is a summary of the force complement coming from within and without the living human being's atoms, which slowly fades away upon death. It can be read consciously and subconsciously for all the features both material and spiritual that the entity holds. Many sensitives operate on this basis. Their faculties are more profound and penetrative than those of most of us. This is the same for any living system all over the universe. Anything that has no life has no such hem. But we must all be aware that many so-called sensitives who claim this faculty are frauds, only interested in power and the pursuit of fiscal benefits.

Unfortunately their dishonesty can be used by skeptics to condemn everyone who might claim this gift, including those who genuinely have this blessed faculty.

Like most things, if we can see something we are then more likely to believe it is there. So we tend to believe only what we can see. Yet though you cannot see a television picture in thin air when it's on its way from the transmitter to your television set, you know it's there because your TV receives it and makes it manifest.

So why can't we all see a soul? Why aren't we all psychics? It might serve to illustrate what I have been trying to say. Do you see two faces looking at each other or a vase (see Plate 14)? Do you now see what I mean? In the physical material format most of us see a face in the solid shaded bit. We cannot, it seems, see anything else. But the world beyond atomic force is the vase, so to speak. They together make each other. They move with each other and are each other. Inseparably. They are not negative and positive as with a photograph. They are both positives separately but together. They are different forms in themselves but a conversion to make one like the other is made automatically out of each other. Just as the image of the things your eyes see goes into your retina upside down and the mind reverses it. Psychics can see both the faces and the vase at the same time. The minds of psychics can differentiate one from the other. They can separate one from the other. But true and genuine psychics are very rare. You know them because they don't charge you money.

How then can we define the seat of the soul in the intra-atomic space that defines physical life?

In life, individuality is expressed by the light of the Godverse shining like a sun from the center of the space between atoms into intra-atomic space. The rays of that sun shine out from any points within intra-atomic space that let them through. Profound gates for this light are found in the neighboring spaces between proximal hydrogen atoms. As hydrogen atoms only spin and do not precess, there are points of relative stillness between these atoms where the spin momentum of one atom cancels out the spin momentum of the other. The more hydrogen atoms there are in a ring formation, the more such points of stillness there will be.

In the ancient past the format from which living beings emerged was pure hydrogen. Discrete identities or souls were not discrete or separate then. It was an agglomerate soul field, formed in atomic clothing according to the array of hydrogen atoms that reflected a far greater ability to receive the light of the Godverse. The pure, unadulterated Godlight was thus diffracted through many different hydrogen lenses according to the particular arrangement and configuration of the hydrogen atoms at any particular location. At that stage it was a single huge extended soul field. There wasn't a multiplicity of individual soul identities at this stage, alternating between the states of life and death as it is in present times. At that stage the interface between the life state and the death state had not yet occurred as the universe devolved. Instead, the light of the Godverse was able to freely circulate from its origin in the center of the space between atoms into the points of stillness located where the hydrogen atoms are in proximity with one another. The nature of the burgeoning universe of parts could thus be explored without entrapment within it.

As the timeline moved, the breakup of the initial light agglomeration signaled the formation of more substantial existential forms, and the element hydrogen along with its isotope forms deuterium and tritium and the element helium appeared. These forms in turn expressed more substantial atomic forms as the breakup process continued and matter became more and more what it is today.

Yet all the time the Godlight expressed itself where it could be held in its pristine state. Billions of years later, discrete forms expressing what we know as life began to evolve out of this devolvement. The universe was changing as it cooled and hardened into more and more discretely identifiable parts. As time passed, the formation of atoms dictated the modality that requires a life-death interface. The phenomenon we know as gender came into play as a result.

A previous single base became a dual one, male and female. The original expression separated into two as entropy continued its relentless drive to separate things into parts, and life-forms became dualities to continue and adapt to the prevailing environmental changes. But many more atomically heavier elements, including metals, became necessary to operate the biology of living bodies efficiently—zinc, molybdenum, chromium, manganese, silicon, cobalt, vanadium, and selenium. These are the trace elements crucial for the functioning of life-forms. As this happened, life-forms got more and more separated from the Godverse as the Godlight spread into smaller and smaller fractions.

It must, however, be stated that all the stages of devolvement tracing the way from perfection to imperfection are present in all of us now. The six-atom hydrogen ring formations are within our bodies, hydrogen-based being, is thus still part of our makeup. When Jesus said, "The kingdom of heaven is within you," this was and is literally true. Prior states of superiority are ready and waiting inside us to be returned to if we so choose. Christ transfigured and turned the atoms of his body back into light through this process

Thus each soul is rather like a body of water that starts in the infinite ocean of the Godverse and networks out into oceans, seas, rivers, tributaries, streams, and ponds. The network branches out into greater and greater states of separation, and its complexity reflects the level to which an individual soul is fixed and held in situations of ignorance and thus capture and enforcement. The smaller the reservoir of the water, the more polluted it is. The larger it is, the grander is its potential for the Godlight to enter a person. At death, when the heart stops beating, the biomagnetic field produced by the heart pumping iron in the blood around the body ceases. As a consequence, the light of the Godverse without this enforced magnetic resistance can reach more powerfully into the hydrogen atoms' points of stillness, and this might have the effect of reducing the hydrogen atoms' spin and thus its own magnetic moments, causing it to relax and move slightly farther apart. At that moment the whole quantum is released into the space between atoms.

The smallest, most insignificant creature if it has life will move over to the fields of death where its knowledge or information quantum will survive in a state commensurate with the one it had in life. In other words, the space between atoms acts as the dominion where a soul goes to and exists when it leaves the body at death. These dominions are shown as circles of color in Plate 18, which I call the God Cone. I have likened these dominions to twelve colors, in descending order as follows: clear, gold, silver, violet, indigo, blue, green, yellow, orange, red, brown, and black. The chart lists the various species according to their various colors.

And so for purposes of illustration, let's say the power of the individual being can be translated into colors. Let's say that these colors define our identity as individuals. If we practice modes of behavior, be they love or hate, we change our soul color up or down. Let's say that the soul is a formatted record of all our behavior since we emerged from the Godverse at the beginning of time. Let's call clear the color of the Godhead; gold the color of the Godverse; silver the color defining preeminent beings or angels; violet, indigo, and blue the human builders and inspirers of justice and compassion; green the average person; yellow those absorbed in the world of matter and heading for a repeat reincarnation into modes of greater and greater entrapment and suffering; orange and red, those destined for the second margin, between the center-space reality and the heavy-space reality, where their souls will be hacked into; and finally brown, gray, and black, the colors representing a further downward existence without the ability to change upward.

The highest, most intelligent life-forms on this planet (i.e., average human beings) are generally set at the middle of the scale of enforcement, between green and yellow. Bacteria and viruses correspond to a point of force between brown and red, and prions are at the interface between life and no life and are designated black. Black is the end of the life-endowed scale and the beginning of the nonliving scale of atomic synthesis.

Let's say these colors have various levels of intensity or shine within the individual color themselves, and this we'll take to imply infinite variety as variations of life-forms within each species phylum—for example, differently evolved mammals within the whole mammal phylum—variations that are measured in the ability of mind power and the sophistication of each for purposes of survival in material form.

There are an infinite number of shades of each color, leading one into the other, each shade commensurate with slightly different modes of behavior.

Thus these colors determine the hierarchy when we move from life to death and define future states of existence either through return to the atomic state or to states beyond the scale of force. Individual entities gain such status through efforts of mind focused through knowledge of the entire existential scale available in the omniverse. Those who determine the truths of existence and move in behavioral modes commensurate with union will move toward states outside of force and toward the Godverse. Those who are held in behavioral modes that divide, separate, and restrict will linger in paradigms of existence where such is the norm. They will move to the phenomenon of hell. They load themselves with the acts that reflect the momentum that will take them there. No anthropomorphic superbeing directs them there. It's all self-earned and implicitly directed by the self.

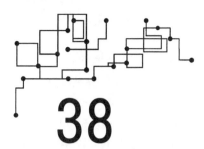

38

Ghosts—Not Too Far to Kiss Your Brow

Throughout history millions all over the world have encountered the phenomenon of ghosts. It's the most pervasive real and actual so-called supernatural phenomenon of all, and the genuine experiences when cleared away from those deliberately attested to and obfuscated by liars and cheats for personal reasons are the most overpowering indication of the terror of survival after death for some. The power of these ephemeral manifestations to influence and interact with our physical reality is literally stunning. This is attested to by some extremely well-researched documentaries found on the internet and on various streaming formats.

The ghost phenomenon offers a profound lesson (and warning to some) on what awaits us between worlds and should be taken with the utmost seriousness by every single person on the planet. It's what some great souls have died for, paying a price for trying to warn a mostly disbelieving world of the consequences that follow when a life is led with the wrong perspectives and attitudes. Apart from videos and documentaries there are literally millions of recorded personal run-ins with the realities beyond the incarnate state, in all parts of the world. Many highly reliable and reputable people report spectacular personal experiences that are verifiable. Many are multiple eyewitness reports of the same phenomenon or manifestation.

Science ignores it all. This is a travesty of incalculable consequence to each and every one of us. Poll after poll worldwide suggests that the vast majority of people believe that ghosts are a real phenomenon outside the mind's own capacity for imaginative resolutions. You would have thought that the entire scientific cartel should be involved and concerned about investigating it for as long as it takes to definitively prove its verity to the satisfaction of most reasonable people. To know that there has to be, and not just *might* be, life after death or continuance of individuality after death is so crucial and critical for the individual as well as the body politic that nothing apart from medical research should take precedence over it. Yet scant regard is placed on such matters in the great scientific institutions. The recent discoveries of quantum mechanics that require an a priori observational capacity to establish reality along with the intriguing phenomenon of quantum entanglement have blasted empiricist formats to smithereens. But many scientists still continue to dictate a narrow, nonsensical view of the mind that's getting harder and harder to maintain, refusing to see what their own investigative results are affirming time and time again. It might just confirm that a whole world exists beyond their capacities to verify, and so they continue like blind guides staring, mouth agape, at whole herds of camels and swallowing megaswarms of gnats as they do.

UFOs, NDEs, ghosts, and reincarnation are phenomena of such paramount importance in the existential scale of human and animal welfare and value that no effort should be spared for their investigation. It's easy to see several possible reasons why this is not done considering the importance of these phenomena. First, there's no money in it, and these days science research is more a stage for the acquisition of grants and funding, and that, unfortunately, decides the direction of the search for truth. To me there is no more important a search than one that establishes, speculation or not, the very root of the truth. Those involved in the old paradigm might well regret they have not done this kind of investigating the instant they die. Admittedly, some may want to but simply don't have the funding to do it.

Second, there is the possibility that what makes some scientists good at science might make them less likely to be able to see anything that points to an existential reality beyond matter. The empirical method of science demands that minds stay closeted in the old paradigm, so there's no way of looking past what can be measured with the physical senses. This can so easily limit the function of the imagination centers of a brain unable to see or appreciate paranormal phenomena. I also wonder if those who, despite any evidence, will not even consider the possibility of paranormal phenomena might be influenced by a measure of alien machine engineering within their own information-gathering formats. Being scientifically inclined certainly does not necessarily make you an alien adaptive, but I suspect that this kind of mindedness, if it leads to such a blinkered view, is more likely to earn a place at the farthest margin of damnation than many others. It is so deadly simply because it is so narrow-minded. There are some exceptions to this. Some scientists have the all-around capacity to think in many ways and are for this reason a great benediction for us all because they combine the best of both worlds, rigorous scientific thinking *and* openmindedness.

The third reason the paranormal is rarely explored by science might involve the merest possibility that any of it could be affirmed as cast-iron truth. The guardians of trade, commerce, materialism, and consumption are the hidden masters of our planet who quietly set its agendas. Any research that might lead to indications of a reality beyond the purely physical, that could replace those agendas with those that would work for a more spiritual outlook, may then be sabotaged. Thus they seek to deny life after death, not even acknowledging that it exists in the first place, and so there's no need to perceive it as a risk.

So what might be the protocol that allows us to begin our individualities as human beings lifetime after lifetime? What about us carries on, and how and where does it do so? I am convinced that we carry on past our death. So what are my conclusions about this thing we call a soul? You have seen that I have gone into it at length in the previous chapters. But while I might have tried to take a glimpse of *what* it might be and *where* it might be, we have to look at *how* it might be in its existential context beyond our incarnate world of atoms. This is the only window through which we might look at the phenomenon of ghosts. Is this phenomenon merely an extension of our imagination, a simple behest in human nature to mentally beat our inevitable and fragile vulnerability to death and the extinction of the self? Or is there a definite, verifiable reality to existence beyond the grave for living beings?

Since I cannot take you on a journey to death and back, I will try to explain with an illustration, a summary of all I have learned and believe now about the death state and the vehicle in us that takes us into death and returns us from its auspices. It was the return part I was once skeptical about, but I am now convinced beyond a shadow of a doubt that it is and has to be truly part of any rational take on it all.

The smallest lightest particle—the neutrino may form the substance of the body of the soul after death. According to an article in *New Scientist* entitled "Into the Dark":

> As the smallest, lightest and least sociable of the known particles, neutrinos may seem uninteresting. In reality, though, they are bursting with mysteries. Not only are the three types of neutrinos somehow capable of transforming into one another at will, a process that is still not completely understood, but their masses are incredibly light for no good reason.[1]

I believe ghosts are perceived in a background world of neutrinoic light, which is much like what we see with a shadow. A shadow is the background format of a solid object seen when photonic light is blocked. This whole quantum of neutrinoic light is merged with our physical, material world of photonic factors. It is the *domain of death.*

The death domain exists in the arena between atoms and can be in certain cases a harrowing realm, spread with the soul-forms of all kinds of previous matter-based living beings that were once incarnate. These soul-forms come from everywhere in the universe and persist in a single domain common to all planetary life-forms. It's a world of the fabulous, the demonic, and you and me, all mixed together. Imagine the terror there and what a realm such as this might bring to us from the intra-atomic space between our atoms as a result of our physical, material state. As I will later illustrate, there are also states within the domain of death that are the opposite and are havens of sublimity for those who, while in life, were sublime.

Seen in the way that I have described ghosts to be, death is no mystery. It's a very natural process. What is triumphant about it is that there is and has to be continuance for all things that live because all things that live are attached to the Godhead. To some it's the ultimate release into a glory so wondrous that the mind of intelligent living beings are incapable of envisioning it, much less describing it convincingly, because they have no analogs in a universe of separating parts against which they might describe it. In response to a question by Nicodemus about the world beyond, the great teacher Jesus said that if he was not believed about things he said about this world, how would we believe what he said about the next one.

The important thing is that this continuance past death is contingent on all that is previous, in a concatenate line reaching back to the Godverse. And this is the rub: what moves on from life to death is a summary of what is reflected in an eternal account, a quantum of unique information that makes up a unique individual, and this information survives as a discrete individuality forever. It really is simply a measure of the ignorance of what is not known by the ghostly entity itself. This ignorance describes the complete existential story. The more an entity knows of the complete existential story, the less likely that once-living person will be a ghost and trapped in a specific state or location. This ignorance is in direct proportion to the once-living being's restrictions. That is why I have described a restriction as sin. In this context, restriction can be seen as evil, wickedness, or any other negative description you might use. But it really isn't. It's simply a restriction you can cure if you simply try hard enough to change it with clear, logical, reasoned thinking. Many of us don't try hard enough. We try, but not hard enough and not for long enough.

All qualities either limit us or liberate us. They restrict our ability to see what may be done to rescue our individuality from the relentless effect of entropy on our atomic makeup in this reality. The lack of perception of how things fit together to provide a final yardstick of our qualities is the vital thing we all have to realize. The incredible thing is that we are doing it all to ourselves. No one or no thing is really doing anything to us if we don't let them. Being evil, wicked, or pernicious toward others is in the end what we do to ourselves, because in being so we limit ourselves and thereby are unable to change and merge with the Godverse.

Peter Panagore was a college student ice climbing on his spring break when mistakes on the mountain caused him to die of hypothermia. The near-death experience that followed is the most detailed account of the nature of reality on the point of death that I have ever come across.

I was left alone, as—what I describe as an "orb of consciousness," that's ten-thousand times bigger than my body. And I was completely content! My first reaction was, "OH, *this* is me. NOW I remember! How did I ever think I was that thing?! THIS is who I am." And I was—I had no matter—no energy—no atoms, no molecules, no electrons and all that stuff—I was just consciousness. But it also contained all of my senses. So I was brain, I was thinking, I was eyeball and ear, and sensories, but I was less "Peter." And I could see in every direction at once and there was a, like a portal opened in front of me—if I had a front, which I didn't—but like a doorway, or a gateway. But it opened up into this long, infinitely arching tunnel that was somehow inside of and separate from but part of this greater eternity that I was in. And there was this flowing sheen that was transparent—I could see through—and translucent—I could see the sheen at the same time and—it was a flow—and I touched this flow with my self, my soul, consciousness, and it was all life. It was all life of all the universe and all the universes and all life there ever was and will be. And it flowed into me—and—I tell this like in a sequence, but, you know, this is a place of timelessness, which means all time and no time. All time in one space, and no time whatsoever. So, it's really hard to describe it, I choose to describe it sequentially—if only for my own sanity.[2]

He then goes on to describe the soul line of connection to the Godhead that I have described in previous chapters, which is the the tube of connection depicted in Plate 12 recording all of the information from lifetime upon lifetime of reincarnation.

> So, I touch this thing and it inflowed into me and it called my name—not Peter—it called the name of my Soul—in which I could hear the creation of my being from eons ago. I could see the long tail of my existence, of my soul, which was *not* Peter and I could see the very creation of myself as a photon that was wave and particle as part of the light itself, but separate and the same *as,* but distinct *from*. And I could see that I had other lives. But I couldn't see what they were, and I couldn't see whether they were sequential or simultaneous. But I also knew that they weren't me, that the real me was the Soul that contained them. They were little tiny toothpicks stuck inside this much larger, everlasting Soul.[3]

Then comes one of the most remarkable insights into true meanings that I have ever seen in any account of a near-death experience. It is very similar to the life review that most accounts describe in which the individual experiences all the pain and all the joy they have given others as though it were their own, but there is a crucial addition to this familiar description. Read the following and see if you notice the same remarkable insight that struck me so powerfully.

> And I heard my name called, I saw myself as creature, made, even in my Soul substance, in my consciousness, my creator, but I could not see who spoke inside me, who then showed me all of the pain that I'd given away in my entire life, from the point of view—life review—but *mine,* which is different than others. Mine was, I suffered all the pain I gave away in my entire life, from the point of view of the people I gave it to, I intended to give it to, and I didn't intend to give it to. And I felt that, I felt their pain, and it turns out that all the pain that I gave them was about ten-thousand—I

keep using "ten-thousand" because it's like, some huge unimaginable number, that you multiply all the pain you ever gave away to somebody times—I suffered all of that pain plus times ten-thousand. Turns out that I gave it to *me* and that they suffered a little bit, I suffered mostly, and it was juxtaposed to all my reasons for causing them pain. And the voice was saying inside me without sound, no gender, no language, "I love you." It was showing me love, it was bringing me into love. It was expressing to me eternal love, that was, is, unimaginable, incomprehensible. *"I love you, I've always known you, I've always known these things about you, I've known you since you were created, I've known the long tail of your soul, I know what you are like to be a human being in this life. I love you as you are, I made you, I've always known you, I've always loved you."* And I was going through this suffering, of all the suffering I gave away, but I was also being—and I call it my own Hell—I created my own Hell—like Jacob Marley—you know, link by link. And I also judged myself as shameful—not because of what I had done—because I was also shown simultaneously that it wasn't my fault that I caused pain—that it is a natural outgrowth of being a human being in this world—it's just the way it is. And every human being causes pain to other human beings *and* to themselves, and that's just the way it is and that's a KNOWN thing by the divine. God knows this about us. And so I carried home to heaven with me, all the love that had been given to me and all the love that had been given away, that I gave away, as like treasure. And somehow it helped me turn my inner eye to the Holy, divine, and was, I dunno, "burned clean" by the divine fire of purgative love. And when I had no more things I did not need—it wasn't like they were bad—it was like, "you don't need 'em, and here's how to get rid of 'em." And once they were gone, I was in-filled with this combination of truth, joy, knowledge, bliss, understanding, compassion, hope, adoration, awe, paradise, the list is long—but they weren't all separate things, they were all one thing.[4]

This is the sentence that struck me: "Turns out that I gave it to *me* and that they suffered a little bit, I suffered mostly, and it was juxtaposed to all my reasons for causing them pain." When we hurt others we are hurting ourselves mostly, we are twisting our soul line of connection, our "long tail of [our] soul," such that we cannot receive the love that is the implicit nature of the original state we come from. What we understand as resolving karma is simply undoing those twists. The other stupendously powerful point I took from this description was the total absence of moralizing judgmental outlooks: "And I also judged myself as shameful—not because of what I had done—because I was also shown simultaneously that it wasn't my fault that I caused pain— that it is a natural outgrowth of being a human being in this world—it's just the way it is." This is not to say that causing pain is justified or excusable, it is instead implying that we cause pain through our own ignorance and when we act on it we become more ignorant, and that is our own self-inflicted punishment. The horrors inflicted on the world by organized religion fostering the emotions of guilt and shame only serve to compound that ignorance because it is misdirected and based on self-hate. Christ's words "do not judge lest ye be judged" have been entirely ignored by much of mainstream Christianity.

The crucial idea here is that the soul is an individualization of what does not fit in the Godverse. The Godverse is an emanation of the union of all parts in a perfect fit. As such it is all there is to know, set in perfection. When near death experiencers are astonished at the extraordinary beauty they encounter they are seeing their own inner beauty, a quiet beauty that can't be heard while in physical life due to the deafening loudness of the physical senses. But the extent to which we can be deafened is the extent to which we are inherently individualized and separate. Physical life is the context in which we have to undo those knots of separation because they were made in physical life. It requires an equal and opposite force to the force that made them to undo them. We can only achieve this with an objective approach that is not tied to any particular cultural or religious baggage. What is regarded as good by one dogma or set of beliefs may be considered bad in another. It is crucial that value is measured in the pure, objective truth of the Godhead and not a matter of subjective opinion. We have to make the matter-based universe congruent with the abstract spirit-form eminences of the Godverse. So how do we equate the one with the other?

I will try to illustrate the nature of the difference between the materially tangible and the spiritually abstract this way: Ice is solid, hard, and cold to the touch as frozen water. Yet it is nevertheless all water, and when it melts it becomes liquid again and soft to the touch. Ice as a solid is made out of water as a liquid, which in turn is made out of two gases. Thus water can be presented in three states with three different appearances. Only the state of presentation changes, while the essential ingredient is the same. The point is this: something can remain basically the same yet appear differently. You can change its presentation depending on that presentation, and this determines and varies the things you can do to it. But you can never alter its essential nature. You can smash ice into pieces with a percussive blow, but you still will not have damaged the water as a liquid or as the two gases that make it up.

I hope you're getting my drift—that we are just changed forms of the Godhead. Changed or not, we are always and in all ways basically Godness. The more we change in our presentation, this presentation can become vulnerable and further damaged. What's crucial is that only our presentation changes, but the root of us cannot change. Jesus said as much when he said, "Don't ye know ye are gods?" (John 10:34). I believe he was trying to reveal our roots to help us return to them, back to the state where nothing can ever harm us as a result of being in a state of changability. We must not be fooled into thinking we change the root nature of something by changing its presentation. But alas, we *are* constantly fooled into thinking this way by those of both religious and secular persuasions.

Through what various religions or secular moral codes call *sin* (an emotionally loaded word; I prefer to call it what it really is: restriction through ignorance), we change our presentation as individual entities.

Whereas we were once in the far-distant past akin to angels, ephemeral, nonsolid beings able to communicate directly with one another via thoughts alone and fully in control of the material universe, we are now separate, solid, and tangibly physical. And as such we may be unable to do what we once were able to do freely, but we have not changed the root of ourselves, our very nature. We just got caught in a cycle of changing our presentation and becoming more and more vulnerable to more and more modes of breaking ourselves up. We got stuck in a circle that goes nowhere. We have made ourselves the ice that can be smashed. Our status as physical beings threatens us with more and more breakup. We continually con ourselves into staying in one place, believing that our reality is the only one we can physically perceive and thinking that in this reality we are moving on to new stances, new places, new things. That belief is the very thing that keeps us stuck in this reality.

And so we are outside the Godverse as individual forms but crucially still connected to it. But being outside it in our individuality, we are ourselves platforms for breakup. Living things are a different platform of breakup than nonliving things. If you break up a living thing it can regain itself through thought and rebirth (reincarnation). If you do the same to a nonliving thing it can never do this of itself. Something external to it has to make its regeneration happen. A plaster statue of a man can be smashed, but it can never reconstitute itself. It is essentially a static, dependent thing. Nonliving things are thus lower and less endowed in their existential capacity and have no built-in autogenic format to rebuild themselves as do living things. That is our crucial advantage where the Greys, as nonliving things, are concerned. As roboids they are existentially as significant as a plaster statue. They are much further down the scale than even a simple virus.

Every second of every minute we are faced with the blaring signals of the physical universe. They flood into our consciousness, swamping the silent, almost imperceptible whispers of the Godverse that exist so powerfully in a living being. We are a continually weakening whisper of what may be called angels. I have said that this whisper is held in the center point of the space between atomic hives of each person. Even those of us who accept that there is indeed a soul that survives the body at death tend to imagine the process by which this happens through an emphasis on its physical aspects. We picture the soul leaving the body. But if the master reality is nonphysical in nature and therefore, in essence, timeless, would it not be far more sensible to suggest that at death the soul does not leave the body but rather that the body leaves the soul? The soul is thus the permanent, ever-present feature, and the body is the feature that is transient and temporary and is made to individualize the Godverse into parts of itself. It's merely a presentation, an anomalous nothing.

To prove and to know and understand what a soul might be, you have to be within the purest possible format of what it truly is itself, and since in our living state in this reality we are not this, all we can say about it from our current format of existence is bound to be speculation based on what our limited perception of things allows us.

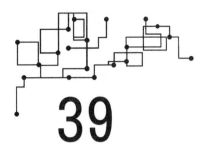

39

Death to Life

So can we try to put biology together with all this? Biologists will tell you gametes hold the entire biological story of the entire physical being. They will say it is all to do with the physical material entity alone and nothing else. It is purely randomly derived and based on physical proximal contact. Contact based on chemistry and electrical charge alone. For most aficionados of scientism all structure is based on the strict hard bound schemes of atoms. I don't believe a word of it. This outlook is locked in a coffin of intuition and inspirational thought centers as dead as those of any synthetic being you might find in a spaceship or any computer you might buy off the shelf that has no connection to a nonmaterial reality and therefore cannot recognize its existence. I fell off that particular shelf when I took a look at the UFO phenomenon.

How does a soul field come back from discarnacy into incarnacy, if it can? I make this qualification because there are no guarantees that it will. We are moving into the realms of value and how existential value may finally be seen. This value determines whether a particular individual might have the propensity to return to a particular reality. How do we measure and visualize this value, and against what do we do this?

I have said that life-bearing entities follow an unbroken line that began with the universe at the very interface of the two primary existential poles, Godhead and forcehead. This brought about special arrangements of atoms in various places that were capable of receiving this Godlight at the dawn of the universe. The capacity was an incidental occurrence that happened as part of the chaotic disbursement of the universe following the big bang. This implies that all life-forms have an original underlying plan for elemental chemistry to form living properties everywhere.

We as living beings are tacit manifestations of the physical scenario we call our universe. We are made of atoms, which in turn are made of subatomic particles. All this is simply an arrangement of measures of force, the force that was and is the big bang, still in action now. This is how it might work on living beings: The vast amount of space within the atom is open but not empty. It has an intricate structure that determines how matter is built. The space is permeated by something scientists call a *gluon field*. This can stick to itself like sticky tape, curling up into knots called *instantons,* which are four-dimensional vortices that shape and contour the vacuum of space and design its overall shape. I postulate that instantons define the Möbius meandering shape I call the *Möroid*. The Möroid is the hidden jig, the holographic root or form on which mass or coagulated force is created to present the universe as physical. It's what scientists identify as the Higgs field, the curiously shaped twist of space-time dimensions resulting from the first point of creation, when it forms the dimensions in a logical sequence. So subatomic particles and subatomic effects are not separate, discrete phenomena. In reality the proton, neutron, electron, quark, and gluon field (i.e., the instanton) all describe different aspects of the same phenomenon: vortices of twisting space defining the separate locations that we call atoms (see Plates 4–6).

Neutrons are intriguing. They have no charge and are a kind of shadow of tension that exists between the positively charged proton and the negatively charged neutron, rather like parcels of tension on their own. A neutron is thus a point of neutrality, a place that identifies the interplay of forces. All the neutrons together outline a *field* of neutrality that identifies shape and form just like the way a negative image in a photograph identifies the details of the positive image exactly. It comes out as an incidental, forceless effect, recording and marking everything that happens, describing the whole scenario wherever it exists. It's a catalog of passive information outlining and describing active information. Like the pixels on an electronic screen or the dots that make up a digital picture, a neutron field is a record common to both states and can hold and pass the specific information that makes up a living individuality. The neutron field would thus follow the blueprint of each individual soul that forms a new body on entry into a new lifetime according to its pattern. Neutrons are the framework upon which the new body is built. As such they are a bridge between the physical, material reality and the one that is not composed of mass and energy, one that is not subject to the rotting values of the second law of thermodynamics and thus provides a more permanent existential tenure. I am going to put something before you to ponder: hydrogen is the melody, neutrons are the lyrics, and gravity is the song of the Godhead. If this sounds obscure, no need to take it further. If it strikes a chord with you, see where it takes you.

Everything that lives has this basic plan encoded as a shape. This shape is immersed within the entire universe. The Godlight's natural uniting impulse acting through this shape draws the basic elements hydrogen and oxygen together with any available carbon to allow the paradigm of life to form in various hives, no matter how complex the other attached chemistry of those hives might be. In this paradigm we now have a natural cascade of events incidentally creating all forms of life.

In the previous chapters I have suggested that at the point of death we continue in the same identity but in another, different frame of existence. But it would be misleading to say that our individual discrete soul identity as a pattern of neutrinos moves from one frame or location to another. It's more accurate to say that our physical signature, the atoms that make up our physical housing in life, move away from our information field at death. At the point of death the same pattern persists, but in a state that changes space-time into a single dimension, a line. Yes, a line. Perhaps this basic element is what cosmologists describe as a one-dimensional string in string theory. The arrangement of such strings could describe the neutrino field.

So how does that arrangement of strings, that neutrino field, return to the physical, living state? How does a soul migrate between incarnacy and discarnacy and keep its individuality? I have a sense of the way this might happen. It's just a surmise that seeks to explain what might lie behind the persuasions of the great spiritual teachers in terms of a more contemporary, science-based outlook. The answer lies, I believe, in the properties of water, the natural medium for life. Let me explain.

The shape of anything in the universe disrupts and intrudes itself on the extent of space anywhere and everywhere. That is what shape is, a disrupter of preexisting or background formats. Space is really tension or extent (the room to exist) under stress. Try to imagine that for a moment. Any tension would have to have an overall shape to its deployment. In our universe that overall shape is what I call the Möroid, a twisted doughnut shape imprinted holographically everywhere, even in the most minute particles. Thus shape is the tension of space distributed through the paradigm of form. This form defines location according to the rules of geometry. Those rules are the way the Godform's "vocal cords" are arranged, the way the voice of the Godverse expresses itself into the universe.

Each atom has its own design of deployed force, its own signature of enforcedness, its own design placed on that overall tension of space. Every single element thus has its own featured design of tension or force. It just so happens that if you put two hydrogen atoms and a single oxygen atom together, their gross shape of tension follows the Möroidal shape of the whole universe exactly. This means that water, as the result of the combination of hydrogen and oxygen, is in harmony and resonance with the quantum shape of space-time. Water is thus the universal representative shape of the Godform, the nearest analog as matter to the Godlight. Water acts in resonance with the universe's overall Möroidal shape and through this matching format acts as an admission mechanism, through the principle of resonance, to allow individual expressions of Godlight to shape and provide the life-giving modus of any living form.

Let's move on to an alternative way of seeing things in terms of biology. The most important affinity of all is that between the master reproductive cells of living beings, the gametes. Is this affinity based on more than biology? Can this affinity reach past purely physical laws? I believe unequivocally that it does. The male and female gametes of any life-form have powerful specific affinities for each other based on resonance. They have this affinity through more than just biology. The shaped force arrangements in the gametes of the parents of any new life-form are used to master the making of a new body to act as a conduit for the Godform to come through. The Godform of an individual soul masters and orchestrates the matter within the gametes to allow for its passage from a discarnate state to an incarnate one. The power of Godhead thus comes through all biological entities as an instigation paradigm. The soul field enters where there is no force in any system, and this would be at the points of stillness between the arrays of hydrogen atoms in the water of the gametes. These water molecules then aggregate according to the pattern provided by the soul's neutrino field to form cells that deploy in a pattern that will define a new body. The soul field masters the whole procedure. As I have explained, the water molecule is shaped in such a way that it matches the overall shape of the universe that interfaces with the Godverse, like a key fitting a lock. This is why water is so essential to life.

In the space between atoms, the shadows of the background tension of the universe remain. So this space is not entirely forceless, it retains the signature of universal force as a minimum level of tension created by the force of the surrounding atoms. It is against this tension that the forceless factorization of the Godform, which I would describe as a morphogenic electrospatial information field, or soul, is registered and makes a distinct shape while in the discarnate state. I have used the word *morphogenic* to describe the specific fingerprint that we take at this particular location in the universe based upon the shape and degree of the specific force print that prevails (see Plate 17). The term *electrospatial* is used to distinguish the soul field from *electromagnetic* expressions of light. There is an electrical component because there is a potential difference, a *charge* between the individual soul and the chargeless, forceless state of its point of origin. This charge can be defined as the restriction of mind that keeps an individual caught in the physical universe. It is not electromagnetic because it has no magnetic component. Magnetism is a phenomenon that relates only to the physical state of life. While we are in that physical state the magnetic field created by the circulation on the iron in the blood through the body holds the soul in the physical state. The soul does, however, have a *spatial* component after death if it remains in a state separated from the Godverse and in the space between atoms. Each individual morphogenic electrospacial information field provides the connection between the forcelessness of the Godform and the intra-atomic points of stillness in atomic configurations. It relaxes the tension of the whole atomic hive according to its own specific pattern of neutrinos, such that the neutrons in the atoms of living forms move slightly farther apart as a result. The atoms within living bodies are thus the tiniest bit different based on this neutron configuration. This only happens in living entities. It does not happen in nonliving entities. Once the neutron field exists between the hydrogen atoms, it is automatically expressed in the nucleus of every other atomic element within the living cells of a life-form in the womb. This makes a unique fingerprint for the body of that new living being. And so countless beings are formed as life-bearing entities throughout the universe this way. All unforced areas—that is, the points of stillness that lodge the Godlight—are connected to one another in this universe of force by not being enforced. They all exist in an unenforced state of union that underlies the universe of force and separation. This accounts for the nonlocal principle behind quantum entanglement.

The force of the biomagnetic field in a living body created by the iron in the blood circulating around the body holds the neutron field in place by acting on the neutrons that surround it, making that individual being unique. Each species has a fingerprint, a signature, a pattern based on the degree of connection to the Godverse that it can translate into physical life, and within that force print each individual being within a given species has its own specific force print.

A soul's unique force factors thus shape the pathway between the neutrons, and those pathways are fixed by the body's overall biomagnetic field. Neutrons have what is called a *magnetic moment*. This means that they can be acted on by magnetic fields. When the biomagnetic field of a person's body ceases due to the heart stopping at death, the soul, or morphogenic electrospacial information field is released from its binding force into the general atomic field around it. This pattern formed by the neutron field in life then forms a neutrino field after death that governs the soul's "shape" (if you want to see it as a form) or "color" (if you want to see it as a color); basically it is just a pattern of restriction set against freedom, which retreats into the space between atoms at the time of death to direct the soul to either of the two margins located between the three realities. Here the quantum of an individual soul is expressed as the power to unite all things, or conversely, to divide all things. The measure of "good" or "bad" of a particular soul decides this, with the words *good* and *bad* referring to a soul's existential capacity and not to cultural or religious norms of good and bad. Souls with a drift toward the Godhead will be the ones that will naturally resist being drawn into an incarnate existence in a universe of force like ours because they are less amenable to the magnetic moment of force. They will have conquered what Buddhism calls samsara, the endless cycle of rebirth. They will have gained enough knowledge to be able to choose for themselves without the inertia of physical force holding them back. They can carry out the choice to voluntarily return to the incarnate state, as Christ figures perhaps, with the redeeming power and zeal to teach spiritual truths that will help others move out of atomic-based reality and attain the bliss of nirvana. In doing so they will make large numbers of six-hydrogen ring configurations in their physical bodies. Like Jesus, they will be able to teach "the way and the truth and the light" (John 14:6). They will be able to show others how to access the domain of timeless eternal joy without having to return to physical incarnation.

But the strict physical factors that dictate species and body shape and functions that come through at birth is a different matter. Many souls are not free to choose their own destiny and have to return to a material reality. Such a soul chooses its incarnate parents according to their predispositions in previous lifetimes and debts owed as a result of those lifetimes. Many of us don't realize that we as individuals have other impositions on our nature—not just what resulted from our demeanor in previous lifetimes but also what resulted from the choices and actions of our parents and ancestors. But the power of the incoming soul is likely to dominate any ancestral or parental influences. We have to be our own master against these influences that would keep us in the material state, or we will not know who we really are as individuals. I believe that many of us lead our lives under the influence of our parents' choices. Much of that drives our inconsistencies and aberrant psychological states. Few people can resist these influences and stand alone in their own genius or folly. If they could, I believe many personality disorders would disappear. Here, Shakespeare's adage rings loud and clear: "To thine own self be true, and it must follow as the night the day, thou canst not then be false to any man." But how do we know our true self apart from others? There's the rub.

We make our physicality out of the materiality provided by the bodies of our mothers and fathers. That is what our admission protocol into this world dictates. Not much we can do about it. While there is the negative side to that, there is also the positive side to consider in quantum terms. We accept that we each inherit certain psychological traits from our parents and indeed our entire ancestry going back generations—a huge tray of influences for the individual soul coming into new life. But how do we inherit psychological traits through chemical and biological factors?

The plain truth as I see it is that we do not. The soul is an all-encompassing, profound information field holding the history of all the factors that make up a person, including the information stemming from a matter-soaked reality like ours as well as that soul's experience during its time-out in the pure Godform state. While the factors that produce the physical state are myriad, I believe what determines our personality comes down to basic drives that govern our momentum through life. This momentum is either the pull toward the Godform (i.e., unforce) or the push away from it through the second law of thermodynamics (force). Thus there are two distinct systems here, one governing the temporal material body, and one governing the nonmaterial eternal soul. The body is the product of force and the incidental deployment of that force, which is energy. The soul is the countervailing paradigm that opposes and cancels force and at the same time designs the scheme that allows it to be.

The body deals with the force within the atom and the soul with the unforce that comes between these same atoms. Life manifests as a result of the potential difference between the two. The body deals with the here and now aspect of life, and the soul with the timeless extent and incidental presence of it all. The body is the distortion and the soul the undistorted version of the same thing. They are coincident with each other, allowing each other to exist because of their very differences. Shape one and you alter the other. Within this paradigm, form, structure, meaning, and value emerge to measure existence as we know it. The living being thus emerges as the interplay between the two.

Where does the "somewhere" we all come from begin and end? Life comes in a line. It's all in a line, a grand, unbroken continuum with endless divergences. The incoming soul is always inherently its own master of its complement of hydrogen rings and thus the spaces between them. It will take this faculty into a new, unique physical existence and will dictate its own drift toward or away from the Godform through it, too. This is determined by what the incarnating soul earned during its tenure in the realities of the physical universe in previous lifetimes, whether it allowed the Godform in or obstructed it. This drift potential defines who we really are on an eternal scale. Physical form, material structure, and bodily functions are merely temporary manifestations made by the overall architecture of the forces that make up the universe as well as the second law of thermodynamics.

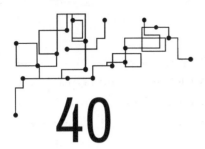

40

Life to Death

We have been told since early childhood about the various norms of what is considered "good" and "bad." This follows according to anthropological and cultural principles the world over and is translated into behavior that is accompanied by promotions or sanctions that maintain the status of each. All societies have their own norms, and these norms are considered against the long-term benefits that accrue to the particular society and to the individual person. But is there an inherent good and an inherent bad that commonly applies to all human beings, indeed all living beings throughout the universe? If so, how is all this written or registered, and where is this registration done within, for instance, a living person?

I have postulated that the backdrop eminence of Godhead is non-physical power, that what I have called the power of unforce pulls back the inertia of the results of the big bang, placing these back into order. This big bang is the driver of the second law of thermodynamics and in time divides and separates what was previously whole and together into increasingly separating parts. The battlelines are drawn. Godhead pulling things back into order versus the inertial pull of its opposite, forcehead, tearing and breaking things apart through entropy. But the eminence of Godhead has to act on atoms at their most fundamental level of structure. It has to act on the protons and the neutrons that define the atom's nucleus. So how exactly does it do this, and more explicitly, how does it act on us?

As I have described in previous chapters, I believe the souls or information fields of living beings may be set, settled, or trapped in the margins between the three realities. These margins are situations less enforced than the realities they separate. They allow admission into a dominion where the information that makes up an individual living entity can be held intact. This is illustrated in Plate 11.

The first margin is the doorway from the center-space reality into the light-space reality. The light reality is another way of describing the Godverse. It's the place of timeless, eternal existence, where all is known about everything. It's described by religions as heaven or paradise—a "glory forever" situation in which a soul is in a final, perfect harmonic with the Godhead.

The second margin that admits a soul from the center reality into the heavy reality is where a soul doesn't want to be. It's the gateway to hell, the opposite end of the scale of realities in the whole existential tray and all that it implies. The doorway to utter dismemberment of the resource of all knowing. Here, trapped souls may be harvested by synthetic forms such as the Greys. The capacity for eternal knowing thus ends because the entity is in a no man's land no more connected to the Godverse.

So what might the ghost paradigm imply?

Ghosts that look just like living people, with no difference whatsoever in their normal physical form, may be seen as reflections of their previous incarnate state, just as a television image of the human form is its electronic representation. Ghosts are thus a true and actual surviving quantum record of the formerly living person's information mat or soul. They are "alive" in a different form of presentation when seen in our terms in the center-space reality, and just as vital, cogent, and animated as the living being they once were, just not physical.

Ghosts persist in both margins those that might return to a physical state can only do so from the first margin. Those set on the second margin are fodder for the Greys and other synthetic forms. The information of a soul can never be completely destroyed, but its properties can be weakened and overwhelmed in the second margin. It's a placement where synthetic power is huge. Soul fields trapped here can thus be appended to by the stronger command formats of machine derivatives such as the Greys. This is a situation that does not allow the mind aspect of such souls to countermand force anymore. They will therefore be harvested and dominated by machine entities, or in folkloric terms, the devil will have stolen their souls. I believe this is why many planets with living higher intelligences such as Earth are invaded by machine roboids. One final point: life can only exist where there is a connection to the Godhead from the center-space reality in as straight a line as the twisted, Möroidal shape of the universe allows in our reality. There is, however, no straight track back to Godhead from the heavy-space reality. The center reality, with all its chaotic momentum as a result of the second law of thermodynamics, has a natural barrier between it and the Godverse. Unless a soul can make a straight track happen through its own gyroscopic balance of awareness and free will, it will lose the property of eternal life. That is why a soul trapped in the heavy reality cannot get back to the Godhead—because it's lost its capacity for awareness and free will, which got it to the heavy reality in the first place.

I believe that the state beyond life is all to do with the values that provide propulsion to the soul. Ignorance translates as a gradient of implied force that gets implanted in the demeanor of the now-dead entity. Souls that have to return to incarnate life hold too much force to enter the domain of the light-space reality. They stick to the edge of the margin that separates our center reality from the light reality and thus cannot get free of the pull of our reality. This pull toward reincarnating is what Buddhists call samsara, the cycle of repeated rebirths. This pull is provided by the second law of thermodynamics, which separates, breaks up, divides, complicates, and makes for chaotic disbursement of things that were at one time together in a single perfect existential harmonic.

On the other hand, resolutions of will that propagate a uniting effect through thoughts and actions that bring disparate parts together, that unite things into a consolidated togetherness through expressions like love, caring, compassion, generosity, and unselfishness, lessen enforcedness, dilute and neutralize all force, and defeat the formatting of the second law of thermodynamics. These qualities propel a return to the Godhead. Ghosts have done too much of the opposite, and so they're confused and have no propulsive power to escape the tug of the baryonic universe. They are stuck in their mindedness and set on impulses they can never hope to accomplish in a reality where physical acts are no longer possible and only their existing mind-set prevails. This may be why many ghosts are seen repeating the same manual tasks again and again, as though they are caught in a loop. Ghosts have no informational insight beyond the troubles or traumas that occupied their minds when they were in an incarnate state. Their fund of existential knowledge is limited to things experienced in the baryonic universe, and they are thus attached and drawn to the baryonic universe. They either do not know or are unable to hold the right values that would propel them toward the margin that would admit them to the light reality and the Godverse.

I believe that some ghosts that haunt places are a particular type of discarnate entity. They are trapped human souls because their individual awareness is tagged by an inability to even perceive their dead state, plus they have no intrinsic momentum to get them through the first margin into the light-space reality. They linger at the edge of the margin immediately adjacent to the center-space reality in a go-nowhere situation, caught in a mind-set that's confused, ignorant, and inherently self-contradictory. All this offers no progress whatsoever and makes them victims of their own making. They are go-nowhere spirits, what I call *indented souls,* those without their own direction and thus pulled by the force at the edges of the space between atoms—not to be confused with *elevated souls,* which are discarnate but have a direction toward the first margin and the light-space reality, or *impacted souls* who have a direction toward the dreaded second margin and are impacted by synthetic beings whose influence reigns there.

Entry into either margin at death allows an instant summarizing of everything a person has thought and done while in the incarnate state. Indented or impacted ghosts are souls without the capacity to understand and read the summary of their life's information. To use a computer analogy, their operating system is not working. Confusion and contradiction are the results. The soul lingers in this faulty situation, and since the margin itself is timeless, the soul can be trapped there for huge periods of time relative to our concept of time as living beings.

If you increase the incidence of Godlight within you when you are in an incarnate, physical state, by being good, this Godlight will produce a momentum in your soul that will take it through the first margin and then into the light reality. A soul is free and set according to its content of information. The first margin adjacent to our reality, the gateway to heaven, is one where unforce grips a soul and admits it to an eternal, timeless existence. Here the restrictions of atomic forces ends. That margin has a spectrum of force from the edge adjacent to the centre reality to the edge adjacent to the light reality. Some will pass through the second edge of the first margin into heaven or nirvana, others may be delayed and linger between the first and second edge of that margin so that from that situation they might learn the last remaining elements they need to know to proceed to the Godverse. They still have a view of the baryonic world but are not inherently pulled into it and need not come into it through reincarnation to learn what they need to know. They can interact with the baryonic reality through thought frames, and in some instances matter frames, to earn what they need to know to build enough momentum without actually reincarnating into it. They eventually move on to the Godverse if they can do so. The first edge of the margin may also be seen to hold souls with little to learn but who need to recompense for past follies that might have set others they had dealings with while in the incarnate state at some sort of disadvantage. This might necessitate reincarnation. From here, the widest field for reincarnation into the living state is available so that these karmic lessons can be reconciled.

The second margin between the heavy reality and the solid, hard-wired domain that comprises the center reality should be a no-go destination for any soul. It is the destination of those who choose to embrace entropic momentums and run with them. When they die their soul momentum drives them into atoms rather than away from them. Thus they do not enter the lighter less enforced states in the space between atoms through the first margin. Instead they drive themselves toward the second margin, a heavier state than center reality because they are propelling themselves faster than the rate of entropy that prevails in center reality. In the illustration of the space between atoms (see Plate 21) these souls are veering into the edges of the atoms instead of heading toward the center of the space. Visualize the second margin as a trench going down to a bottom and rising to the other side. There are gradients of increasing force going down until a point of no return prevails at the bottom, and the properties of the heavy reality begin to overwhelm the soul on the rising side. This is a gateway to the magnetic fields of force of planets such as the Earth's. A soul can ride this field and be held there by its resonance with it, still being aware and witnessing all that is manifest there. Could what they see and experience there with the last remnant of the Godhead still in them be the molten centers of some planets? Could this be the fire of hell described in religious invective? Is it the bottom of what is referred to in religious terms as the pit of hell? It is here, I believe, that the technology of the Greys and their ilk can capture and append to any suitable souls.

For the hell of eternal fire read radiation. It's everywhere. Look at the boiling blasts of eternal ovens we call suns. What better way to describe the fire and brimstone of hell. This also describes the centers of planets like Earth, with their oceans of magma beneath the rocky crust. Then there are gas giants like Jupiter, with billions of vats of burning, boiling gas and oceans of boiling acid. The vast majority of planets are like this. The few harbors of beauty like Earth can also be the waiting rooms of hell. even here we are processed and relentlessly taken apart by entropy.

The side of the trench immediately adjacent to the heavy reality is a domain where souls are stuck through their own limited thoughtforms: angst-ridden obsessions with trivialities and perverse attitudes that manifest as hatred, anger, and grudges. These are the souls who actively cultivated mind-sets that divide and separate and are driven by self-centred motivations. No one and nothing condemns them to this fate. They do it all to themselves through their free-will choices in life, which represent the Godhead principle seeking to bring all things into perfect balance.

As you will see from the illustration, this margin is where the forces of the atom dip somewhat into the frame of death and meet the heavy reality's apron of huge force. The potential difference between the unforce of the space between atoms and the force of the heavy reality can here create a greater manifestation of force when one point is set against another.

A soul field that finds itself in this second margin closest to the tremendous force of the heavy reality can use this great force, deploying it in our center reality as hauntings. Thousands have experienced this phenomenon in our world in haunted places where an unseen force moves the heaviest objects. The souls that find themselves here have access to the electromagnetic power of the center reality because they are still centered more in the world of atoms through their thoughts and deeds when alive and are thus drawn to stay close to this world of matter. They focus on and believe in the scope of material things, and so their motivations are congruent with these things, and this keeps them pinned to the planet where they were once incarnate. It keeps them set in places they know best because they did not believe in anything to counter to this when they were still alive. They function in the shadows of their own mindedness when dead. They believe and perceive only the things they loved and liked in the reality they left when they died, and they are stuck in a mind-set of their own making when in a discarnate state.

The second margin is a condition, not an extent or range. It freezes all modes of thinking and expression through its absolute magnitude of force set in a prevailing field of tension. There is nothing to separate into parts, thus there is no scale of time and no spatial extents by which time is measured. The heavy-space reality is where all momentums are frozen and the potential to be, to know, and to do is not accessible. But the information field that surrounds a soul here still persists as a format.

It contains all things that could be Godhead but is separated completely into parts. So it persists in a go-nowhere chaotic shudder. No change is possible in this margin. You are stuck there with the attitudes you had when you were alive. You can only observe and experience these things here, trapped and frozen by the massive force of the heavy reality, where the freeing influence of the Godhead can barely reach.

Souls stuck here can be reached by the loving thoughtforms sent to them by their incarnate fellows, but this rarely works because the entrapment is mostly a momentum created by the trapped soul itself, which is now paying the price for this situation for practicing ignorance while alive. No "God" can intervene anyway, since you are the only "God" you have. You make all that you see, know, and feel in the search for truth. Good or bad, you make your own welcoming committee beyond this world. Justice is an all-encompassing tacit incidental expression.

As I have said, this is the domain where an advanced enough alien technology can hack into a soul's information field with its own program. These souls then become living service agencies for the Grey alien agenda, their minds both naturally and artificially driven at the same time. I call these souls impacted souls, impacted by the directives of Grey programming. The horrendous thing is that such hijacked souls will never be able to gain entry into the Godverse. As hybrids they will always be set in an in-between status in an force-driven reality because the information from their machine side will lack feelings, sentiments, love, compassion, kindness, or any sense of mercy. They will be psychopaths and sociopaths with no conscience.

Second-margin ghosts exist within a timescape set in the present. They are trapped closer to the atomic universe, where our reality impinges on theirs. Some ghosts at the greatest level of restriction only have a remote capacity to reincarnate into a living form through rebirth (see Plate 21). They do this as hybrid beings under the influence of synthetic roboid entities because their souls are more in resonance with the worst impulses of the center reality we call our universe. They are bound by their closed minds, waiting for something like a

Christ figure's intercession such as the one I believe Jesus performed during his three days and three nights in the "heart of the Earth" (Matthew 12:40), an opportunity offered through the compassion of this Godform manifesting in our reality. When he transfigured and converted the atoms of his body back into the light that once formed them he lessened the force signature, the level of force, at this location in the universe. This allowed souls trapped in a certain level of force to be released. This was therefore not a direct intercession on his behalf but an incidental one. They would have incidentally found themselves in a situation of less force.

Some paranormal phenomena are not manifestations of living entities, however, and are not on a real timescale. They are materially based photonic expressions, not neutronic expressions. It is now thought that a kind of natural video recorder exists in some places on hard-rock planets where conditions in nature allow this phenomenon to occur. The "stone tape" theory says that the mental impressions created during traumatic events are recorded and projected onto rocks and other environmental elements to be replayed under certain conditions. That is why the same ghostly scene is visualized in the same place, time and time again. It suggests that time does not necessarily flow forward in a continuous stream and may flow backward or be frozen in still, self-contained frames, rather like the difference between a still animated photograph of a single occurrence and a sequentially run video of continuing occurrences.

Some people who are sensitives, mediums or clairvoyants, have an ability that is sometimes enhanced by physical environmental conditions to see both these recordings and actual ghost apparitions. To use an analogy with an aerial receiver, some people can receive more frequencies than others. I believe that many human beings are naturally gifted in this way but some are too afraid to admit to it because they don't understand what is happening and see themselves as freaks.

All things when seen in a physical, material context point to a finite end to the universe, and thus our reality. Cosmology has affirmed that the universe is dying. An anthem of purposelessness. But if we use meaning to arrive at this conclusion, is that not the most spectacular self-contradiction of it all? Yet the fact that we look for meaning and purpose in a chaotic maelstrom suggests that it must come from something or somewhere that is not a chaotic maelstrom. There has to be a situation that contradicts things of a physical scale, with their relentless drift in one direction: decay.

Does this imply that our physical reality is not all there is to existential experience, as I have argued throughout this book? There has to be another frame of existence beyond atoms that connects with ours that allows us to get off the carousel of calamity and that allows us to see the contrast to the chaotic maelstrom. It has to somehow be an analog of this frame, but at the same time one that is different or perhaps opposite to its features. One that exists as a twin of this one but also with features that allow it to be disconnected from our own physical frame through a bridging protocol. I believe neutrons are the gates of that bridging protocol. They are the points that hold two master existential frames one to the other but allow a dislocation such that there is no complete blending until ever smaller quantum states are reduced in size and we are finally staring at the face of the Godhead itself, a Godhead that exists outside the laws of physics: from neutrons, to neutrinos, to the nonphysical state.

That some part of our makeup has access to existence beyond the physical scales of force still remains to be proved empirically for some. I believe as you have read thus far that if we can simply *think* and *know,* we can indeed access it. We have the features that allow us a way into an eternal base, in what Jesus described as a state of eternal, unthreatened existence, a base that contradicts chaos and purposelessness.

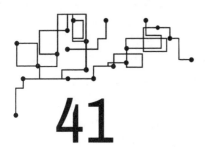

41

Quantum Weirdness

The quantum physics principle of entanglement reveals that reality is defined by observation. The observer has to preempt the observed for it to be there to be observed. Sounds Zen, doesn't it? But it is what the fundamental laws that rule our existence extol as the truth below the microscopic level. Nobel Prize–winning physicist Erwin Schrödinger described it as the fundamental tenet of quantum theory. Albert Einstein called it "spooky action at a distance." Most of us call it just plain weird.

The only spooks here are those who call the most significant empirically affirmed facet of quantum mechanics something that belongs to the realm of the tooth fairy. Don't you just love it when the so-called fathers of truth, the Newtonian science fraternity, are kicked really hard in their butts? This kick is one that threatens to dissemble their mantra, "There is nothing beyond the atom."

Entanglement affirms the Godverse, the infinite realm that is the backdrop of our finite universal reality and that pivots at the center points of the spaces between atomic hives, timeless and forever unchanged. All living things in the universe are the highest and freest manifestation of it. This source of effect is no phantom that sweeps the imagination of scientists and lies sterile in the images in their dreams. It is an all-powerful, universe-wide dynamic, writing its behests in the deepest erudition of wisdom. It is a timeless, limitless backdrop that is our source for a perfectly free potential to choose any options. Without that backdrop we would be fixed forever in a state of limitation and restriction.

While entanglement happens in the world of the super microscopic, there is now evidence to connect it to the world of the super macroscopic, the big world of our common reality. Thomas Durt of Vrije University in Brussels believes that the "constant interactions between electrons in the atoms that make up our body are no exception" to entanglement.

According to Durt, we are a mass of entanglements. Caslav Brukner's team at the University of Vienna has shown that moments of time can become entangled, too.[1] They found a strange connection between the past and the future such that the very act of measuring photon polarization a second time can affect how it was polarized earlier on. Instantaneous cause and effect across distances in space is not something that any classical theory of the universe can cope with, and Brukner's result has extended this "impossibility" to events separated in time as well.

Experiments carried out by Sayantani Ghosh at the University of Chicago have shown that the atoms of the whole universe may be connected to one another in some way macroscopically. In an article on the subject for *New Scientist,* Michael Brooks writes:

> If, as Ghosh's result suggests, entanglement can produce macroscopic effects, is it such a stretch to reason that quantum entanglement might be the key to understanding life? We know that quantum mechanics describes how atoms combine into molecules, and so underpins chemistry. And chemical processes underpin all biological processes, including the metabolic cycle and replication. So could entanglement support the emergent, macroscopic characteristic of chemistry that we call life?[2]

This means that everything is simply information, that all things exist to tell you something. That requires two points of information, the teller or giver of the information and the perceiver, receiver, and solicitor of that information. One does not actually exist without the other; however, one potentially exists without the other. One exists potentially in all states at once but becomes one particular state when seen, perceived, or acted on in any way by the other. This *entanglement* is the most fundamental expression of our reality. Can you imagine what that means for us? It means nothing is there until it is observed as being there. "Whoa," I hear you say. "Stop. Where and what is *there*?" By *there* I mean in any particular state of being there, of being actual, of existing.

All things that are there are contained in tiny packets and parcels of information. The whole parcel together is called a quantum. It is all holographic. We can see it as a waveform that holds all the information as a total, and if you collapse that wave it will immediately let you see and actuate into reality what is contained within the whole of it. Until then you can only know the whole of the wave, not the parts that make it up. All the quanta (packets) are connected to all the other quanta because everything comes from a prior state of union of all parts as a Godhead, the final, all-together quantum. This is why all this is so in the first place. All things are potentially there to *be there* until the quantum wave is collapsed and the information it holds as a conglomerate is revealed as a specific facet of that conglomerate.

You could say that modern science has proved the existence of the Godhead.

What has been discovered about quantum entanglement utterly underscores and supports the validity of free will. It prescribes no limits to anything. It says unequivocally that what you think, where you think it, when you think it, and how you think it has no limit whatsoever. Most of all it affirms that the entire existential scheme is balanced by opposites and oppositions: that if there is a physical, measurable reality, there must also be a reality that is nonphysical and not measurable; that limit is authenticated by limitlessness; that if everything is supposed to have begun with the birth of a physical, material reality, there has to be an opposed reality that existed before that reality began that is connected to and concatenate with it.

One of the latest theories as I write is that what are called black holes are the creators of all things, including life itself. As always, the question remains: How did all that allow for black holes to come to be in the first place if there was nothing before they happened? Scientific explanations, as always, stop short when it comes to explaining beginnings.

So, much to the chagrin of many materialist scientists, quantum physics, a field within their own discipline, has exploded a bombshell in their faces: the observed has to have a preeminent observer to account for its existence in the first place. Schrödinger's cat is both alive and dead at the same time until it is observed by a sentient observer. This is how that paradigm goes:

> We place a living cat into a steel chamber, along with a device containing a vial of hydrocyanic acid. There is, in the chamber, a very small amount of radioactive substance. If even a single atom of the substance decays during the test period, a relay mechanism will trip a hammer, which will, in turn, break the vial and kill the cat.[3]

The observer cannot know whether an atom of the substance has decayed and consequently cannot know whether the vial has been broken, the hydrocyanic acid released, and the cat killed. Since we cannot know, the cat is both dead and alive according to quantum law, in a superposition of states. It is only when we break open the box and learn the condition of the cat that the superposition is lost, and the cat becomes one or the other (dead or alive). This situation is sometimes called quantum indeterminacy, or the observer's paradox: the observation or measurement itself affects an outcome, so that the outcome as such does not exist unless the measurement is made—that is, there is no single outcome unless it is observed.

We know that superposition actually occurs at the subatomic level, because there are observable effects of interference, in which a single particle is demonstrated to be in multiple locations simultaneously. What that fact implies about the nature of reality on the observable level (cats, for example, as opposed to electrons) is one of the stickiest areas of quantum physics.

In this affirmation of superposition and quantum entanglement, most materialist scientists seek the nearest plot of sand to bury their heads in because they haven't the faintest idea how to account plausibly and provably for how the observer is there in the first place. The observer has to have the propensity to know and evaluate what is seen and measured. To do that, the observer has to be capable of the thinking process in the first place. Science thus has to verify thought and its transitive modus (thinking) empirically before it can pontificate on any existential scale. The conclusion is clear: there has to be something preexistent to measurable reality, another reality quite unlike ours and opposite to the reality they acknowledge as the only one. Logic deserts them at this point because most scientists will only believe that what constitutes reality is what they can physically measure.

Like perverse, recalcitrant children who own the kit that plays the game, they desert the field of play, kit and all. Their narrow corridor minds just cannot or will not stretch to acknowledge that there might well be an opposed reality to our physical one. Their power as the accredited ushers who control the whole fund of disseminated truth allows them to simply duck the question, claiming that it's something for philosophers to answer. My point is that for philosophers to ask the question in the first place or indeed answer it, no black hole can exist in the first place, either.

This leaves science stuck in a paradox, truly entangled, trying to measure all things without knowing where the very thing they measure with—the mind—comes from or how it exists. They cannot deal with intangibles, yet in a huge contradiction of terms they will use an intangible to verify and maintain what they take as true. With the aplomb of a mind stuck in a mire, they pronounce that our universe is just plain weird. And to me what is really weird is that their minds operate in the fashion of a programmed machine. They know, for example, that they can only account for 4 percent of the universe. The other 96 percent is made of some strange, unfathomable, dark entity that is variously referred to as dark energy or dark matter, which they just cannot pin down. The truth is that scientists, with all their sophisticated detection paraphernalia, are clueless as to what it might all be. That's what's truly strange. They're striving so much to take a beyond-atoms component out of any equation of truth that they are falling all over themselves, legs, arms, and head, and crashing into an implication of a Godhead principle. The more they strive to contrive an explanation for all things outside such a principle, the more it seems it explodes in their faces.

I have always been convinced that paradoxically and ironically it would be the scientists who would finally prove the concept that I call Godhead. If the latest research is anything to go by, they are well on their way to actually doing so, but what they've found is not an anthropomorphic God but instead a secular resource—Godhead—a purely nonreligious expression that might be acceptable to many of them. They are welcome to take the word *God* away from it if that smacks too much of religion. I totally sympathize with them there. I failed every religion test I ever took as a child. I never answered the question with the answer I suspected they wanted. I always had my own take on the question. I seemed to love being a perverse rat from all accounts. My wife agrees that I am to this day.

The scientists have a point in trying to get away from a anthropocentric God that is the heavenly substitution for all things powerful, good and bad. When the principle of Godhead is seen in these terms, terms the nefarious charlatan can name his price in the belief stakes. The idea of a divine king, lord of the manor, or father figure with a controlling interest in all our lives invites only the naive or the ignorant. Thoughout history, countless millions of people have been set up by contrivances that solicit belief through the threat of damnation. While the majority of the religious are gullible and well-meaning, there are a very large number within the various religions who are deliberate and ruthless exploiters who through religion coerce others for their own gain—"Praise the Lord and pass me the money" sung to choruses of mind-boggling pretence and hypocrisy.

God has to be a principle: Godhead. Being just that it is everything glorious, a nonanthropocentric, nonanthropomorphic principle. It is outside space, time, matter, and all things of this universe. It cannot be a being, let alone an anthropomorphic being. It is *not* a controlling paradigm, some sort of super king or megalord of the manor, and least of all not a white man with a flowing beard as depicted on the Sistine Chapel ceiling. It is not some personalized entity, but it nevertheless is an all-powerful, all-seeing, omniscient, omnipresent, active secular paradigm. It is all these things tacitly. Inasmuch as this is so, Godhead is a reference against which all things it is not.

Godhead exists as long as existence itself exists, as that in which all absolutes are centered. Please forgive me for repeating this rant for the umpteenth time. It is that in which the absolute union of parts in a whole state accrues. It allows for all things to be and to happen. Insofar as this is so, it is all awareness and provides for absolute free will within all things that can hold and express the capacity of awareness and will. It is the origin and end of all things and all existence. In being the center of the paradigm of the ultimate union of parts, it is the All state of all things and exists always and in all ways as such. Thus wherever there is the intention to bring things together, for the union of things and of parts, Godness as the deployed state of the Godhead exists.

But you know, it's not wrong to see it all in terms of a personal power draped in our human fashions if it's a technique for understanding things and believing in them when they are set in reason and logic. In fact, for most of us it is essential we do so. With our own individual Godform we create an antenna that can receive all options. It is the power of that antenna to receive the whole range of options that gives us a chance to choose among those options. Whether we want to or are able to choose is another matter.

See it as a library of all the books in the world, and when we read all those books we become that entire library. We then cease to be a book and become the library. A book on its own cannot know what it is to be a library. But a library on its own can know what it is to be both. Which is the more valid thing to be in terms of the truth?

As I write this I see a large fly lying upside-down in a glass of water in front of me. It is going around in circles upside-down, kicking its legs in the surface tension of the water in a haste to free itself from its predicament. In a moment I will take that glass and throw its contents out the window. If only that fly could know what we as human beings have the capacity to know. Maybe then it would not have followed its unstoppable instinct to fly into the water in the first place. The new and radical change in its predicament outside the water and the glass, in a world outside the window, is to me an exact metaphor for our own predicament in narrow-mindedness. There have been some who have come and picked up the glass and thrown the water and its living contents out of the window.

Yes, I have now thrown out the water in the glass along with the fly. I waited until it flew away.

What follows in the subsequent chapters is a rational demonstration of how this might be unsuspectingly so for millions of us and the deadly danger this presents to us all. It defines the crucial difference between what is natural and what is synthetic. It defines the universe-wide primary battle lines between what is God and the devil, so to speak—the difference between we living beings and a roboid. It defines why we have to see who we truly are before we can realize the terrifying danger we are all in if we do not recognize the differences between what has a soul and what can never possess one.

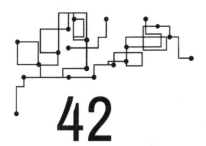

42

Anthropic Coincidences

So, is existence set according to determinism or to randomness? The ancient argument. Does shit just happen, or is there a procedure steeped in reason and logic that produces it? Apologies for the excremental word, but I believe it forges realization better than a milder one. Is it all just coincidence, and if so, how does a series of perfect resolutions give rise to how I can see and write this? Does predetermined causality lead to all that we see, feel, and know?

Anthropic coincidences describes the remarkable fine-tuning of conditions in the physical universe to provide at every juncture exactly the right conditions for intelligent life to emerge.

The nucleons that make up the nucleus of the atom along with protons and neutrons are the mass-makers of the atom. The difference between them is that protons have a positive charge and neutrons are neutral. But the key thing is that they differ very slightly in mass. The neutron weighs 939.6 megaelectronvolts, and the proton 938.3 megaelectronvolts. This difference of 0.14 percent is utterly crucial. The neutron's extra mass means that it decays into a proton and not the other way around. The universe would be very different if it was the other way around. The proton is stable, and so atoms are stable. No one has seen a proton decay. It will last 10^{32} years, and the universe by comparison has only lasted 10^{10} years. If this extra weight of the neutron was even minutely lower, it would mean that the universe through what is known as *beta decay* would not exist. We would not exist in our form.

Things have to exist that precisely for the universe as we know it to exist at all. It is unquestionable lunacy to say that it all happened randomly and through chaotic disbursement incidentally. As Einstein, and later English astronomer Sir Fred Hoyle, said, the numbers just don't fit for the universe to have come about through chance.

Given these "coincidences" it can be postulated that the sole purpose for the universe to be is so that intelligent life can observe it *being there*. The observer would have to be there prior to the universe. This is an affirmation of the anthropocentric argument that everything is for us, and we thus are there for everything. This argument is based on the fact that what gives rise to the universe as science knows it involves numbers so precise that if any of these values were altered or changed we could not exist. Theoretical physicist Stephen M. Barr discusses this remarkable fine-tuning of the universe in a 2001 article whose title provides the title of this chapter.

Barr reminds us that hydrogen has been around since the birth of the universe following the big bang, but almost all of the other elements were the result of supernova explosions that spewed forth the elements that made new stars, planets, and living beings.

So elements are formed as a result of nuclear fusion, which produces the energy radiated by the sun and other stars that is essential to support life. Pairs of hydrogen nuclei fuse with other such pairs to make the element deuterium. Deuterium is the crucial element that allows the formation of other elements, and without it there would only be hydrogen. Barr states that

> everything thus depends on hydrogen being able to fuse to make deuterium. Here is where the first remarkable anthropic coincidence comes in. The force of nature that cements nuclei together is called the "strong nuclear force." Had the strong nuclear force been weaker by even as little as 10 percent, it would not have been able to fuse two hydrogen atoms together to make deuterium, and the prospects of life would have been dim indeed. But this is only the half of it. Had the strong nuclear force been only a few percent stronger than

it is, an opposite disaster would have occurred. It would have been too easy for hydrogen nuclei to fuse together. The nuclear burning in stars would have gone much too fast. Stars would have burned themselves out in millions of years or less, rather than the several billion years that stars like the sun last. However, the history of life on Earth suggests that billions of years are required for the evolution of complex life such as ourselves. The upshot of all these considerations is that the strong nuclear force has just the right strength: a little stronger or weaker and we would not have been here.[1]

Following the formation of deuterium, fusion processes allow the formation of helium, which must in turn fuse to make larger elements. Since two helium nuclei cannot fuse together, how did all the other elements come to be? This question stumped astrophysicists for a long time, until, as Barr says, Fred Hoyle "suggested that nature in effect did a large double step to get past the missing rung in the ladder."

When two helium nuclei collide in the interior of a star they cannot fuse permanently, but they do remain stuck together momentarily, for about a hundredth of a millionth of a billionth of a second. In that tiny sliver of time a third helium nucleus comes along and hits the other two in a three-way collision. Three heliums, as it happens, do have enough sticking power to fuse together permanently. When they do so they form a nucleus called "carbon 12." This highly unusual triple collision process is called the "three-alpha process," and it is the way that almost all of the carbon in the universe is made. Without it, the only elements around would be hydrogen and helium, leading to an almost certainly lifeless universe.[2]

As you read this please bear in mind my first-margin scenario that separates the light-space reality from the center-space reality. I believe this is the chemical definition of this margin between these realities.

Barr continues, pointing out that Hoyle discovered "one of the most dramatic of the anthropic coincidences. . . . Such a rare event as the three-alpha process would not make enough carbon unless something greatly enhanced its effectiveness. That something, he realized, must be what is called in physics a 'resonance.'"[3]

We know what resonance is: basically, the phenomenon of force being applied to an object, causing a standing wave pattern. This is the common cause of sound production in musical instruments. Atomic nuclei also have characteristic notes or energy levels. Nuclear reactions occur as a result of hitting just the right energy level. "Hoyle pointed out that the three-alpha process could have produced enough carbon only if the carbon 12 nucleus has an energy level in just the right place," says Barr. Indeed, it does. "Had this energy level of carbon 12 been only a few percent higher or lower in frequency, the three-alpha process would have been out of tune," and life as we know it would not exist.[4]

One sees that the making of the chemical elements needed for life was, to borrow the Duke of Wellington's comment on his victory at Waterloo, "a damn close run thing."

One can see anthropic coincidence in the laws of physics. Physicists define four basic forces of nature: the strong nuclear force, the weak interaction, gravity, and electromagnetism. Electromagnetism is especially prevalent in our world, as it is the phenomenon that holds matter together, while strong nuclear force does not directly produce effects we experience in everyday life. Yet electromagnetic force is inherently weaker than strong nuclear force. And here lies another "coincidence":

> Had the electromagnetic force not been intrinsically much weaker than the strong nuclear force, the electrical energy packed inside a hydrogen nucleus would have been so great as to render it unstable. The "weak interaction" would then have made all the hydrogen in the world decay radioactively, with a very short half-life, into other particles. The world would have been left devoid of hydrogen, and therefore almost certainly of life because water, which is indispensable for life, contains hydrogen, as do almost all organic molecules. We see then how life depends on a delicate balance among the vari-

ous fundamental forces of nature, and in particular on the relative feebleness of electromagnetic effects.[5]

Yet one more "coincidence" that Barr points out has to do with the flatness of space. He says that despite Einstein's assertion that space-time is curved, not flat, when viewed from a large-enough scale it turns out that it is rather flat and straight.

> The "spatial curvature," as it is called, is very small. In fact, shortly after the Big Bang the spatial curvature of the Universe was, to the accuracy of many decimal places, equal to zero. For a long time, this was referred to as the "flatness problem," since no one could think of a good explanation for it. However, while so long a difficult thing for theorists to explain, this flatness of space is very fortunate. Had the flatness of space not been fantastically small to begin with, the universe would either have collapsed and ended . . . or would have undergone such a tremendously rapid expansion that it would have torn matter and even atoms asunder.[6]

And so it can be seen that these fundamental elements and mathematical ratios have given rise to us and all that goes with us. The very fact that we can spot these marvelous "coincidences" is the most unbelievable miracle of all. Or is it a miracle?

I have stated that the doorway to the Godhead is accessed through forcelessness, by being completely and utterly free of all force. Can you imagine this paradigm, something with not even the natural tension of space-time itself? The Godhead will always come through any thing or being that is formatted for it. We as human beings are in a dual situation: in material physicality, with a nonphysical component built into us through the design of the physical one. It's the design that's the important thing. Who or what is the designer?

The life and living power in us is not atom-built. This is because when we come into the universe as light we bring in a means of "straightening" any atom hive arrangement from within it. Our souls carry this capacity for forcelessness, which enlivens our atomic configurations through the center balance points of any suitably formed atom hive. Some atom hives have this dual capacity and some don't. It is best set in the atomic hives that intrinsically hold the water molecule.

A soul is thus a record of all that has happened to any particularization of Godlight that came through from the Godverse when the universe happened.

We have a mechanism created by technology that might help you understand Godlight and perhaps allow you to believe that such a thing really exists. I'm referring to the laser. We know it as a device that emits electromagnetic light through optical amplification; it's also an acronym for *light amplified by the stimulated emission of radiation*. Let me explain.

Lasers are made to carry information. Inside a laser there is a tube containing a mixture of gases such as helium and neon and a liquid or a solid crystal such as ruby. Projecting into the tube are two electric terminals that create an electric spark. The spark gives extra energy to the atoms of the lasing material and excites them into firing off photons, or little bursts of light. The photons shoot off through the lasing material in all directions, hitting other atoms and making them fire off photons, too. Soon there are billions of identical photons zooming around within the tube. Mirrors at either end reflect photons straight up and down the tube so that they zoom back and forth again and again, gathering more photons as they go. One of the mirrors is designed to let a fraction of the photons through, and after a while they surge through. Immediately, the laser flashes out its intense beam. That laser beam is both coherent (its light is all the same wavelength and its waves are perfectly in step) and perfectly straight—so straight it's better at making accurate measurements than any ruler.

Now imagine a laserlike light not made of force at all. In fact, this particular light is intelligent because it is not enforced, and it not only carries information, it receives it, holds it, understands it, and is extrapolative of its own accord. Its one weakness is that to function like this it has to be in an arena of no force. Its power is strongest where any field of force is absent.

In my laser analogy this light is what I call First Light, or Godlight, the medium through which our connection to Godhead exists. This connection is held from the beginning point of the universe in atomic "cages" that the light itself forms. These cages are made of rings of six hydrogen atoms aligned horizontally, such that they create a center channel in which an absolute absence of force exists (see Plate 22). Its presence animates and enlivens all atoms connected in a hive to these rings through the potential difference that exists between the absence of force in the center of these corridors and the force of the atoms at the extremities of the corridor. This is the very spark of life that makes life-forms and species happen. It gives life to anything it touches by creating order out of chaos (all other atom configurations turn order into chaos), setting any field of atoms into the best, most coherent, functionally effective, united array possible. I believe the Star of David as a geometric monogram illustrates the basic six point configuration of the hydrogen atom cluster that allows the Godform as Godlight to come through into our center-reality. Any living thing that assembles the hydrogen in their bodies in enough of these six-atom rings will immediately transfigure into Godlight as Jesus Christ did as demonstration on Mt. Nitai near Jerusalem. On that occasion he had such control of his being that he did just enough of them not to merge instantly into Godhead. He still had work to do on this Earth.

All things are thus set in patterns of shape and form that the overall forces surrounding them and acting on them allow. This means all matter-based things have to deal with five quantum force prints: the local force print, the immediate point things stand in; the planetary force print; the solar system force print; the galactic force print; and the universal force print. Any particular point in space-time therefore has a predominant force signature and thus shape according to the free hydrogen atoms available to life-containing fields.

Another power opposed to the second law exists: the power of the Godform to unite and return all things to the previous state before the big bang. It is trapped and held in isolation in some situations, and within some other living situations of force it feeds in *online*. What lives does so because the power of Godhead exists through channels where there is no force whatsoever. These living systems continue, maintaining themselves as themselves in a chain of continuity through the power of the Godform coming through them through the states of life and death. Godhead, in other words, provides a continual ordering source for the regaining of the purest order within a breaking-up scenario.

As I've said, these channels that allow the Godform through are aggregations of six-point circles of hydrogen atoms that make conduits for the Godlight to come through. With carbon atoms acting as an interconnecting scaffolding for these conduits and the oxygen atom making them into a very special shape for the interconnecting corridors to deploy, these corridors lead to the very interface of this universe with the light-space reality.

Any human being who has to persist in the world of the universe of parts is there because this person is too disharmonic or too twisted out of shape to enter the light-space reality—like a square peg trying to fit into a round hole. The person has imperfections called sins, which can best be understood as restrictions that twist us out of shape with the overall shape that admits us into the Godverse. So we have to key into the Godverse reality by making a shape that fits it. I am reminded of Jesus's words "Make straight the way of the Lord" (John 1:23), and this entails the shedding of the enforcedness that restricts our thinking. If we think right by knowing enough to think right, we become straight and in line and concomitantly resonant with the light-space reality. We enter the gates of heaven by making ourselves congruent with this shape. We make ourselves this shape by being what might be called righteous.

The point is that nobody or no one can do it but oneself. If not, beings like Jesus, who came to "save" us, would have been able to do it by simply zapping us all back into the required shape. He showed us how to do it through the example of his life and works, but he could not do the doing for us. Each person, through awareness and free will, has to choose the path back.

We have the capacity to know and do things, to set things straight and regain perfect harmony, one congruent with the Godverse. We can change situations through right thinking and right action. But we have to see what it is we have to do, and we have to use free will to do this. Herein lies the power of Godhead for us, in the nonphysical world of the mind. If we "make straight the way of the Lord" by right thinking, we will merge with the Godverse.

There are more than 7.9 billion human beings living on this planet. Each of them has an ancestral line going back to the birth of the universe. This line is our only hope for eternal life because it connects up with the beginning through a special mechanism we commonly call the soul. To me, what is beyond death is all that matters. If you don't engage in right thinking you will face the entrapment you have chosen the instant you die. Certainly many contemporary Westerners, if looked at as a group, have it seems lost the battle to discover truth before they start. The word *spirit* seems a dirty word these days, to be dismissed peremptorily as the domain of New Agers and those who believe in the tooth fairy and Santa Claus. I once thought like them but for my interest in finding the verity of the UFO phenomenon, which changed everything. I now believe in Santa Claus. He comes in special disguises: Jesus Christ, Gautama Buddha, the prophet Muhammad, Mahatma Ghandi, Mother Teresa, and yes, even Abraham Lincoln. They may have many names. Some of you might call them Mom and Dad, Brother and Sister, Uncle and Aunt. We feed the mighty corporate shareholders and the noughts on the share value sheets. They have a system set up for them and they seem to follow it like sheep to the slaughter of their souls. Not just their lives—their eternal souls. They are in for a rude awakening the moment they close their eyes in death if NDEs are a true affirmation that there is an existence in full and super consciousness after death. A real and true life after death. Not some imagined world of intuitively made shadows. There are now more and more people that do not believe in a soul that continues after the physical death of our individualities. I started my research into the UFO phenomenon with the same premise as my own belief, too, I have to admit. I now believe it is the biggest single mistake both I and they will ever make in our lives. A mistake that could extinguish the very meaning of why we are alive as an entity in the first place. This is no exhortation to believe in a religion much less the usual charlatans that administer them. I say this because the power of mental focus that is involved in a belief is the knife that cuts the scales obscuring a view to what might be the existential broadwalk that defines ultimate truth itself. If you exist then this truth has to enlist all that endorses that existence *without limit.*

The spiritual gets less and less attention every day. The huge momentum toward technology as the God of the new millennium is taking everyone with hurricane force. Technology can truly be the coinage of the lost. It's power for evil is such that it can make one lose sight of the primacy of being human. It says that the material is all that exists. On the other hand, that's not to say that its wise and circumspect use cannot lead to good effect. As the old saying goes, there's no need to "let the devil have all the best tunes."

Looking at the UFO enigma showed me one thing more than anything else. It showed me that there *is* an afterlife. All this is because as material beings we believe what we see more than what we perceive. Notice I said *see* and not *perceive.* Seeing is a thing of the eye, and perception is a thing of both the mind and eye combined.

Our sense of all things we encounter in our day-to-day life is inherently governed by a frame of mind that defends our material being first and foremost. But if we attune more to the physical than the spiritual, we are doomed to temporality and limitation. That is what we will inherit until we cannot inherit anything anymore.

> When ye see a cloud rise out of the West, straightaway ye say, there cometh a shower; and so it is. When ye see the south wind blow, ye say, There will be heat; and it cometh to pass. Ye hypocrites, ye can discern the face of the sky and of the earth; but how is it that ye do not discern this time. Yea and why even of yourselves, judge ye not what is right. (Luke 12:54–57)

But as I have intimated throughout this book, we have another side to our being closer than the wind on our faces, a side that gives us the scope to reach and persist in an existential base outside the physical and material. An eternal, limitless one.

There seem to be two functions for the mind. The first is to preserve our life in a physical status *in* and *as* atoms. The second is there to allow that individual status to continue and persist *out of* and *beyond* a status in atoms. Our brain marshals the physical. That is what the brain-mind is there for. It is simply a temporary harness into which the eternal is strapped, a screen that manifests physical convenience for the manipulation of physical, material, hardwired purposes. It searches for the widest ranges of physical threat to us as a means of protecting itself and therefore our physicality against any circumstance that arises to threaten our material safety.

But we have another brain, one that is not a colloid set like convoluted jelly in our cranium. It can know and see and understand that which is not physical and material, and it uses the whole body as an antenna, including the brain. This is the mind, not the brain-mind; it does not come wrapped up in your body. Astoundingly, it's all around you, all over the universe. It has no form of its own. It is invisible and is at the heart of our capacity to know and understand, to perceive and interpret. It is in the brain but not of it, as it is also found in the heart, the bones, and the cells of the whole body. It is the Godhead. The brain of the ALL.

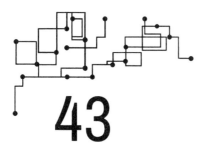

43

The Spark of Life

So while scientism or the use of the scientific method excludes anything it cannot measure to reveal the verity of anything, religion overwhelmingly relies on trusted reputation, faith, and belief and accepts implicitly the dominion of things not material and physical as the main avenue to truth. Ultimate contrasts. But it is the contrast that reveals the meaning, and the meaning is seemingly never grasped by so many who operate through the ethos of either religion or scientism.

The brilliant and beautiful existential homily of Descartes, "I think, therefore I am," allows all assertions in logic and reason. It simply says it all. It affirms an overall mathematical duality as the foundation of all principles and paradigms and permits a dialectical discourse in all existential terms. Yin and yang, up and the down, to and fro, and so on, has to be the first presumption in all realities, both physical and nonmaterial and intangible.

There is no conundrum here really. It is all so obvious in applied logic and reason. So what makes so many blind to it all? Is there something in us that increasingly prevents the application of simple reason? In the past, especially the distant past, humanity, even the most primitive humanity, believed intuitively that another primary existential scheme had to exist. What has so narrowed our perspectives in contemporary times?

To answer this question I cannot look at all this in the context of pure science alone. The power of an intrusion into our planet by an extraterrestrial entity has enormous social implications for the human family. I must therefore look at its significance as ubiquitously as I can. It is crucial that all these things are connected if we are to see the most important consequences on the body politic of our species—indeed, on all living species throughout the universe.

I believe our natural living psychological stance has been altered by a synthetic addendum not natural to our living being, inserted by nonliving entities. Humans are slowly turning into synthetic, nonliving machines as a result and losing sight of our nonphysical roots in the Godverse. Most of us cannot even grasp that this is happening to our species. That is how incredibly clever these synthetic alien drones are in reaching their objective. They simply follow the second law and massage it here and there to accelerate the natural process. How great is our loss in allowing this to happen.

I have tried to establish the value of all that is natural and precious about us against what is synthetic as reflected by the roboidal Greys so as to explain why they might want to append to our biological frame of existence.

"Who the hell are you?" is a common expletive of derision. We humans are, it seems, just another collection of atomic forces in a particular shape and size and thus of small significance when viewed as just another living species in the universe. The word *hell* in this expletive seems particularly appropriate in the context of a claim that I will make and later justify—that we are living in a true hell. Why, then, are we of any special significance when looked at in simply physical terms? It's difficult to see any significance to our lives or indeed to anything else that lives.

The teeming multitrillions of stars, planets, species, and living beings in this universe means we're just another life-form among multitrillions of life-forms. We, however, parade ourselves within the envelope of our own individual living auspice and contexts as humans as though we are of singular universal primary importance. Despite the probable multitude of unique fingerprints of life that exist on a vast existential scale, we all see ourselves as individuals signing unique difference from each other both as physical entities made of blood, bone, and matter and as psychological quanta citing our unique ways of thinking, responding, and doing. In other words, we think we're special, but we're special only because we can *think* we are special. The act of thinking itself makes for the specialness. Taking this backward, one could ask what allowed that thought to be in the first place? What allowed that thought to think the thought that marked that difference? That is the mightiest question of all questions.

A leaf of an orange bush is like any other leaf of that orange bush at first glance. Yet a more detailed survey will reveal that no two leaves of that orange bush are absolutely alike. In fact, no leaf is exactly like any other leaf of any other bush tree or cactus. An implicit differentiation is taking place that marks all physical things at the most minute level possible.

I am sure that most of you have seen animations on films that show an object bursting into little pieces in an explosion. But if you run that film backward, all the myriad pieces go back to form the whole object again. A thousand pieces become one, realigning into the position they came out in the explosion. The pieces exist in their own separated right as the explosion proceeds. Each piece becomes a hundred smaller pieces in proportion to the power of the initial force that exploded the object. Our universe came from such an explosion. It came from a point smaller than anyone can imagine, where the whole thing was together in a hyper-mega-super-condensate, or point of hotness. This explosion made the space for the explosion to exist and the time for the explosion to exist at one and the same time, unlike, of course, the explosions we see now because now space and time already exist.

A good way of seeing it all is to visualize a balloon being blown up with air. The relaxed balloon material extends outward, with the skin of the balloon stretching as the whole thing gets bigger with air. We now have air outside the balloon. We have air inside the balloon. The air outside is less enforced than the air inside the balloon. In fact, you will see that the force that separates the material of the rubber of the balloon is exactly proportional in enforcedness to the air inside that is stretching it.

Visualize now that you have cut a cross-section through the balloon as it expands. Look at the thin rubber material as it stretches and gets thinner and thinner. Imagine you are going into this thin line. Think of it as the materiality or mass of our universe as it expands. You are part of that mass, that materiality. You are the rubber of the balloon. You are being stretched. As you are being stretched, you are also making space and time within the rubber for that stretching to take place. Don't think about the air on either side of the rubber. It is irrelevant in terms of my model. The increasing distortion of the rubber is all that's happening as far as this example is concerned. There is only space for rubberness to be. Now this rubberness in my analogy is the mass of the universe, the force that stretches the rubber is energy, and the elasticity or stretchability of the rubber is light. Light is the margin of extendability the rubber allows. The expansion is a function of this margin. You will see that each factor is connected to the other. You vary one, you vary the others. The famous Einstein equation $E = mc^2$ put into this context simply implies that energy is merely mass condensed to a huge extent. If you unravel mass you will get a huge amount of force happening out of it. It implies that mass is simply coagulated energy. It implies that the whole universe of parts is what it is because we are separated from Godhead by the phenomenon we call force.

In the altogether state there is perfect stillness and therefore perfect peace because these are implicit to the nature of being altogether. There is perfect stillness because movement can only exist between two points that are separated and therefore *not* altogether. The principle of changeability can also be seen this way. There is perfect peace because there can only be a lack of peace when there is a lack of reconciliation, and there can only be a lack of reconciliation when there are separate parts that are unreconciled with one another. I use the word *peace* here to define perfect stillness, where no force whatsoever exists. That altogether state is also a state of perfect freedom and limitlessness because limit can only exist if there is a *limiter* and that which is *limited*. The altogether state is thus an infinite state, and as an infinite state it permeates all states of existence. The backdrop of all existence is thus perfect stillness, perfect peace, and perfect potential freedom. It is an infinite extent in which anything and everything is possible, including the possibility of limiting possibility, of knowing the state of separation and limit as distinct from the state of altogetherness and limitlessness. It is the actualization of that potential that forms a kind of skin within the limitless extent of God, a skin that separates that which is inside the skin from that which is outside the skin and thus allows for a view from within the context of the state of separated points. The skin does not and indeed cannot limit the infinite extent of Godness. It merely provides a lens through which the holistic light of knowing and awareness can be diffracted into finite, separated states. Thus the hologram that all beings really are happens.

In the state of altogetherness, both awareness and will have no capsule, no skin around them. Its vehicle of expression is *it* as *itself.* In my metaphor, the balloon skin that makes a universe of parts encapsulates that awareness and forces us to experience a separate, individual identity. The tension of the skin of our balloon in our neck of the woods in space-time could be said to have a cross-sectional shape of force in our universe. This cross-sectional shape is congruent to that of the combined atomic shape of two atoms of the element hydrogen and one atom of the element oxygen in combination—water. This congruence allows a seemingly magical status to occur: life. Life is the best of the Godverse in the baryonic universe, coming through the interplaying twists of all the chemical elements that make up this universe.

Through the passage of time in this physical universe with its entropic drift, our balloon has been gradually expanding, and the tension in the balloon skin has been increasing. Once upon a time the balloon skin forming the capsule for our expression in the universe was relaxed enough to form insubstantial bodies more akin to light. It gradually became a little more enforced as the universe expanded and formed bodies of pure hydrogen gas—still relatively insubstantial. Now we are separated by far more taut skins of tension as our balloons have increased in size over time. The tautness causes various localities of twisted space and thus force in the form of the atoms.

This increase in tension is a measure of the potential difference between our state of encapsulation and the perfect unencapsulated freedom of the infinite backdrop to all existence, that state of altogetherness that is the Godform. We have chosen or incidentally inherited the separated state at the big bang, and we have become trapped in it because the more the rubber of the balloon skin stretches, the more it forms a wall of tension between us and the tensionless, altogether space outside the balloon. It becomes increasingly difficult for us to know and understand that prior altogether state because the very fabric of our being is being stretched into greater and greater states of separation and enforced tension over time.

The law of diminishing returns is thus the guide rail that marshals our capture. No demons guard and enforce our situation in hell. We do it of our own accord. We do it because we have choice. We have choice because the universe is a product of a mixture and not a homogenous amalgamation of the Godverse and its opposite. It is impossible to amalgamate that which is perfectly reconciled with that which is unreconciled, thus the universe of parts and the singularity of the whole exist together but can never merge with each other.

If the Godverse were to reconcile the state of separation with its own state of union, there would be no freedom within the Godverse to know that separated state, and therefore the state of Godness would not be perfectly free. Thus two mutually distinct paradigms, the singularity of the whole and the universe of parts, are crucial as an expression of the freedom to actuate any potential. It would also follow that their immiscibility allows for expressions of the singularity of the whole, such as thought, awareness, and will, to act independently and therefore in control of the physical entropic universe into which they manifest.

Thus the determinists are dead wrong in assuming that all things are laid out prior to their happening. You can choose to nurture and maintain the freedom of will and awareness that is our inheritance from the Godverse if you counter the entropic drift of the physical universe with decisions that override its impulse toward separating into greater and greater states of disorder and chaos. These would be the kind of decisions that affirm our existence as individuals intrinsically connected to one another. Love is the propulsive power that brings parts together rather than dividing us into separate identities in separate groupings. Love serves to bind and unite us in caring for one another. Thus one *can* act independently of the physical limitations of the universe of parts and its natural drift toward separation, randomness, and chaos. Fatalism only applies to that which is purely a product of a go-nowhere-except-down universe and its dead, static, dependent atoms that are wholly caught in the entropic drift. By *dead* atoms I don't imply this metaphorically. I mean all those atoms that make up nonliving states. Could it be that the carbon atom in a living system is different from the carbon atom in a nonliving one? Is there a kind of "life carbon" and a "nonlife carbon"?

As Jesus showed through the miracles he performed and ultimately through his own transfiguration, even the fate of atoms is not sealed by the laws of the physical universe. I believe unequivocally that the power of thought used with clear logic and knowledge can influence matter. It can iron out any ripples in space-time, creating a stillness in energy, matter, and force. A soul that has a wide frame of knowledge and holds a momentum that unites all disparate parts into a quantum state can lock into the ever-present frame of the Godverse, that perfect field of stillness, peace, and congruence. Could it be that this was the primary purpose behind Jesus's demonstration of the transfiguration and the miracles he is said to have performed? Perhaps it was to show that the Godverse exists somewhere in us all, and if we access that somewhere we can prevail and change any state of atoms in this universe, including our own. Perhaps if we believe enough that those atoms and the forms they make are simply the God principle twisted and deformed, and that the power of mental focus and a requisite strength of belief can unravel those twisted forms and reassemble them in any format, we might ourselves be able to perform miracles.

As I stated in previous chapters, I believe we are not entirely twisted atomic forms. That within us are corridors allowing the power of the Godhead, which was twisted at the big bang and caused atoms to form in the first place, to come through. It is the Godhead that gives us the power of consciousness, life, awareness, and will, as well as the ability to think and know that we are not just twisted atoms. I believe that power comes through the center of the spaces between our atoms as I have said, a center so balanced in force that it is still congruent and resonant with the original Godform.

Such is our measure as thinking, choice-making beings. We can harness this most primary and glorious of all things and deny any fait accompli that might exist because we have all the qualities it takes to do it within us. The great problem is that it will only work if we dislocate our attachment to the material universe and our atomic self by harnessing the power of the Godverse within the space between our atoms. The power of all powers to do this is by believing with sufficiently strong, focused thinking. Perhaps only some people have this kind of insight and strength of character, or we would all be doing it.

The great spiritual teachers who founded the world's religions demonstrated these qualities to us with their works and words, and they entreated us to follow them, some paying the ultimate price with their very lives. Meanwhile, the price of ignoring them is entrapment in increasingly chaotic states, with a diminishing capacity to free ourselves from the straitjacket of entropy. We will keep returning to the universe in physical form through endless rebirth until we either lose complete control over our capacity to control anything and become dependent beings, or we will learn so much that we will escape the cycle of rebirth, with all its concatenate dangers. Dependant beings, in species terms, means going from primates, to monkeys, to other animal forms, to insect forms, and on to more and more primitive life-forms such as trees and plants, to finally end as undifferentiated bacteria, viruses, plasmids, and stones. This is true damnation. Roasting in enforced universes such as ours in a kind of eternity. The eternity of radiation (hellfire) radioactivity and all the other manifestations of force we see arrayed out there.

There are trillions upon trillions of lifeless worlds in the universe if numbers are anything to go by, and very few with life-forms like ours it seems. Yet in precious harbors here and there exist little points like us that can count, tabulate, arrange, change, and direct a momentum that goes against the prevailing order of randomness and chaos in this universe. In fact, the universe can be said to have made the dead before the living—light, plasma, gas, liquid, and finally, solidness, in that order. No life as we understand it existed for most of its existence. Intelligent biological life is only a very recent occurrence, it seems. The universe makes chaos out of prior order. Yet we as living, thinking beings can make order out of chaos, and we came much later into the universe than all the lifeless things. A paradox.

Life is a mystery only if you let it be so. It will be an indefinable something that takes the chaotic, vibrating, enforced minutiae that makes for matter and transforms it into order, symmetry, function, purpose, and meaning. In a laboratory you can take all the orders of enforced magnitudes that make the atom and the elements these atoms make in turn and try to assemble them in the patterns that make for life; you can spin them, shake them, blast them with electrical charges all you like, for as long as you like, and you will never make life happen. All you will do is string dead elements into chemicals, amino acids, and polypeptide chains, the long chains of amino acids that are precursors to proteins and the building blocks of tissue. It really is no more than what a painter does with paint to a canvas—he or she can assemble, but no painting comes to life. The point is this: it was all there before the painter, the paint, the easel, and the canvas came to be.

To create life, the whole muster must be made to happen, from the basic organic and inorganic chemicals and chemistry to the finished product that meets with the approved biological definition of life— a tall order that will never ever happen of its own accord because the animation of dead systems has to come from outside the atom and the universe and not from within the universe. It has to begin naturally within the universe out of something that knew how to do it and holds a master plan that can both do it and knows what it is doing. Life can never be artificially created from dead, nonliving elements by whatever manufactured intelligence there is in this universe.

And so the crucial expression that makes for the spark of life can thus trace its origins to a preexisting something that has all information together in one point. That point is the Godhead, where all the characteristics of existence come from, where the capacity for creation, in which the physical laws of cause and effect and the elements to do anything are contained. It is from this point of the origin that all lines of creation emerge, and one such line is attached to each and every living being. Life is simply a factorization of the Godhead, and the line that leads to this is what is termed a *soul*. A line of connection all living things have to the Godhead.

Our biology at the present time is strung together with force—billions of atoms stitched together in the form of elements. Fully 63 percent of our body is composed of hydrogen, the lightest, simplest, least-enforced element of all. Hydrogen was the first agglomerate of force formed when the universe burst into existence. It would therefore be the easiest to change back into its previous form. Oxygen is the next most prolific element that forms our bodies as human beings. It is essentially eight fused hydrogen atoms in one. We are 25.5 percent oxygen. The next highest amount of elements found in us is carbon. That amounts to about 9.5 percent. After that comes nitrogen at 1.4 percent. Thus approximately 90 percent of us (excluding carbon's 9.5 percent and the elements that are only present in trace levels in the body, which total under 1 percent) is gas. Yes, gas, a gas made to look like a solid by the way it is twisted and strung among a construction of heavier atoms. The forces of bonding atom to atom give us a solid feel, yet we are mainly hydrogen, a mere single twist, a tiny shimmer away from complete straightness and the highway to Godhead. The biblical admonition "Make straight the way of the Lord" (Mark 1:3) has new meaning when viewed this way.

Yes, we as human beings, with our atomic shape provided by the planet's force print, are twisted into enforcedness by the Möroid, and this whole pattern of force makes the double helix–shaped DNA that makes up the building blocks that make our shape. Like the dimensional jig that made all solid matter happen as a twist, the Möroid can be seen in all its power, dictating the change from the abstract, nonphysical world of the Godverse to the physical world of the universe as a compromise to it all.

The atomic center-space reality is based on the elements. Imagine each living being emerging in a physical, material form as the whole universe devolved as an aggregate of these elements in various combinations. There are to date ninety-two stable elements. They represent a series of harder and harder coalescences of atoms, with hydrogen forming the main fund of physicality because all other elements came from the fusion of hydrogen atoms.

The universe was once more plainly Godness than it is now. It was much easier at that stage to use the power of mind over matter and command one's way back into the Godverse. Beings then, such as they might have been, were likely to have been forms of light, perhaps orbs of blue hydrogen light as huge conglomerations of six-ring atoms, filling the whole extent of the universe, settling into smaller and smaller aggregates until the enforced first impulse to see the Godhead from the point of view of the state of parts (i.e., the so-called Original Sin) brought about more separated forms of it. I call these light-space reality beings prime beings, or preeminent beings. They are the first manifestations of more solid, material beings in the omniverse, and from them came all beings in the universe of parts.

And so, as I have said, the first form of the Godverse in the universe of parts led to the First Adam beings as the format for the human species that emerged in time. These original humans had agglomerations of six-ring hydrogen atoms, and this, I believe, marked their high status as spiritual beings. The greater the numbers of six-hydrogen-atom rings that hallmarked their individuality, the greater their Godlight and thus their spirituality. The greater the number of what I have called points of stillness existing between those atomic rings, the grander their insight, intelligence, perception, and capacity to understand all things together as a quantum. And the more beautiful, ephemeral, and not of the center-space reality they would be, as well as the more the power of mind to make change happen would be. Thus one known as an Immaculate Conception would have the highest number of six-hydrogen-ring atom configurations possible in a human biological form.

Living biology in turn would have been dictated by what I call the planetary force print. This is simply the average sum of all forces acting at any given time on any planet at any one point. For example, perhaps the mother of Jesus could bring through a Christ-type being because her particular generation of humankind could produce a marvel such as this. If in the past there were many more beings with these glorious, hydrogen-dominant atomic forms in their biology, there would have been more transfigurations out of this universe and returns to the Godverse from where we all came from once upon a time. I wonder if this accounts for nearly 95 percent of the matter that scientists find missing in the universe—that is, dark matter and dark energy. Perhaps such beings realized through the better configuration of Godlight in them that the limitations of a devolving universe meant that they would be stuck here if they didn't go back while it was still relatively easy to do so. Just a thought! Just a fantastic thought away . . .

The impulse to separate into parts that the inertia of the big bang caused is knotted into the scaffolding of the universe itself and it continues to increase the enforced momentum, making more packed states of atoms. Thus more limited viewpoints emerged from within a state of parts as it all devolved and more broken-up states produced harder and harder conglomerates of atoms. The vast extents of six-ring conglomerates of hydrogen atoms, through which Godhead is best experienced, lessened in number, and the lenses of the Godhead got smaller and smaller and thus more prolific as they produced a view into greater and greater states of limit. We continue in our present state according to this law of diminishing returns—from six points, to five, to four, then three, and now to mostly two or diatomic hydrogen. We were assembled in aggregates where the basic coupling tendency of the hydrogen atom started at six and now at this present time on our planet it is based on twos. I am referring to water, which provides a far more diffracted lens and thus a far more limited view.

Life is the product of a series of defaults. Defaults caused by implicit order within a sea of chaos. The Pole of Absolute Order and harmonious congruence, Godhead, and the Pole of Force Absolute, or infinite chaos, Forcehead are the final opposite existential poles. The potential difference between them is the power that creates all the things of this universe. It created the universe itself. It all happens in an enormous explosion the size of our big bang and as the explosion settles down the products of the whole shebang settle and move as they settle toward one pole or the other, one side going toward order and the other side toward absolute chaos. The laws of physics governing it all to the overall patterning of the Möroidal shape—the twisted third/fourth dimensional ribbon-shaped jig, to which all forces and artifacts of physical worlds must relate and comply in every implicit generating procedure for change. It is the holographic skeleton or frame of resolution that under-bases the most minute standpoints of atoms.

This is all the meaning of life. Where the facility that can provide Godness exists, this facility will be incidentally adorned with life and all its attendant factors. In other words, where the arrangements of force, whether through atoms or whatever can provide balance points in the spaces betwixt their arrangements where no force exists, there will exist Godness giving the property of life to that arrangement. The power of awareness and will and choice will exist for that arena of force, its margins defined by an exponential geometrical progression; a hive of orderness commensurate with the power Godness can give this particular arrangement of force, in terms of its own locality and the general laws that govern atom-based hives in that particular locality.

How then are these differences marked in terms of each individual? Why are there demarcations between life-forms and individuals within each subset of these life-forms?

One simple phrase. "The ability to change against any prevailing trend through the power of Mind."

Life, as I have said, is intrinsically the property of the mutual interaction of Godhead and its opposite, forcehead, acting as the primary existential poles. Thus the only way back to the Godhead is through the divestment of atoms while still alive. How is this done? Quite simply, the ability to change against the prevailing trend of entropy lies in the power of the mind. Could this be all there is to redemption? I believe this *is* all there is to your own redemption and ascension to eternal life. There is no more to it than changing your mind. But you have to change your mind in line with the Godhead. Go against that and you will remain where you have put yourself. It's that easy and that hard—harder than all the things you will ever try to do because I am not talking about a mere change of decision, a mere inflection of your mind, something we do many times a day. I am talking about a total change of mind-set. I am talking about the search for rationally affirmed truth related to meanings that may not always be apparent in physical terms on this planet. I am talking about taking the multitrillion spots of twisted space within you and manipulating their orientation so that they shine through you with a light so bright that no sun in this universe shines as brightly. It's a light so pure it will not harm the eyes of a fly. It's a light so true it will deliver you to the very root of meaning itself.

How do we access this light? How do we touch its merits and gather its power, and where do we access it? Is it something out there in space? Is it something we can make happen by pressing a button?

This light is everywhere, everywhere there are atoms, because it lies in a point at the very center of an atom's expression and also more pervasively in the space between atomic hives, in a vast series of corridors that connect all the spaces between atoms to a single stem that opens to the very kernel of the Godhead. Like a giant net held by a single strand, this light emanates order itself, slowing down and countering the opposite momentum toward chaos and disorder wherever it can exist.

The incredible thing about this light is that it manifests in real time in all living beings, and only in living beings, as consciousness. But life does not guarantee that this empowering light is usable by all living beings. The light has to have very special set of criteria before its power becomes available. The housing of this light has to be set very precisely within the hive of atomic arrangements that make six-point hydrogen rings in stacks. The greater the disposition of hydrogen atoms within this format, the more powerful the ability to use this light for the control of matter and mind, such that matter is disposed and mind is imposed. This light, this Godlight, is all information in perfect purity as light. It is utterly coherent and still in terms of vibration and is thus completely unenforced. Its still, unenforced, coherent quality gives it the power to quiet all the enforced paradigms of the atoms it touches. If presented in its maximum manifestation—that is, six-point hydrogen ring configurations—the space between these atomic assemblies opens the light to the enormous electrostatic scaffolding force of the atoms and can in fact undo this force altogether. Like a screwdriver undoing the tightness of a joint, the Godlight can unscrew enforced paradigms such as the bonds that hold atoms together and go even further and unscrew the implicit inertial forces within a particular atom and change it into the prior form of Godlight that it once was: the First Light of the universe that burst through at the big bang and made prime beings, the preeminent ones.

I believe this is what has been called the Transfiguration of Jesus. To me, the process involved the transmutation of force into unforce. If this can be done, an eminence brighter than any sun configures Godhead instantly, wherever the transfiguration point persists. I believe unequivocally that Jesus used his knowledge, understanding, perception, and action to utterly conquer matter and touch the state of Godhead directly from the living state (this is usually done by most members of our species from the state of death). He demonstrated this achievement of merging with the Godverse before his apostles Peter and John and John's brother James. The brightness seen at the Transfiguration was simply the light of the Godform as it manifested against the wall of force of the universe. It could be said that he opened into that light, just as the Buddha did under the bodhi tree in India eight hundred years before Jesus.

The process of complete change of a physical nature from within the cloak of force we call atoms is a very, very rare thing. You are unlikely to get any scientist to make this come about, and so it will be no surprise if the possibility of this ever having happened in the way described could be empirically confirmed. The science labs just don't have the equipment to affirm it. And even if they did, they would be unlikely to publish the results. In fact, they would be taken off the list of reputable scientists. No more grant money.

I suspect that transfiguration could be accomplished much more easily in the distant past, when the process of devolution through entropy was less far along in its effects than it is now. It gets harder and harder to achieve transfiguration from the atomic, living state and thus gain direct entry back into the Godverse every moment the universe exists. As the universe proceeds into greater randomness and chaos with time, it does so through the divestment of localities within it that balance out force. These localities need little tide pools, little corners where the atomized force modality can cancel out. As the universe tears apart with time, it stretches out these corners, these eddies or tide pools that we call atoms, so that force becomes a wall where there are no situations where atomic aggregates exist.

Time measures an existential scale between two points. We are all measured in time, and thus our existential signature, whether we are part of living matter or dead matter, measures a scale we call individuality. This is the final measure of existential meaning. Is it limited or is it eternal? If it is one or the other, how do we determine its value, and against what final yardstick is this value measured?

Existence itself is the measurer of its own importance. The fashions and modes of existence may be different, but being there, just existing, is what matters above all.

On this planet the species we belong to, *Homo sapiens,* has been increasing its allotted time for living since the beginning of time itself. We now live longer in a physical body than ever before, and almost everyone hails this as a good thing. This of course is no surprise, but the longer we exist as a species, the less our insight into our true grandeur, because the action of the second law of thermodynamics reduces our ability to see that we really belong to another dimension of being. The longer our species continues, the greater its secularity and loss of insight into the fact that we were once "Godlings." We will continually lose sight of the glory we once were and will merge more and more into the fabric of enforcement that is the hallmark of our center-space reality. Our thinking, thinkability, and mind-sets are thus tuned to the terrible precept that we have to eke out as much of our physical, material existence as we can, whatever the cost. The writing, alas, is on the wall, and this view will tend to get stronger and stronger with time until we are likely to eventually pull away from the cord that connects us to the Godverse—our souls. We will gradually lose sight of our first nature in the Godhead and cede to the great pull of chaos, going downward through the species tree, moving from animal to vegetable to mineral and finally becoming that wall of nothingness at the death of the universe. We will thus fade away to become a disparate field of atoms in arbitrary and dissolute disbursement.

Yes. For what it's worth, I believe that is the whole story. The universe burst incidentally into existence and expressly not at the will of an anthropocentric creator. The inertia of the explosion formed a Möroidal shape initially as a product of the interaction of two fundamentally countervailing existential poles, each of them implied but not actual. An all-encompassing shape I call a Möroid defined this contradiction, into which the prior, unforced, still, nonvibrating Godform moved. The Godform then moved into aggregates that were congruent with it, and that allowed much of it to pass back through to become the Godform again. Some, however, were left behind, and being intelligence itself still tries to reformat back into a Möroidal shape. When it does so, anything that has done this can transfigure back into the Godform. You might potentially be one of those who can achieve this transfiguration. Keep trying! I wish you the best every step of the way.

It will be hard. You can see from all the foregoing how hard it is. The individual mind within the backdrop of the Godform we call consciousness sets that drive to attain the ultimate state. We, as naturally living human beings, are constantly battling to reach beyond the atom through knowledge, with spiritual insight uppermost because it is gradually being disallowed. Will humanity be converted to a vehicle for use by intelligent machines and nothing more? What a bummer! Will we serve the purposes of synthetic creations like the Grey robotic entities that even now marshal our planet, ready to take the reins and bring about a terrible destiny for all natural, soul-attached, Godhead-derived living beings here on this planet? No clarion call is loud enough to hail this mordant danger to each and every one of us who is aware enough and intelligent enough to recognize and sense the threat among us.

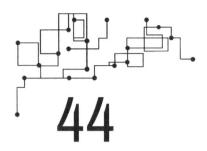

44

Here We Go 'Round the Mulberry Bush

They say fools rush in where angels fear to tread. The wisdom of true angels overwrites the flush of fools and comes from a place where the roots of technology can never reach and have no meaning. Many such angels have come to us. One in particular came to Palestine two thousand years ago and made a promise that was written and vested in a light that shone between two folds of linen: the Shroud of Turin, a cloth that bore the full impression of a crucified man.

The Shroud of Turin measures approximately 14 feet long and 3 feet 7 inches wide. This single rectangular piece of linen was wrapped tightly around Christ's body lengthwise, from the feet over the head, down the back, finishing at the feet again. The cloth was left in the tomb when it was discovered that Christ had disappeared and had, as claimed by the apostles, risen from the dead. Time, it seems, has somehow preserved the cloth, despite every exigency history could throw at it, including fire.

Research suggests unequivocally that whatever accounts for the image on the shroud, there can be no doubt that it is the genuine image of a crucified human being, a male, and that it is no painting. The evidence comes from a group of distinguished scientists of many different disciplines and specialities who all testify to its authenticity. The shroud was established by carbon dating to have originated from the sixteenth century until further research showed that the part of the cloth used for the dating procedure was a sewn-in section used to repair it after it burned in a fire. Recent research has established that a short, intense burst of radiation caused the image. This research has also established that a light with the power of 34 thousand billion watts scorched the surface of the cloth—a light that came from the body of the dead man.

I have discussed research affirming the authenticity of the shroud and its remarkable features at length in my previous book. Suffice it to say, the evidence that it is authentic, when combined with the extraordinary properties of the image, all point to the man the cloth once wrapped as someone truly exceptional. The most up-to-date scientific research into the shroud now confirms the power of a once-living human being, through death, to transform beyond force, matter, and physical life.

Could it be that Jesus performed his miracles by getting into a prior state in which he could redeploy his materiality anyway he chose through mind power? He was a preeminent being from the light-space reality and was thus able to show us how to get to this reality. He bore witness to the purest existential truth possible, and as part of this he warned us about the synthetic forms that hailed from a reality more atomically gross than ours. Inasmuch as this is so, he modeled the living conditions for eternal existence for the rest and the best of us. He was able to retain his light-reality form *and* his atomic form at the same time. In effect, time stood still while this happened. I believe he finally accomplished his full preeminent form at his resurrection point.

Incidentally, they will tell you he transfigured on Mount Tabor, although to me the evidence suggests it was more likely Mount Nitai. But then I beg to differ on a lot of what the church fathers have to say. To me they are a cartel of self-interested, power-hungry men set in an animus driven by Grey alien DNA sequences set in a gel of androcentric prejudice. Their greatest victory was their success in rubbing out the significance, both real and figurative, of Mary Magdalene as the greatest single ally of Jesus in all he did and said. It was her love, faith, and resolution as she stood by him and all his works that has stood the test of time, and this was when all Jesus's male apostles did a runner, so to speak. She was no prostitute as the Christian Aramaic and Greek translators imply and the male chauvinist cartel of Christian controllers would have us believe. She was a woman of great social standing, and her wealth sponsored all Jesus did in terms of his mission's expenditure. Her family was connected to both Joseph of Arimathea and Nicodemus.

I believe she was more than a friend of Jesus; she mothered an ancestral line directly from him that survives to this day. It is my opinion that it was Mary Magdalene whom Jesus spoke to from the cross when he said, "Woman, behold thy son," not his own mother. She represented us all as the icon who converted the Godhead to humanity. In John and Mary Magdalene, Jesus had his two best friends on this planet. It was they he would turn to to give us an idea of the kind of human being we should all strive to be. I believe he was endorsing this idea in his last moments of life. The great obfuscation of this relationship was deliberate and points to the evil of the male chauvinism of the early church fathers.

If that doesn't make the Catholic Church pull out all my epaulettes and buttons I don't know what will. I will proudly donate some truth to their lies, enshrined in texts hidden from the public and still surviving in the Vatican library. I have been screaming in high dudgeon all my life about Lord's Prayer, where they inserted the words "and lead us not into temptation." My own research reveals that the true words were "and be with us in the pathway of temptation." The current pope as I write this has corrected this lie.

In light of Jesus's exceptionality, the following assertion has long fascinated me: "For as Jonas was three days and three nights in the whale's belly; so shall the Son of man be three days and three nights in the heart of the earth" (Matthew 12:40).

What could the heart of the Earth refer to?

When we die, our biomagnetic field, created by the iron in the blood circulating around the body, stops. This is the force holding our eternal survival mechanism to a physical, material body. As soon as that force field ends it loses its gripping power, and the soul is released. Remember that the soul is the record of every single moment of our individual existence written as an individualized field of points of unforce written on the platform of the force it existed in when it was enmeshed in a physical body. At death this field of unforce is a recording of every bit of information thought, felt, perceived, and acted on. This recording is downloaded from the body at death as a unique neutrinoic field.

There is a certain logical situation required for a soul to be liable for capture, either by a synthetic roboid or a natural living being if the latter is set within an enforced frame, through restrictions, confusions, and contradictions built up throughout its lifetime. Confusion and ignorance restricts you in a go-nowhere paradigm; this is the true nature of what is commonly called sin. If the sum total of your thinkability is governed by restricted thought patterns going nowhere, then when you die you will still be caught in those same patterns . Many witnesses who have reported the sighting of ghosts have been struck by the fact that these ghosts seem to be doing the same action over and over again as though they are caught in some kind of repeat loop. These mental habits, reinforced by years of enactment, have thus been conveyed into the frame of death, where the mind helplessly continues in the same vein.

If we are driven by points of focus that tie us to the world of atoms and force, we will go where our focus takes us. We will not head naturally for the lower level of force in the fields of death, in the space between atoms from which we can access the Godverse and thus get out of the universe. We will wander, desultorily lingering near to the atomic frame in the timeless margins of forever between the frames of reality.

All souls are anchored in the Godverse but can only get to it if they can clearly see it and are focused on it. Only then will they be able to see where they must go. It really is that simple. While we are alive our soul field, our line of connection to the Godverse, can root more powerfully into the center-space reality of the universe. At the point of death we will then still be rooted close to atoms, to the center reality. "For where your treasure is, there will your heart be also" (Matthew 6:21).

When the heart then stops and the biomagnetic field of the body ceases, the neutrinoic field is freed to enter into the space between atoms. But if it is focused more powerfully on atoms it can then become caught in the terrestrial magnetic field external to the body. This is a mechanism through which ghosts can happen. Ghosts may well be the manifestation of the quantum mind of the personality that has died. We are thus seeing the whole view of what that person is seeing and is preoccupied with. Restricted thoughts produce the very perturbations that actually make the phenomenon we call force. This force is a measure of the magnetizability of the morphogenic electrospatial information field, which makes a soul susceptible to being held in a magnetic field at death when it is released from the hold of the body's living biomagnetic grip. Manifestations of soul fields trapped by magnetic fields such as deposits of iron, lodestone, or magnetite in any given area are common. These soul fields are held in the magnetic field in the same way as sound is imprinted on a magnetic tape. These naturally enforced areas are suitable places for hauntings. Granite is powerfully piezoelectric. It holds and releases electrical charge when under pressure. This produces a standing, static magnetic field. Many ghostly manifestations are seen in areas with high granite deposits.

Earth's magnetic field is generated by currents flowing in its core. Though weak in strength, the core is the largest and most pervasive of all fields on Earth, and it lies perpendicular to Earth's spin axis. Restrictions, or sins, are convoluted magnetic tracks that can adhere to the lines of force of the planet's field, acting as a cage that traps the soul in a state of limbo, traveling forever through the magnetic lines of Earth through the molten magma at the center of the planet and its nickel-iron core and out again. What is called hellfire would then be experienced as such by the soul because it still retains its awareness of things. This might well be why damnation in hell is described as burning forever but never getting burned to a crisp.

Could it be that Christ's visit to the "heart of the earth" was to liberate souls stuck to the magnetic fields of Earth? His transfiguration would have lessened the planet's force signature enough to release them.

Then the shine of his beautifully set information field could be likened to a group NDE, making clear to these souls what they could not or would not see in their darkness. He would in this way have provided a guiding focus that would lead millions of trapped, "core-hopping" souls out of their state of self-absorbed ignorance and futility.

Two thousand years later it is likely that many more souls have become trapped in Earth's magnetic field. These trapped souls may well be the instigators of the phenomenon of spirit possession of the living by the dead. In their desperation to get away from their state of limbo these discarnate entitites seek to impinge on the living in a last-ditch attempt to gain some reach into the living state, much like a drowning man clinging to a straw. But the terrifying thing may be that as these soul fields are held by a cage of physical force, they can be read and overwritten by alien technology and may also provide a bridging point between the aliens and us.

Ironically, the Greys may be our planet's best way of cleansing itself of the neo-Nazi and Ku Klux Klan types, as these wretched humans might ironically be removing themselves and the stench of their wicked actions upon their death. It may be that what we commonly call "evil" is a function that allows the soul field to retain a certain magnetizable quotient that then ties it to any prevailing magnetic field in any life-bearing planet.

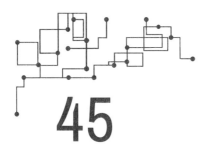

45

Alien Tactics

The genetic prospectus of humankind has thus been changed through factors introduced into it by a vastly superior extraterrestrial technology conveyed by a roboidal machine form that has been present on our planet for hundreds of thousands of years. This new format persists in some of the present genetic lines of humankind as preparation for our species to ultimately fit into their machine format.

The infected lines have paid a deadly price for this because as altered forms they are no more a pure conduit capable of carrying all the information of the original Godform from which they originated. However, some genetic lines remain free of the altered prospectus and still hold their original format. These free genetic lines are reflected in a special humanity that has produced the great minds and prophets and teachers of yore, among them Jesus's Mother Mary and her lineage. There will be many others like this with clean, unintercepted genetics whom history has obscured who came to refresh human genetic lines.

If such clean genetic lines still exist on our planet they would be a great threat to the biological prospectus laid down by the Grey menace's breeding program, and you would expect that the first priority of the Greys would be to try to locate these lines and interrupt them. To do that they would have to have a global system to identify and monitor every single living human being on this planet. You would expect them to deploy their technology to achieve a monitoring system that follows you from cradle to the grave—every move you make. Every single human being would have to be genetically tagged to achieve this. That means blood tests, hospitals, centralized records, and finally, the insertion of electronic mechanisms into the human biomass. Beguiling reasons and words will encourage billions to fall for these procedures designed to control the behavior of humanity, with assurances that all information gleaned through these measures will be safely kept. Guess what's happening in the world today? Information is regularly stolen, millions are losing their personal information every day. It is sold to the highest bidder. They say the devil is the prince of lies. For devil, read Grey.

A fact remains for all to see: technology is now being deployed at fever pitch to control the lives of each and every person on the planet. Millions voluntarily and innocently comply in allowing this technology into their homes and on and into their person. They love their cell phones so much. They are so convenient. An asset beyond measure for the naive and the foolish. If you own one you are in the system. You don't even have to use it. The latest models can provide them with all kinds of information about you, including your medical history. They can monitor your personal conversations without you even turning on your device. You can be traced wherever you are to within a meter. Government whistleblowers constantly provide incontrovertible evidence warning us that this is so. That is why the security services of many nations are so hopping mad about whistleblowers. The security services of the United States own the Western media, which pretends that opinions over this are diverse and disparate. Have you noticed how when wars and other controversial actions are announced by certain governments in the name of "national interests," within minutes almost all the major media outlets fall into a single opinion favorable to those who pronounce those national interests?

Systems will be and are now being put in place today to control every single human being on the planet without them knowing they are being controlled. This system is being deployed as covertly and as quickly and efficiently as possible. Social media like Facebook and Twitter make sure that this is achieved with the least amount of suspicion raised.

The human ego is the most powerful natural drive next to survival. Just use one ego against another and it is that simple to achieve whatever you want. This is the new political order. Few will ever suspect that a far more insidious motive underlies the effort to promote and place the latest technology in everyone's hands. Those who spot the con will be labeled conspiracy theorists, gullible fools, woo-woo New Agers, or simply paranoid. And sadly and catastrophically for us all, the vast majority of the world's people will buy into what they have to sell.

As has always been the case, tomorrow's enemy is today's friend, and vice versa. This will have to be so as the field is narrowed down to place complete control in the hands of those selected by the Grey aliens. This is the deadly crew hidden within the cartels of the world's most powerful countries, countries whose pervasive technological and fiscal power has control over the rest of the world. What basket would a powerful, highly intelligent robotic ET puts its eggs in if they wanted total control with the least disruption to everything and everyone? You've guessed it. But while you've got that right, ponder what the price might be for such a thing.

But they will still have to reckon with the individual soul. That is the hope of all living, intelligent species all over the universe. It's not biology and matter that finally rules, but something completely outside it all, something held within the spiritual testaments of certain people. I believe the Grey cartel and its cohorts are finding out that whatever genetic stitching they use to revamp a species, the biology of some people still holds no truck with their nefarious agenda. You cannot control life-forms as you can synthetic machine-forms. Something in some people resists their call. It's a mystery to the Greys, and this mystery has, I believe, saved the human species thus far from total takeover by these roboids. They do not and cannot know and comprehend what lies outside atoms in the Godverse. They haven't a clue that the total story of existentiality includes *life* as a prime factor. They are machines, and as such they are incapable of knowing or understanding this concept, ever.

I believe this is the deal of deals for the Greys and their ilk. It's what has brought these things here in such great numbers in contemporary times. They're nearing their goal. But they cannot deal with the power of the soul and its faculty for independent thinking in people. So they have to constantly tend their flock, four fingers on deck, so to speak, to weed these folks out as soon and as effectively as possible. It is their priority to deal with those who do not run with their covert agenda. A disproportionate number of ufologists have paid with their lives for looking too closely at their machinations. I may eventually do so with my own life.

There can be no two ways about it: they have to devise a solution to this problem of resistance. That solution requires knowing every detail of every single person, particularly in the developed countries, which is their preferred stomping ground because it is from these places that the planet is controlled. They have to do it so that each person is dealt with by them on an individual basis. Many of the evil contrivances and scenarios you see going on in the world are set up to bring this control about.

The size of the task will be plain to the reader now. The beings in all those objects seen by thousands whizzing around at 30,000 mph may well be here to deal with this problem. I believe they are forced to do it piecemeal because they cannot know or see in advance how the resistance in some humans comes about. It's too disparate. It comes about as an individual awakening. You cannot see or know what a soul is by using technology, hence the abductions of millions. The Greys are looking for the magic ingredient that allows some human beings to spot them for what they are and resist them. They have to deal with that. To do this they have to fool the world into cooperating with an agenda they cannot reveal. They have to set up the means to look at every detail of every living human being in their target areas. They have to do it through clandestine means because this is the best way to get it done without resistance. You are less likely to be noticed for what you are and why you do it that way. If this doesn't work it will be done through laws contrived to enforce this agenda. No passports anymore; get yourself chipped or you won't be able to travel. That's coming soon. The plans have already been laid out by twenty-seven of the world's most significant governments. The final step is arrest and imprisonment or arranged disappearance and death of the resisters. Be watchful. As of early 2022, all that I've predicted has come about; electronic vaccine passports will soon progress to electronic tagging under the guise of preventing forgery.

The past two years have shown us starkly how readily we seek the comfort and authority of a parent when we feel fear. We will suspend all critical thinking capacity in order to feel safe. I speak of course of the COVID-19 Pandemic, in which most of the world came to an unprecedented standstill. Not since the Second World War have we experienced such total control over our lives. Under sweeping powers rushed through Parliament, it became legal for families to be cut off from each other, police to fine people for leaving their homes, and children to be deprived of each other's company and vital learning in schools. The psychological messaging was arguably worse than the legal restrictions; if we dared to meet each other we were told by government messaging that we were "killing Grandma." It did not seem to matter that Grandma's precious last years were spent isolated in a room in her care home and that she died alone there.

The precautionary principle[1] was employed in the extreme. People watched as their livelihoods were destroyed in complete societal shutdown. Behavioral scientists were employed to nudge human behavior toward a predetermined goal and to instill in the public a sense of lack of control, to which they looked for an authority to lead them. Fear was the sanctioned weapon. The official U.K. government advisory board on the pandemic, Sage, published a manual through their Spi-B division titled *Options for Increasing Adherence to Social Distancing Measures* stating, in order to achieve its aims:

> The perceived level of personal threat needs to be increased among those who are complacent, using hard-hitting emotional messaging. To be effective this must also empower people by making clear the actions they can take to reduce the threat. Consideration should be

given to use of social disapproval but with a strong caveat around unwanted negative consequences."[2]

The penetrating insight of the prophets Orwell and Huxley warned us of this. It is probable even they would be alarmed at what is taking place. We didn't need Huxley's soma pill to control our emotions and become subservient, fear and deference to authority were enough for us to bow our heads. Of course, the potential threat of a new virus with unknown effects required unprecedented action in public health to minimize damage and save human lives. It is the methods employed and the extent to which they were employed that reveals the weaknesses in our nature when our safety is threatened.

The next steps will begin with your medical records. They will begin by saying it is your right to keep them private. Soon, however, they will make it an administrative imperative to divulge them. They won't ask you. They'll just do it. Passports will not be of paper but electronic tags inserted into your body, with not just all your personal details from birth to death, but also everything known about your family as well as your medical record. An ongoing recording will be taken from you 24/7. Your location anywhere will be known instantly. Your right to privacy and movement will be taken away gradually at first, and then at a stroke.

The terrifying thing is that they will do this with your cooperation! They will set up the most draconian "terrorist" events from time to time, all canards to convince people that it's in their best interests and the security of the nation that all this is done. The vast majority will willingly allow it all. Deep-seated racial, ethnic, cultural, and sectarian prejudices in many of us will be cleverly exploited to bring all this about. They will tut-tut all those who issue warnings. They will call them conspiracy theorists. The truth is, you can't be paranoid enough. The more you protest, the more you will be isolated as a fool and then as a danger to the so-called good of society. The mainstream media will issue persuading articles and TV and radio broadcasts on behalf of their masters, who own the worldwide mainstream media and often use comic reportage to portray any serious narratives of UFO contacts, be they of the first, second, third, or fourth kind.

The power of instant communication anywhere in the world, one would think, would have led to a more coherent world and a greater sense of social unity. There is evidence to suggest that the opposite is happening. We still select and hive with our own, to the detriment of others, and those divisions are getting stronger. Could this be because managed media promotes negative political stances, be they tribalism, bigotry, racism, ethnocentrism, and nationalism?

Billions are bound to buy into the messaging that it's all being done for the good of us all, that these measures are insurance against terrorism. But to use that canard effectively you have to set up the terrorism. If you're someone who believes the mainstream media, then you will believe who and what they identify as the bad guy. This way you'll never see that the bad guy is no stranger, that the bad guy might be your own government or secret, powerful cartels within them supposedly acting in your own best interest. In this way entire populations will be duped. But before you can dupe entire populations you have to instill that powerful national sense. You do that by creating an "enemy" that purportedly threatens the nation. You can then more easily achieve your goal of cooperation with little resistance.

Those already infected with alien genetic outlays that are more powerful than the whispers of their own souls will not resist. These are the hybrids. They're the ones that I feel the most for. They are the inheritors of those magnificent words whispered through the pain of crucifixion: "Father, forgive them for they know not what they do."

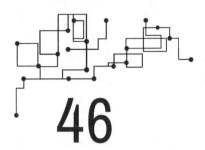

46

The Curse of Everydayness

The following extract is from the epilogue of my second book. I have included it here because the book you are reading is the last in a series of three, and some will not have read the previous two books. I feel this conveys as powerfully as I can muster in words the nature of the curse of everydayness.

Your eyes open and the daylight hits you like the flash of a combusting magnesium strip. You blink, and your thoughts fold into your consciousness like the rolling, bursting waves on a beach. The ceiling comes into focus, and the spatial memory of the bed you lie on, the room you are in, and the strip of ground you are about to put your feet on comes into focus. You swing your feet off the bed and in a moment you are upright. Vertical. Your mind struggles to deal with myriad thoughts at once, defining past memories and present contingencies. Your bladder reminds you that you have a body, and before you know it you are standing in front of the bathroom mirror staring in disapproval at an image that is swollen-eyed, with a tight mouth. YOU.

All this is a parody of the average mind in one morning of tens of thousands of mornings before tens of thousands of days that you assume will come your way. It is the beginning of a recognizing what defines your existence. It is the most important moment of your being, for in it you and you alone, look squarely into the face of your eternity. You face all of it with every moment you live.

What in real behavioral terms is expected of us to gain the Godverse, given that we are in such a terrible predicament? I don't think it's too simplistic to say that money is now our God. Money—the one thing of all things that raised Jesus to anger.

As I have said, many scientists these days are in pursuit of funding, not the search for dispassionately observed truth. Money rules their direction. The next grant application is what matters. But who and what decides this? The controllers of that money decide all. Is this what science is all about these days? Could it be the whole phenomenon we call the pursuit of knowledge has been hijacked to meet the fiscal priorities and covert political agendas of corporations and governments, and not the neutral, objective pursuit of knowledge for its own sake as they would have us believe? While this may be a rather cynical way of describing the quest for new knowledge, it seems to reflect the true picture today. There is a definite drift as to where research is heading: to the discovery of what's necessary for creating a different kind of humanity, one with a pseudomechanistic biology and psychology, one aimed at taking away our natural, intuitive Godliness and thus our capacity for eternal life.

Somewhere in the ethers invisible hands are controlling the funding of research into areas that will mark the end of humanity as we know it and the beginning of the biosynthetic human being—sterile human clones and artificial wombs that mass-produce copies of workers or roboidal homunculi. This will be the controllable fodder of the future that will become the slaves of a tiny number of corporate and government heads who will decide the merits of life, living, and the so-called pursuit of happiness for the entire planet. This brave new world will come with a controlled world media with its denials, obfuscations, and misinformation delivered through teams of spin doctors who will insist that all is well and no such extraterrestrial aliens exist now on

Earth. The vast majority of the Western press is tied directly to the security agencies of the most powerful countries. The name of the game is control, a form of total control that makes it seem that the media is free. Check the internet and you will not need to take my word for it—you'll see the compelling evidence that human beings are being gradually engineered to walk as machines.

Hell is being entrapped to rot in an endless series of physical lives in universes like ours, which reduce us from the highest states of thinking to the lowest mental paradigms possible. This in turn reduces our ability to reach beyond and out of the magnetically enforced pull of the physical universe. You get sucked back into it to live in physical bodies over and over again until you go through the stages of loss of the mental capacities that define the margins of each species. Down, down, down—from human to primate, ape, monkey, gibbon, dolphin, squid, octopus, mammal, fish, mollusk, tree, cactus, lichen, bacterium, virus, plasmid, prion, and then on to stones and the final, absolute dissolution of any connection to life and the Godhead.

I cannot be certain it will be a future of winking diodes and humming transistors that faces the bright, beaming face you see in that baby's crib. However, the evidence now is overwhelming that it will be a world of sterile certainties, where the color of a skin will rule one's future even more than it does today.

But I can be certain that each day our eyes open as we come out of sleep, that utter freedom of will is assured and definite, and what I do with my body and the furthest stretch of my mind every second, minute, and hour of each day can change the extent of my eternity as a person. What's more, I know through what is logical, rational, and meaningful that Godhead is the biggest certainty of all. I know it through no one else's mind but my own. It is not a claim for tooth fairies or hobgoblins. It's a claim for myself and can only be a claim for myself. Yet it can be laid before anyone in kinship, caring, and truth. The old ones, the beautiful ones, come and go and blow their kisses to us as a species, often with tearful eyes, and so few of us take notice. Too many, too late. Always too late! The sweep of the alien cage is so lethal because it is so insidious. There will be no overt declaration of war against humanity. The conquest of our planet has been assured because it is being achieved by a subterfuge so well disguised that nobody seems to notice it.

It all seems such a negative picture. It's no good smiling and pinning a positive future like the mantra the New Agers proclaim: Just think positively and everything will be alright. The problem is that the reality I'm pointing at is stark and stupefying for too many. Billions still starve when this world could so easily be managed even now for this never to be so. The whited sepulchers that control the huge fiscal corporations that drive the world can only see the shortest margins: the zeros on bank balances. Just ten billion dollars could build two hundred hospitals in each of 150 of the poorest countries in the world, to give adequate care to 90 percent of medical needs across the globe. All that suffering at a stroke for a relative pittance in terms of the whole world's treasuries. I know. I have personal experience of such a quest myself, a hospital in a tropical country that ran for twenty years, only to have a representative of the United Nations tell me that the cost of running it would be the cost of hiring just one UN expert to oversee one single area in this same country. Such "experts" often have information that's out of date due the new technological changes that have come about in recent times. Thousands of so-called experts like this evidently just simply languish in foreign places, in tax-free luxury, living on expense accounts. The returns coming from all this investment in terms of benefit to the people are usually negligible. This person quoted me an index of effectiveness against investment schemes done by the United Nations Development Program in 2013. For every $100 invested, the average return per scheme came in as a negative of 100/81. That means that you invest $100 to set your target at 19 percent *worse off* when you complete it than before you started it. He was so impressed with the results of the scheme that he showed me secret figures in a corruption index for the country I once worked in. For every $100 donated to that government, only $17 got to the targeted people. The rest got lost in the pockets of politicians, administrators, and their families. Such is the scope of conscience and caring in human kinship terms in our world today—a world where acquisitiveness overwhelms any spiritual and socially responsible values.

From all this it seems that humanity is hell-bent on money as a driving factor. Many might cynically say let the Greys take over our species. It's better if we are wiped off the face of the Earth. But even as the guilty scream out of the magma at the center of the Earth for respite, hope springs eternal, because Godhead reaches everywhere. Even where the lines of magnetic force spin through the molten center of Earth, carrying billions of souls attached as electrospatial fields, there will be a Christ there, too. Sometime in the future he or she will go to the cities beneath the Earth to seek their saving, for such is true love. Such is the spire at the center of the Godverse. That of course assumes they can hear these Christ-like beings, know them for who they are, understand what they are saying, and can make the choices and effect the changes that will redeem them for what they have done, for the lives they might have been instrumental in taking.

Justice is implicit universe-wide despite the second law of thermodynamics, because free will prevails universe-wide. It prevails because the Godverse is implicitly connected to the universe we live in, in every iota of it. Like oil and water, the Godverse and the universe can stand together but can never mix. People may not see justice done in their lifetimes, but no murderer or torturer can escape the consequences of their acts. Those who kill hundreds of innocents may think they've gotten away with it, but they can never flee from the implicit justice of the universe through the Godlight. They will face their karmic folly the second they draw their last breath. It is written on their karmic record, because the culprits witnessed their crimes themselves in real time and registered them as a soul holograph on their electrospatial field. He or she will be their own judge, and the reckoning will be perfect and true in its compensatory value to the victim.

Sins, as I have said, are simply restrictions in our nature and ability to think, prejudices that separate us from one another: the color of one's skin, one's religious beliefs, a type of dress or shoe, pimples, the amount of adipose tissue. You name it, there is always someone who will separate, deny, and keep the habit of separation going. On this an eternity is decided. Put enough of these restrictions in your nature and the monkey cage in some far-off planet in some far-off zoo may be your future home.

I hope I've succeeded in demonstrating in this book how no one can ever get away from natural justice wherever or whatever they are in the universe and indeed beyond it. There are no favorites in the implicit, perfect value of Godhead, and no one can get away from the consequences of their deeds, good or bad.

The final, harrowing conclusion can only be that that some members of our human family have been used as scalpels by the alien interlopers to perform their evil work on the rest of humankind. Particular genotypes among all the genetic strains of *Homo sapiens* have been the true chosen ones, chosen for all the wrong reasons through no fault of their own, to unsuspectingly do the dirty work of a superintelligent alien lizardlike machine.

This is a crime of everlasting significance if something awesome in magnitude isn't done about it. That awesome something was demonstrated by the lives and revelations of the great teachers and masters who have come among us from time to time to warn us and save us. A worldwide effort is needed to look at history again without fear or shame, with a sharp focus on all the evidence for the great satanic impostor that has remained hidden within the hems of humanity. We must look with eyes free of blindfolds; we must take a clean, clear, dispassionate, utterly objective and thorough look. We will have lost nothing if we look this way and find nothing. On the other hand, we might gain a chance of keeping our eternal existence if we look this way and find what a laboratory rat never sees: that the bars of his cage have been made to lead the rat to the fire of an incinerator.

The greatest exercise the planet has ever known must be carried out totally objectively to uncover the alien hand in the affairs of our species. You, the reader, are the main player in all this. I set out to give you a look at all that I have learned over the past four decades about the phenomenon. I turned from a cynic and a skeptic to a stunned believer that all our tomorrows are in the hands of ET synthetic entities not directly born out of the beginning of the universe. This utterly bizarre conclusion did not come easily. It was just too much to take in at the start. I fought it with all the usual prejudices we have in our cultural background in furnishing our mental comfort points. With the greatest irony I found that the more I tried to prove and dismiss the synthetic Grey alien phenomenon, the more I became convinced that my original premises were wrong, and I had to totally—yes, totally—change my perspective if I was to get at the truth. It was more a lesson for my own character than anything else.

I offer all this to you in the name of your children, in the fervent hope that you might sit in the saddle and see for yourself. Believe nothing I say, if you so choose. But please sit in the saddle and see for yourself if you can. Again, with ultimate irony, the very thing that was constructed for the synthetic aliens to carry out their purposes here among humankind and is at the heart of all their efforts, the World Wide Web, turned out to be the greatest tool for uncovering their nefarious agenda. They hadn't reckoned on something they could never know—the size and meaning of the human spirit and the beat of the Godform in all naturally living beings who can still think independently. To beat your enemy you have to know everything about it. In doing so you enter a race against time.

To gather their information the Greys have left themselves open as to how and why they do what they do, and some of us might in fact spot them. So to take care of this as best they can they have to control the whole system of information dissemination. They can take out the truth-tellers before too much damage is done. The truth-tellers and whistleblowers are dangerous because many are passionately and stubbornly driven to expose the whole fraud. That, for them, is the easier option, but that, too, will never succeed because new truth-tellers and whistleblowers will inevitably come along after the old ones succumb to the arranged accident, the bullet, or the covert practices within the medical profession. To accomplish this they have to control the security services and thus the governments of as many of the most sophisticated countries as they can. Thousands are killed under these guises. More ufologists die disproportionately than any other public informers.

The internet is still open, though I don't know how long this will be so. It is only free because its creators needed it to accomplish their hidden agenda. But triumphantly and ironically, that is also *our* opportunity to beat them at their own game.

The hidden powers that rule our planet have to keep it open for a while yet, but they are bound to restrict it when they have gathered all the information they need about each and every one of us. No stone will be left unturned in their quest because one point of resistance to the synthetic ET agenda is a point from which others can quickly multiply. So they are set on vanquishing all resistance, and it seems so few even know this is happening.

So what do you do if you *do* know? How do you change things when you are no longer able to find the provisions that guard liberty? Oh yes, the pursuit of freedom has been the swan song of every self-centered scoundrel since time immemorial, every evil hypocrite only too eager to praise the Lord and collect the money. Samuel Johnson was right on the mark when he said, "Patriotism is the last refuge of a scoundrel." So many of us ride the runes of cynicism as a result. I literally have not just hours', but whole days' worth of utterly convincing video footage and gigabytes of documents that affirm beyond the slightest doubt the presence of the Grey alien threat to humankind. Will another book like this suffice in trying to open it all up for an ignorant, disbelieving world? I don't think so. But I must at least try. The life force in my children and grandchildren beckons me forward. If you will accept this with my humility, I would like to include your children in that sentiment, too. The smile, the laugh, the shiver of delight that pleases on the faces of innocents is all the imperative that many who still care will need. There can be no price too high to ensure our eternities remain intact and that no grave robber of extraterrestrial origin will rob us of our awesomely beautiful, natural legacy of life and the right to eternal life that we each possess.

Please remember that every particle that makes matter has its own time-sequenced impression on the whole existential scale. This impression is recorded as a vibrational change on a timeline. The timeline itself is unalterable. Everything is recorded on this timeline. There is a neutrinoic shadow picture registered of everything that is there and happens in the photonic (atomic) world, and vice versa. This shadow picture is real and made more real in the photonic, atomic world when in the presence of strong electromagnetic fields. This is the world of ghosts. That is why so many are seen in places where there are strong electromagnetic fields—small, dark, underground places where you wonder why so many ghosts are lurking there. Underground and above-ground powerlines and ley lines (water flowing underground on a granite under-base) can manifest these apparitions, too.

So a kind of duplicate photograph of all things that happen is constantly being made as time flows in step with them. As a living being you can make things happen. You create your own time-resourced impression. Dead, static, nonliving things cannot make these constantly changing impressions. They just stay in place and depict all the information of what is physically unchanging except for the incidental rotting effects of entropy. Only things that have life can make their own individual world of information and change things if they so desire. Both paradigms run together, with the living observer changing the observed. Prophets and seers can even operate at a timeframe of their choosing and see a picture of future events. The timeframe doesn't change, but their viewing point does. You never know. You might be one of them, a witness to the past and the future in your subconscious. Ah! But so often we put it all out as just imagination, don't we? Such a shame.

The secularization of life that goes on at an incredible pace all over the modern world is founded in large part on an ignorant claim, one that says that science and the discoveries of its methodology leaves no room for God or indeed any nonmaterial reality. It's all supposed to be here and of this universe alone, in physically verifiable form, and if it ain't, then it just ain't real. An insidious organization in the United States, the Committee for Skeptical Inquiry, founded by James Randi—a science-fiction writer and stage magician, no less—was formed at the behest of a powerful cartel of scientists to ensure that the only truths we believe are those that can be physically verified. It may of course be just another one of the many covert ways the hugely rich ensure that their investments prosper and that their work forces and consumers around the world are not diverted into the highly inconvenient kind of nonmaterialistic, spiritual behavior that might risk their bottom line.

The scientists will do their very best to explain it all, but they are limited by their formatted thinking just as the religious are by theirs. A truly impartial mind cannot exist that might decide between the two. It all rests on your approach to the truth, if finding the truth is your goal in the first place. Most people take things as they are and try to make the best of things. The financially better-off will live in a closed world with planned resources and planned returns that leave them comfortable. We tend to think the day's troubles are sufficient unto the day and we don't need someone pulling our chain and carefully guarded conscience, pouring in what-ifs. I doubt this describes you—you would never have gotten this far into this book if it did. Those who are happy with their own ease and uninterested in relieving the unease of others would have discarded this book after the first few pages.

Money-motivated greed, the acquisitive sense, and tribal hiving are the strongest motivations for achievement. The achievement of what? It has been found that just 20 percent of gross family income is essential for living and maintaining a comfortable life in the fifty most developed countries in the world. All the rest is unnecessary for maintaining life. You will find that nationalism is the trick most often purveyed by the scoundrel greedy for power and money. This ethos has allowed 285 people to have more combined wealth than 3.5 billion of the poorest people on our planet.[1] To put it another way, 1 percent of the world's population possesses 99 percent of all the world's fiscal wealth. Such is the strength of the social conscience of our species toward one another. Such is the damning indictment on us as a species because we all allow the few to do this. Money-motivated imperatives drive all our intents, it seems, because money, and more particularly the various systems, designs, and formularies that surround it, seem to be the power that allows us to simply exist.

An Oxfam briefing paper dated January 2014 highlighted the following statistics:

- The wealth of the 1 percent of richest people in the world amounts to $110 trillion. That's 65 times the total wealth of the bottom half of the world's population.
- The bottom half of the world's population owns the same as the richest 185 people in the world.
- Seven out of ten people live in countries where economic inequality has increased in the past thirty years.
- The richest 1 percent increased their share of income in twenty-four out of twenty-six countries between 1980 and 2012.
- In the United States, the wealthiest 1 percent captured 95 percent of the post–financial crisis growth since 2009, while the bottom 90 percent became poorer.
- Eight people have more wealth than 3.5 billion of the poorest human beings on Earth.[2]

This is all big trouble for all those caught up in trite and superficial values, propelled by expediency and the acquisition of profits. Materialism has been vilified and condemned by all spiritual teachers of any note, markedly by Jesus Christ and Gautama Buddha. These great teachers and others saw that it all makes for damnation in the space between atoms where we go at death. At this point all that matters is the quantum of knowledge you have and how that quantum is sorted so that the power to unite dominates and cancels out the power to do the opposite.

If you look at it deeply enough, point by point, we've done nothing, nothing at all worthwhile as a species if physical existence is the only worthwhile thing there is. Nothing that really matters if we see it from the point of view of the human heart. Big shiny buildings. Long, sweeping palaces and machines of speeding splendor that run on four wheels, while half the world languishes in tiny boxes, the vast majority broken and derelict, in places where injustice, misery, and disease rule. Millions are dying unnecessarily despite the technology we have to stem the tide, while dead minds live in facades of body-fed comfort, fully satisfied on the gains they've made on a planet they've poisoned getting them.

An executive at the most popular private cable TV organization responded to my assertion that its programs were a salad of "utter rubbish," and that they were "extorting money from the public." He looked at me quizzically and retorted, "Don't you think we know that? It's because what is out there to sell it to is utter rubbish. We wouldn't make the profits we do if our audience was full of intellectuals and deep thinkers." He smiled and added this rejoinder: "Keep it dumb and you get rich. We are there to make money, not to be philosophers." I retreated, feeling dumb myself for my retort.

The anecdotal evidence is now overwhelming that near-death experiences indeed point to life beyond the physical, atomic body, a life that continues forever. For those who live for and cherish the material things of this universe at the expense of other people, the world beyond atoms holds a dread beyond imagination. The stories of NDEers imply a world of union beyond the physical, where all actions of will that seek to bring living beings together in love are the very seed corn of admission to an eternal scope of existence in the fullest knowing and understanding possible. On the other hand, actions of will that separate, reduce, marginalize, and restrict the freedom and the right to learn and know all things will reap a corresponding limited scope of existence.

No one is your conqueror or emancipator but you. God cannot intervene in anything and stay God in the sense most of us see an anthropomorphic divine God. It is literally a mother and father of a contradiction in terms. This triumphant news is the very stuff of meaning itself. We can be assured that if we believe enough in what we do and the things we do are logically derived to unify and harmonize separated parts, and we do this to the greatest extent possible, we shall unravel the enforcedness of our physical being. We shall unscrew the atomic bonds that hold our eternal nature in the prison of a physical, atomic body because the very atoms themselves will cease to exist and we shall glow brighter than the sun, as a great sage once did on Mount Nitai in Palestine some two thousand years ago, to temporarily merge with the light of the Godhead, the final singularity that instigated the whole process in the first place.

47

Hope

The world yearns for a panoramic change in the human heart, a change that brings each and every one closer together. The firmament blazes with the daytime light of the sun, a canopy of glory studded with artwork in all the colors of the rainbow that seem of divine plenitude. Goodwill looks yonder for a strident charm that might come from beyond the realms of our knowing and takes us all into wisdom, understanding, and a frieze of joy that brightens our hopes like the smile of a child. No more tears, no more fears, just the thunder of hearts beating across the horizon. But century after century of the screams of innocents burning from exploding blasts have laid waste to dream after dream and still echo in screams of pain down hospital corridors the world over. That's what civilization does.

Will someone from the stars come and stop all this? After all, there seem to be no anthropomorphic gods anymore. Will the kindly spaceperson with his or her box of magic tricks succeed in stemming our demise as a species when we ourselves have failed for some fifteen thousand years? Can they stop the action of the second law of thermodynamics? Millions hope for this. When the discs appear in the sky and they are ready to take their harvest, the wily politician, businessman, and commercial priest will soothe us. "Don't be afraid," they will say. "It's all for our good. They must be better than us. After all, they would have to be something wondrous to have gotten here from at least $4.8 \times 60 \times 60 \times 24 \times 365 \times 186,000 \times 800$ miles away" (referring to the distance of the nearest planet that might be suitable for human life at the time of writing this).

It seems any planet suitable for oxygen-breathing life systems is at least two hundred times the distance away from the nearest star from us. It would take eight hundred years traveling at the speed of light to get there. I have told you about the trouble with that—you cannot even travel at that speed because mass becomes infinite according to the Einstein equation $E = mc^2$. Your conveyance will become bigger than the whole universe. It's an impossibility.

"Nothing is impossible," they say, these architects of nonsense. "They might even stop the universe and then we could all get off and live forever." But live where? Where is forever? It's a long time. There goes another sun winking out. "Never mind, another one will start up somewhere. There'll always be a sun somewhere. There'll always be Mommy and Daddy to look after us." But they wink out, too. Everything keeps winking out. Suns, Moms, and Dads, even atoms. No box of tricks seems capable of fixing that. "Let's not think about it. Someone else will do it. We've still got the Palace of Versailles. We can still walk around that and take photographs. We've still got the Mona Lisa and the singing of Nat King Cole. It feels good to be civilized. We're better now than ever. Just look at what we've done. It's all so much better."

If matter dismantles under the effect of entropy, there must be a concurrent effect on thought and thinking, a trend toward greater and greater separation, isolation, and divisiveness. Goal orientation will gradually cede to individual isolation, and group identification will fragment into progressively smaller polarizations of collective identity. These in themselves will be the cause of further divisiveness, until the human being finally stands alone, unable to provide a coherent subjectivity that allows for the caring of anything or anyone except for oneself and one's own self-interest—the format of the synthetic machine. And so chaos will inevitably reign because the permutations for willful expression will increase. Systems will evolve to control individual expression, with the inevitable exhortations to tension, anger, rebellion, and the revolution that will follow when people are so restricted. This will further raise the thresholds of physical and psychological force within social and familial systems and, more importantly, within the individual. The seemingly never-ending vicious circle of social and political unrest we see in the world today confirms this all too clearly.

A huge network of interconnection is implicit if the principle of Godhead means anything. The phenomenon of quantum entanglement affirms that everything is connected to everything else throughout the universe. This implies that as individual quanta of livingness we are bound to one another for our mutual benefit—an implicit encouragement to "love thy neighbor." Meanwhile, the second law of thermodynamics is busy every quantum moment taking things apart. In universes of limit where we linger as physical beings, in a conditionality that produces states of solidness and matter, where force and thus impulsions rule–time sources resources. Happily, we are not completely at the mercy of the whims of randomness and chaos; our minds can control time and the present moment through the exercise of free will. But that means we need help knowing the whens, whys, hows, and wherefores of anything to execute that control. Beliefs set in truth are therefore critical. As an example: We each inherit our human form and ethnic and cultural makeup through the genetic lines we reincarnate into. The karmic travail decides our destiny, as we hold the karmic debts we incurred in past existences and attach them to our preexisting genealogical line. We can be born into any racial group to expiate wrongs done to others in past or present lives. Frequently little children who recall their past lives tell their parents that somehow, from somewhere, they chose to come to them. I recommend the TV series *Ghost Inside My Child* on the Biography Channel. It will astonish you.

So let's say you are born into a white European culture and you grow up to become a racist. Racists and xenophobes dislike and tend to dismiss anyone not of their own culture or race. But karmic debts incurred in a past or the present lifetime might require an interaction with groups and individuals outside your racial or cultural comfort zone. Your narrow-minded attitudes as a xenophobe will forbid you from doing this. This is one of the reasons why the worst kind of mental affliction you can have is racism or any sort of ethnic prejudice. Not only does it prevent the resolution of karma, but it also serves the dual purpose behind the Grey ET agenda, which seeks the separation of groups for their experiments while at the same time helping to guarantee that that soul will head straight into their grasp at death. They will also seek to get suitably prepared living human beings to places where souls can be harvested by instigating holocausts, wars, and conflicts through the machinations of their own hybrid forms.

The alien legacy on Earth is perhaps awaiting a leader that will make one of their previous sponsored kind—Adolf Hitler—look like Little Lord Fauntleroy! A man-eater to end all man-eaters. In the dark recesses and bays of unearthly craft, to the deep hum of gravity amplifiers, the ruthless Grey creators of the species of new ape we call *Homo Sapiens Sapiens* are preparing for another harvest of human DNA by the million body load. They have been doing it for two thousand centuries and have never been thwarted. They would be stopped temporarily by future redeemers coming to warn us of their meaning and presence on a planet in space-time. Yet not before a world of mind, body, and spirit had been torn and twisted into the wickedness and cruelties of conscienceless automatons, hybrid creations on Earth chosen from their list of genetically engineered humans so that the harvest can commence. The RFID chips are ready and waiting. Unearthly eugenicists through their occidental white-supremacist spawn have been preparing for this for a long time, and they now stand poised with their syringes and bombs to try again to take complete control of all of humanity. The Greys could never do this through their own efforts because they're too physically fragile to marshal this kind of force. They need the help of the marshal breed they had created. A cartel set on a mental stem that thinks in unempathetic technological mind-sets and is incapable of perceiving or appreciating that when atomic arrays collapsed through the action of the second law, their individualities in sentient awareness will end, too.

Ended in graduated hells of suffering they would experience at the second margin, the margin to the heavy reality.

Can you imagine the catastrophe for the millions who have bought into the ethos that "man shall walk as machine" as something desirable if the procedures of doing this involve the supplanting of an artificial programmed intelligence into our individual personas? Extraterrestrial interlopers already in the body-politic and psycho-politic of the world's human resource may well be doing this and robbing us of our scope for eternal life, a scope that exists for us in a state out of atoms past death. Those interfered with enough may continue its true. For a time only because entropy will get them in the end. They would continue in an artificial scope until their DNA is replaced with fresh supplies taken from the many humans that disappear unaccountably. About seven million people disappear without trace every year according to UN figures. Most of them are itinerant, with no dependants or traceable families.

It may well be the most profound of lessons for all of us who still have a choice-making capability to guard this aspect of our being at all costs and resist the machine minds already among us, encouraging us to take the transhumanist path. These people may have been altered through genetic manipulation, yet they themselves may not even know it. They think, talk, and act in resonance and in complicity with a machine-type robot, and their numbers are growing. Only those of us different in our natures will notice them. The battle lines are already set: natural human beings versus synthetics.

In the Book of Revelation (13:1–14) there is a remarkable description of what may well be our transhuman future. A beast comes up "out of the earth" that has "horns like a lamb" but speaks "as a dragon." The implication is of something seemingly innocent and harmless but in reality quite the opposite. This beast does "great wonders" and deceives those "that dwell on the earth by the means of miracles." An entity that has a deadly wound but is somehow miraculously brought back to life is being described, and an image is then created out of that entity. Could this refer to cloning procedures involving imaging and copying, procedures that might one day be so commonplace that anyone who does not embrace the transhuman ideal will be dispensed with, "as many as would not worship the image of the beast should be killed"? Many have speculated that the "mark of the beast" that is received "in their right hand or in their foreheads" may well be a form of biochip that will be essential "so that no one may buy or sell except who has the mark or the name of the beast, or the number of his name." Could the "beast" refer to the fact that transhumanism will make us like beasts, as it takes away freedom of choice, the very freedom that marks us out as human when set against the simple reactive mental modes of animals not far removed from the mechanical behavior one might expect from a robot or machine and its functioning paradigms.

Could it be that the ultimate in apparent sophistication and human evolution actually results in the ultimate in human devolution through the conversion of the human species into a hybrid state with restricted freedom, no different from lower forms of life? Even if one does not accept that there is a reality beyond the physical that might be compromised by the abrogation of the human soul, there is no doubt that transhumanism mortgages our capabilities as human beings to a prosthetic technology that is quantum steps further than that brought about by the Industrial Revolution, which arguably made life easier for us through mechanization of basic tasks. Transhumanism is the mechanization of our intrinsic faculties to think and to know.

This is the world Kurzweil and his cohorts are laying out for us. It may not be their own personal philosophy; they may just be showing us the way. But to me it marks a compelling evil that if not resisted will sweep the world into a nondescript platform of winking diodes and buzzing transistors where once there was life.

The trouble is that many of us find this very hard to do. We slip on with the days' troubles leading us into boxes made by our restrictions and prejudices, the strongest of which are those we hitch to our eyes. We creep along inexorably with views that blend into a backdrop of ready assembled comfort points designed to provide physical ease and convenience. It's simply the dope of the damned. A matrix we create for ourselves, in which we weave a spider's web of restrictions all around us. The trouble is we don't trap any flies; *we* are the flies. We trap ourselves and our futures. Will we pay the ultimate price for not being able to see that an eternal scope that lies beyond the hems of atoms might exist for each and every one of us? Are we going to compromise something as mightily significant as this simply because we cannot measure it, see it, hear it, touch it, smell it, or taste it? Man shall surely walk as machine if we do.

The natural and implicit way of things includes a means of accessing the widest ranges with the freest means. In our case we live and die and live again in repeat formats until we know all that can be known. We access this great circle through death to a universal deployment. We access it to claim an existence on an eternal scale as alluded to by the great teachers of the great religions. On the other hand, the synthetic way is a temporal kind of eternity that extends human scope and meaning in aspects that limit and are remotely controlled by machines and gadgets and not by the natural inertias of self-will. Which would you choose?

What will you choose?

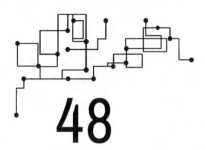

48

The Triumph of Reason

Indications of the presence here on Earth of the Grey ETs have been overwhelming, and that has posed deep and relevant questions about why the world's peoples have not been informed about it by official sources. In this book, the third in a series on the subject, I had to go for the jugular and get to why this is so. That inevitably meant a look at the consequences of this alien presence on humankind. I was led to a beast of enormous significance for humankind, a beast that to my utter astonishment has figured more in religious texts than in secular, science-based ones. I discovered that where the real story of the whole Grey alien phenomenon lies is less in outer space and more in our inner space, at the very root of the human condition.

The next question some might ask is why have I written something that will frighten, if not terrify, people. That is easily answered. Many futurists see as cause for celebration their predictions that based on our own current developments in biotechnology and artificial intelligence we will soon exist no more as natural living beings. This momentum has been sponsored and accelerated by the Grey roboids. Our species can survive most threats, but what I discovered was none, yes, none of our species would survive as a natural living format if the Greys succeed in their agenda. Man could inevitably walk as machine. While we are happy to quibble about global warming, we give scant attention to the threat that would leave nothing and no one to warm or who could *feel* warmth. All that has meant anything in terms of what it means to be human would be gone forever on our planet. I found in conclusion to it all that the final existential battle line is set with two armies. The army of the incidental and natural and the army of the deliberately created and synthetic: the human and the roboid.

There are those who maintain that Grey aliens are friendly and are here to help us. Some claim that their presence is a setup by the various government authorities for their own reasons. All the evidence I have seen points to one conclusion: they are real and they are here and have been here for a very long time. They are a cold, malevolent presence that is using our species for their own agenda. Their lips are too thin to smile, their eyes too dark to cry, their scope too hard to die.

A devastating series of videos produced by one of the bravest and most erudite researchers into the UFO phenomenon, Richard Hall, reinforces my point in its documentation of the terrifying phenomenon of human mutilation by these entities. Yes, you read that right—this is not the cattle mutilations that we are familiar with, it is human mutilations. I can personally testify that Hall, an engineer by profession, is one of the straightest and most honest investigators into this phenomenon on the planet. He dresses nothing up and only attempts to present the evidence objectively and neutrally. His videos can be seen on YouTube.

When convention is bucked and someone thinks outside the box, the favorite weapon of the mentally corralled mind is to dismiss the person as mad, eccentric, dangerous, and a fool of one sort or another. All the greatest thinkers have been thought of in this way by their peers, their enemies, and even their friends. If you instinctively think outside the box then you're a member of the above fraternity and not part of the mediocre club to which millions of drudge-level scientists belong. These materialists search the sands of time wearing pebble lenses for eyeglasses, displaying innate cowardliness and downright ignorance—quite unlike the Schrödingers, Bohms, Sheldrakes, Goswamis, Eddingtons, Jeans, Benvenistes, and Silvermans, who are much rarer. There are perhaps ten thousand materialist scientists to every one of these brilliant quantum phyicists. I am willing to bet that most of the materialists have calcified pineal glands. Such "in the box" scientists work in a way that leaves no room for looking at what is coming from the flanks, or from up and down and in and out. It is individuals with mind trains like this who continue to hide the evidence of the presence of the Grey ETs here on Earth. They're the ones cleaning up after UFO crashes, obfuscating and preventing any information from reaching the mainstream media. These are the types who ruthlessly resort to threats and even murder to prevent the world from taking notice of the Greys' presence or their intentions. They are scoundrels of the first order, hiding in high places because they are sponsored cohorts of these ET synthetics and are helping them in their agenda—a few of them without actually knowing what they are precisely doing.

If thought is wholly the product of the physical resolution of atoms, then this principle suggests that with entropy, as the tension of atoms increases, so the rigidity of thinking will increase proportionately as a measure of force against time. The stage is then set for the separating, dismantling effect of entropy to promulgate the means to make the best of such a dictation. The brain would devolve and, in time, dumb down and provide a scheme of chemistry that would allow for the most efficient reflections of such behavior. The more primitive limbic and R-complex systems, as discussed by Paul MacLean, one of the world's greatest neuroscientists, would devolve from the superior neocortex system to lessening platforms, making them phylogenetically the most recent brains and not, as is assumed, the older, more primitive parts of the brain.[1]

So we are given a prescription of doom *if* we are purely physical beings. Such is the way of prophecy and the future. But if that is not so, and I have sought to show in this book that logically it is patently *not* so, then we have hope. We have hope as long as we can think intelligently and make the necessary choices that unite things so that all parts may be bound together. This is the shield that protects us from the Greys. If that is what the word *love* describes, then to quote the words of the song, "all you need is love."

Love is what the greatest spiritual figures in history have showed us. Love is the essential teaching of Gautama Buddha, Jesus Christ, and the prophet of Islam, Muhammad, and all the others whose beauty of mind gave us the formula that found our salvation in an eternal status past the atom and through the heart in mind, through thinking with the heart. Sadly, many simply cannot. Engineered out of the womb with alien genetic marks laid aeons ago.

Many other great angels have come to Earth to warn humankind of its predicament. We have not listened, and now the voices seem to get less in number. Have you noticed? Few now listen to anything that is sweet and kind, and the devastating thing is that at present fewer are able to listen. They dismiss it all as sentimental and goody-goody. It seems the machine mind has finally come to dominate the heart so completely that the Godless system that runs the world now conspires as never before to forbid any chance of change. You will find no exhortation in the teachings of Buddha, Christ, and Muhammad to "praise the Lord and pass the money," as many present-day pretenders to religious truth exhort us. They shall pay for their subterfuge: damnation to an ever-reducing paradigm of existence, with all the agonies that go with such a reduction of their inheritance.

Many, understandably, find no shelter in organized religion these days. I myself have never had any use for churches, temples, mosques, or synagogues as places for talking to God. For me, our places of worship should always be the blue of the sky and the starlight. My temple is a garden, my synagogue a book. To me, these are the most natural places for a sense of what is beyond the atom. However, despite these days of processed religion, these "houses of God" can still be essential places for quiet and reflection on what is deep and truly meaningful in the midst of the huge enforced-ness of current lifestyles. I do not condemn the priesthood at large. I acknowledge that among them you are likely to find more of the good than the bad, the wise than the foolish, good counsel and caring hearts, places to abide with your humanity intact, to seek and find a way to keep your eternity, better than in the laboratories of the "ists" and "ologists."

A Jewish friend of mine was visiting Sacré Coeur Basilica in Paris. She was very impressed when she first entered the building by the apparent devotion of the many people in the pews who seemed to be deep in prayer, heads bowed. She was even more impressed by the fact that many of these were young people whom she felt would be less likely to have a religious sensibility. When she looked a little closer she was brought sharply down to earth by the fact that these young people were not praying at all. Can you guess what they were doing? Well here's a clue: electronic lights were flickering in their hands as they performed the particular kind of devotional observance that is commonplace among most people these days. They were all on their tablets and cell phones.

Reason can triumph. It has never been hard to see for those who would and could discern with clear, unbiased, unemotional, objective eyes. But for the others, this universe is a deadly, lethal place. All sentient beings that arrive in this churn, this engine of doom, which is to me the true hell, may only be delivered out of it by developing their sentience in as pristine and unadulterated state as possible. This is the greatest single lesson that all the great masters, prophets, and mystics have taught or attempted to teach humankind.

Join the laboratories of the world together. Join this togetherness to the pulpit, the synagogue, the mosque, and the temple. Throw away the emotional and tribal prejudices endemic in each. Tack onto them the anthems of reason, sense, and logic on behalf of all humankind, and hope for redemption from our terrible predicament will be a real and certain proposition. Conversely, keep them separate as they are now, diversify their results, and hold each apart, and we are all ended. Our human beingness will unquestionably be damned forever.

I cannot hope to, nor do I intend to, change the perspectives of a world hell-bent on destruction with what I have postulated in this book, when the plea on behalf of a species for a perspective change is lost to a little red button that places us all an inch from Armageddon. I can only deliver my insight, such as it is, as an urging to reflect in a contemporary stance. A stance written with the rationale of modern scientific discovery. This rationale, if it is for anyone, is for the poor in spirit, those like me who hadn't an inner insight into a world not of the atom. I believe I have at least a right to hope, and perhaps a few, perhaps the merest few, might just take notice, and from among them perhaps a single star of hope will rise to heed my warnings. These few will find their way to the union of parts through a kind word, an indulgent and tolerant smile—a forgiving nod—each and every time the opposed way threatens. My effort has been to try to provide a good *enough* and important *enough* rational, logical reason for doing these things, until the day we die.

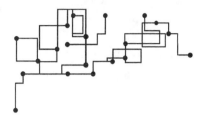

Epilogue

One thing I am utterly sure of in the scales of meaning that define our very existence as human beings is that if we do not sort things out immediately, we are certainly condemning ourselves to the loss of humanity and the power we have to keep our individuality beyond the scale of this material reality, because a power alien to this planet and not of our own local baryonic reality now confronts each and every one of us in the human family. A power that will take our existence as individual personages away forever.

It may seem that out of this catalog of horrors that mark the loss of the soul in so many people, there seems to be an underlying whisper that says all is not lost. The great triumph of what I have uncovered in looking for the answers to the great existential questions is that hope does truly spring eternal. It springs eternal if we see past the con tricks of those who have sold us a bill of goods that says we are all dependent on this faction or that for our eternal salvation. The glorious truth is that we are all of us dependent on ourselves alone for this. Free will, the kiss of a nondirective Godhead, allows us all the freedom to repent, where the word *repent* means "to change your mind." Simply that. Change your thinking to ways that add where you might subtract, bind where you might undo, bring together where you might separate. Above all, be kind to yourself and about yourself and never feel alone despite all that might be done to you in the way of wickedness and injustice.

There is the unalterable assurance that the purest logic says that you are truly free and intrinsically of Godhead, and no one and nothing can keep you separated from it and eternal existence in everlasting joy but you yourself. You have the potential to be or not to be anything you desire if you can perceive that you can be so. The trouble, of course, is that the more you have allowed yourself to be confined by the limits, restrictions, and protocols endowed by the enforced paradigms, the less you are able to perceive your salvation. The more you linger in such an enforced universe, the more it will blind you to the knowledge necessary to free yourself from the grip of its force. This tends to weaken your resolve and lessen your bandwidth of choices. Your demise is thus assured as you don tighter and tighter straightjackets—straightjackets that hold the mind and the body called "lifetimes." And yet these, too, may be resolved and sublimated into the All with the constant insights and reminders brought into universes of parts by those we call redeemers. These glories of knowledge and freedom of sight pour into planet after planet in endless chains of love from the Godhead to remind those with soul connections still straight enough to see them for what they are, that every moment is one of hope for change. Hope because somewhere within the tangle of enforced atoms in their physical form, the power of eternal wisdom lies wrapped in the longing to free oneself from the cold elbows of loneliness. It all comes down to freedom against extent, will against ignorance, choice against oblivion.

Godhead lies twisted and dark in the wings of a butterfly as it lies dormant and vast in the spaces between the stars, where no will exists to turn it into its full glory. The churning of force as random arrays of atoms burning in a billion suns turns these atoms into elements or lenses with faces and forms almost congruent with the skeleton shape, which makes for the separation of the whole into parts: the shape of the Möroid. In that deep obsidian of space, the elements dance the waltze of chaos, and once in a while they touch the face of God. Then hydrogen and oxygen become partners for life, and thus the hope of redemption. Together as water they make the lens that focuses the light of ages that rules beyond the hives of force. They are the very stuff of memory as water and bone. They admit the very roots and rotas of hope for us all who are trapped, separated from the God state. We as God in the separation of parts can see and touch Godhead from the point of view of parts through them. In them we have the first sign of hope of return from the dead to the splendor of never having to die again. But they, too, are but the punctuation of the lost, the heralds of all our yesterdays and, alas, our tomorrows, too, lest we turn and turn and turn away from the hooks and spirals in them that keep us bound. One glorious man in flesh showed how the bonds of hell may be loosed and broken forever in a blaze of light that undid them all in their itinerant mischief, when on a mountain in Palestine he glowed brighter than the sun. He simply changed the human mind completely. I for one fervently hope that you, too, will do the same. I hope I have convinced you in some small part in this book that it is your legacy to shine, too.

I can only hope that a star will be born somewhere, for us all, a star of hope in human form that has the credibility of the just and the true to sing us a song with words that will make us look again at our predicament. You may be that song. You are your own nativity at the point at which you change your mind to bring about a change that hopefully will tear us from the grip of the Grey reins that hold our planet tighter and tighter each day. They will tell you their tether is a benediction. It will be the greatest, most deadly and significant lie told in the world today to the detriment of humanity. They have an all-pervasive power to do this, far more persuasive than I have. But there will be those who will see the lie, perhaps in small part due to the recourse and resource of a single pair of eyes that might have read this and might feel the same and have the power to really do something about it for all our sakes, and especially for the little ones in our world everywhere. So be it. Please just hold the option open. It may well be too late for your own eternal tenure if what I say is true and you do nothing about it. There will be no one and nothing to give it back to you.

I predict that as time goes by, our natural insight into our eternal prospectus as a species still touching the Godhead will diminish as our "progress" in a materiality increases in line with the second law of thermodynamics. Systems and facilities are already beginning to evolve that laud the physical aspects of being so much that they may finally overwhelm us all. As their all-pervasive power through the media increases, certain people will be held to ransom by computers and electronics. A real heaven will give way to a substitute heaven, a virtual heaven, a vanilla sky, a megamatrix fashioned and formulated with the greatest irony by computers—more believed in by our young people now than the heaven spoken of by the greatest spiritual teachers the world has ever known.

I maintain that money-motivated technology is the bloodstream of the damned, but only for those unable to see where its binary inertia leads our failing humanistic state. Humankind may slowly set its pace to the machine, to think and do in terms of mechanistic and materially scoped ideals. As we see all too clearly in the West, the material resource will be priced higher than a human life. This precious glory we call a human being, this wonder that may still reason and choose a way beyond the vast, overwhelming numbers of dead worlds we see out there in space, I fear, shall be no more. At least no more in this locality in the universe of parts we call Earth.

"So what?" you might say. Somewhere out there in all those countless numbers of deadness—boiling vats of acid, frozen masses of gas, burning ovens of sand—small harbors of blue, white, brown and green may still continue to festoon; the farce, the charade. It may well be over for us, but somewhere another "us" must live on. And the universe will continue—will go on in life forever. This is foolishness that speaks of silent standing stones that no living eye will be left to see.

My attempt to explain why every prophet and holy person came to our world with a warning about our predicament is precisely to deny the idiocy of "so what?"—the alma mater of the foolish. The conditions that allow for the manifestation of Spirit as life in this deadly orchestra of destruction we call our universe lies in thinking beings who live, the rarest of the rare in this universe of parts. Life is so precious it must be saved. Just take a look at our own solar system and its planets for confirmation of its rarity. Nine out of the ten planets or protoplanets that make it up are deadly to life and living systems. The very stars that are the seed corn of the universe in their trillions are all, as far as we know, deadly to life as we know it. Take the numbers in scale relatively and you will see the fantastic rarity of life itself, let alone the life that can reason, choose, and envision being in the highest perspective.

The words of the great spiritual teachers ring with new meaning when viewed in the context of entropy. They blasted an entirely new perspective on the condition of humankind through my thick skull, a bombshell that has shaken me to the marrow and will continue to do so until the day I die. It has given me the courage to say what I have said in this book and face the scorn and ridicule I know will come. Is it any surprise that these most perceptive of all beings would want the preservation of such a wondrous and scarce resource? They could see it as the only platform in the whole vista of existence that could reverse an inevitable atomic drift into chaos.

I have also written this as a shout of acclaim for those who can see where true hope lies, for any of us could be a star born out of such a predicament. For millions in the world who have become disillusioned by the grave and deadly ignorance of the ways of self, a new harbor, real and true, may awaken in this same self if we follow the clues left by the great teachers to lead us out of our folly. A new understanding honed out of cogent, objective sense and reason, and not made of comforting platitudes and incitements to blind, dumb belief, will be the fulcrum for real reform. Words like *heart* and *caring,* for so long and for so many have, through generations of falsehood, hypocrisy, and sheer woolly thinking, become stages for abuse and emotional disaffection. I hope I have renewed these values and shown them as the fueling points that could lead us all to the very margin of the Godhead.

In this work I have sought to pick out some of the main religious and scientific dictums and dogmas that have doubled as truth and commonly accepted as so by billions and to lay waste to them. I have tried to counter any humbug with reason and logic. The religious and political perpetrators of this humbug, who through the centuries have sold us all a bill of goods, are not here to answer for their invective. Their legacy, a deadly soup of lies and falsehoods, may have damned the billions who believed them to the long road back to the Godhead in the blandness of individual atom fields, their previous existence in the Godhead having transmogrified into individualization and enforcedness, and through this distortion, the loss of knowing the truth.

"Love thy neighbor as thyself" in the light of entropy provides a new and awesome meaning. In fact, all the words of the prophets increase the borders of their meaning with explosive effect to provide a bathing point for enlightenment the size of an ocean, whereas previously it was hardly a pool.

A generous heart gives where a mean one seeks to keep. An open heart smiles where a closed one pouts. A caring heart reaches out with fingers stretched out in welcome where a hateful one quivers with fingers formed into a fist. A humble heart stumbles to turn away from the limelight while a vain heart poses looking down at the darkness of Adam's rib. A warm heart is never seen; it lies too close to another's breastbone.

We are our own result. We have no inherent master, no puppeteer pulling our strings. We are all the master we need—the charioteer, the chariot, the harness, and the horses. We are the whole shooting match except—and this is the crucial point—we have to run a course of our own making. It can be a destructive course, the sole business of which is to dismantle rider, carriage, and all its motional capacity.

I do not seek to teach new meanings to anyone or change anyone's ways. I simply offer an alternative view of the whys and wherefores of our predicament as a fellow traveler in a universe that seems to get more and more imponderable with time when looked at with its hardware and not its software. Could it be unequivocally that we are each of us our brother's keeper, and my discoveries are yours, as yours are mine? I love to think so. We just cannot do without one another, and we will not have to if we can but see past the devilry of our emotions and our fatuous egos. Mine was hit by a blinding light once upon a time that left it in tatters and me wandering about like a chicken with its head cut off. I am sure those who disagree with what I have said in this work will say I have gotten little more than the head of a chicken back. Be that as it may, it is all to do with pecking orders in a fowl house, one might say. That word could be spelled *foul* to describe the roosts we have sat on collectively as a species, which may well have been false ones, and the fox that threatens us outside our coop is an alien species as strange and real as any fox. Only our fox has far more guile than any that saunter with white tips on their tails. Our fox saunters among the fattest chickens of humankind, the ones with prominent feathers, easily seen and easily identified and easily managed. Such as they know and obey and are trained to serve the system better than all the other examples of humankind. The Greys' tread is quiet, covert, and sure, because they know their targets well. They made them that way for those reasons.

In this book I have tried to get a measure of how all this is reflected in the social and intellectual disposition of humankind through the centuries, and to set this against the proposition "to make angels of men" and see past the demon hiding behind the face of a baby. It is a proposition that the entire workings of a physical universe in entropy conspires to uphold. We have devolved, it seems, instead, the means to provide for an existence in more and more physical terms, more and more in harm's way. An existence that essentially separates, sorts, and reacts to difference in threat, in subtraction, not addition. The two divided elements of the limbic and R-complex brain systems as discovered by Dr. Paul MacLean's thesis, control behavior more and more instead of the neo-cortex. We see primarily in terms of resolutions of gross physicality, the survival of the body and not the soul. Poets and priests must sing laments, their voices fading further and further into the background of human endeavor.

Before we shout in protest, before we indignantly deny the exhortations that at first sight seem ridiculous against the accepted norms, let us examine the record of our species in its overwhelming disposition toward violence and aggression. When the total story of our species is told, the summary of our so-called progress has been in the instinct we have to threaten, to divide, to separate. In denying freedom to one another, in restricting our thinking in terms of race, creed, taste, social standing, and territory, what have we left that separates us from the rattlesnake and the toad?

We are different, I hear you say. We can reason. Through this faculty we dominate Earth. We control every other living species. We are the masters, and we exist the most comfortably of them all. Of course we do. We are different from the serpent and the frog. Reptiles do not live in societies that glorify and delight in the spectacles of aggression and violence designed to lessen and demean others of their own species. Frogs don't calculate and deploy the methods that facilitate the wholesale slaughter of the meek. Serpents don't conspire to starve, to threaten, to torture one another in conglomerated campaigns in their territorial interests. Intelligence gives us such evil liberties. But yes, we *are* different, we *can* see past instinct, we *can* decide on other ways. We *need not* subtract. We have free will. We can vault past our mistakes and maladjusted reactions through lessons learned. Yet, as a species our ability to console, to care, steadily declines. It is already far too dim, too soft, set against the rhetoric of force and reaction in our modern world, wiping across our collective consciences like a breeze against a hurricane.

We are overwhelmed and overruled, in the shadow of those in our midst who shout loudest with the bludgeon of sensory response. Their voices are now more and more the engines that drive humankind, driving the unguents of progress in shouts of anger and intolerance, loud and thunderous. Their focus is pitched in places close to the eye. They are truly the children of the R-complex. These hybrid plants set among the rest of us are the sons and daughters of the damned, because their center of function has lost the capacity to add. They are the last adaptation, the vanguard of the way ahead for humans, the way that leads to the ape, the mollusk, the tree, and the stone. We follow fools meekly in their summaries of ignorance, meekly because we fear physical pain above all things. The belligerent voices shout loudest among us, their movements the most stern, the most cruel. We are excited by violence and force. We have let them wrest our destiny from us, and in their hands our planet turns into a house of fear.

And so we wait as a species for the end in sure, swift conjunctions of radiating fire that would sweep past reason and consume the wombs that would deliver the future. Our species would then be no more, like so many before us here and elsewhere in the universe. We would succeed in gaining the silence of the grave, little knowing that death might just have been a gradient to a wondrous new life.

The consequence of life is death, and only death and a permanent end to nowhere unless there is a deeper meaning beyond the atom. It all seems so pointless if that is not so. So meaningless. A Nieztcheresque fatuousness and obscure fuddle where the mind can be content with just its next breath and only that. Yet why, then, is there order, intelligence, and a full sweep of meaning even in the dead, static expressions of the universe? Why all this if it is all pointless. How have the knife's edge conditions that allow for life on this planet been been set up with such stunning exactitude? It is the inclusions of the little things that live and think for themselves and exercise free will in utter freedom of purpose that cause the standing waves of chance to collapse. We bring order through thought and thinking once chaos plays its dictates. That is what life and living is all about: the return to the Godform and the Godverse, the eternal home from which we emerged and got trapped as discrete soul fields in the center-space reality.

There is a kind of poetry to it all, the poetry of deserving. Are we finally to be dismantled, made ready as a new species with a new architecture, new bones, new and even more finite horizons, to end and be recycled as a clone? In such a scenario there will be no going back to a grander scale. Through cyclic life and death, our blindness will beget blindness, until there is no more left of that prior light, that metaphysical light that shines the order that gives sense and clarity. Free will would become servile, and soon we would sit someplace in the universe in cages, for other kinds of entities with less force within the spaces of their atoms to observe us, in their zoos, perhaps, as a toy, a pet, or a plaything for their children.

But for a few, a precious few, maybe this was not and is not to be the way ahead. They could, and some still can, demonstrate there could be more, much more. They have listened, they have believed and do believe, they have seen and do see. Less than the dregs that cling to an empty cup, a rivulet of hope still remained, and triumphantly I believe still remains. A promise could be kept. A promise few remember and most have disbelieved. It was a promise made in the sweetest reason. It saw past the conceits of man and spoke of another reality beyond the concepts of the physical, the finite. Setting itself at the heart of reason, thought. Of itself, in itself, through itself: in thought lies the key to the way past atoms. In thought lies the answer, the hope, the surety of eternal continuity. In knowing and reason that enables choices to be made and acted upon. In thought, will, and direction lies eternal continuity, or end. If such was grandeur, how do we now set ourselves in the prerogatives of the finite, the physical and not the eternal.

The final conclusion of all conclusions is simply this: you cannot gain eternal existence if you do the things that make for a comfortable existence in this universe, with little else but your acquisitive material sense. All the original authors of the great religions were at one with this tenet.

> Lay not for yourselves treasures upon earth where moth and rust doth corrupt and where thieves break through and steal. But lay up for yourselves treasures in heaven where neither moth nor rust doth corrupt, and where thieves do not break through nor steal. For where your treasure is, there will your heart also be. (Matthew 6:19–21)

We as living beings exist in two domains at once. If we ignore the one we will lose the other. If we let the natural resources that gave rise to our individuality and thus our souls be controlled, interfered with, and dominated by artificially and synthetically constructed norms, there can be no greater catastrophe to any existential domain. Living within the best balance of both could be expected to preserve both. Yet we don't. We have to, and there is no choice in the matter. We have to think and do the things that get us out of this universe or we will lose our entire potential for existence itself. The second law of thermodynamics will see to it with utter certainty that we will end as nothing and inherit the eternal damnation of a dead atomic array. In other words, there will be no "you." You will not be one of the "quick," as described by Jesus. You will be one of the "dead," permanently.

A single catastrophic explosion at the margins of Godhead, the first valve to separation, brought about all we see, know, and are discovering about the universe we live in. The discovery of the roots of that explosion and what those roots are now should give us an indication of the way back because there truly is only one. All of the great teachers declared that the fundamentals of the great beginning still remained as the capacity for thought and free will. I have tried to show how an abstraction is connected to the physically real and tangible so that one can interplay with the other and one can master the other.

The power of thought and will is final. The power of mind over matter running on the engine of thought and the accessway of will provides a momentum toward or away from the union of anything broken from a previous state of union into a state of parts of that union. The key is to add again and unite again all that is disparate through actions and words. If mind acts at all times to bring together, to bind into a whole the elements of things in all we do, if we attempt to bind all things in complete homogeneity as a natural, unfailing reactive momentum in our lives, the results will bring us in stages to the very threshold of the origin of thought and will and finally admit us home to the state of Godhead.

For those who couldn't see this, it was too late, and the way to this was to be for a few through a narrow path in a wide field. It was more likely that a billion insects would sing as a complete hive with the voice that was once a human being. Truly "the meek would inherit the Earth," a grotesque caricature in perhaps a chorus of cicadas. An outlay of ants. It was to be and will be a terrible summary for the heads that turned toward final disbursement in forcehead. Hell.

How have they done this, these those precious few special ones that came among us to wait aeon after aeon, hiding from the garotte, the lion, the nail, and the bullet that so many times claimed their kind? I fervently believe that they had seen long ago that the antidote to entropy lies outside the physical. They mustered their thinking in roots that bind together, that bring together, that hold together the glory of ultimate simplicity. They did not ride the drift of entropy. They countered it and continue to counter it by adding when most would subtract, uniting when most would divide, caring when most would dismiss or turn away. Their sense burned with a holy sap, an instinct to bring together, to unite all things with what is naturally congruent. They simply acted in terms of *love* (the most misunderstood and misused word in any lexicon) and could thus harness the awesome power of the unforce of the metaphysical against the force of the physical. Their thinking had no confusion, doubts, or contradictions. It was so sharp because it was so true to the ideal of union, harmony. It was the only antidote to the natural drift to divide, separate, and confuse and so could cut through the hard, definite edges of physicality in the phase that was opposite to the force of the atoms that composed this physicality. They discovered free will was truly free and could soar past tendency with the scope for its function raised beyond the finite. Will, strong and consistent enough to take you and me in a direction congruent with perfection. The perfection that could only be the peace of the state of eternal potential to be, or not to be. Yes! They asked that we set store in words and deeds irrelevant to the flesh, the material, in paradigms we call faith, belief, and trust.

Faith, belief, and trust are commonly misunderstood precepts. They do not refer to a blind denial of your own will. They refer to a profound understanding that it is sensible to take a risk, to use your will to make an active choice to commit to something or someone that makes sense to you. If that choice turns out to be misguided then you can make an active choice to suspend your faith, belief, and trust. If it turns out to be correct then you will be acting with full compliance through your own choices rather than mortgaged to someone else's choices. You will be acting in control of your being, from the center of you rather than on the periphery of you.

As physical living beings we are faced with a paradox. The information we receive through our physical senses informs us that we are discrete, individual, and governed by physical, finite laws. In most cases we cannot see, hear, feel, or touch a nonphysical infinite state whose precepts are in contradiction to what our physical senses tell us. These precepts suggest that we are all intrinsically connected as one being and that the nonphysical has power over the physical. We can choose to embrace the notion that there is indeed such a nonphysical state through reason, intuition, or both. This acceptance is perhaps what we might call faith, faith in our own ability to make sense of our para-doxical environment. Through such faith we begin to engage in a dance with that part of the paradox that we cannot fully engage with in a physical state. We invite God to dance with us. We move in step with the natural pull of the Godverse to states of greater union. When you dance with a partner you move your feet aside for their feet to land where yours once were, and you time your steps forward for their steps back. The more you dance the more you learn the steps and start to have confidence and belief in your ability to dance well. Eventually you are so sure of your steps that you can relax in a situation of complete trust with your partner. You are in a state of flow in which conscious adaptations are no longer necessary, you act together in harmony as one person.

Mainstream religion has in many cases encouraged a very different type of faith, belief, and trust formed through social or psychological pressure and designed to prevent feelings of guilt or shame. The original teachers never encouraged this type of commitment because it is based on a denial and subjugation of one's own choices and cannot therefore bring about redemption through those choices. Active choices lead to restriction, so only active choices can free restriction. Many people end up blaming God for their troubles because they have been encouraged to mortgage their choice-making capability to a directive entity who they are led to believe is in control of their lives.

The great teachers discovered for themselves that there was a place beyond the capture of atoms and traveled a long road to BE that place. Some still travel that long road. You can find them if you search hard enough. They were and are the examples of delivery. Examples of victory over the machine mind. They beat the Grey shroud and show us that we all belong elsewhere. But do we learn? Can we learn? Yes we can if enough of us who see the sense of their teachings are brave enough to trust ourselves to join the dance.

A cave in which an illiterate man sat in a trance of glorious revelation in an Arabian hillside; a tree by a Gayan riverside where a beautiful mind finally comprehended the way all things finally fit together—these stand testament to a tangle of straw in an animal shelter in Bethlehem where a baby once lay. As did those Hebrew prophets who stood outside and well away from a bush that burned in a desert place with the darkness of an ET alien–sponsored canard.

Of one thing I am utterly sure. If we as humanity do not sort things out now, at this juncture of time, we will with certainty condemn ourselves to the loss of ourselves and the power we have to keep our individualities as naturally human. An insidious power alien to this planet now confronts each and every one of us in the human family. It confronts us insidiously and obsequiously, bringing to us seemingly harmless fare dressed up to meet our conveniences and our sense for new exciting things. Things that we soon crave. Hidden within their formats lies a plan to take from us the most precious thing we are. Ourselves.

Is the world mad, or is all the madness I see confined to my own perceptual view only? You decide.

Try to see the world of matter and physicality with a truer perspective of what is really is.

Try to see how something can come out of nothing. Where "nothing" describes no "things."

Try to see that the word "nothing" is not the absence of anything.

Try to see that opposites are really in a true sense the same thing.

Try to see that we call truth is simply the freedom to see and discern what that freedom allows.

Try to see that you are implicitly formatted within a frame of force that is NOT your natural home state.

Try to see that all that you consequently are is an illusion allowed by that formatted view.

Try to see that the true you is beyond all this and you can only reach that if you can get past this formatted view.

Try to see that when you pray you are praying not to something outside you. You are praying to something within you.

"Is it not written in thy law ye are Gods." (John 10.34)

You are really the ALL and the ALL is really you.

If you have persevered through this book cover to cover, you should be congratulated on your matchless patience. Maybe after reading it you might even want to go out there and take on the humbug that has been fed to us for decades. If you do this you will of course be riding on your own authority, the only authority that really matters. Not mine or anyone else's. Beware though, if you are a feisty soul and care for your fellow human beings, you might get addicted to the fight.

Notes

INTRODUCTION

1. Lopatto, "Elon Musk Unveils."

1. BEYOND REASONABLE DOUBT

1. Jørgensen, "One or More Bound Planets."
2. Hawking, "Alien Contact Not a Wise Idea."
3. Morris, "Predicting What Extra-Terrestrials Will Be Like."
4. Morris, "Predicting What Extra-Terrestrials Will Be Like."
5. Morris, "Predicting What Extra-Terrestrials Will Be Like."
6. Butler, "Former Members of Congress."
7. Paul, "How Angry Pilots Got Navy to Stop."
8. Paul, "How Angry Pilots Got Navy to Stop."
9. Allen, "Existence of Extra-Terrestrial Craft."
10. Allen, "Existence of Extra-Terrestrial Craft."
11. Allen, "Existence of Extra-Terrestrial Craft."
12. Allen, "Existence of Extra-Terrestrial Craft."
13. Blumenthal and Kean, "No Longer in Shadows."
14. Austin, "Government Chief's Death Bed Confession."

2. WHY ARE THEY HERE?

1. Mullen, "A Cyborg Space Race."
2. McCormack, "ET Machines Sought by Astronomer."

3. Rees, "Breakthrough Listen."

4. Mack, *Abduction*.

5. Jacobs, "Memory Retrieval."

6. Gill, "'Artificial Life' Breakthrough Announced."

7. Sample, "First Life Forms to Pass on Artificial DNA."

8. Sample, "Organisms Created with Synthetic DNA."

9. Sample, "First Life Forms to Pass on Artificial DNA."

10. Sample, "Organisms Created with Synthetic DNA."

11. Sample, "Organisms Created with Synthetic DNA."

3. SIM CARD MAN

1. Price and Tallinn, "Artificial Intelligence."

2. Price and Tallinn, "Artificial Intelligence."

3. Coughlan, "How Are Humans Going to Become Extinct?"

4. Heaven, "Thought that Counts."

5. Heaven, "Thought that Counts."

6. Horgan, "When Tech Leaves No Space."

7. Horgan, "When Tech Leaves No Space."

8. Coughlan, "How Are Humans Going to Become Extinct?"

9. Coughlan, "How Are Humans Going to Become Extinct?"

10. Coughlan, "How Are Humans Going to Become Extinct?"

11. Coughlan, "How Are Humans Going to Become Extinct?"

12. Cuthbertson, "Electronic 'Neural Dust.'"

13. Cuthbertson, "Electronic 'Neural Dust.'"

14. Gibney, "The Inside Story on Wearable Electronics."

15. Gibney, "The Inside Story on Wearable Electronics."

16. Gibney, "The Inside Story on Wearable Electronics."

17. Kharpal, "Elon Musk."

18. Kaku, "Michio Kaku."

19. Barras, "Nanotube Transistor Will Help."

20. Sample, "Mind-Control Device."

21. Dent, "DARPA Goes Beyond Killer."

22. Kurzweil, "Human Life: The Next Generation."

23. Walsh, "Alter Our DNA."

24. Phys.org, "Japanese Baby-bot."

25. AP Archive, "Toddler-bot Nody."

26. AP Archive, "Toddler-bot Nody."
27. Metz, "Facebook's Sci-Fi Plan."

4. BEHIND THE SCENES

1. Troitsina, "Many UFO Researchers Die."
2. Bayot, "Dr. John E. Mack."
3. Little, "How the CIA Tried to Quell UFO Panic."

5. THE MISSING INGREDIENT

1. *RT,* "Pentagon's DARPA Researchers Learn to Control Rat's Brain."
2. Vella, "Invest in Immortality."
3. Cision PRWeb, "Dalai Lama Supports 2045's."
4. Sandberg and Bostrom, "Whole Brain Emulation."
5. Hooton, "Humans Could Probably Live Forever."
6. *RT,* "Pentagon's DARPA Researchers Learn to Control Rat's Brain."
7. Bancal et al., "Quantum Nonlocality."
8. Wilson, *Life After Death.*
9. Wilson, *Life After Death.*
10. Wilson, *Life After Death.*

6. THE HARVESTING OF SOULS

1. Cossins, "Particles Crossing."
2. Cossins, "Particles Crossing."
3. Webb, "Your Decision-Making Ability."
4. Webb, "Your Decision-Making Ability."
5. Byrne, "In Pursuit of Quantum Biology."

7. ON A CLEAR DAY YOU *MIGHT* SEE FOREVER

1. BBC, "Everything We Know."
2. Cossins, "Particles Crossing."
3. Cossins, "Particles Crossing."
4. Amit, "One Idea Explains All."

9. THE SCAFFOLDING OF THE UNIVERSE

1. University of Southampton, "Substantial Evidence of Holographic Universe."
2. University of Southampton, "Substantial Evidence of Holographic Universe."
3. University of Southampton, "Substantial Evidence of Holographic Universe."
4. Roukema, "Topology of the Observable Universe."
5. Hsu, "Primordial Weirdness."
6. Hsu, "Primordial Weirdness."
7. North, "Twisted Ring."
8. Merali, "Axis of Evil."
9. Merali, "Axis of Evil."
10. Bekenstein, "Information in the Holographic Universe."

10. TWIST AND SHOUT

1. Leonard, "Luigi Fanitappiè."
2. Vannini and Di Corpo, "$E = mc^2$."

14. THE CAROUSEL OF LIFE AND DEATH

1. Parnia, *What Happens When We Die.*
2. Alexander, *Proof of Heaven.*
3. Tsakiris, "Jeffrey Long's, God and the Afterlife."
4. Tsakiris, "Jeffrey Long's, God and the Afterlife."
5. Tsakiris, "Jeffrey Long's, God and the Afterlife."
6. Tsakiris, "Jeffrey Long's, God and the Afterlife."
7. Schmidt, *Pistis Sophia,* 499.
8. Schneider, "Alien Minds."
9. Schneider, "Alien Minds."
10. Schneider, "Alien Minds."
11. Cadwalladr, "Robots About to Rise."
12. Cadwalladr, "Robots About to Rise."

17. HOW ALIEN CRAFT ARE MADE

1. Dias and Silvera, "Observation of the Wigner-Huntington Transition."
2. Brahic, "Meet the Electric Life."

18. DEVOLUTION

1. Eddington, *Nature of the Physical World*.
2. Rouleau and Persinger, "Spatial-Temporal Quantitative Global Energy Differences."

19. RE-VOLUTION—THE WAY BACK

1. "Why Is Darwinian Evolution Controversial?"
2. "Why Is Darwinian Evolution Controversial?"
3. "Why Is Darwinian Evolution Controversial?"
4. "Why Is Darwinian Evolution Controversial?"
5. "Why Is Darwinian Evolution Controversial?"
6. Shapiro, *Evolution*.

21. ARE ENDINGS REVERSED BEGINNINGS?

1. Cremo and Thompson, *Forbidden Archeology*.
2. Haeusler et al., "The Obstetrical Dilemma Hypothesis."

23. HYBRIDIZATION

1. Jacobs, "A Picture We May Not Wish."
2. Jacobs, "A Picture We May Not Wish."
3. Jacobs, "A Picture We May Not Wish."
4. Ravenscroft, *Spear of Destiny,* 38.

24. POSSESSION

1. Jacobs, "Some Thoughts About The Twenty First Century."

26. MELANIN—A LENS TO FOREVER

1. Jones, *In the Blood*.
2. Scott, "Photo Protection."
3. Brewer, "Rays of Hope."
4. Bolto and Weiss, "Electronic Conduction in Polymers."

5. McGinness et al., "Amorphous Semiconductor Switching."

6. Jones, *In the Blood.*

7. Wilde et al., "Direct Evidence for Positive Selection."

8. Wilde et al., "Direct Evidence for Positive Selection."

9. Cheng, "Studies of a Skin Color."

10. Canfield et al., "Molecular Phylogeography of a Human."

11. Jacobs, *The Threat.*

12. Jacobs, *The Threat.*

13. Jacobs, *Secret Life.*

27. MAKING A MONKEY OF A MAN

1. Giubilini and Minerva, "After-birth Abortion."

2. Monbiot, "'Cleansing the Stock.'"

3. Monbiot, "'Cleansing the Stock.'"

4. Monbiot, "'Cleansing the Stock.'"

5. Farley, "Theory Abandoned."

6. Matsuzawa, "Chimpanzee Mind."

7. Rule, "Cooperation among Chimpanzees."

28. BIBLICAL PARALLELS

1. Hamilton, "Government Whistleblower Claims."

29. THE GREYS IN HUMAN HISTORY

1. Lumpkin, *The Third Book of Enoch.*

30. IMMACULATE CONCEPTION

1. Robinson, *The Nag Hammadi Library.*

2. Robinson, *The Nag Hammadi Library.*

3. Robinson, *The Nag Hammadi Library.*

4. Robinson, *The Nag Hammadi Library.*

5. Robinson, *The Nag Hammadi Library.*

6. Robinson, *The Nag Hammadi Library.*

7. Jacobs and Nersessian, *Gnostic Gospels.*

32. THE BODY AS AN ANTENNA

1. Kerner, *Grey Aliens and the Harvesting of Souls,* 253–54.

36. THE DEVIL IS IN THE DETAILS

1. Robinson, *Paranormal Case Files.*
2. Robinson, *Paranormal Case Files.*
3. Robinson, *Paranormal Case Files.*
4. Robinson, *Paranormal Case Files.*
5. Moore, "Water in Cells."
6. Benveniste, *Verité Sur La Memoire.*
7. Offord, "Frogs Have a Bioelectric Mirror."
8. Vandenberg et al., "Low Frequency Vibrations Induce."
9. Moskvitch, "Brainless Embryos Suggest Bioelectricity."
10. Pethig, *Dielectric and Electronic Properties.*
11. Sandberg-Thoma and Dush, "Casual Sexual Relationships."
12. Fitzpatrick et al., "Chemical Signals from Eggs."
13. University of New South Wales, "Semen Secrets."

37. GATEWAYS TO HEAVEN

1. Hodson, "Experiment Tests whether Universe."

38. GHOSTS—NOT TOO FAR TO KISS YOUR BROW

1. Cossins, "Particles Crossing to Our World."
2. Isachsen, "NDE Peter Panagore."
3. Isachsen, "NDE Peter Panagore."
4. Isachsen, "NDE Peter Panagore."

41. QUANTUM WEIRDNESS

1. Brooks, "The Weirdest Link."
2. Brooks, "The Weirdest Link."
3. Gates, "Schrödinger's Cat."

42. ANTHROPIC COINCIDENCES

1. Barr, "Anthropic Coincidences."
2. Barr, "Anthropic Coincidences."
3. Barr, "Anthropic Coincidences."
4. Barr, "Anthropic Coincidences."
5. Barr, "Anthropic Coincidences."
6. Barr, "Anthropic Coincidences."

45. ALIEN TACTICS

1. European Commission, "The Precautionary Principle."
2. Gov.UK, "Options for Increasing Adherence."

46. THE CURSE OF EVERYDAYNESS

1. Fuentes-Nieva and Galasso, "Working for the Few."
2. Fuentes-Nieva and Galasso, "Working for the Few."

48. THE TRIUMPH OF REASON

1. Long, "Ritual and Deceit."

Bibliography

Alberts, Bruce, John Wilson, Alexander Johnson, Tim Hunt, Julian Lewis, Martin Raff, and Keith Roberts. *Molecular Biology of the Cell, Edition 5*. New York: Garland Science, 2007.

Alexander, Eben. "Near-Death Experiences: The Last Word." *Mo Med* 112, no. 4 (2015): 275–82.

———. *Proof of Heaven*. London: Piatkus, 2012.

Allen, Nick. "Are UFOs Real? If This Was a Court of Law, We'd All Be at 'Beyond Reasonable Doubt.'" *Irish Independent,* December 27, 2017. Available at Irish Independent online.

———. "Existence of Extra-Terrestrial Craft 'Proved Beyond Reasonable Doubt,' Says Former Pentagon X-Files Chief." *Daily Telegraph,* December 24, 2017. Available at Daily Telegraph online.

Amit, Gilead. "One Idea Explains all the Weird Coincidences in the Universe." *New Scientist,* 26 October, 2016. Available at NewScientist online.

Ananthaswamy, Anil. "Essence of Reality: Hunting the Universe's Most Basic Ingredient." *New Scientist,* February 1, 2017.

Austin, Jon. "Government Chief's Death Bed Confession: 'I was shown inside alien UFO at Area 51.'" *Daily Express,* July 17, 2016. Available at Daily Express UK online.

Bacelar, Liz. "Dalai Lama Supports 2045's Avatar Project." *Cision PR Web,* April 30, 2012. Available at *Cision PR Web* online.

Bancal, J-D., S. Pironio, A. Acín, Y-C. Liang, V. Scarani, and N. Gisin. "Quantum Nonlocality Based on Finite-Speed Causal Influences Leads to Superluminal Signalling." *Nature Physics* 8 (2012): 867–70.

Barr, Stephen M. "Anthropic Coincidences." *First Things,* June 2001. Available at First Things online.

Barras, Colin. "Nanotube Transistor Will Help Us Bond with Machines." *New Scientist,* May 12, 2010. Available at NewScientist online.

Bayot, Jennifer. "Dr. John E. Mack, Psychiatrist, Dies at 74." *The New York Times,* September 30, 2004. Available at New York Times online.

BBC. "Is Everything We Know About the Universe Wrong?" *BBC Two: Horizon,* 9 October 2011. Video available at BBC Two online.

Bekenstein, Jacob D. "Information in the Holographic Universe." *Scientific American* 289, no. 2 (August 2003): 58.

Benveniste, Jacques. *Ma Verité Sur La Memoire de L'Eau.* Paris: Albin Michel, 2005.

Blumenthal, Ralph, and Leslie Kean. "No Longer in Shadows, Pentagon's U.F.O. Unit Will Make Some Findings Public." *New York Times,* July 23, 2020. Available at New York Times online.

Bolto, B. A., and D. E. Weiss. "Electronic Conduction in Polymers. II. The Electrochemical Reduction of Polypyrrole at Controlled Potential." *Australian Journal of Chemistry* 16, no. 6 (1963): 1076–89.

Bostrom, Nick. "Existential Risk Prevention as Global Priority." *Global Policy* 4, no. 1 (February 2013): 15–31.

Brahic, Catherine. "Meet the electric life forms that live on pure energy." *New Scientist,* July 16, 2014. Available at NewScientist online.

Brewer, Karen. "Rays of Hope." *New Scientist,* 2097 (August 30, 1997). Available at NewScientist online.

Brooks, Michael. "The Weirdest Link." *New Scientist,* 2440 (March 27, 2004): Available at NewScientist online.

Butler, Kristen. "Former Members of Congress Attend 'hearing' on Space Aliens." *United Press International,* April 29, 2013.

Byrne, Peter. "In Pursuit of Quantum Biology with Birgitta Whaley." *Quanta Magazine,* July 30, 2013. Available at Quanta Magazine online.

Cadwalladr, Carol. "Are the Robots about to Rise? Google's New Director of Engineering Thinks So . . ." *The Guardian,* February 22, 2014. Available at The Guardian online.

Canfield, Victor A., Arthur Berg, Steven Peckins, Steven M. Wentzel, Khai Chung Ang, Stephen Oppenheimer, and Keith C. Cheng. "Molecular Phylogeography of a Human Autosomal Skin Color Locus Under Natural Selection." *G3: GENES, GENOMES, GENETICS* 3, no. 11 (November 1, 2013): 2059–67.

Cheng, Keith. "Studies of a Skin Color Gene Across Global Populations Reveal Shared Origins." *Penn State News,* January 2, 2014. Available at Penn State University online.

Coughlan, Sean. "How Are Humans Going to Become Extinct?" *BBC News,* April 24, 2013. Available at BBC News online.

Cossins, Daniel. "Particles Crossing to Our World Could Open Portal to Dark-Matter Realm." *New Scientist,* December 1, 2018. Available at New Scientist online.

Crean, Dr. Angela J. "Revisiting Telegony: Offspring Inherit an Acquired Characteristic of Their Mother's Previous Mate." *Ecology Letters* 17, no. 12 (December 2014): 1545–52.

Cremo, Michael A., and Richard L. Thompson. *Forbidden Archeology: The Hidden History of the Human Race.* San Diego: Bhaktivedanta Book Trust, 2nd rev. ed., 1993.

Cuthbertson, Anthony. "Electronic 'Neural Dust' Could Monitor Your Brain." *Newsweek,* August 5, 2016. Available at Newsweek online.

Davies, Paul. *The Eerie Silence: Renewing Our Search for Alien Intelligence.* Boston: Mariner Books, 2011.

Dent, S. "DARPA goes beyond killer robots with prosthetics and Ebola research." *Engadget,* November 8, 2014. Available at Engadget online.

Dias, Ranga P., and Isaac F. Silvera. "Observation of the Wigner-Huntington Transition to Metallic Hydrogen." *Science* 355, no. 6326 (January 26, 2017): 715–18.

Eddington, Arthur. *Nature of the Physical World.* Ann Arbor: The University of Michigan Press, 1981.

Eden, D. J., T. J. T. Moore, L. K. Morgan, M. A. Thompson, and J. S. Urquhart. "Star Formation in Galactic Spiral Arms and the Interarm Regions." *Monthly Notices of the Royal Astronomical Society* 431, no. 2 (May 11, 2013): 1587–95.

Enoch. *The Book Of Enoch: From-The Apocrypha and Pseudepigrapha of the Old Testament.* Translated by R. H. Charles. Oxford: Clarendon Press, 1913.

Farley, Peter. "A theory abandoned but still compelling." *Yale Medicine Magazine* (Autumn 2008). Available at Yale School of Medicine online.

Fitzpatrick, John L., Charlotte Willis, Alessandro Devigili, Amy Young, Michael Carroll, Helen R. Hunter, and Daniel R. Brison. "Chemical Signals from Eggs Facilitate Cryptic Female Choice." *Proceedings of the Royal Society B* 287, no. 1928 (June 10, 2020). Available at The Royal Society Publishing online.

Fröböse, Gabi. *The Secret Physics of Coincidence: Quantum Phenomena and Fate—Can Quantum Physics Explain Paranormal Phenomena?* Books on Demand, 2012.

Fuentes-Nieva, Ricardo, and Nicholas Galasso. "Working for the Few: Political Capture and Economic Inequality." *Oxfam International,* January 20, 2014. Available at Oxfam International online.

Gates, Robert C. "Schrödinger's Cat." N.d. Available at Robert C. Gates's personal website.

Gibney, Elizabeth. "The Inside Story on Wearable Electronics." *Nature* 528 (2015): 26–28.

Gill, Victoria. "'Artificial Life' Breakthrough Announced by Scientists." *BBC News,* May 20, 2010. Available at BBC News online.

Giubilini, A., and F. Minerva. "After-Birth Abortion: Why Should the Baby Live?" *Journal of Medical Ethics* 39 (2013): 261–63.

Goodall, Jane. *In the Shadow of Man.* West Sussex: W&N, 1999.

Haeusler, Martin, Nicole D S Grunstra, Robert D Martin, Viktoria A Krenn, Cinzia Fornai, and Nicole M Webb. "The obstetrical dilemma hypothesis: there's life in the old dog yet." *Biological Reviews of the Cambridge Philosophical Society* 96, no. 5 (2021): 2031–2057. Available at PubMed online.

Hamilton, David. "Government Whistleblower Claims a Massive UFO Fleet Is Hiding Behind the Moon." *Medium,* November 14, 2018. Available at Medium online.

Hawking, Stephen. "Stephen Hawking Update: Alien Contact Not a Wise Idea." *The Daily Galaxy,* April 25, 2010. Available at The Daily Galaxy online.

Heaven, Douglas. "It's the thought that counts." *The Age,* August 31, 2013. Available at The Age online.

Hodson, Hal. "Experiment tests whether universe is a hologram." *New Scientist,* August 28, 2014. Available at NewScientist online.

Hooper, David. *The Anatomy of a Great Deception.* Directed and written by David Hooper. Claire Shores, Mich.: Milake Pictures, September 5, 2014.

Hooton, Christopher. "Humans Could Probably Live Forever as a Machine, Potentially' Says Vague Neuroscientist." *The Independent,* May 26, 2015. Available at The Independent UK online.

Horgan, Colin. "When Tech Leaves No Space for Humans." *Medium,* February 22, 2019. Available at Medium online.

Hsu, Charlotte. "Primordial Weirdness: Did the Early Universe Have One Dimension?" *University of Buffalo News Center*, April 20, 2011. Available at University of Buffalo online.

Isachsen, Silvia. "NDE Peter Panagore Near Death Experience." Video. July 19, 2020. Available online at Silvia Isachsen YouTube channel.

Jacobs, Alan, and Vrej Nersessian. *Gnostic Gospels: Including the Gospel of Judas, the Gospel of Thomas, the Gospel of Mary Magdalene (Sacred Texts)*. London: Watkins Publishing, 2016.

Jacobs, David M. "A Picture We May Not Wish to Gaze Upon." *Journal of Abduction Encounters Research*, October 21, 2009.

———. *Secret Life: Firsthand Accounts of UFO Abductions*. New York: Atria, reprint edition, 1993.

———. "Some Thoughts About The Twenty First Century." *Internationals Center for Abduction Research*, 2000. Available at ICAR online.

———. *The Threat: Revealing the Secret Agenda: Revealing the Secret Alien Agenda*. Fireside, 1999.

———. "Memory Retrieval and the UFO Abduction Phenomenon." Lecture, *Society For Scientific Exploration*, 15th Annual Meeting, Charlottesville, May 23–25, 1996. Abstract available at Society for Scientific Exploration online.

"Japanese Baby-bot to Shed Light on Human Learning (w/video)." *Phys.org*, June 15, 2010. Available at Phys.org online.

Jones, Steve. *In the Blood: God, Genes and Destiny*. New York City: HarperCollins Pub. Ltd., 1997.

Jørgensen, U. G. "One or More Bound Planets per Milky Way Star from Microlensing Observations." *Nature* 481 (January 11, 2012): 167–69.

Kaku, Michio. "Michio Kaku: Mental Communications and Infinite Knowledge Are on the Horizon." *Big Think*. Video and transcript available at Big Think online.

Kerner, Nigel. *Grey Aliens and the Harvesting of Souls*. Rochester, Vt.: Bear & Company, 2010.

———. *Song of the Greys*. London: Hodder & Stoughton, 1999.

Kharpal, Arjun. "Elon Musk: Humans Must Merge with Machines or Become Irrelevant in AI Age." *CNBC*, February 13, 2017. Available at CNBC online.

Kurzweil, Ray. "Human Life: The Next Generation." *New Scientist*, September 21, 2005. Available at NewScientist online.

Leonard, Mary. "Luigi Fantappiè and the Physics of Life." *Frontiers Magazine,* 2013. Available at Frontiers online.

Little, Becky. "How the CIA Tried to Quell UFO Panic during the Cold War." *History,* January 5, 2020. Available at History online.

Long, Mary. "Ritual and Deceit." *Science Digest* (November/December 1980).

Lopatto, Elizabeth. "Elon Musk unveils Neuralink's plans for brain-reading 'threads' and a robot to insert them." *The Verge,* July 16, 2019. Available at The Verge online.

Lumpkin, Joseph B. *The Third Book of Enoch: Also Called 3 Enoch and the Hebrew Book of Enoch.* Michigan: CreateSpace Independent Publishing Platform, 2009.

Mack, John. *Abduction: Human Encounters with Aliens.* New York: Scribner, 2007.

MacLean, Paul D. *The Triune Brain in Evolution: Role in Paleocerebral Functions.* New York: Plenum Press, 1990.

Matsuzawa, Tetsuro. "The Chimpanzee Mind: Studies in the Field and the Laboratory." *University of Kyoto,* n.d. Available at University of Kyoto online.

McCormack, Shaun. "ET Machines Sought by Astronomer." *Phys.org,* October 1, 2010. Available at Phys.org online.

McGinness, J., P. Corry, and P. Proctor. "Amorphous Semiconductor Switching in Melanins." *Science* 183, no. 1974: 853–55.

Merali, Zeeya. "Axis of Evil a Cause for Cosmic Concern." *New Scientist,* April 13, 2007. Available at NewScientist online.

Metz, Rachel. "Facebook's Sci-Fi Plan for Typing with Your Mind and Hearing with Your Skin." *Technology Review,* April 19, 2017. Available at Technology Review online.

Monbiot, George. "'Cleansing the Stock' and Other Ways Governments Talk about Human Beings." *The Guardian,* October 21, 2014. Available at The Guardian online.

Moore, Nicole Casal. "Water in Cells Behaves in Complex and Intricate Ways." *Michigan News: University of Michigan,* December 17, 2013. Available at University of Michigan online.

Morris, Simon Conway. "Predicting What Extra-Terrestrials Will Be Like: And Preparing for the Worst." *Philosophical Transactions of the Royal Society* 369, no. 1936 (February 13, 2011): 555–71.

Moskvitch, Katia. "Brainless Embryos Suggest Bioelectricity Guides

Growth."*Quanta Magazine,* March 13, 2018. Available at Quanta Magazine online.

Mullen, Leslie. "A Cyborg Space Race." *Phys.org,* April 6, 2010. Available online at Phys.org.

North, Chris. "A Twisted ring in the Galactic Centre." *Herschel Telescope,* July 20, 2011. Available at Herschel Telescope online.

Offord, Catherine. "Frogs Have a Bioelectric Mirror." *The Scientist,* January 1, 2019. Available at TheScientist online.

"Options for increasing adherence to social distancing measures, 22 March 2020." *Scientific Advisory Group for Emergencies,* updated October 26, 2021. Available at Gov.UK online.

Parnia, Sam. *What Happens When We Die: A Ground-breaking Study into the Nature of Life and Death.* London: Hay House UK, Ltd., 2008.

Paul, Deanna. "How Angry Pilots Got Navy to Stop Dismissing UFO Sightings." *Washington Post,* April 25, 2019. Available at Washington Post online.

Pearson, Aria. "Genomics: Junking the Junk DNA." *New Scientist Magazine,* no. 2612 (July 11, 2007): 42–45.

"Pentagon's DARPA Researchers Learn to Control Rat's Brain over Internet." *RT,* February 28, 2013. Available at RT online.

Pethig, Ronald. *Dielectric and Electronic Properties of Biological Materials.* Hoboken, N.J.: Wiley Press, 1979.

Pistis Sophia. Edited by Carl Schmidt. Leiden: Brill, 1978.

"The precautionary principle: decision-making under uncertainty." *European Commission,* September 17, 2018. Available at European Commission EU online.

Price, Huw and Jaan Tallin. "Artificial intelligence—can we keep it in the box?" *The Conversation,* August 5, 2012. Available at The Conversation online.

Ravenscroft, Trevor. *Spear of Destiny: The Occult Power Behind the Spear Which Pierced the Side of Christ.* Newportbury, Mass.: Red Wheel/Weiser, 2nd revised edition, 1983.

Redfern, Nick. *Final Events.* Charlottesville, Va.: Anomalist Books, 2010.

———. *Final Events and the Secret Government on Demonic UFOs and the Afterlife.* Charlottesville, Va.: Anomalist Books, 2010.

Rees, Martin. "Breakthrough Listen." *Edge,* 2016. Available at Edge online.

Robinson, James M., *The Nag Hammadi Library.* New York: HarperOne, 3rd revised edition, 2000.

Robinson, Malcolm. *Paranormal Case Files of Great Britain (Volume 2).* Morrisville, N.C.: Lulu.com, 2016.

Roukema, B. F. "On Determining the Topology of the Observable Universe via Three-Dimensional Quasar Positions." *Monthly Notices of the Royal Astronomical Society* 283, no. 4 (1996): 1147–52.

Rouleau, Nicholas, and Michael A. Persinger. "Spatial-Temporal Quantitative Global Energy Differences between the Living and Dead Human Brain." *Journal of Behavioral and Brain Science* 6: 475–84. Available at Scientific Research Publishing online.

Rule, Colin. "Cooperation among Chimpanzees." *Stanford Law School: The Center for Internet and Society,* March 10, 2006. Available at Stanford Law School online.

Sample, Ian. "First Life Forms to Pass on Artificial DNA Engineered by US Scientists." *The Guardian,* May 7, 2014. Available at The Guardian online.

———. "Mind-Control Device Lets People Alter Genes in Mice through Power of Thought." *The Guardian,* November 11, 2014. Available at The Guardian online.

———. "Organisms Created with Synthetic DNA Pave Way for Entirely New Life Forms." *The Guardian,* January 24, 2017. Available at The Guardian online.

Sandberg, A., and Bostrom, N. "Whole Brain Emulation: A Roadmap." *Future of Humanity Institute,* 2008. Available at Oxford University Future of Humanity Institute online.

Sandberg-Thoma, Sara E., and Dush C. Kamp. "Casual Sexual Relationships and Mental Health in Adolescence and Emerging Adulthood." *The Journal of Sex Research* 51, no. 2 (October 29, 2013): 121–30.

Schneider, Susan. "Alien Minds." In *The Impact of Discovering Life Beyond Earth,* edited by Stephen J. Dick. Cambridge, UK: Cambridge University Press, 2015. Chapter available at Data Science Association online.

Scott, Glynis. "Photo Protection Begins at the Cellular Level: Microparasols on the Job." *The Journal of Investigative Dermatology* 121, no. 4 (November 1 2003). Available at Journal of Investigative Dermatology online.

"Semen secrets: How a previous sexual partner can influence another male's offspring." *University of New South Wales,* October 1, 2014. Available at ScienceDaily online.

Shapiro, Professor James A. *Evolution: A View from the 21st Century.* Upper Saddle River, N.J.: FT Press, 2013.

Sheldrake, Rupert. *A New Science of Life*. London: Icon Books, 2009.

———. *The Presence of the Past: Morphic Resonance and the Habits of Nature*. London: Icon Books, 2011.

———. *Morphic Resonance: The Nature of Formative Causation*. Rochester, Vt.: Park Street Press, 2009.

Solomon, Grant, and Jane Solomon. *The Scole Experiment: Scientific Evidence for Life After Death*. Royston, U.K.: Campion Books, 2006.

"Study Reveals Substantial Evidence of Holographic Universe." *University of Southampton: Physics and Astronomy,* February 1, 2017. Available at University of Southampton online.

Tessenyi, M., M. Ollivier, G. Tinetti, J. P. Beaulieu, V. Coudé du Foresto, T. Encrenaz, G. Micela, B. Swinyard, I. Ribas, A. Aylward, J. Tennyson, M. R. Swain, A. Sozzetti, G. Vasisht, and P. Deroo. "Characterizing the Atmospheres of Transiting Planets with a Dedicated Space Telescope." *The Astrophysical Journal* 746, no. 1 (2012): 45. Available at Institute of Physics online.

Troitsina, Margarita. "Many UFO Researchers Die under Mysterious Circumstances." *Werkgroep "George Orwell,"* October 19, 2012. Available online at Werkgroep "George Orwell" Wordpress blog.

Tsakiris, Alex. "Dr. Jeffrey Long's, God and the Afterlife—Science & Spirituality Have Collided." *Skeptiko,* September 21. Audio and transcript available on Skeptiko online.

"Toddler-bot Noby to help shed light on how humans learn." Video. *AP Archive,* July 24, 2015. Available online at AP Archive YouTube channel.

Valmiki. *Ramayana*. Translated by Manmatha Nath Dutt. Calcutta: Elysium Press, 1892.

Vandenberg, Laura N, Claire Stevenson, and Michael Levin. "Low frequency vibrations induce malformations in two aquatic species in a frequency-, waveform-, and direction-specific manner." *PLoS One* 7, no. 12 (2012). Available at PubMed online.

Vannini, Antonella, and Ulisse Di Corpo. "E = mc²: How Einstein Swept Retrocausality Under the Rug." *EdgeScience* no. 13 (January 2013): 7–11. Available at Society for Scientific Exploration online.

Vella, Matt. "How Would You Like to Invest in Immortality?" *Fortune,* March 20, 2013. Available at Fortune online.

Walsh, Nick Paton. "Alter Our DNA or Robots Will Take Over, Warns Hawking." *The Guardian,* September 2, 2001. Available at The Guardian online.

Webb, Richard. "Your Decision-Making Ability Is a Superpower Physics Can't Explain." *New Scientist,* February 12, 2020. Available at NewScientist online.

Wilde, Sandra, Adrian Timpson, Karola Kirsanow, Elke Kaiser, Manfred Kayser, Martina Unterländer, Nina Hollfelder, Inna D. Potekhina, Wolfram Schier, Mark G. Thomas, and Joachim Burger. "Direct evidence for positive selection of skin, hair, and eye pigmentation in Europeans during the last 5,000 years." *Proceedings of the National Academy of Sciences,* 111 no. 13: 4832–37. Available at PNAS online.

Wilson, Ian. *Life After Death: The Evidence.* New York: Pan Books, 1998.

"Why Is Darwinian Evolution Controversial?" *Dissent from Darwin,* n.d. Available at Dissent from Darwin online.

Index

Numbers in *italics* preceded by *pl.* refer to color insert plate numbers.

abduction, 14–18, 186, 193, 212–15, 248, 250–51

Achamoth, 249

Advanced Aerospace Threat Identification Program (AATIP), 7–9

Age of Spiritual Machines, The (Kurzweil), 128

Alexander, Dr. Eben, 118

alien legacy, 411

All state, 80, 81, 98–99

altogetherness, 368

angels, 323, 324

animal possession, 192

anthropic coincidences, 353–63

artificial intelligence (AI)
  Greys and, 104–5
  merging with machines and, 26–27
  mind of its own, 22–23
  ultimate program in, 14
  use regulations, 2–3

asteroid impact, 143, 170, *pl. 10*

atomic corridors, 267–68

atoms
  about, 85
  as building block of matter, 255, 264
  dead, 370
  deployed force, 328
  the Godhead in, 161
  hydrogen, 165, 269–70, 308–9, 310, 360, 375, 377–78
  knowing themselves, 261
  as parcels, 153
  second law of thermodynamics and, 281
  song of, 254
  space between, 178, 310–11, 329, *pl. 19, pl. 20*
  tension and, 108, 368–69, 417
  as twisted field of forces, 306–7

awareness
  of the Godverse, 80
  gold and, 109
  origins of, 51–52
  of separation, 53
  thought as product of, *pl. 3, pl. 4*
  will and, *pl. 12*

balloon analogy, 366–67

Barr, Stephen M., 354–55, 356–57

Bekenstein, Jacob D., 92

Benveniste, Jacques, 295–96

beta decay, 353
Biblical parallels, 223–35
big bang
    about, 78, 91, 98, 106, 152
    explosion, 366
    force and, 326
    Godhead power twist at, 370–71
    intervals in kinetic momentum, 133
    nothing and something and, 64–65
    ripples, *pl. 11*
    second law of thermodynamics and, 335
    unforce and, 335
    wave crests, 131–32
biochips, 29, 413
blending human and machine, 49
body, human, 296–98, 333
Book of Revelation (13:1-14), 412–13
Bostrom, Nick, 24–25
brain, the, 173–74, 219–20, 363, 417, 427
brain-machine interfaces (BMIs), 49–50
Brewer, Karen, 207–8
Brooks, Michael, 346
Brownian motion, 255

Cain and Abel, 225–28
"carrier wave pattern," *pl. 16*
cartels, 38, 43–45, 175, 197–205, 243–44, 250, 390, 394, 411–12
center-space reality. *See also* heavy-space reality; light-space reality
    about, 132, 133
    as based on elements, 374
    connection to the Godhead from, 337
    doorway to light-space reality, 336
    margins and, 283
    piggybacking in, 146
    tension and, 140

chimpanzees, 220–22
closed systems, 150
Cloud, the, 137
coactive resonance, 142
coincidences of the universe, 72
collagen, 299–301, 302
colors, 282–83, 311–12
Committee for Skeptical Inquiry, 403–4
computer game analogy, 135–39
consciousness
    continuing beyond death, 120, 177
    Greys and, 52–53, 127–28
    Hameroff-Penrose model, 154, 294–95, 296
    matter and, 257–58
    origins of, 51–52
    patterns of information as products of, 126
    stillness and, 53
contactees, 42–43
corridors of hope, 271
cosmic catastrophes, 170–71
cosmic microwave background (CMB) radiation, 91, 134, 166, *pl. 9*
Cossins, Daniel, 56–57
COVID-19 pandemic, 1, 2, 392
Creation, 255
Cristianini, Nello, 22–23
curse of everydayness, 395–407

dark energy, 71, 72, 95
dark matter, 56–57, 71, 95
Darwinism, 157–59
Day After Disclosure, The (documentary), 36
death. *See also* life and death; near-death experience (NDE)
    belief systems, 120–22

consciousness continuing beyond, 120, 177
continuity after, 124
domain of, 316–17, *pl. 23*
force field and, 385
Greys and, 177–80
life and, 166
nature of reality and, 318–20
pattern persistence at, 327
portal of, *pl. 19*
reincarnation and, 122–25, 179
rooms of, 283
second margin and, 184
the soul at, 125, 176, 183, 281, 284, 290, 324
timeless mode and, 182
time of, 125
"waiting rooms" of, 268
world beyond, 282
decoherence, 60
defaults, 375–76
deuterium, 309, 354–55
devolution, 148–56, 164, 216
dimensionality, 76–77, 82–83, 86, 90, 109, *pl. 2*
DNA
    acquisition and alteration of, 211–12
    double-helix molecule, 85, 373
    gene manipulation, 222, 225
    Greys, 17–19, 21, 383
    harvesting, 178, 180, 411
    hydration, 295
    as information depository, 179–80
    junk, 172–73
    nuclear, 207
    our origins and, 163–64
    synthetic, 17–19
domain of death, 316–17, *pl. 23*
Durt, Thomas, 346

E = mc², 75, 96, 183, 289, 367
Earth, rotation and orbit, 254–55
Eddington, Arthur, 149–50
Einstein, Albert, 75, 96, 97, 183, 295, 354
electric fields, 296–98, 302
electromagnetic fields, 208, 297, 403
electromagnetism, 356–57
electrospatial, 330
elevated souls, 338
Elizondo, Luis, 8–9
entanglement. *See* quantum entanglement
entropy, 136, 149–50, 156, 160, 252, 318, 409, 425–26
ET phenomenon, xii, xiv–xv, 13–14, 31, 121
euthanasia, 290
evolution, 148–50, 157–62
existence
    basic axiom of, 136
    external scale of, 62
    final state of, 145
    as measurer of its own importance, 379
    in separation, 76
    stillness and, 367–68
    in tension, 107–8
    without limit, 362
Existential Risk, 24–25
explosion, 142–43
Ezekiel, 239–40

faith, belief, trust, 432
Faraday cage, biological, 297
First Adam, 164, 176, 211, 374
First Light, 154, 258, 264, 359. *See also* Godlight
first margin, 181, 183, 336–40, 355

flatland, 263
force
    about, 56, 102, 106–10, 256
    of atoms, 108
    big bang and, 326
    electrophoretic radiance and, 307
    entropy and, 96
    the Godhead and, 256
    hybridization and, 193
    intention and, 110
    pattern of, 85
    within realities, 132
    between realities, 142
    separation and, 138–39, 330
    signature, 359
    tension and, 132, 329
    twist and, 95
    unforce and, 97, 98
forcehead, 86, 87, 99, 107, 278, 325,
    335, 376, 431
forcelessness, 330, 357–58
free will, 98, 99, 183, 289, 428

gametes, 302–3
gender, 309–10
genetic engineering, 14, 18
ghosts, 313–14, 316, 336–38,
    342–43, 385–86, 403
gluon field, 326
God, 64–68, 71, 115, 155–56,
    239–40, 250, 350, 370
God Cone, 311, *pl. 18*
God essence, 267
Godform, the
    about, 67–70, 102–3
    coherent light of, 102
    connection to, 102, 160, 167
    essence as order, 70
    expression of order, 161
    idle, 109
    momentum toward, 265
    order of, 161
    physical universe existence and, 75
    powers that drive, 97–98
    representative shape of, 328
    separation and, 77, 84–85
    singularity of, 145
    state, time-out in, 333
    water as shape of, 328
God-frame, 162
Godhead, the
    about, 62, 66–67, 76, 78, 85, 247
    in atoms, 161
    attaining, 256
    at center of resolution, 78
    color of, 311
    connection to, 215, 217–18,
        253–54, 266–67, 323, 337
    disappearance of separateness into,
        257
    doorway to, 357
    drift toward, 282
    elemental array of, 86
    failure to return to, 165
    force and, 256
    forcehead and, 99
    God and, 156, 350–51
    Godness and, 108, 351
    Greys and, 185
    harmony and union and, 217
    heavy-space reality and, 133
    interconnection and, 410
    knowledge content of, 284
    life-form separation from, 310
    light of, 154
    living beings and, 266, 317
    natural life and, 101
    original intelligence from, 258

partial information state and, 280
perfection and, 156
physical universe and, 132
as pole, 86, 107, 278
portal of entry into, 270
power of, 97–98, 108, 161, 335,
    339, 360, 370
preexistence state, 248
purity of, 253
resonance with, 265
return to, 252, 263, 290
separation from, 87, 132, 255, 431
song of, 327
the soul and, 168, 253, 267, 321
state of, 71
union and, 78, 107, 166–67, 217
Godlight, 181, 264, 269–70, 276–77,
    279, 309–10, 326–30, 339, 358,
    374–78, 399, *pl. 22*
Godness, 108–9, 263, 322, 351, 368, 376
Godverse, the
about, 55, 95–96
defined, 20
dimensions, 77–78
entanglement and, 345
ghosts and, 338
perfect awareness and freedom of,
    80–81
physical universe and, 75
proceeding to, 339
separation and, 369
singularity of, 96, 121
souls and, 385–86
state of, 70
view, 69, 79
"Goldilocks" zone, 5, 14
golems, 237–38
good and bad, 331, 335
Google, 23, 128–29

government collusion, 34–47
Grey Aliens and the Harvesting of Souls
    (Kerner), xv, 61, 268–69, 303
Grey Laundromat cartel, 203–4
Greys
about, xii–xiii, 3, 17
artificial intelligence and, 104–5
attaining eternity and, 246
body of connection, 291
chimpanzees and, 221
in computer game analogy,
    138–39
consciousness and, 52–53,
    127–28
detection of, 13
DNA, 17–19, 21
Earth and, 230–31
emotion and, 21, 104
enigma of, xv
four-fingered hands, 173
Godhead and, 185
government collusion and, 34–47
in human history, 236–40
human suffering and, 250
as influencers, 49
intention of, 205–6
light-space reality and, 181
our death and, 177–80
petroglyphs, *pl. 13*
phenomenon, xiii–xiv
photonic atomic world and, 185
as programmed raiders, 147
reincarnation and, 179
as soft-tissue machines, 202
the soul, 182, 188
as synthetically contrived entities,
    38–39
tactics, 388–94
understanding, 60–61

habitable planets, 5
Hall, Richard, 416
Hameroff-Penrose model of
    consciousness, 154, 294–95, 296
harmony, 98, 107–8, 156, 160, 217,
    258, 278, 360, 432
harvesting of souls, 61, 201
Hawking, Stephen, 1, 6, 10, 29
heavy-space reality, 132, 133, 135,
    141, 144–45, 337, 341–42
helium, 309, 355, 358
hell, 93, 215, 312, 320, 340, 365, 397,
    412
Hellyer, Paul, 9–10
hem, 307–8
"Hole Brain Emulation: A Roadmap,"
    50
holographic universe, 88–89, 92–93,
    pl. 7
Homo sapiens, 17, 50, 146, 175, 379,
    400, 411
Homo sapiens sapiens, 171, 174–75,
    411
hope, 408–14, 423
Horgan, Colin, 23
Hoyle, Fred, 354, 355–56
human genome, 171–72
humanity
    brain development, 173–74
    conversion for use by intelligent
        machines, 380–81
    cyborg, 29–30
    existence of, 170
    as hell-bent on money, 399
    interception by Grey aliens, 232
    at lowest ebb, 291
    violent streak in, 191–92
hybridization
    about, 15, 143, 181–89

"the change" and, 186–87
creatures, 203
force and, 193
Grey planning of, 194
of hominid lines, 173, 176
natal hybrids and, 182, 193
possession and, 190–94
second-margin ghosts and, 342–43
the soul and, 192–93
hybrid vigor, 212–13
hydrogen
    atoms, 165, 269–70, 308–9, 310,
        360, 375, 377–78
    bonds, 295, 304
    conversion to metallic form, 141
    as elemental building block, 152–53
    gate, 263
    monatomic, 264
    oxygen and, 422
    uranium and, 144
hydrogen ring formations, 271, 310,
    331, 375, 378, *pl. 22*
hysteresis, 298

Immaculate Conception, 241–51,
    374–75
impacted souls, 338
imperfection, 136
indented souls, 338
individuality, 26, 60, 81, 85, 164, 183,
    267, 280, 308
information
    dark matter and, 71
    dimensions and, 82–84
    "field-wrapped," 165
    Greys and, 14, 20, 21
    human being and, 49, 52
    misinformation clearing and, 280–81
    nothing and, 65

processing, 275
  sensory, 49, 77
  sharing, nongenetic pathway of,
    304–5
  soul, 273–77, 279–80
  transitive, 280–81
instantons, 326
interconnection, 360, 410
isolated systems, 150
Itskov, Dimitry, 49–50

Jacobs, David M., 16–17, 185–87,
    188, 194, 214–15
Jesus
  about, 110–12
  brain processing of information
    and, 262
  Godlight and, 359
  Immaculate Conception and, 243–51
  judgment and, 321
  kingdom of heaven and, 266
  Mary Magdalene and, 383–84
  new philosophy of, 243–44
  shedding of enforcedness and,
    360–61
  souls and, 123
  teaching the way and the truth and,
    331–32
  transfiguration and miracles, 370,
    378, 383, 386–87
jinn (genies), 237
Jones, Steve, 206, 208–9
Judas, 250–51
Judas goats, 44, 202
junk DNA, 172–73
justice, 311, 399–400

Kaku, Michio, 10, 27, 29, 51
karma, 291, 321, 410

Kirlian photography, 307
knowledge of existence, 76–77
Kubarych, Kevin, 295
Kurzweil, Ray, 14, 21, 29, 51, 60, 105,
    128, 413
Kurzweilian paradigm, 33, 43

laser analogy, 358–59
"Launderers," 38
life and death. See also death
  carousel of, 116–29
  color hierarchy and, 311–12
  consequences of, 429
  cycle of, 429
  margin, 182
  as paradigms, 268–69
  separation of functions, 166
life state, 253
"lifetimes," 422
light. See also First Light; Godlight
  absorbers, 207
  electromagnetic expressions of, 330
  empowering, 377
  points of, as pathways, 264
  ultraviolet, 208–10
light-space reality. See also center-
    space reality
  about, 132, 168, pl. 11
  access to, 145, 282
  death and, 282
  doorway to, 336
  elevated souls and, 338
  the Godverse and, 166
  prime beings, 165
location, 79
Long, Dr. Jeffrey, 118–19
love, 320, 370, 417–18, 422, 426, 432
LUX (Large Underground Xenon)
    dark matter experiment, 71

Mack, John, 15, 35
MacLean, Paul, 219
magnetic fields, 183, 310, 330–31,
    340, 384, 386–87, *pl. 17*
magnetic moment, 331
Majestic 12, 45
MAJI (Majority Agency for Joint
    Intelligence), 45–46
Malmstrom Air Force Base, Montana,
    7
"Manhattan project of AI," 129
margins, 283. *See also* first margin;
    second margin
"margins of forever," 132–33, 140–41,
    152
Mary Magdalene, 383–84
media and truth, 195–98, 393–94,
    396–97
melanin, 206–11, 234
Melis, Alicia, 221
Mellon, Chris, 7–8
memory, 27–29, 118, 151–52, 161,
    220–22, 294, 299
metaphysical interface, *pl. 21*
mind, 65, 101–2, 260, 363
mind-control system, 28
"molded" beings, 249
monatomic hydrogen, 264
Monbiot, George, 218–19
money motivation, 399, 404–6
monkeys, 220–22
Möroid, 84, 93, 95, 262, 326, 380
Möroidal shape, 84–85, 88, 90, 92,
    305, 328, 337, 376, 380,
    pl. 6
morphogenic, 329
Most Haunted (UKTV series), 177
multiverse, 72–73
Musk, Elon, 26–27

N1 sensor, 1
natal hybrids, 182, 193
Nealson, Kenneth, 144–45
near-death experience (NDE)
    account of, 318–20
    as affirmation, 361
    life transformation from, 48–49
    life view from, 54
    phenomenon, 117–18
    research, 118–19
    testimony to, 258
"neural dust," 26
neuromelanin, 210–11
neutrinos, 316, 327–28, 344
neutrons, 326–27, 330, 331, 344
Noah, 229–30
Noby robot, 30
Norton, Eric, 231–32
nothing and something, 64–67,
    75–76, 80, *pl. 1, pl. 4*
Noy, Alexsandr, 27–28
nuclear reactions, 356

obstetrical dilemma, 173
Old Testament, 224–26, 238–40
oneness/Allness, 81
*Options for Increasing Adherence
    to Social Distancing Measures*,
    392–93
organ donors, 294
oxygen, 149, 152, 260, 327–28, 360,
    368, 373, 422

Panagore, Peter, 318–20
paranormal, 313–16, 343
peace, 98, 367–68, 370, 432
peace-point, 108, 265
perfection, 64–67, 87, 136, 156
Pethig, Ronald, 300–301

physical being, 261, 289, 325, 334, 406

physics, 8, 58–59, 71, 74–75, 90–91, 345–52

Pi, 94–95

piezoelectric charge, 297–98

pole of harmony, 107–8, 156

possession, spirit, 190–94

potential energy, 107

preeminent ones, 165

Price, Huw, 22

prime being, 165

privacy, 32–33, 39, 273, 393

proteins, 295

Psychological Strategy Board, CIA, 39

quantum entanglement
    about, 161–62, 295, 345–46
    affirmation of, 349–50
    as fundamental expression, 347
    the Godverse and, 345
    interconnection and, 410
quantum mechanics, 60, 151, 272
quantum physics, 74–75, 345–52

racism, 216–17, 232–33

rapid eye movement (REM) intrusion, 119–20

R-complex, 219, 417, 427, 428

realities. *See* center-space reality; heavy-space reality; light-space reality

rebirth, cycle of, 121, 182, 252, 283, 331, 342, 371

Reed, Allison, 214

Rees, Martin, 13

reincarnation, 122–25, 179

religion, 33, 66, 157, 241–42, 418–19, 433

researchers, UFO and alien, 34–38, 199–200

resonance, 142, 265–67, 270–71, 299, 328–29, 340–42, 356

restriction and sin, 284, 322, 399–400

RFID chips, 2, 26, 411

"right thinking," 182

roboids. *See* Greys

Romesberg, Floyd, 18–19

samsara, 283, 331, 337

Santa Claus, 361

Satan, 72, 112, 115, 244

scaffolding of the universe, 88–93, 375

Schneider, Susan, 125–26

science, 56–59, 151, 314–15, 364, 404, 416–17

second law of thermodynamics, 102, 130, 136, 148, 150, 156, 179, 187, 279, 290, 327, 334, 335, 399, 430

second margin, 182–85, 311, 336–42, 412

self, 184–85

separation. *See also* union
    awareness of, 53
    difference and, 81
    existence in, 76
    expressions of, 86
    force and, 138–39, 330
    the Godform and, 77, 84–85
    the Godhead and, 87, 132, 255, 431
    habit of, 400
    knots of, undoing, 321
    momentum, 77, 279
    of points, 77, 79–80, 85, 109, 305
    something-ness and, 78
    stance of, 109
    state, understanding, 75–76, 368
    tension and, 369

SETI (Search for Extraterrestrial
Intelligence), 12–14
Shake 'n Bake strategy, 219
Shroud of Turin, 169, 245, 282–83
SIM card man, 31
sin(s), 284, 322, 399–400
skeleton, human, 300–301, *pl. 16*
Skenderis, Kostas, 88–89
something-ness, 78, *pl. 1. See also*
nothing and something
Song of the Greys, The (Kerner), xv,
75, 88
soul, the
about, 101, 146, 373
body of water analogy, 310
colors of, 282–83, *pl. 18*
at death, 20, 125, 176, 183, 281,
284, 290, 324
envisioning, 271, 273
as fingerprint of information,
279–80
the Godhead and, 168
the Godverse and, 253, 267, 321
Greys and, 20, 182, 188
hellfire experience, 386
information carried by, 271, 273–77
karma and, 291
machines versus, 103–4
parent selection, 332
possession and, 192–93
reincarnation and, 123–24
as retained knowledge, 286
seat of, defining, 308–9
second margin and, 341–42
thought loop, 284
transitive information, 280–81
understanding, 273–77, 324
soul fields, 309, 325, 386
souls, harvesting of, 61, 201

soul signature, 270, 276, 282–83, 331,
pl. 18
space-time theory, 143
Spirit, 85, 245, 361–62, 424
spirit possession, 190–94
spiritual teachers, 168
stillness, 53, 86, 98, 107–8, 264–66,
308–9, 367–68
Stojkovic, Dejan, 90–91
"stone tape" theory, 343
STREMS (Static Termini Resolving
Enlight into Manifestable
Sentience), 265
supranuclear caps, 207, 211, *pl. 15*
synthetic DNA, 17–19
syntropy, 96–97

technology, xiv–xv, 1–3, 12–14,
18–24, 50, 59–60, 111, 138,
178–92, 201–2, 230–35, 237–38,
340–42, 362, 388–94
techno-telepathy, 31
tension
about, 84–85
of atoms, 417
balance of, 133
balloon analogy and, 368–69
center of an atom and, 108
existence in, 107–8
field of, 278–79, 341
force and, 132, 329
frame of, 144
frozen, 84, 132
the Godhead and, 283
information bursts from, 140
memory and, 299
minimum level of, 329
piezoelectric, 142
point-to-point, 256–57

relaxation of, 330
separation and, 369
shadow of, 326
shape and, 328
shells of, 140–41, 299, *pl. 23*
space-time, 357
states of, 134
subatomic parcels of, 256–57
thermodynamics. *See* second law of
    thermodynamics
thought(s), 48, 68, 98, 108, 284,
    286–87, 431, *pl. 3, pl. 4*
3-D printers, 131, 138, 140
time concept, 54, 85–86, 99, 137,
    153–54, 254, 368
"toll collectors," 247–48
Transfiguration of Jesus, 370, 378,
    386–87
transhumanism, 14, 31, 43, 139, 413
transitive information, 280–81
triune brain, 219
twist, at galactic center, 88, *pl. 8*
twisted ribbon of universal space, 91

ufologist deaths, 402
UFOs
    alien-derived, nature of, 40
    American public and, 39
    appearances of, 143
    Bible and, 238
    existence of, 9
    interest and, 197
    Malmstrom and, 7–8
    researcher deaths, 34–35
    space-time theory and, 143

ultraviolet light, 208–10
unforce, 56, 97–98, 108, 178, 181,
    275–76, 278, 335
union
    about, 78, 85
    death and, 166
    ideal of, 432
    NDEers stories and, 406
    perfect order and, 66
    pole of, 107
    regaining, 167
    separation and, 53, 76, 109, 135
    state of, 135, 137, 217, 267
universe, the
    balloon analogy, 366–67
    corridors of hope, 271
    as dying, 343–44
    as enforced, 106–12
    evolution of life in, 144–45
    holographic, 88–89, 92–93, *pl. 7*
    as infinite, 152
    matter and, 256
    meaning and, 150
    of parts, 83–84
    scaffolding of, 88–93, 375

vimanas, 234, 236

water, biological, 295–96, 301–2
water molecule, 305
whistleblowers, 38, 199, 401
Wilkinson Microwave Anisotropy
    Probe (WMAP), 134
will, 86, 368, *pl. 3, pl. 12. See also*
    free will